Winners & Losers
Sport and Physical Activity in the '90s

For Matthew and Emily Fisher
in the hope that all children everywhere will grow up
having more safe, healthy and positive opportunities
in sport and physical activity.

Winners & Losers

Sport and Physical Activity in the '90s

Jill Le Clair
*Humber College of Applied Arts
and Technology*

Thompson Educational Publishing, Inc.
Toronto

Requests for permission to make copies of any part of the work should be mailed to:
> Thompson Educational Publishing, Inc.
> 11 Briarcroft Road, Toronto
> Ontario, Canada M6S 1H3
> Telephone (416) 766–2763 Fax (416) 766–0398

Canadian Cataloguing in Publication Data

Le Clair, Jill, 1947-
  Winners and losers

Includes bibliographical references and index.
ISBN 1-55077-037-3

1. Sports - Social aspects - Canada. I. Title.

GV585.L43 1992   306.4'83'0971   C92-093118-9

Cover photographs
Top:
Jeff Adams and Marc Quessy, *courtesy Athlete Information Bureau;*
Angela Issajenko, *courtesy Macmillan Canada;*
Ken Dryden, *courtesy Hockey Hall of Fame and Museum.*
Bottom:
Gaetan Boucher, *courtesy Athlete Information Bureau;*
Silken Laumann and Kay Worthington, *courtesy Athlete Information Bureau.*

Printed in Canada.
  2 3 4   95 94

Table of Contents

Woma 124
Nature 136.

Preface

This book provides a lively introduction to the social issues underlying Canadian sport. It is entirely Canadian in focus, although material is included on sport and physical activity in the United States and other countries.

This work contains a vast amount of information on sport and physical education in Canada. A recurring theme is the need for sport to be more accessible and more broadly-based. Unlike other books in this area, material on women, minorities, and persons with disabilities appears throughout.

Instructors looking for a comprehensive, introductory-level textbook on Canadian sport will find this book particularly helpful in the classroom. The language is straightforward and the material is easy to understand. New concepts are highlighted and explained. The review questions, concepts and discussion guide at the end of each chapter provide the basis for a spirited discussion in the classroom.

A most interesting part of the book is the fifty-six profiles of prominent athletes, many based on personal interviews by the author especially for this book. On each profile usually hangs a tale that goes beyond the individual athlete's story and raises broader issues for Canadian sport today and tomorrow. Readers should find these short profiles informative. They will also provide an opportunity for the reader to brush up on some of those "names" in Canadian sport.

The key features of this book are:

- the content is Canadian (with cross-cultural comparisons).

- women, minorities, and the disabled are integrated throughout the discussion of all aspects of sport and recreational activity.

- the social issues of equity, ethics, choice and change are part of all subject areas.

- fifty-six profiles of prominent athletes, many based on personal interviews for this book, provide for lively discussion.

- new concepts are introduced and explained—the book tries to be jargon free, while recognizing that certain concepts, if explained clearly, are useful learning tools.

- the material is clearly presented with charts, diagrams and boxed material to introduce this new information in an exciting manner.

- because many of the issues are topical and even controversial, there are many opportunities for students to evaluate and debate issues for and among themselves.

- for instructors, there is a Instructor's Manual containing chapter learning objectives as well as additional test questions and discussion topics to provoke lively classroom debate.

A challenge in writing this book was that, like most things, Canadian sport is changing rapidly. Attitudes towards such things as drug use and the participation of women in organized sport have changed enormously over the last few years. Understanding changes such as these enables us to become empowered, make better choices, and create new arrangements that are more appropriate to our needs.

We hope this book will encourage students and others to take an active interest in the future of sport in this country. What sport becomes in the 90s and beyond will depend on what each of us contributes today.

Sport Profiles

Acknowledgements

I want to thank the students at Humber College for their enthusiasm, iconoclastic thinking and varied ideas during the development of the book. It has been a great pleasure teaching these students and learning from them as well.

Michael Hatton and William Hanna at Humber College were helpful and encouraging throughout. Mike Badyk and Bill Bayes, my friends and colleagues were also very encouraging from the beginning. Stanley Klein provided useful and perceptive comments after reading the first draft. Wayne Dods kindly read each draft, made good suggestions and was supportive over the years. Lorraine Boucher was patient and very helpful in finding research material.

Many athletes and sport administrators, agents, coaches, educators and lawyers were very kind and gave generously of their time for interviews, as did sport enthusiasts and fans.

I also want to thank the other people who helped me along the way: my mother Pip Le Clair, Joan Barton, Kathy Belfontaine, Phyllis Berck, Gary Berman, Marilyn and Philip Brown, C-Tech Computers, Louise and Kit Campbell, John Cape, Kelly Crockett, Emily Daniels, Francis Farrugia, Emily Forrington, James Glancey, Leo Hoilka, Clay Huckle, Carol Jackson, Gordon Johnson, Bruce Kidd, Victor Kolman, Daniele Laumann, David and Diana Le Clair, Alexandra Le Clef Mandl, David Lees, Ralph Legrow, Howard Lewis, Professor Ioan Lewis, Thomas Lord, Shirley Marsden, Jim MacDonald, Greg Malszewki, Anne Montagnes, Barry Nye, Ian Parsons, Caroline Ogilvie, Joe Pantalone, Tessa, Piers, Zoe and Kirsty Phipps, Harry Rokkos, Karen Salt, Chris Schenk, Gail Sleeman, Dawn Smith, Ian Sutherland, Ken Tipton, Jacqueline von Hettlingen, Mary Usher-Jones.

The biggest thanks go to Keith and Faye Thompson who worked day after day at the sometimes seemingly endless task of putting the book together. It was a delight to work with such thoughtful and energetic publishers.

From the Publisher

Your Opinions

We would like to have your opinions on this book. If you have any textual material or photographs that you think might be useful in future editions, we would appreciate hearing from you.

Instructor's Manual

An Instructor's Manual is available to assist those instructors using this book in their classrooms. The Manual outlines in detail the key learning objectives for each chapter and provides additional test and resource material to liven up classroom discussion and debate.

This manual is available free to instructors using this book as a required textbook in a course of study. Please contact the publisher to receive a copy when completed.

Speaker

Jill Le Clair is available to speak about her book to students and other groups or associations interested in sport and physical activity in Canada. Please contact the publisher to make arrangements.

Winners & Losers

Sport and Physical Activity in the '90s

Ken Dryden, former goalie of the Montreal
Canadiens.

Chapter One

WHY STUDY SPORT

"Winning isn't everything—it's the only thing."
Vince Lombardi

"Losing is a little like dying."
George Allen

"It doesn't matter if you win or lose it's how you play the game."
English public school creed

"Movement is to be enjoyed to its full."
T'ai chi saying

People care about sport and physical activity. Even those who say they hate sport, say it with passion. The thrill of success and the pain of disappointment are part of this emotion. There is the delight in friendship and camaraderie, the love of the sunshine, the water, the grass, and the wind. There is also the misery of failure, painful injury, exclusion and dashed hopes. *Is it any wonder that sport exerts such a powerful influence?*

However, in North America today there is an enormous emphasis on *winning*. Rewards come to those who are defined as *winners*. Ben Johnson received little recognition for his third place in the 100 metres at the 1984 Olympics. Striving to do your best and coming in third does not bring the huge rewards and "big bucks."

Similarly, when an top athlete falls from grace, the penalties are severe. In Ben Johnson's case, when he tested positive at Seoul in 1988, the International Olympic Committee (IOC) took back his gold medal. Then, after he admitted his drug use at the Dubin Inquiry, the International Amateur Athletic Federation (IAAF) wiped out Johnson's time records, even though he had passed drug tests at the time the records were set. Johnson is said to have lost hundreds of thousands, perhaps millions, of dollars as a direct consequence of his drug use.

The Toronto Star (J. Goode).

Silken Laumann, winner of two gold medals in 1991.

THE SOCIAL CONTEXT OF SPORT

In answering the question why study and analyze the world of sport, the words of C. Wright Mills, the well-known American sociologist, seem as appropriate today as when they were written thirty years ago:

Ours is a time of uneasiness and indifference ... It is the social scientist's foremost political and intellectual task—for here the two coincide—to make clear the elements of contemporary uneasiness and indifference (Mills, 1970: 11–13).

By studying the social context of modern sport world we can begin to understand why we are uneasy about such things as the emphasis on winning, drug use, and the high incomes of the professional athletes at the top.

THE REAL THING

Success in North America usually means winning. Vince Lombardi, the very successful coach of the Green Bay Packers, is often quoted: "Winning isn't everything, it's the only thing." Lombardi expected every football player on his team to do his best. He did not mean that any action was justified in order to win, which is often how his quote is interpreted in the 1990s.

Some commentators feel Ben Johnson was unfairly treated because he was forced to admit in public what many other international athletes were doing secretly. Was Ben Johnson unfairly treated? Was he a victim of the sports system? Are top athletes, who are paid very large sums of money to compete and win, to blame if they cheat or are they merely victims in a sports system that has gone astray? Media personalities make pronouncements. People in restaurants and at barbecues raise their voices to emphasize their views.

Social Values and Sport

Values are the underlying beliefs upon which people live their lives. It is from these values that individuals make decisions about what they want to do. If, for example, obtaining the gold medal is more important than how you get it, then any behaviour will be justified.

The values of those who train and coach athletes, for example, can vary enormously. Some coaches are only concerned about sport performance, others are interested in the athlete's academic or personal achievement as well.

Athletes sometimes are encouraged by coaches, fans, sponsors and even by governments to do all that is necessary to be considered a winner. Athletes do not receive financial support from Sport Canada unless they perform well. Being a winner means placing with the top competitors, preferably first. In this context, sometimes the underlying objectives of sports become unclear to the athletes themselves. Andy Higgins, the University of Toronto track coach, testified at the Dubin Inquiry (which investigated drug use in Canadian sport) that Sport Canada officially insisted that coaches train their athletes to compete cleanly. "But there was also another message that kept coming from everywhere." He said coaches felt some pressure from officials to put their athletes on drug programs in order to win.

"That message was that the kind of performances expected were of a very high level and in certain events they were totally unreasonable."

"There was a double bind and a double message and our coaches were starting to feel this ambiguity, and there was a sense of pressure" (Ormsby and Hall, 1989:A4).

Similarly, as Dave Skinner, managing director of the successful Canadian Alpine ski team, points out:

"High performance in sport is a good idea, as long as it is not identified with winning alone. The confusion between winning (the symbol) and excellence (the goal) is fostered by the very system that condemns it" (Christie, 1989:A1).

~ SPORT PROFILE ~

Elizabeth Manley—"I'll still be an athlete when I'm 80."

b. 1965, Belleville, Ontario. Elizabeth Manley is the first woman in Canada to land a triple combination in competition. She personifies the polite, modest, generous and determined image all Canadians like to have of themselves. She is one of the best figure skaters in the world.

At the 1988 Winter Olympics in Calgary, the media followed every move of the East German figure skating competitor Katarina Witt and the American Debi Thomas. The event was labelled "The Battle of the Carmens" because the skaters had chosen the same piece of music.

Suddenly, Elizabeth Manley powered onto the ice with a magical performance — and she looked like she was having fun as well! The onlookers at the Calgary SaddleDome roared their support when Manley chose a program of enormous difficulty and won the silver medal (Orr, 1988: F4). A photographer suggested she bite the medal to see if it was real, which she did, and it was.

Elizabeth Manley was labelled a winner because she came up with a medal when many had not expected her to. However this bright, bubbly personality has also overcome very hard times.

In 1982, Manley's life had seemed out of control. While training in Lake Placid she gained a great deal of weight and went almost bald, so much so that she had to wear a wig (Manley, 1990: 91–93). After losing her place on the world team, she decided to retire. But in 1983 top coaches Sonja and Peter Dunfield offered to move to Ottawa for her, and soon she was back in the tough competitions.

Manley turned professional after the Olympics and, as she explains in her book *Thumbs Up,* joined the Ice Capades "for the glamorous life of the ice-show star" (1990:213). However, she found " … the pressure is the same, whether you're an amateur or a professional. You can't train for twenty years and then just give up that edge. I'll still be an athlete when I'm 80" (Nagler, 1989).

In order to discuss or analyze modern sport, which is so preoccupied with this idea of winning, we must also examine the idea of losing and the negative connotations associated with losing. George Allen, the former NFL football coach, said "Losing is a little like dying" (Leonard, 1977:18). Losing is tied up with a sense of failure or shame, of not being good enough. If the only people who count are those who place first, second, or third, everyone else is a loser *by these terms.* Similarly, those who are not encouraged to participate in sport, or are actively excluded, are already pre-labelled as losers. Successes and rewards will not come to them.

As we can see, then, our definition of sport is socially constructed. Sports issues are continually being debated and re-defined according to how societies and individuals *value* certain types of activity. Who should be rewarded and at what rate? Why are women not part of the NFL, the NHL, and the NBA? Why aren't disabled athletes included in the Olympics? Why are there so few people of colour in managing and coaching positions on professional teams? These aspects of sport are all shaped by the society we live in.

Athlete Information Bureau (C. McNeill).

Elizabeth Manley biting her silver medal at the 1988 Calgary Olympics.

Physical Activity—A Part of Being Human

The new born baby wiggles and cries the moment it separates from its mother. This is the beginning of active life. Movement is part of what makes us human. As the child grows and develops so too his or her motor movements expand and develop. The world extends beyond the crib and home to the garden, the street, the school and the parks or fields.

Studies on primates, the closest animal species to humans, find that chimpanzees, baboons, monkeys, macaques and gorillas all indulge in play. They "work" finding food, climbing, walking and hiding from or attacking predators. Then they play. They run in circles, tap each other on the head, roll on top of each other and tease each other. These activities have no productive goal but rather are physical in nature.

Physical activity is rooted in our biological past and yet not all people are active. Many merely buy tickets to view sport or sit down and watch sport on television. For some it is even too much of an effort to get up from the television to get something to eat! Others spend all day working with their minds and hardly moving their muscles. They are not enjoying what is supposedly a part of being human. How has this come about?

Because physical activities are such a normal part of everyday life, they are often taken for granted. It is often only after an injury that an individual suddenly realizes the amazing abilities of the human body. The delight in running, the excitement of jumping, the thrill of racing down a hill on a bike or on skiis, the exhilaration of diving into water—these are what makes a person return again and again to their favourite sports. Tennis-great Billie Jean King describes the beauty and pleasure in playing tennis when everything goes well:

> That perfect moment happens in all sports. In basketball, it might be that split-second hesitation just before a player gets off a jump shot that you know is gonna go swish. In baseball, players say they can't feel the ball on the bat at all when they've hit a home run, but they know, they just know (King, 1974:200–201).

Every athlete has also felt that pleasure when the muscles are working well, the conditions are perfect and the thrill is there. There is a sense of freedom, a feeling that anything is achievable. Those moments are truly beautiful for both the participant and the observer.

The Struggle Within Sport

When we look closely at sports and sports organizations, we see the constant struggle between groups over programs, policies and

Understanding The Whole Picture

Every athlete has experienced times when everything seems to go wrong. The bike breaks down. The wind changes direction. The muscles tighten up. The coach chooses someone else. The sponsor cancels the funding. The money is not there to go to the training camp. Sometimes it is hard to figure out what happened, what went wrong. Sometimes common sense just fails.

We experience the world but that does not mean we automatically understand all of it or even that part that we ourselves make up. It is often difficult to see all the factors involved in any situation. The emotional component colours our view and sometimes significant aspects are obscured or hidden. Kathy Belfontaine, a psychotherapist and social worker, points out that it is often "hard to see the picture when you are in the picture yourself." Often it is even frightening to think about the picture. Perhaps what will be seen may not be too pleasant, or might make the person feel helpless. Because physical activity is such an important part of our lives, controversy about it can touch an emotional core.

Marie Curie, the scientist once said: "Nothing in life is to be feared, it is only to be understood. Now is the time to understand more, so that we may fear less." By critically studying what goes on around us it is possible to see things more clearly. It is then possible to understand how each of us as individuals "fits in" and how society operates. Only then is it possible to make effective choices.

Applying this to sport, it is only by getting a better grasp of the broader social context that it is possible to understand modern sports activities. Only then can we decide what form we want sports and physical activities to take and how we can help to bring it about.

---

funding. Sometimes groups work together, sometimes they work in opposition. Sometimes interests overlap, sometimes they are mutually exclusive. Boycotts, the police and even the army become part of how sport is to be defined.

All of this struggle and conflict makes up sport as we know it today. The fighting does not just take place in the boxing ring, on the ice, or in the stands. Members of minority groups have had to fight the objections of those who didn't want to see them in certain sports at all. Athletes try to get their unrecognized sport recognized by official sport organizations. Fans complain about changes in the rules. Lobby groups demonstrate outside events to push their point of view. Women who were once defined as frail and helpless, shocked the public when they dared to ride bicycles—what is more, in divided skirts! Professional athletes go on strike for better pay and working conditions. The gay community fights for the right to use the term "The Gay Olympics." The World Hockey Association starts a new league that it claims is bigger and better, and certainly pays higher salaries—for a while. The sport associations of the disabled organize to be included within the Olympics for the able-bodied. Sport groups negotiate with each other over jurisdiction.

Through this process the definition of what is appropriate or suitable constantly changes. People who are excluded from participating fight to be included or attempt to eliminate or redefine the activity.

Athlete Information Bureau (E. Langsley).

Canadians at the Women's Rugby World Cup, Cardiff, Wales, 1991.

~ SPORT PROFILE ~

Brian Orser—"The Toast of Canada"

b. 1961, Penetanguishene, Ontario. Brian Orser began skating at six years of age. His career is typical of most high-performance athletes in his event—a steady climb through the rankings over a period of more than fifteen years. His achievements stand out clearly:

- 1975 Canada Games gold
- 1977 National novice singles title
- 1979 Juniors title
- 1979 Vienna Cup
- 1980 International Grand Prix title
- 1981–84 National senior champion

- 1983 Gold Skate Canada
- 1983 Silver
- 1984 Silver Sarejevo Olympics
- 1984 World Champion
- 1988 Silver Calgary Olympics

At the 1988 Calgary Olympics, Brian Orser's competition for a first place finish with American Brian Boitano was nicknamed the "Battle of the Brians." The two Brians had competed internationally for ten years.

The scores were so close that no one was sure who had won, until the computer showed Boitano's small margin of victory. Boitano had skated so strongly that Orser had no room for errors. Many Canadian journalists discussed Orser's loss at great length. He was judged by them to be a loser. They seemed totally unaware of the close nature of the competition.

As a journalist described the scene more accurately the next day, "If either the Danish judge or the Swiss judge had given Boitano a tenth of a point less or Orser a tenth more for technical merit, then Orser would have the gold and be the toast of Canada today" (Orr, 1988: B4).

Social Science and Sport

The values of the wider society are naturally reflected in sport activities. Why are there not more women in the Olympics? Why do Americans watch so much football? Why have the Gay Olympic Games faced opposition? Why is it that a typical 30-year-old Swede is said to be in better shape than a 30-year-old Canadian? Why are there few black quarterbacks in the NFL? Why do athletes use blood doping? Why are various sport organizations considering drug testing? The answers to these kinds of questions can be found by looking at the social context of sport today.

Social scientists analyze what they see around them and study sport in a manner that differs from that of an ordinary person. Often fans watch games for years and develop an extensive knowledge of their particular sport. Yet, at the same time, it is hard for these fans to evaluate what is around them. This is equally true, if not more so, of the athletes who participate in sport. Their focus is on training, competition and winning, rather than the social context of their sport.

Social science engages what C. Wright Mills called our *sociological imagination.* The sociological imagination involves an *historical,* an *anthropological,* and a *critical* sensitivity to the world around us (Giddens, 1987:13). To understand contemporary Canadian hockey,

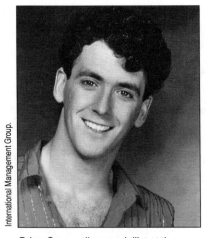

International Management Group.

Brian Orser, silver medallist at the 1988 Calgary Olympics.

Can Social Scientists Have No Opinion?

Social scientists try to be objective or **value free**, meaning that they are totally without biases. This is a difficult thing to do, as each and every one of us has unique experiences that influence how we see the world around us.

If you had a coach in high school who forced you to sit on the bench every time you made an error in judgment, you most likely would think that coaches seem to punish players' mistakes rather than encourage them to learn from their mistakes. You are, of course, entitled to your opinion. But perhaps not all coaches are like the coach you worked with. Was she or he typical? What are the pressures on coaches and on this coach in

particular? What was the sport? What was the record of the school? It is essential to ask these questions before anyone can say "Oh, my coach ... was a typical coach."

The very questions a researcher decides to ask indicate certain biases. If the Milk Marketing Board declares milk to be the best food for athletes it would be no surprise!

Every research study is, therefore, part of a broader perspective and everyone studied operates from within a certain framework. It is important that this perspective is made explicit by the researcher and is understood by anyone evaluating a particular piece of social research. So the best thing to do in reading any material is

to ask what the source is and how was the research conducted and by whom.

Here is a another example. In many high school history books students will find the following statement: "'Universal suffrage' was won in 1848 in France." The textbooks explain that all French citizens won the right to vote after revolutionary struggle. However suffrage (the right to vote) was only given to men (Eichler, 1985). Women, known as suffragettes, continued to fight to get the right to vote for many years. In fact Quebec was the last province in Canada to give women voting rights—in 1940!

for example, it is crucial to take into account both the *historical background* to Canadian events and the *cultural elements* that make up Canada as well as to have a *critical view* of the present. Only then is it possible to understand specific issues such as the predominance of hockey in Canada, the Canadian "style" of hockey, the recent presence of Soviet players, the debate over hockey franchises, etc.

In looking at the positive drug test of Ben Johnson, for example, a social scientist would place the test results in the context of the history of the Olympic Games, the relationship of the athlete's experience as a Jamaican-Canadian, and the attitudes towards drug use in high-performance sports.

Sport studies are done by social scientists at the *macro level* and at the *micro level*. At the macro level, sport and sport organizations are analyzed on a large scale. In these kinds of studies, researchers evaluate organizational and institutional structures often involving large numbers of people. They examine such aspects as the relationship between the International Olympic Committee (IOC) and the Canadian Track and Field Association and in turn its relationship to the Ontario Track and Field Association and the Mazda Optimist Club (of which Ben Johnson was a member).

COMMON SENSE VS. RESEARCH

Our impressions of the world do not always tell us the whole story, and sometimes even tell us a false story. Because we are so closely involved in events, it is sometimes difficult to be objective.

Social science strives to put aside superficial impressions and "common sense" conclusions in order to arrive at an accurate assessment of what is actually happening.

ON THE TREATMENT OF THE SEXES IN RESEARCH

Good research today is expected to meet the guidelines outlined by the Social Sciences Research Council in their handbook entitled *On the Treatment of the Sexes in Research*, written by Margit Eichler and Jeanne Lapointe. Men and women may have different attitudes and behaviour in the area of sport and this must be taken into account.

"Awareness of sex as a social variable therefore implies a dual perspective in research, a duality that must also be reflected in appropriate language" (Eichler & Lapointe, 1985: 6).

Social Science Methods

As in the natural and physical sciences, in order for research findings in the social sciences to have any lasting value, certain general procedures need to be followed to ensure that the results accurately reflect what is going on.

The Research Problem

Framing the research problem is probably the first and most important phase of social research. The research problem refers to the precise matter to be investigated. The research question usually indicates the researchers own sense of what is important.

Developing Hypotheses

The next step is usually to develop a clear *hypothesis* to be tested. An hypothesis expresses a relationship between variables. *Variables* are those elements that may influence or cause a certain thing to happen. For example, what relationships are there between such factors as family income, ethnic background, sex, age and the participation of children in track and field or hockey? The researcher then decides which techniques are going to be used to collect data.

Data Collection

Quite often social research involves surveying a particular group. A *survey* involves asking people their opinions on certain things. Even at this stage bias can affect the results if the sub-group being interviewed is not random. A *random* sample is achieved when the specific group being surveyed represents the wider population about which you wish to generalize the results. Typically, the researcher wants people of different ages, both sexes, a range of incomes and from various ethnic groups and geographic areas. To take an extreme example, if the researcher did a survey on sport preferences and only did the research in the Yukon on retired people, there would

be very different results from doing the same research on teenagers at Hubbards Beach in Nova Scotia!

There are other dangers with social surveys. The very way in which a question is presented can influence the results. For example, the sport researcher can ask *open-ended* questions that allow for any answer or *closed* questions — ones that limit choices. They often come up with different results (Shimizu, 1988: 22–27). Asking the question "Do you prefer hockey?" allows for only a "yes/no" answer. What if the person likes ball hockey? Will they answer yes? Will the person give the same answer to the question "Do you play hockey?" Would the researcher get the same answer if the second question was "Which sport do you play?"

Analyzing the Data

Having collected the data, one must now analyze it. Broadly speaking, the data and the type of analysis can be of two types: quantitative and qualitative.

Quantitative techniques are generally used to analyze large amounts of discrete information. Computers are often used to process the information quickly. **Qualitative** analysis is when people are interviewed in depth to get detailed descriptive information and more personal impressions from those surveyed. Here the emphasis is placed more on description and interpretation. Obviously, the distinction between these types of data analysis are not always clear and both can be used simultaneously.

Drawing Conclusions

Assuming the research is carried out with due regard to scientific procedure, the researcher can then draw the *research conclusion*. These research conclusions will redefine or substantiate the initial hypothesis and form the basis for further research.

Windows on the World

The way in which you view the world, of course, ultimately influences what you see. There are three main schools of thought — **structural-functionalism**, **conflict theory** and **symbolic interactionism**. What follows is a highly simplified description of these three approaches.

Structural functionalists see society as an integrated whole, something rather like a system or biological model. They see sport as inspiring members of the society to work together and they emphasize common values and co-operation. They tend not to stress conflict and power, but focus on the integration of society.

Looking at the Blue Jays organization, for example, functionalists might focus on the fact that when the Jays seemed likely to take the pennant the team pulled Toronto, and even the country, together. They would not focus on the fact that John Labatt Ltd. owns the team, that there was a short-lived strike in the summer of 1985, and the fact that there are few Blue Jays who live in Canada. The shared values, common goals and supporting mechanisms to keep an organization together are seen to be central.

Conflict theorists, as their name suggests, focus on the conflict in society and power struggles between groups. In looking at the Toronto Maple Leafs, they might focus more on the relationships between management, the coaches, team members and the shareholders. This perspective is often seen to be critical or radical. It usually involves a concern with changing how things are to make them "better" or fair. Conflict theorists tend to see society as being made up of those who own and control society and those who are employees and work hard but do not control society. Who owns the teams, who pays the salaries? Who makes the decisions? Why do strikes take place? Why do athletes become professionals? What is the source of conflict between players and coaches at high school? Why are there arguments over the use of recreational centres? Why are there fights between parents over ice-time for their children?

Conflict theorists see conflict and change as inevitable as different interest groups struggle over power and resources to get things done in their favour.

Symbolic interactionists do smaller-scale studies. In these studies, the perceptions of the participants themselves are most important. Such studies can yield valuable information not only about how the individuals perceive the world around them but also about the broader social structure.

The important element in this approach is how those in the situation define their world, their roles and their values. How do they make sense of the world? What are the symbols that function in their world view? What does the Olympic gold medal stand for? Is it merely a gold medal? What does it mean to be a player on a professional sport team? What does it mean to play for the Leafs?

Structural-functionalism, conflict theory and symbolic interactionism are general approaches to the world. It is important to bear in mind that in practice there is considerable overlap in the kinds of things investigated and the research findings.

Micro-level studies, as the name implies, look at people in small groups and examine what happens within them. What are the dynamics between team members, their interactions with coaching staff? What is the effect on a team when players who speak other languages and come from other cultures (such as the Soviets) are introduced?

Serious study of the social context of sport is a fairly recent phenomenon. In the past it was not taught separately at universities and colleges and research on sport and society was not funded. As a result, teachers and researchers were hesitant to choose sport as a focus for their studies. Today, however, there are many journals that

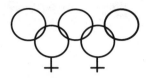

NEW OLYMPIC SYMBOL

This new Olympic symbol was developed by a group of participants attending the Canadian Olympic Academy at Dalhousie University in 1987. The group included Pat Galasso, Susan Gywnne-Timothy, Daniele Laumann and the author. It was thought that this symbol emphasized the importance of women in the Olympics and provided a powerfully different image.

The Terry Fox Run, Nationa Office.

Terry Fox, creator of the Marathon of Hope in 1980.

publish research specifically related to athletes and sport. Some examples are: *Journal of Sport Sciences, Canadian Journal of Applied Sport Sciences,* and the *Journal of Sport and Social Issues*. As sport has become a more dominant feature of society, its place in academic research has become more important.

Sport as a Commodity

When we look at sport in North America we find that it has increasingly changed from being an activity that many engage in to a product that is watched, bought, and consumed:

> In 1983 some 78 million attended professional and college baseball games; 76 million flocked to the horse races; 54 million to college and professional football contests; 42 million to college and professional basketball games; and another 20 million to hockey matches (Quoted in Eitzen and Sage, 1986:15).

Sport is also increasingly dominated by corporate demands. What sports can be marketed most effectively, show well on television and generate the most profits? The sport teams of high schools, colleges and universities tend to act more and more as feeders to the "big time" professional sport systems.

The athletes themselves increasingly serve the needs of the business sector. Is the athlete marketable? Does he or she present well? What angles can be used to present them? *Globe and Mail* sportswriter Stephen Brunt calls this image of the presentation of an athlete, such as a boxer, "the subtext." "What's his 'story'? Is he motivated by a loving father or a crippled brother, by his love of country or city or state, by the desire to combat child abuse?" (Brunt, 1989:100). The skills of the athlete have become part of the entertainment industry. The super-stars are packaged in the same way movie stars once were. Is this what we want sport to be?

Amateurs and Professionals

Recreation is that group of physical activities that is largely outside the direct driving force of marketable commodities. Unlike professional baseball and hockey, participation in rowing, canoeing, running, *t'ai chi*, sailing, cycling are for fun. No one directly makes a profit. There may be coaches, trainers and various experts but the goal is different.

The modern Olympic Games, first held in 1896, were originally defined as athletic competition for *amateurs*—more for fun than for profit. Strict guidelines were enforced to exclude those who played sport for money. Nearly one hundred years later, the Games have

~ SPORT PROFILE ~

Terry Fox—Marathon of Hope

b. 1958, Port Coquitlam, British Columbia; d. June 28, 1981 at 22 years of age. Terry Fox was an active basketball player in high school but in 1977 was diagnosed with osteogenic sarcoma (bone cancer) in his right leg. His leg was amputated six inches above his knee. Fox was so overcome by the suffering that he witnessed while in the hospital that he decided to run across Canada to raise funds for cancer. His journey was called "The Marathon of Hope."

Terry Fox's "Marathon of Hope" took place in 1980 with the simple objective of raising the awareness of all Canadians about the critical need to find a cure for cancer. Fox began the run in Newfoundland. Initially, few paid much attention to this gutsy, committed, somewhat angelic-looking young person, but gradually the media and the public began to notice the courage and determination of this young man. In spite of the terrible pain and incrasing weakness, Fox continued running.

Sadly he was only able to complete the 5,342 kilometres to Thunder Bay in northern Ontario before he became too ill to continue. Cancer had spread to his lungs. Terry Fox's fierce determination resulted in raising $24.17 million for cancer research. This amount satisifed his goal of raising one dollar for every Canadian. By March 31, 1990, "The Marathon of Hope" and the annual "Terry Fox Runs" raised in excess of $90 million to support the research efforts of the National Cancer Institute of Canada (NCIC).

"The Terry Rox Run" raises funds for use in cancer research primarily through an annual event which is held every September. The NCIC is the sole beneficiary of the funds raised. NCIC utilizes these funds for innovative cancer research seeking the secrets behind the early detection, treatment and cures for all cancers.

But the importance of Terry Fox's achievements reach far beyond raising the millions of dollars. Fox redefined the perception Canadians and others around the world had of persons with disabilities.

Fox was completely dedicated to hope for the future and achieved what many fully-abled individuals could not have done. Most importantly his memory lives on.

"The Terry Fox Run" strives to maintain the heroic efforts and integrity that Terry Fox represented. It is a grassroots organization. It does not allow any commercialization, nor does it seek any government funding other than small amounts for part-time help on a short-term basis.

The sucess of the runs is made possible by the dedication and hard work of over 100,000 volunteers who organize in excess of 2,500 run sites in Canada. Across the country over 500,000 participants walk, jog and bike in memory of Terry Fox to raise funds. Nine "Terry Fox Run" offices in Canada with 20 full-time employees support the magnificent work of the organizers.

During 1990 there were also 65 international run sites in such countries as Belgium, Germany, England and Australia and various cities in the United States. Approximately 24,000 people participated in these international runs which raised over $400,000 for cancer research.

Source: Compiled from material supplied by Betty Fox—The Terry Fox Run National Office, October, 1991.

changed considerably. In 1988, Olympic television coverage was extensive. NBC "paid $300-million (U. S.) for exclusive domestic rights to the Games, … presenting nearly 180 hours of coverage—75% of it live" (Campbell and Christie, 1988:A15). During the Games it was impossible not to see sporting activities on television.

The physical size and the numbers of participants in the Olympics of today are staggering. In 1896, 311 athletes from 13 nations, all of

"FIRST NATIONS"—THE USE OF WORDS

Different words are used by various authors to describe North America's first peoples, depending on the historical period in which they wrote and their political perspective. Any of the following terms are used: aboriginal, indigenous, native, and Indian peoples.

There has been much debate over these terms. Some feel aboriginal is too narrow a term, others that native people is inappropriate and that Indian can be confused with East Indian or is somehow demeaning. In the 1990s, many people prefer to use the terms "first peoples" or "first nations" because they feel it best expresses the special history of native peoples in Canada and the United States.

Alwyn Morris holding his eagle-feather, 1984 Olympics.

them men, attended the first modern Olympic Games in Athens. In 1988, almost fifteen thousand athletes attended the Olympic Games in Seoul and approximately a quarter of them were women. The complexity of the facilities and the billion-dollar expenditures have matched this growth as well. The Olympics are no longer a gathering of amateur athletes on a small-scale!

At the first Winter Olympics, which took place in 1924 at Chamonix in France, sixteen nations were represented, with 281 male competitors and 13 women. Nowadays, in order merely to bid to be the host city for the Winter Olympics, complete facilities for the athletes, coaches, officials and media have to be available. Also, communication and transportation systems must be available for participants and observers. In order to cover the range of sports, Calgary had to construct five different venues (or sites) when it hosted the Winter Olympics in 1988.

The focus on young athletes and their performance at the highest level tends to get lost in the huge budgets and big buildings. No wonder some athletes feel like the gladiators from Ancient Rome. They are at the centre, yet somehow they are not. The enlargement of the Olympics and their commercialization reflect changing attitudes towards sporting activities.

Who Is Defined as A Winner or Loser?

What is thought to be appropriate sporting activity varies from country to country and even between ethnic groups within one country. In some countries sport is still thought to be inappropriate for women, for example. Even in the 1988 Olympics, some countries insisted on having a man lead their country's delegation into the stadium. In the past, the colour of an individual's skin prohibited an athlete's participation.

Such attitudes are based on stereotypes and prejudices. The implementation of these ideas is **discrimination.** Discrimination can take many forms and has been an important aspect of sport, as it has in society. Values about how individuals should be treated affect an athlete's career and also influence whether an individual will decide to dedicate himself or herself to achieving success in sport.

There is heated discussion over the experience of athletes of colour in professional sport. In the United States, talented black baseball players were excluded from participation in major league baseball until 1946, and as a result, they were forced to play in the Negro Leagues. Even the most talented black athletes did not have the chance to prove themselves in the major leagues. Nor did they have the opportunity to make the high salaries earned from working within

~ SPORT PROFILE ~

Alwyn Morris—Overcoming All Odds

b. 1958, Kahnawake, Quebec. Other canoeing club members referred to Alwyn Morris as "just a little shrimp" when he was a 110-pound, 14-year-old who wanted badly to compete. He spent most of his first year in the club doing jobs like sweeping out the clubhouse and remembers being yelled at and told to get out of the boats.

Above all, Alwyn Morris was, and is, tenacious and determined. By 1975, he had grown to 5'8", 130 pounds and had become national kayaking champion. In spite of the fact that there was little coaching and help with his training, Morris still wanted to compete and win. He explains: "Being headstrong is important. It has helped me more than it has hurt me over the years."

Morris was able to withstand racial taunts and prejudices when people said to his face things like "you stupid savage," "you're the token Indian," and possibly even more demeaning (especially for an athlete because of its denial of hard work and training), "Of course you're going to do well in kayaking, you're an Indian."

Like many members of his family he was interested in and skilled at various sports. His grandfather, Tom Morris, competed in lacrosse and had hoped that Alwyn might have followed in his footsteps. His grandfather had always stressed the importance of doing well, focusing on the work at hand and ignoring detractors.

This special relationship with his grandfather became even more important as it became clear to everyone, including Morris and his teammate, Hugh Fisher, that they were going to finish in the medals in the 1984 Olympics. Morris wanted to express his cultural heritage and honour his grandfather on the Olympic podium—at the moment of his triumph. He pondered for many months on the nature of that expression. Some suggested he wear a traditional travelling cap, others that he wear special clothes. But none of these seemed appropriate.

The eagles would always be in the trees watching and following while Alwyn Morris trained with other athletes, who had become like his family, at the University of Victoria. The water, the trees, the concentration on technique, the fatigue, the quiet and the eagles—they were all linked. Then, just before the Olympics, Morris was invited to a meeting of native peoples from across the United States at a local Friendship Centre. There they presented him with a beautifully beaded feather—an eagle feather! To Alwyn Morris, it seemed predestined—the kayak, training for the Olympics and the eagle all seemed inextricably linked. He just knew what his symbolic gesture at the Olympics was going to be.

Morris approached his coaches with the proposal to mount the podium with the feather and heard no objections. Political gestures are not allowed at the Olympics, but everyone recognized Morris' special relationship with his grandfather and his heritage as a member of the Mohawk Nation of Canada's First Peoples. So, while he received his gold and bronze medals, he proudly held high his beaded feather, a symbol of his heritage.

However, that is not the end of the story. Today, he heads the Alwyn Morris Foundation to encourage sport and health for First Peoples in Canada. He has been central in the planning of the First Nations Sport Secretariat. His aim is for all native children to feel proud of being part of the founding nations of Canada and to have the opportunity and support to become winners in the world of sport or any other field they choose.

Alwyn Morris overcame all the odds—little money, limited coaching in the early years and racial prejudice—to become an Olympic and all-round winner.

Quotations from a personal interview by the author, April 1991.

CAROL ANNE LETHEREN

An interesting "first" for Canadian women was the choosing of Carol Anne Letheren as the Chef de Mission, the head of the 567-member team at the Seoul Olympics. She had a twenty-year background in sport administration and coaching.

Athlete Information Bureau and COA (C. McNeill).

Debbie Fuller, champion diver from Quebec attended university in Florida.

that system. Don Rogosin has called these talented athletes the "invisible men." "Though the Negro League was virtually ignored by the dominant white culture, in the black community it was a cultural institution of the first magnitude" (Rogosin, 1983:4). The separate and not-equal sport system of the pre–1950s in the United States has been replaced with integrated sport, but many argue that racism continues. Reggie Jackson, the baseball player, recently said "We have a serious problem that isn't going away" (1987:41).

Similarly, racial discrimination has been a part of Canadian sport in the past as well, although racial discrimination was never officially enshrined in Canadian law. Native Canadian athletes, for example, have largely been ignored. Very few members of the First Nations' communities have become part of the wider sport community. For the most part, their needs and concerns have not been recognized or served.

Olympic ideals can make a person give up almost everything in the hope of obtaining a gold medal. Disabled athletes, for example, have spent years fund-raising simply to get their achievements recognized. Before Terry Fox and Rick Hansen, the media paid very little attention to the terrific dedication of disabled athletes. The distances, heights and times attained may not match the statistics of the international able-bodied athletes, but disabled athletes are certainly equal in their commitment to training, dedication to sport, skill of performance and desire for excellence.

Women in Sport

Images of winners created by the media reflect the values and structures of sport. Sport movies of the forties and fifties, for example, portrayed the heroes of the major leagues, and all the players in the movies were white. It is still difficult today to find movies about women and their athletic endeavours in spite of their achievements. If individuals are not allowed to participate in a formal sporting activity they cannot even try to become part of the winning group.

In Canada, this was highlighted when ten-year-old Justine Blainey wanted to play hockey at her skill level and in her own neighbourhood. There was no local girls' team at her level, so she tried out for a boys' team. She successfully met the criteria in terms of skill and ability. However, the Ontario Hockey Association said that it did not want girls on any of their teams. There followed a three-year court battle for the Blaineys. In December 1987, the Ontario Human Rights Commission decided that she did have the right to play on a boys' team if she had the skills.

Prejudice in Sport—Discrimination

Basis of discrimination	Labelled
Sex	Sexism
Skin colour: a) the Major Leagues in the USA b) South Africa	Racism Apartheid
Religion: Jewish	Anti-Semitism
Sexual orientation	Homophobia
Physical appearance: those mentally or physically challenged or disabled	Handicapped
Economics: lacking financial resources	Class chauvinism or elitism
Ethnic or cultural or regional group; this can be based on differences in clothing & lifestyle or language	Ethnocentrism

The Federal Government recognized that sexism exists in sport and issued its *Sport Canada Policy on Women in Sport* in December 1986. The document declared that:

Sport Canada's goal with respect to women in sports is as follows:

TO OBTAIN EQUALITY FOR WOMEN IN SPORTS

Equality implies that women at all levels of the sport system should have an equal opportunity to participate. Equality is not necessarily meant to imply that women wish to participate in the same activities as men but rather to indicate that activities of their choice should be provided and administered in a fair and unbiased environment. At all levels of the sport system, equal opportunities must exist for women and men to compete, coach, officiate or administer sport. (Government of Canada, Fitness and Amateur Sport, 1986:14).

Changes in governmental policy came about because of the pressure from the general public and lobby groups, such as the Canadian Association for the Advancement of Women and Sport and Physical Activity (CAAW&S), the National Action Committee on the Status of Women (NAC), an umbrella organization of 650 different women's groups, and the Legal and Education Action Fund (LEAF), which takes specific cases to court. There are also individuals in the government and within sport organizations who have worked hard to encourage better opportunities for girls and women.

UNESCO'S INTERNATIONAL YOUTH YEAR, 1985

UNESCO, in the International Youth Year in 1985, reiterated its commitment to physical education and sport as essential ingredients in the development of an individual's abilities, good health and self-fulfilment.

The International Charter of Physical Education and Sport (1978) declared in Article 1 that "every human being has a fundamental right of access to physical education and sport, which are essential to the full development of his (or her) personality" (UNESCO 1985: 29). However if you are born in one country, as opposed to another, your likelihood of having access to sport activities and facilities may be much greater.

Many Third World countries (developing countries or "have-not" nations) are struggling to provide health programs, education facilities or the fundamentals of food distribution to their populations. Discussions about exercise and games seem unimportant given widespread starvation and inadequate health, housing and services.

CITIUS, ALTIUS, FORTIUS

Sometimes, even the most positive expression about physical activity can be distorted in the reality of competition. The motto of the Olympics is "Citius, altius, fortius" or "Faster, higher, stronger." However the spirit of Olympism is much more that this. The Olympic Creed as outlined by Baron de Coubertin, founder of the modern Olympics, stated that:

> The most important thing at the Olympic Games is not to win but to take part, just as the most important thing in life is not to triumph but the struggle. The essential thing is not to have conquered but to have fought well.

Coubertin wanted to encourage sport participation and excellence. He emphasized the process of competing, not simply the goal of winning medals.

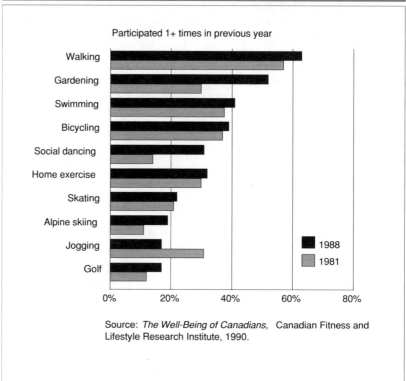

Source: *The Well-Being of Canadians,* Canadian Fitness and Lifestyle Research Institute, 1990.

Sport Canada's new policy is an important step for Canadian sport. The policy that there should be equality in sport for girls and women will have ripple effects throughout the country in the years to come. Some provincial governments in Canada are already drafting new policies on women and sport and these are expected to be ready in the early 90s. The key question now is how these various policies will be implemented.

Who Are We Going To Be—Winners or Losers?

A game played in New Guinea by the Motu people involves children making two circles. The inner group of children tries to swim underwater to get past the outer circle of children. The game is called *paro* and the emphasis is on cooperation. There is no winner. The game reflects the values of their culture, where the emphasis is on developing excellent swimming skills and not on winning the games as such (Calhoun, 1981:115).

Are You Fit?

- Do you yawn regularly throughout the day?

- Do you feel tired when you wake up in the morning and often do not really want to get out of bed?

- Do you become fatigued from tasks requiring minimal energy, such as climbing a flight of stairs or walking around a shopping mall?

- Do you run out of energy by the middle of the day or early afternoon?

- Do you experience a drowsy feeling for much of the day?

- Do you look or feel flabby?

- Do you fall asleep early in the evening while reading or watching television?

- Do you experience difficulty in coping with daily pressures?

- Do you experience nagging aches and pains?

- Do you find it difficult to relax?

- Do you often have an irritable disposition towards others?

- Are you often too tired to participate in leisure activities?

- Are you vulnerable to a variety of health problems, such as frequent colds and back pains?

- Do you generally lack energy and vitality?

Source: Robert V. Hockey. 1985. *Physical Fitness: The Pathway to Healthful Living.* Toronto: Times/Mirror/Mosby: 9

In North America, on the other hand, many children's sports are the training ground for the highly competitive professional sports such as basketball, baseball, football and hockey. The emphasis is on winning games and encouraging the potential super-stars who will go on to play professionally. The focus of many children has switched from playing and having fun to an emphasis on defeating the opponent (Blair, 1985:82). Even in such areas as gymnastics—where there is no professionalism as such—three-year-olds are now training.

In spite of this—or perhaps because of it—physical fitness in general has not been a priority in Canada. Studies show that the physical fitness levels of young children fall the moment they go to school. Children and teenagers tend to be physically unfit and overweight. The writer George Leonard describes his non-enjoyment of sport as a child:

> During my youth, organized sports was a world separate from mine. Physical education was something dreary and threatening, smelling of stale sweat, sounding of jeers and challenges. Athletics was something you "went out for," something *out there.* A team was something you "made"—or didn't make (Leonard, 1977:22).

Moreover, we know that children copy their parents' behaviour. An American study, The National Children and Youth Fitness Study II found that "approximately 50% of parents of young children say that they *never* obtain vigorous exercise" (Ross, Pate et al.:1987:92).

Fitness at school, an important part of early education.

VIOLENCE AND AGGRESSION IN SPORTS—A REFLECTION OF SOCIAL VALUES

Are the values that athletes operate under contrary to the rest of the world, or they are merely a reflection of the outside world?

Where there is an overemphasis on winning, pressure grows to stretch the rules—intimidating umpires and using unauthorized equipment, psychological warfare, physical assault or whatever seems to give "the edge." These become part of expected behaviour.

Aggression on the field or on the ice also seems to lead to aggression off the field. Horrible incidents have occurred after competitions have ended. Should it be necessary for athletes to be violent to win?

Drug use, for example, seems to be on the increase. As quickly as new testing methods appear, so up pops a new drug—to beat the system. Should athletes feel it necessary to take performance- enhancing drugs in order to compete at the elite level?

Fitness for international competition is not the same as fitness for a healthy life. It may be that a bodybuilder has to survive on 600 calories a day prior to competition "to peak" effectively, but it is clear that this kind of diet is a disaster for everyday living. Fitness is entirely individual and specific. The fitness performance profiles for gymnast, Mary Lou Retton and boxer Mike Tyson are quite different, as are the profiles of any top athlete compared with an average citizen.

Wellness is a concept that is used to describe all-round fitness and lifestyle. To be a winner in the context of wellness includes living in an environment that encourages physical activity and is not damaging to health through such things as pollution. It is also necessary to look at what the aims and goals are for school and recreational programs. If only the special, the above average and the gifted are placed on the teams, what happens to the average and uninspired majority?

Fitness is linked with diet and lifestyle. What does it mean if a person regularly works out and seems quite "fit," but smokes a pack of cigarettes a day?

What Kind of Sports System Do We Want?

There are many different viewpoints on sport issues. Everyone has to make up his or her own mind on these issues. However, it is necessary to think about some of the basic questions as these issues are discussed. What kind of sport system do Canadians want? Do Canadians want to win medals at the Olympics and pour public money into systems for elite athletes? Or, would we rather have a healthy, fit population and, to this end, put our money into recreational and health programs at the municipal and local levels? Should professional sport be more equitable? Should athletes "have" to take drugs to make them competitive internationally and professionally? In sum, what kinds of physical activities and sports do we want to encourage? What do we want our governments to spend our money on?

The media can and do play an important role in defining what sport is. Television promotes some sport activities and excludes others. The sports experts/reporters/journalists define the issues and frame the sport. They are central to the promotion of teams and sports personalities and play an important role in defining winners and losers. Closer attention to what the way sport and physical activity are portrayed in the newspapers, magazines and on radio and television will be particularly important in shaping the future of sport in this country.

Physical Fitness for All — The F.I.T. Formula

Physical fitness has five basic components:

- the amount of energy available to the muscles;
- the efficiency and capacity of the heart, lungs and blood;
- circulation;
- muscular endurance;
- muscular strength; and
- general body flexibility (Dyer, 1982: 17).

The F.I.T. formula

Many people are now doing aerobic exercises simply because they enjoy them. They are often done in a club where there is a social element involved.

The interest in aerobic exercise — from a fitness point of view—lies in the fact that most people today do not get their heart and respiratory rates elevated through their ordinary every-day activities. Many people take the car to pick up milk when the corner store is only a block away. Their work at home or in the workplace does not give the body an extended workout. Therefore, for many people it becomes necessary to raise their heart and breathing rates through exercise.

The formula used to encourage people to train effectively is the F.I.T. formula. The abbreviations refer to Frequency, Intensity and Time.

F = Frequency

I = Intensity

T = Time

It is important for a person to exercise frequently. It is better to exercise three or four times a week for half an hour than to exercise once a week for two hours. **Intensity** refers to the need to exercise at an intensity where the heart and respiratory functions are raised to improve performance. If a person just jogs along so their breathing remains normal, they are not stressing their bodies and no improvement will take place. **Time** refers to the length of time the person has these rates elevated. To be effective it is important that it is at least for 15 to 20 minutes at a time.

Taking one's pulse

For a person to monitor their heart rate effectively, they must learn to take their pulse. This is done easily by resting two fingers on the side of one's neck to feel the pulse. It is easier than on the wrist, but you must be careful not to press too hard, because this will slow down your heart rate and you will have an inaccurate reading.

What one is looking for is the number of beats per minute. The fastest way to arrive at it, so you can continue exercising, is to count for 10 seconds and then multiply by 6. Say it is twelve beats in 10 seconds: 12 x 6 = 72 beats per minute.

Do the count several times and then average them.

Am I exercising adequately?

The question now is, "Am I exercising adequately?" Then you have to do another calculation to find out what your target range for exercise is.

Target range

This is the pulse range within which a person should exercise to get more fit, but not to put too much strain on the body. It is linked to age as well. There is an upper limit and a lower limit. If you are above the upper limit, ease up. If you are below the lower limit, speed up.

There are several different ways to obtain the target heart training rate. One formula is outlined in the Fitness Canada handout:

Upper limit: 200 minus the age of the person. **Lower limit:** 170 minus the age of the person.

Using the formula with a person 21 years old: Upper limit = 200 –21 = 179 beats per minute. This person should ease up after 179 beats a minute. Lower limit = 170 - 21 = 149 beats per minute. This person should speed up below 149 beats per minute.

There are several different formula that may be used but it is generally agreed that it is necessary to get the heart rate elevated while exercising, walking, etc. Assuming one's health is otherwise good, to see improvement in cardio-respiratory endurance, one must train with one's heart rate elevated to at least 60% of its maximal rate. For a healthy student in his or her late teens, it may be more desirable to train at higher than the maximal rate (Bucher & Prentice, 1985: 57).

These figures are just rules of thumb and everyone should consult with their doctor before embarking on a exercise program.

Olympism: Philosophy of the Olympic Movement

For Pierre de Coubertin and those who helped establish the modern Olympics, the Games were to be more than an athletic event. They would be the focal point for a broadly based social movement which, through the activity of sport and play, would enhance human development and make the world a better place in which to live.

To this end, de Coubertin and his colleagues tied the staging of the Games and the work of the International Olympic Committee to a set of ideals which has come to be known as "Olympism."

Olympism is a state of mind, a philosophy even, encompassing a particular concept of modern sport, according to which sport can, through an extension of its practice, play a part in the development of the individual, and of humankind in general ... and to strengthen understanding and friendship among peoples.

These ideals can be summarized by the following six goals:

Mass Participation:	The expansion of opportunities for sport and play for *all* people.
Sport as Education:	The creation of opportunitites for personal growth through lessons learned on the playing field as well as through the application of sport in the classroom.
Fair Play:	Integrity, fairness and respect are the principles of fair play. With them, the spirit of competition thrives, fuelled by honest rivalry, courteous relations and a graceful acceptance of results.
Cultural Exchange:	The creation of opportunities for the international appreciation of cultures by making the visual and performing arts part of the Olympic celebrations.
International Understanding:	A movement that transcends racial, religious, political and economic differences, that promotes understanding, and thus contributes to world peace.
Excellence:	The pursuit of excellence in any endeavour. De Coubertin said that the quest for success is not a goal in itself but a means of aiming higher.

CITIUS	**ALTIUS**	**FORTIUS**

Source: Canadian Olympic Association.

ParticipACTION—Twenty Years of Toning Canada

Participaction is a non-profit, government fitness agency that has dedicated the last twenty years to encouraging Canadians to get fit. Its name and logo are instantly recognizable to virtually all Canadians.

It launched its campaign twenty years ago with the assertion that the average 60-year-old Swedish person was more fit than the average 30-year-old Canadian. The TV advertisement proclaiming this ran during half-time shows, shocking many Canadians.

The agency has rolled from success to success and is widely considered to be an important contribution to the fitness movement in Canada.

Participaction receives wide support from government, corporations and the media. The latter donate an estimated $15 million in free media space each year.

From the beginning, the agency has emphasized moderate activities to get Canadians fit—basically, whatever you want to do. It avoided promoting any particular activities, emphasizing enjoyment rather than exertion.

Russ Kisby, the organizations president since the Swede campaign, explains "We've always wanted people to know they don't have to be marathon runners to benefit from exercise. We want people to go hiking, cycling or just leave the car behind on that next trip to the corner store."

The current interest in fitness activities has much to do with the aging of the Canadian population. The post World War II "baby boom" generation is approaching middle age with concerns about living longer, healthier lives. But the role of Participaction in encouraging and giving direction to this need has been very important. Every Canadian has been affected by its message—for the better.

Source: Adapted from "Fitness Agency tones up Canada", *Financial Times of Canada*, December 2, 1991.

There are many conflicting ideas about what sport is. Sport is sometimes identified with nationalism and even militarism, yet it can serve to cross boundaries between nations. Sport is part of the entertainment industry but much of the delight attached to sport has nothing to do with money at all. Sport is often identified with white, male "macho" figures, but it also provides a vehicle for the expression of strength on the part of women, minorities and persons with disabilities. Sport is about ability and physical skills. Once a person is included in competition, his or her talent has to be recognized. Any stereotype or negative image is washed away in the reality of the sport performance.

What will sport become in the 1990s and beyond? It will become whatever we, as concerned citizens and sports enthusiasts, make it become.

Athlete Information Bureau and COA (T. O'Lett).

The martial arts—sports for fitness and fun or for fighting?

REVIEW

Questions

1. Why is it important to understand the social context of sport and physical activities?
2. Why is it sometimes difficult to see the whole picture?
3. How do social scientists study sport?
4. What are the main analytical perspectives used when examining the social context of sport?
5. On what basis have certain groups been excluded from sport?

Concepts

-   Values
-   Hypothesis, variables, survey, random sample
-   Qualitative, quantitative research
-   Structural-functionalism, conflict theory and symbolic interactionism
-   Discrimination — sexism, racism, elitism, ageism

Discussion

1. What kinds of things do we take for granted in sport?
2. What changes have you seen in sport in the last few years?

Terry Fox takes a break during his
Marathon of Hope run.

Crowds await anxiously as the skier on the 90-metre jump soars into the air at the Calgary Olympics, 1988.

Chapter Two

WHAT IS SPORT

"To get to any professional level you have to be very disciplined. You have to have a tremendous work ethic because if you don't you won't be around very long."
Raghib "The Rocket" Ismail, Interview with the author

"Great running is an art that is intensely personal, no two men do it quite alike. When a cat makes a beautiful run, it's poetry and jazz. That's why no coach can 'make' a great runner. Great runners are works of God."
Jim Brown, NFL football player

PROFILES IN THIS CHAPTER
- Bobbie (Fanny) Rosenfeld
- Rick Hansen
- The Firth Sisters
- Fergie Jenkins
- Gaetan Boucher

What is sport exactly? In North America most research has focused on organized sport. When the term "organized sport" is used, it refers to sport where there are formal rules and regulations, officials, a history around the sport and specific kinds of rewards in the way of trophies, titles or money.

This book is primarily concerned with organized sport. However it will also discuss informal sport, games, fitness and recreational activities. These areas are equally important because many people participate in informal sports and recreational activities. If the narrower definition is used, these other activities are excluded.

Organized Sport in Canada

The sports covered by today's media are well-known to everyone. Television newscasters and sports writers publicize those sports that are part of the sports industry and tied to national advertisers and huge sport complexes. Other events, however, are not so well known, such as the Arctic Winter Games and the Northern Games. The First Nations' and Inuit peoples' games, for example, include events that are unfamiliar to southerners:

Baseball is a popular sport among young people throughout Canada.

SEVENTH ANNUAL NORTHERN GAMES

Sports and activities at the Seventh
Annual Northern Games:
Wrist Pull
Arm Pull
Bench Reach
Head Pull
Two Foot High Kick
Alaska High Kick
One Foot High Kick
Knuckle Hop
One Hand Reach
Airplane
Kneel and Jump
Bow and Arrow

SOURCE: Fawcett. 1977.

Cycling is for fun— First Nations
children on their bikes.

... Hic Skinning, Tea Boiling, Bannock Making, Fish Cutting, Muskrat Skinning, Tug of War, Canoe Racing, Duck Plucking, Harpoon Throwing, Seal Skinning, Fiddling, Juggling, Traditional Dress, Good People Contest, Sewing, Handicrafts, Drummers and Dancers (Inuit and Indian) (Fawcett, 1977:199).

Moreover, the focus of these events often is not merely to develop excellence in athletic skills: "The fundamental purpose of the games is to encourage mass participation, by all ages, cultures and walks of life, in a broad range of athletic activity" (*Arctic Winter Games*, 70:40).

In order to be part of a winning team, or to be defined as a winner, an individual has to be part of a system that allows him or her to be so defined. Unless skills or games are covered by television and the other media, those who participate in them will be almost invisible. There may be a stunning athlete who participates in the Pink Triangle Soccer League, for example, but few people know of this amateur league.

The games played at schools and the sports that receive the most attention from the media change over time. In 1867, when the new Dominion of Canada was formed, organized physical activities of various kinds took place. The traditional physical activities of the First Peoples took part, for the most part, separately from the new Canadian settlers. The influence of Britain was evident through the military garrisons and educational institutions. Cricket was an important sport, as were horse racing and curling. However, both cricket and curling were regarded as "alien" or British games (Metcalfe, 1987:21). Also, informal competitions and games such as "coon hunts, cock fights, rifle matches, wrestling and fisticuffs were common" (Metcalfe, 1987:16).

Gradually, with the growth in population and increasingly larger towns, the introduction of trains and the industrialization of the country, organized or modern sport as we now know it came into being. By the end of the nineteenth century, formal organizations were established for such sports as lacrosse, hockey and rugby. Competition, in the context of clubs, became more important and distinctively Canadian sport came to be emphasized. George Beers, for example, deliberately set out to make lacrosse Canada's national sport by promoting it and publishing a rule book. Baseball is often thought of as fairly new phenomenon because of the recent presence of the Montreal Expos and the Toronto Blue Jays, but baseball was the sport of the working or poorer classes 100 years ago. "By 1867 Hamilton (Ontario) boasted no fewer than seventeen baseball clubs" (Metcalfe, 1987:26).

The different socio-economic classes engaged in different sports. Those who were more wealthy played cricket, curled, rode horses,

Snow Snake — Kow-a-sa — A Cultural Tradition

Snow snake was one of the most popular games in Canada and the northern United States among the First Nations. It was considered the national game of the Iroquois. Snow snake competitions involved sliding or throwing a pole along a frozen track. Scores were individual but players formed teams. Betting took place and the prizes were often the snakes or poles themselves.

The snakes were two to ten feet in length, but most were six to eight feet long. "One end of the snake was enlarged and curved, giving the appearance of a snake's head. It was held so that the 'head' curved upward and this shape enabled it to easily pass over the irregularities on the icy path" (Oxendine, 1988:105-106). The poles were carefully decorated with eyes and special carvings and were beautiful works of art. They were polished and oiled to help them travel faster.

The trail was an important part of the competition and a grooved path was made by dragging a log through the snow or ice in a large open area. Sometimes water would be poured to make the trail smoother and faster. Then the competitors threw the poles, somewhat like a javelin throw. There are reports of throws at the same speed as major league pitching (100 miles an hour) and distances as far as a mile.

In the southern United States where the climate is warmer, a similar game is played on hard ground.

Today there is a growing interest in the sport, and competitions take place in many communities. In fact, some competitors are reluctant to let anyone else handle their snow snakes because the use of special polish and oils helps give an edge; in the same way skiers are protective of their choices of waxes and polish. It is a perfect sport for our cold Canadian climate and is an interesting example of the cultural context of sport.

held rifle-shooting competitions, rowed and snowshoed. Later in the century golf, yachting and lawn tennis would become important. For most of the working population, however, sporting activities took place primarily on special holidays and at events such as picnics, since people did not have a great deal of free time.

Organized amateur sports were developed primarily in Montreal and Toronto by the middle and upper classes. They had more leisure time to indulge in recreational activities. The commercialization of some sports began to take shape as well. Horse racing, ice hockey, baseball, rowing and lacrosse became professional sports. The National Hockey Association (NHA) was formed in 1910. Previously, amateur clubs had competed for the Stanley Cup. "The first professional league was the International Hockey League, which ran from 1904 to 1907. It was located in three small northern Michigan towns, Pittsburgh, and Sault Ste. Marie, Ontario" (Metcalfe, 1987:169). With the development of artificial ice, hockey games could be consistently promoted and the profits assured, as the owners could be sure that the games could take place.

The combined changes of **urbanization**—the movement of people from rural areas to urban areas or cities—and **industrialization**—the manufacture of goods by mass production—had a profound effect on physical activities. For the first time large numbers of people were gathered together for specific activities. At the same

THE MOST POPULAR PHYSICAL ACTIVITIES

JUNE:

- walking
- swimming
- bicycling
- calisthenics
- jogging/running
- baseball
- golf
- tennis

NOVEMBER:

- walking
- calisthenics
- bicycling
- swimming
- jogging/running

SOURCE : *Physical Activity Patterns in Ontario III: A Research Report from the Ministry of Tourism and Recreation.* Ministry of Tourism and Recreation, Ontario. 1986:5-9.

time, technological changes took place that allowed the transportation of spectators and the creation of large facilities with artificial electric light for evening events.

Today, organized and professional sport activities are fully entrenched as an essential part of our lives. In addition, people have more leisure time to participate in physical activities and to watch them. In June 1984, for example, 65% of Ontario's adults were active at least once a week and 44% were active three or more times a week. The most popular activity was walking. Activities vary from season to season, of course, and the Canadian weather also affects participation rates. Sports participation today also varies considerably according to one's sex, income and education. According to this study, more women (48%) were active three or more times a week than men (41%) in June; and in November 30% of women as against 26% men. However, more men expend high levels of energy. Those earning higher incomes were more active, which is not surprising as they tend to have more time and money for physical activities; 77% of those with a university degree participated whereas the figure was 38% for those with only public school education.

It is clear that many people are involved in various forms of physical activities today that would not be included in the category of organized sport. So, for our purposes, it is useful to distinguish three different categories of sport—organized, informal, and corporate sport activities (Eitzen and Sage, 1986:16). Fitness, and recreational or leisure activities are also discussed.

A Definition of Sport

The origins of this Middle English word "sport" are rooted in "to disport" meaning that the activity provided amusement, diversion and fun. Theoretically, all these elements should also be included today. Sometimes, however, these aspects are minimized.

In categorizing athletic activities, it is necessary to look at the reasons people participate at a given level and who benefits as a result of the activity. Athletic or physical activities range from being not very structured, with little competition and no direct rewards or benefits, to activities that are highly structured, very competitive and with very specific rewards. Sports sociologist Harry Edwards has classified the different aspects of physical activity using a range of factors (Edwards, 1973). Researcher Erik Allardt categorizes sport more simply by asking whether it has formalized rules, whether the emphasis is on physical strength or technique, and whether there is bodily aggression against other players (1970:27). The degree of institutionalization and the forms of organization can be significant too (Luschen, 1970b).

TABLE 2-1:

Classifying Physical Actvity: Sport, Game, Recreation, and Play

1 Very little.   2. Somewhat. 3. Present.   4. A great deal

❏	1.	Little outside influence.
❏	2.	Fantasy or make-believe a part of the activity.
❏	3.	Restraints on where the activity may take place.
❏	4.	Restraints on length of participation.
❏	5.	Little practical or utilitarian benefit (financial, material, power, status).
❏	6.	Little competition.
❏	7.	Little emphasis on rules.
❏	8.	Little emphasis on the individual.
❏	9.	Voluntary participation in the activity.
❏	10.	Little emphasis on ranking and roles and positions.
❏	11.	Little preparation in advance of the activity.
❏	12.	No formal history or tradition.
❏	13.	Little emphasis on group.
❏	14.	Physical exertion involved.

Source: Harry Edwards. 1973. *Sociology of Sport.* London: The Dorsey Press: 58–59 (modified).

RAGHIB "THE ROCKET" ISMAIL — ATHLETE ON A PEDESTAL

"Talking to the media comes with the territory of being a professional athlete. Some athletes like the attention and love to be bothered and want to talk to the media every day.

"I don't like to talk about myself much. It makes me feel uncomfortable with people asking questions. The reason I don't like it, is because you always hear people in society complaining how athletes always think they are on a higher pedestal than someone else, but they don't realize that by them constantly wanting to know about you and making you the focal point of certain things it's like they're raising the athletes.

"If you keep telling someone something a hundred times, the hundred and first time they're going to start believing they are kind of special. Not everyone is strong enough to be able to keep a level head and go on about their business."

Raghib "The Rocket" Ismail, interview with the author, June 1991.

Organized Sport, then, is a competitive activity that uses vigorous or complex physical skills, has rules, officials and a tradition in a cultural context (Coakley, 1986). In organised sport, the athlete is motivated by either personal or public rewards.

Let us now look in more detail at the various elements of this definition.

1. Sport is a competitive activity.

The dictionary definition of competition is: "to seek or strive for the same thing as another" (Webster,1965). Competition can take many forms. The competitor may be competing against the clock, as in downhill racing, or the athletes may be racing head to head, as in swimming. The competition can be in the form of team competition, one group against another. Competition can even take place against a record and the other person may no longer be living!

ROLE OF THE ATHLETE

An athlete in our culture is expected to do a number of things:

1. Set an example for others, especially children.
2. Be dedicated to their chosen sport and train hard.
3. Be a good team member.
4. Be respectful to coaches and organizers within the sport.
5. Represent their country and act as ambassadors.
6. Look like an athlete—be neat and clean.

2. Sport involves vigorous or complex physical skills.

The physical skills displayed in sport can be vigorous as in hockey or Sumo wrestling, or they can be complex as in snooker or skeet shooting. The latter two clearly are less vigorous but they do involve complex physical skills. Anyone who has ever made a bet at a pool table and tried to show off has probably found this out the hard way. Using this definition, then, neither chess nor checkers would be considered sport, but horseshoe throwing, croquet and *bacci* would be.

3. Sport has rules.

The definition we are using holds that there must be rules, but rules and regulations can be enforced in different ways (Coakley, 1986). There are three aspects of rule enforcement in sport.

(i) *Who participates*: There are the rules and regulations that determine who can participate and how. Provincial hockey associations, for example, ensure adherence to regulations.

(ii) *Equipment*: There are controls on the technical equipment that can be used. What size balls can be used? What protective gear is essential? What should be the size of the court? Can artificial turf be used? Are aluminum bats illegal? Should video replays provide the last word for referees?

(iii) *Officiating*: Those who participate in the regulatory agencies help train young athletes and officials (such as judges, umpires and linesmen) and ensure that the rules established are in fact respected.

4. Sport has a tradition in a cultural context.

The cultural context refers to the values and the ways in which sport is played. In North America, for example, it is part of our culture that football players are male and aerobics is viewed as a woman's activity. Male ballet dancers in the past were considered effeminate. Such stereotypical views about physical activity are often widely held and become part of the cultural context of sport. Culture influences the very sport activities that a nation participates in. In Canada, hockey is viewed as the "national" sport (although it used to be lacrosse); in Italy or Brazil, soccer gets the most sports coverage and is the game most often played in the school yards; in the Dominican Republic and Japan, baseball is the dominant sport. If we look at who participates in sport and physical activities we find that culture influences participation as well.

Hard Work and Dedication

Sport is not easy. It requires not only athletic talent, but just as importantly dedication and hard work.

Because of an unquenchable love of the sport, sometimes a person will work very hard in order to achieve a title even after he or she has reached an age at which one might expect that person to retire. Debbie Brill went to the Commonwealth Games at Edinburgh, in the summer of 1986 at the age of 33, because she did not want to give up high jumping. Jimmy Conners, tennis star of the 1970s and 1980s, competed at the French Open and the British championships at Wimbledon well into the 1990s. Tennis has changed dramatically in his lifetime and is now a power and speed game, but he retained a devotion to the sport and hoped for a chance of centre court victory.

Past athletic achievements and memories are not easily forgotten either. Men in their thirties and forties can be seen walking around suburban shopping malls wearing their hockey jackets from ten or fifteen years earlier. They worked hard to get them and they are still important symbols years later. Everyone has seen the dens lined with sport trophies. Girls put ribbons from horse competitions on bulletin boards in their bedrooms.

Often it is necessary for athletes to leave their home and friends at an early age to pursue their favourite sport. For many of these students, it means hard work both at school and in the summers.

Success in sport does not come easily. It depends in part on talent and very much on a dedication and love of the game.

5. Rewards and motivation in sport

The last aspect of our definition of sport refers to the question of motivation and rewards. Here there are two main elements: (i) *public rewards* and (ii) *personal rewards*.

(i) *Public rewards*: These are the direct benefits and rewards to the athlete. They include: money, incentive bonuses, medals, titles, trophies, ribbons, badges, letters, scholarships, public recognition, etc. Some people feel that professional athletes are only concerned with the financial rewards they can earn. But clearly the motivation has to come from other factors because the commitment and the training cannot be sustained merely through money. Also, in many sports there are few financial rewards available. There are not many sponsors lining up to support the biathlon or the high jump!

(ii) *Personal rewards*: These are sometimes not apparent to the outsider. They often include goals set by the athlete or individuals unknown to others. The goals of elite athletes are often in the public domain. Everyone knew that Ben Johnson and Carl Lewis were competing for the title of "the fastest man on earth." However, the man recovering from a heart attack whom we see walking quickly along the roadside might have set a goal merely to walk two kilometres in half an hour. He would certainly win no awards for that effort, but for him it is a goal he has worked long and hard to achieve.

Athlete Information Bureau (C. McNeill).

Hard work—Silken Lauman at a race in 1988.

Horror or Pleasure—The Bullfight

Bullfighting is a national sport that highlights different values about the appropriateness of certain kinds of sporting activities.

Traditional bullfighting in Spain focused on the skill of the *matador* in killing the bull. He was expected to show great bravery and skill in facing the bull. Today the focus is on the skilful use of the *muleta* (the small red cloth) and the cape. The *matador* must show no fear in the face of danger. (Zurcher & Meadows 1970:115–116).

When North Americans attend bullfights it is common knowledge that they cheer for the bull! Their emotions are stirred not by the courage of the *matador* but by empathy for the plight of the bull.

Animal rights activists do not see bullfighting as a sport but as cruelty towards animals. They have no interest in the tradition of training and bravery of the *matadors*.

Velcro Bullfighting—The Canadian Twist

Portuguese-Canadian bullfighting in Listowel, Ontario, adds a new twist to a sport often regarded as brutal—velcro.

"Instead of jabbing the bulls with traditional spear-ended banderillas, the matadors use those fitted with velcro. The spears cling to a mat fitted on to the animal's back" (Stoynoff, 1991: A3). Portuguese bullfighting is "nothing like the Spanish. It's all done with much respect for the bull—to highlight the art, the spirit. The matadors are like cultural heroes" (ibid: A3).

There is no blood, nor wounded bulls in the humane Canadian-style bullfight.

Canadian Olympic Association.

Bobbie (Fanny) Rosenfeld, a winner in many sports.

Public or external rewards often act as motivators for athletes but they do not provide the complete answer. When mountain climbers are asked: "Why did you climb Mount Everest?" they reply "Because it's there." This sometimes seems bizarre to others, but is not far-fetched for the climber. Often people will attempt tasks for reasons that are entirely private. The general public does not know the reasons. This can apply to "ordinary citizens" as well. People are motivated for all kinds of reasons. Immediately after John Bassett's death, his daughter Carling Bassett said that she wanted to continue to play tennis the best she could in his memory.

(She) fulfilled one of Johnny F.'s final wishes: Keep playing and play well. She did. Less than two weeks after his death, Bassett "re-dedicated" herself to tennis, advancing to the quarterfinals of the French Open. She also paid him tribute after winning the Canadian singles title last month in Mississauga (Ormsby, 1986).

Bobbie (Fanny) Rosenfeld—Canada's Female Athlete of the Half Century

b. 1903 Ekaterinburg, Russia, moved to Barrie, Ontario, as an infant; d. 1969. Fanny Rosenfeld is Canada's Female Athlete of the Half Century, yet like many talented Canadians she is not well known. In Canada we hear about Babe Ruth and American achievements but we rarely see movies of our very own heroes, especially if they are women. There are biases as to who is likely to be promoted as a hero.

Rosenfeld was unusual in that she was a very talented, all-round athlete. She became known to the Toronto racing community when she decided to enter a 100-yard dash at a picnic, surprising herself and everyone else by beating the then-Canadian champion sprinter, Rosa Grosse.

She played on championship basketball teams, won the grass tennis court championship in 1924, won hurdle races, threw the javelin, played softball and hockey. She said hockey was her favourite, but her track and field performances were more popular with the public.

Rosenfeld was an impressive competitor—she set three records in 1928, which lasted into the 1950s: 18 feet, 3 inches in the running broadjump, 120 feet in the discus, and 8 feet, one inch in the standing broadjump. There were no fancy track clothes provided by sponsors, so Rosenfeld competed in the 1928 Olympics in Amsterdam wearing the baggy shorts that belonged to her brother! Athletic events were not part of a high-profile business as they are today.

Constance Hennessey, who was a founding members of the Toronto Ladies Athletic Club (in 1920), described Fanny in this way:

"She was not big, perhaps five-foot-five. She didn't look powerful but she was wiry and quick. Above all she was aggressive, very aggressive physically. No I don't mean that she made a lot of noise or had a belligerent manner. She simply went after everything with full force.

"She was a fine hockey player. She checked hard and she shot like a bullet. On the basketball court she drove with the ball if she had it, she drove after it if someone else had it. She was just the complete athlete and I am certain she would have been good at any sport. Certainly she was as good as one could see in track and field, hockey, basketball and softball (Wise and Fisher, 1974: 79)."

Arthritis forced Rosenfeld to retire from competition in 1933. She then worked for many years for the Toronto *Globe* newspaper as a sports writer. Her determination was balanced with good humour and caring for others. She worked hard to promote sport and sport for girls and women in particular.

Today there is a memorial to her in her home town of Barrie and a beautiful park next to the SkyDome in Toronto is named after her. Her family attended their openings and the group included her sister Ethel and nephew Gary Berman. Her great niece and nephew Joshua and Tara Berman, who were there also, hope to emulate her commitment to excellence. In this way, we see the Fanny Rosenfeld tradition continuing.

One hopes the biases that have caused women such as Rosenfeld with exceptional talent to be ignored will soon vanish.

The reward could also just be the very special pleasure that the physical activity brings to the person—the sound of the stick on the ice and the sense of pleasure when the puck slides into the goal; the smells of the grass in the afternoon work-out when the tackle meant a successful down; the good feeling from making a perfect catch; the sense of satisfaction from making an impossible slide; the triumph when the angle of the dive was just right; the delight when you know you couldn't have run any faster because the stride was perfect. These are the kinds of things you cannot write on a trophy or put on the wall or in a bank account.

TABLE 2-2:

Defining A Sporting Activity

ORGANIZED SPORT ACTIVITY	INFORMAL SPORT ACTIVITY	RECREATIONAL ACTIVITY / PLAY
ice hockey	street hockey	shooting pucks
football	touch football	throwing a ball
NCA* triathlon	cycling to school	wheelies
Little League baseball	park baseball	practising pitches

Source: National Cycling Association.

The personal search for excellence, competing against the very best person or team in your sport is also part of the reward of sport. It is also something that those who watch, or coach, never know. Only the actual competitors truly know the respect each athlete feels for the other. They understand the work, the courage and the effort because they have walked in similar steps to reach the same goal.

What are the Aims of the Physical Activity?

In order to categorize different sport activities, it is essential to put the activity in context. Who organizes the physical activities and what are the aims of the organizations or those who participate?

In organized sport activity there are formal structures where the regulations of the sport are enforced. In organized sport, athletes can be excluded from playing if the rules and regulations are not followed. The tennis player John McEnroe, for example, has been suspended or fined on numerous occasions for inappropriate behaviour, being rude to officials, spectators and other competitors. Zola Budd, a runner who was born in South Africa and moved to England in order to avoid the ban against South African athletes, was excluded from the Commonwealth Games in the summer of 1986 and the Olympics in 1988 because of her questionable British citizenship and South African residency. Pete Rose, the manager of the Cincinnati Reds, received a lifetime suspension from baseball for his gambling activities in 1989.

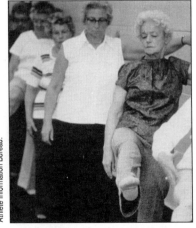

Athlete Information Bureau.

Seniors' fitness—exercise is now more popular among seniors.

Physical Activity in Context

The same physical activity performed in a different context might be labelled sport in one context and recreational in another.

When a person is out windsurfing and speeding with the wind, the activity is labelled recreational. The same person sailing in a windsurfing competition is seen to be participating in a sporting activity. In recreational activities the emphasis is on enjoying yourself with no officials present. It certainly does not mean that the activity is taken any less seriously and often a strong competitive element is present.

Bike-riding, to take another example, can take place in a number of different contexts. If an athlete enters a triathlon, that participation would be considered a formal sport. If the person went on a non-competitive distance tour with his or her local club, it would be informal sport. Going on a scenic ride to a local conservation area would be labelled a recreational or leisure-time activity. In the latter example, there is physical activity involved, but it is not competitive, nor are there officials involved. A child playing in the lane doing "wheelies," on the other hand is indulging in play.

Corporate sport is organized and run on a business basis by a corporation. The focus is on running the business at a profit and on marketing the sport by linking it with products that can be sold to sports fans. The classic form, of course, is the one we are all familiar with—commercials. The products can include sporty cars and clothes. The focus is on sport as entertainment. The sport is marketed as a product in order to maximize exposure and eventually profits. The athletes within the system may love the sport themselves but often feel like *Meat on the Hoof,* as Gary Shaw described his college football experiences. Athletes are "a commodity to be manipulated, hazed, drugged, used, traded and discarded" (Leonard, 1977:20)— and this was written about college football in the sixties! These business organizations have links to other aspects of the business world and directly to the media. Obviously, they are a very powerful group in shaping the consciousness of the nation.

What we find increasingly is that both informal and organized sport activities are influenced by corporate or marketable sport. Children copy major league baseball players they see on television and try out for little league teams. The form and structure of the sport experience imitates professional sport. The activities of children are being prepared, organized and evaluated on the basis of their potential for professional sport. (This is discussed further in later chapters.)

Recreation and Leisure

A logical question to ask after arriving at a definition of sport is: when is a sport not a sport? What do we call those activities that meet all the criteria of the above definition—competitive, vigorous or

Rick Hansen—The Phenomenal "Man in Motion World Tour"

b. 1957, Port Alberni, British Columbia. A truck accident at the age of fifteen left Rick Hansen with both legs paralysed. He decided he would not let this interfere with his interest in sport. He captained his wheelchair volleyball team to win three national titles and participated in many basketball championships and marathons.

Hansen's list of athletic achievements is truly phenomenal: 5 world track records; 1 Pan-Am Games record; 12 track gold BC Games; gold 800m.; silver 1500m; bronze 4 x 100 m. relay, 1980 wheelchair Olympics; BC wheelchair tennis singles titles 1981–82; participation in a special event, the 1500m. at the LA Olympics; and there are many others. He was also the first disabled person to graduate from the University of British Columbia with a degree in physical education.

Hansen is probably best known for his 25,000-mile wheelchair tour around the world. This trip took him through 34 countries. The purpose of the "Man in Motion World Tour" was to raise $10 million dollars for spinal cord research, rehabilitation and wheelchair sports *and* to create awareness of the potential of disabled persons.

Hansen explains: "Since the time of my accident, two major dreams have inspired me. One is to help those people with spinal injuries and the other is to wheel around the world" (Sokol, 1985a: 140).

complex physical skills, with rules, a tradition and rewards—yet have no officials? For our purposes these kinds of activities are called informal sport or recreational activities. **Recreational activities** are those activities where there are no enforced rules as to how the activity should take place. Competition and physical activity may or may not be present. The focus is on enjoyment.

Recreational activities are usually not competitive and the focus is on enjoyment and fun or play. The same physical skills are present, but the focus of the activity is different. A few examples make this point clear. An athlete may participate in a hockey league where there are rules and regulations enforced by officials with rankings and trophies at the end of the season. Here the participation is in organized sport. He or she might also play street hockey on Sunday afternoons, which would be labelled as an informal sport activity. There are rules, it is competitive and it is physical. The enforcement of the rules may vary, and the number of players most likely will be flexible. Neighbourhood participants are very clear as to what is considered to be appropriate behaviour. The focus of the game may be different, in that there are no trophies, but the physical activity is still very important. All the other aspects of defining an activity as a sport apply: competitive, specific rule expectations, tradition, etc. but the activity is not formally institutionalized.

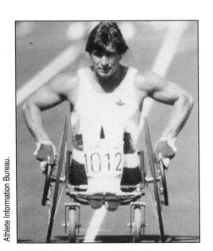

Rick Hansen, competitor and fund-raiser for spinal cord research.

Patterns of Physical Activity

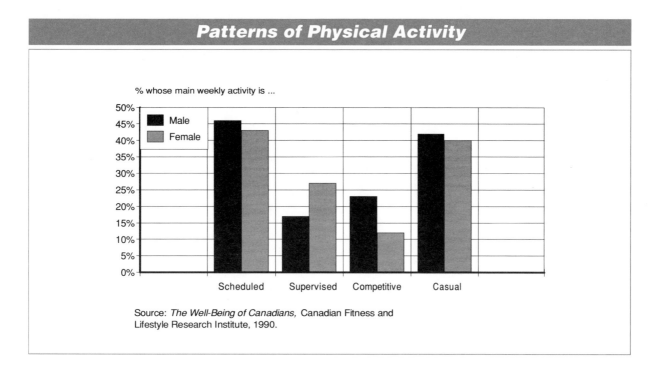

% whose main weekly activity is ...

Source: *The Well-Being of Canadians,* Canadian Fitness and Lifestyle Research Institute, 1990.

The participants are involved with the activity for the pleasure associated with the activity in and of itself. Another factor may be the prestige associated with the activity. Admiring glances at the lines of the handmade canoe, the newly designed windsurfer, the sleek lines of the yacht, or the curves of the improved skateboard may take place. The purchases associated with these products certainly make up a recreational sporting industry, but the goals of the participants are different.

In order to clarify the different categories of sport further, we should also distinguish between competition in the context of organized sport and a sport contest. A **contest** is a competitive activity where there are no official rules and regulations established by tradition.

When Carl Lewis and Ben Johnson raced, there were regulations as to the length and surface of the track. There was sophisticated electronic equipment to measure the speed and officials to ensure that the starts were correct. This is an example of a sporting competition. A contest is an informal competition. One person racing another to the bottom of a ski hill is a contest. "The last one down buys the coffee" is a typical example of a non-institutionalized competition. Whether the activity is downhill skiing or running, the purpose is to see who is the fastest. The events are competitive and physical and there may

TABLE 2-3:

Percentage of Population Engaged in Outdoor Recreational Activities (U.S.A.)

	Professional	Clerical	Service Labourer	Student
Camping in developed area	39	33	28	41
Camping in a primitive area	26	20	26	29
Sailing	19	14	6	20
Fishing	51	47	56	67
Outdoor pool, swimming, sunbathing	56	54	47	63
Walking to observe nature, bird watch	66	47	46	57
Hiking or backpack	43	28	29	42
Other walking or jogging for fun	76	67	64	88
Bicycling	53	49	53	87
Golf	28	14	11	22
Tennis outdoors	46	37	27	67
Cross country skiing	7	2	2	6
Snowmobiling	8	7	10	12
Attend outdoor sports events	73	69	61	82

Source: Geoffrey Godbey. *Leisure in Your Life: An Exploration.* Toronto: Saunders College Publishing. 1981 (modified).

even be a tradition, but there are no officials or codified rules. Who has not been cheated of a win by a fellow competitor who shrugs off your anger at losing by saying "You never said we had to go down the same run?"

Another aspect of recreational activity over which there has been a great deal of discussion is the term leisure-time activities. **Leisure activity** is activity that is done outside the context of work and is fairly unstructured and not very competitive. Here activities such as playing touch football or soccer would be included. Yet we must keep in mind that a similar activity played by a professional athlete becomes a sport.

Recreation and leisure time activity varies from society to society and from economic group to economic group. A study conducted by the U.S. Department of the Interior, the *1978 National Outdoor Recreation Survey*, presents a number of different categories of

~ SPORT PROFILE ~

The Firth Sisters—Remarkable Cross-Country Skiers

b. 1954, Aklavik, Northwest Territories. Stephen Firth, a Loucheux-Métis trapper was relocated from Aklavik to a new government village called Inuvik, one hundred miles above the Arctic Circle. Here his twin daughters, Shirley and Sharon, became part of a cross-country ski program established by a Chamonix, France-born skier and Oblate missionary priest, Father Jean Marie Mouchet.

From its beginnings as a community project with young and old involved, this program was developed by Father Mouchet to link with the National Fitness Council of the Federal Department of Health and Welfare. With a small budget of $25,000, they established the Territorial Experimental Ski Training (TEST) program in Inuvik (Bryden, 1987: 159).

In 1967, five hundred skiers went through the program and finally ten athletes were selected for the Inuvik ski team. Thirty- and forty-kilometre training sessions often took place in temperatures as cold as 45 degrees below zero, and in the dark as well. The aim of the program was to encourage and support athletes from the north to attain their best in international competition.

The Firth sisters enjoyed competing against each other. It was as if they spurred each other to do their best. Dominating women's cross-country skiing, both won race after race through the 1970s. In 1978, at the Canadian Seniors in Sault Ste. Marie, Shirley Firth won three gold medals in the 5km., 10km., and 20 km. races.

Shirley and Sharon Firth are the only Canadians in the history of the Olympics to have competed in four consecutive Winter Games. For them, seeing many parts of Canada and the world were as important as competing in the Olympics.

occupations and their relationship to leisure activities, some of which we would not call sport activities. The participation rates vary with occupation and are linked to other factors such as cost, availability and lifestyle.

Golf, for example, is much more popular with professional in-dividuals than with service workers or labourers, obviously due to the constraints of time and money. It is interesting that 22% of post-secon-dary students managed to play golf at least once. This reflects the fact that such students tend to have more free time and tend to come from more affluent families.

Cultural Attitudes Towards Leisure

A difficulty in assessing leisure and recreational activities in multi-cultural cities like Toronto, Montreal and Vancouver is the lack of literature on the ethno-cultural influences. Not only is research sparse in this area, but definitions of ethnicity are not consistent or clear. Many cultural differences seem to have an affect on sport and leisure participation. Among these are: the family as the unit of leisure, gender segregation, length of time in the new homeland and "iden-tity-maintaining" aspects of leisure (Hall & Rhyne, 1988b:4).

Cross-Country Ski Association.

Shirley and Sharon Firth, champion cross-country skiers.

It is unclear whether **ethno-cultural** variations in leisure are due to the values, traditions and customs of a particular group (the ethnicity explanation) or to **socio-demographic** variations among groups (such as income, education, age and gender). It is also possible that groups such as the Chinese, Portuguese and South Asian may have their access to leisure institutions limited because of language limitations.

Play and Spectacle

Playing is usually associated with children, but it does apply to adults as well. The girl hopping up and down her hopscotch diagram on the sidewalk is playing. The person constantly dunking basketballs in a net in the driveway is playing. Here there are no rules, no officials and sometimes even no goals.

Play is unstructured fun, where rules and regulations are not enforced. Usually competition is not present in any serious manner. Some psychotherapists have argued that one of the problems of contemporary living is that many adults do not know how to play. Playing is part of the joy of living, and if that enjoyment is denied an individual this will influence their whole personality.

Recreational activities, contests and playing are normally activities that take place in an informal context on a private basis. However, there is one other category that is important to consider—that is, sport as "hulk and bulk" spectacle.

Spectacle is the term used to describe physical activities where the emphasis is on entertainment and show rather than on the sporting or athletic elements. There has been a good deal of controversy over this question. Many devoted sport fans feel that their sport has been changed from a "serious" sport into entertainment. Sports about which this has been said include boxing, roller-derbies, and wrestling. Gradually, the emphasis came to be more and more on entertainment rather than on the sporting component.

Whenever professional wrestling is mentioned in a sporting context, people smile and think of Macho Man or Hulk Hogan. Wrestling is a sport that is now primarily considered to be entertainment. In fact, a large portion of the audiences at such events are often children. Although Hulk Hogan has made professional wrestling an even more popular sport, a fan who takes the outcomes seriously is ridiculed. The reason sports like wrestling and roller derbies are classified as spectacle, rather than as sport, is that the emphasis is not on the competition but rather on the entertainment and spectacle elements of the sport. The clothing, the personalities, the conflicts are all exaggerated. It is for this reason that people generally remember the

Athlete Information Bureau (T. O'Lett)

Champion bobsled team—C. Lori, A. Swim, K. Leblanc, H. Dell.

> ## ~ SPORT PROFILE ~
>
> ## Fergie Jenkins—Sport, History, Talent and Freedom
>
> *b. 1943, Chatham, Ontario.* Fergie Jenkins is the first Canadian to be inducted into the Cooperstown Sports Hall of Fame, because of his outstanding achievements as a baseball pitcher. However, like most Canadian young men, he played hockey and was on a Junior B Champion team.
>
> As a child Jenkins was energetic and athletic but by fifteen he had a dream to succeed in baseball in a way that had not been open to his father. Ferguson Jenkins Senior had played for the "Chatham black panthers, an all-black baseball team that barnstormed, and won a series of provincial titles" (Brunt, 1991:D1). But there were no professional baseball openings in the major leagues for black athletes at that time. His high school English teacher, John MacGregor, was convinced Jenkins had talent and arranged that he would be seen by a baseball scout. Gene Dziadura, a former player, and Tony Lucadello, a Philadelphia Phillies scout, coached him for three years to
>
> help improve his skills. Jenkins was picked up by Philadelphia and then found himself playing with a class D team in Miami.
>
> Fergie Jenkins has family ties to the south. His mother's family fled Kentucky in the mid 1850s. By means of the Freedom Train they escaped slavery to live a more independent although often difficult life in Canada. When Jenkins went to play baseball in the southern United States in the early 1960s he found life very different from that in Ontario. On the field black and white players worked together. Off the field lives were separate. Just as in the old South Africa, players drank from separate fountains and used separate washrooms. Black players were not permitted to stay in the same hotels and were billeted in the homes of black families. Jenkins describes his most irritating daily experiences: "At the Greyhound Bus stations we'd have to eat around the back. We couldn't eat in the restaurants. I'd give a teammate five dollars to get me something. I'd get mad but just for a
>
> few minutes" (FreshAir June 1991). Racial slurs and abuse from the stands were not all that the black players faced. Discrimination also meant life-threatening situations. On a number of occasions he was advised not to go out to the parking lot but to stay in the clubhouse because the Ku Klux Klan were meeting there. Fergie Jenkins explains: "In Canada we read about these things. I lived it in the United States." Jenkins was courageous and single-minded. As he puts it: "I went to play baseball and that's what I did."
>
> Jenkins is quietly loyal as well. In 1980, he was arrested for having drugs in his luggage on crossing the border into Canada. Bowie Kuhn the baseball Commissioner suspended Jenkins, who refused to name the drug users on his team. The suspension was lifted after arbitration, but to the present time he has never exposed his teammates.

personalities rather than the sporting skills involved. Often even the rules and the behaviour of the officials are part of the entertainment. While the referee is busy in one area of the ring, mayhem breaks out as a wrestler in another corner of the ring, to the roars of the crowd, is busy breaking the rules and hitting his opponent on the head. There are "scripts" to the competition, so the audience knows the "good guys" will win and the "bad guys" will lose.

In intercollegiate wrestling the focus of the sport is quite different. The athletes train, the officiating is taken very seriously and the emphasis is on the athletic skills of the participants. Theoretically, it is the same sport but in fact the focus is quite different.

The Underground Railway

There are a number of talented Canadian athletes whose family history goes back to the days of slavery in the United States. Fergie Jenkins, the great baseball pitcher, is one of these athletes.

The Civil War struggles over slavery in the United States are quite well known. What is not so well known is the history of Afro-Canadians.

John Graves Simcoe was the first Lieutenant-Governor of Canada. He had been influenced by the ideas of the English abolitionist William Wilberforce but found that the ruling circles in Upper Canada (with a population of 14,000) took slavery completely for granted.

In the second session of Upper Canada's Legislative Assembly, Chief Justice Osgoode drafted a bill "prohibiting the importing of slaves into the colony" (Hill, 1981: 16). It passed but was not enforced. However, black Americans began to trek North to Canada because it was known that black people could be free here.

In 1833, the *British Imperial Act* abolished slavery in the Empire. South of the border, however, the *Fugitive Slave Act* was passed by the American Congress in 1850 so that slave owners could arrest fugitives who had fled from southern states. This lead to bounty hunting and kidnapping.

George Brown, owner of the Toronto *Globe*, was a founding member of The Toronto Anti-Slavery Society, formed in 1851. The Society declared it would fight slavery by every legal means *and* help the "houseless and homeless victims of slavery flying to our soil" (The *Globe* quoted in Hill, 1981: 20). Harriet Beecher Stowe's book *Uncle Tom's Cabin* opened many people's eyes to the horrors of slavery.

The major route to freedom taken by runaway slaves is shown in the attached map. The Underground Railway did include sympathizers within the railways but it also included other methods of transportation. Many people from different walks of life risked their lives to help slaves escape to Canada. Alexander Ross, a Canadian doctor, who sometimes used his interests as an ornithologist to cover his activities, helped escapees, as did a very brave fugitive slave from Kentucky, John Mason.

Former Maryland slave Harriet Tubman is perhaps the most famous and certainly was very courageous. She conducted many dangerous trips to bring slaves across the border, and even had a price on her head of $40,000. There is considerable variation in the figures but it is thought that at least 30,000 fugitives reached Canada between 1800–1860.

Source: Daniel G. Hill. 1981. *The Freedom-Seekers: Blacks in early Canada.* Agincourt: The Book Society of Canada Limited.

Some sport analysts argue that other sports are in danger of becoming spectacles rather than sports as more and more pressure is brought to bear by commercial advertisers to increase the entertainment value of sports. Hockey is a case in point. The film *Slap Shot* was severely criticized because of the assumption in the film that hockey had to include fights in order for it to be a marketable product. Others feel that hockey as a sport has been "diluted" in order to open franchises and provide entertainment.

It can be seen that the same activity in different contexts can be labelled differently. A physical activity can be a sport, a recreational activity, a contest, an informal or formal game, play or spectacle.

Participation and access to sport have changed dramatically over the past twenty years largely because of the high-pressured marketing of sports and the growth of the sport equipment industry. Even in the area of recreational and leisure-time activities, the number and type of products available have increased enormously. Whereas our parents had a pair of running shoes that they used for running, tennis, walking, and the gym, today each of these activities is seen to need a specific type of shoe. In some ways, technical differentiation and specialization inhibits participation. To sell you skis, the salesperson feels it is essential to know what kind of skiing and what style of skiing you practise—"Do you skate?" is a skiing question. The same is true of bicycling. Does the recreational athlete need a mountain bike, a ten-speed, an eighteen-speed, an alloy frame? The industries have made more and more choices available.

Ideology and Sport

How sport is defined is much more than mere classification by the kind of activity performed. Sport, like other social activities, may be defined differently according to the beliefs held by a group or an individual. **Ideology** is the collection of values a person or group has about the organization of the world. It is what they feel is significant and how their world is structured. It is based on the people's perception of their relationship with the economic and political structures of their society.

Ideologies can be dominant within the society or they can be held by a minority. Stanley Klein, medical anthropologist, explains:

> … societies produce ideologies and subjects and so are historically conditioned artifacts. However, the function of ideology is to make both the world and its people appear not artificial and contrived but obvious, natural, and inevitable. Self and world are inextricably connected such that the reality of the former assumes and is psychologically premised on the integrity of the latter (Klein, 1987:37).

The outside world becomes part of how we define ourselves. We see ourselves as winners or losers through society's eyes.

Conflict over ideology usually turns nasty when it gets to money. Everyone is in favour of equal opportunity, but what will it cost? Government officials will say very seriously that they are concerned about the disabled, but will they allocate the money for ramps for access into public buildings, will they fund the disabled games? This is the true test of ideological beliefs.

WHY NAMES MATTER

Negro Leagues, Black Athletes, Afro-Canadian

The words we use are often at the centre of debate. The words used to describe people of colour have changed over time and have been at the focus of heated political debate.

Years ago it was considered most polite to use the term "Negro," so we read about the American Negro Leagues in the 1940s and 1950s. By the 1960s, many black Americans began to argue that the term "Negro" was derogatory and was a word used by white people to describe black people. "Black and I'm Proud" was one of the themes to establish a recognition of the independence and respect that the community demanded. So when we read about the outstanding athletes like Jackie Robinson and Willie Mays they are described as *black athletes*.

In the 1990s, many members of the black community prefer the term African-Canadians or Afro-Canadians because it highlights the historic links between North American black people and their historic roots in Africa. Others feel the term "people of colour" is preferable because it is more inclusive.

Therefore, we find different words and terms are used by different writers at different times in history. These usages reflect the social and political perspectives of the period.

~ SPORT PROFILE ~

Gaetan Boucher—The Commitment to Winning

b. 1958, Ste-Foy, Quebec. Gaetan Boucher, like many Canadian boys, was a good skater and liked hockey. However, he gave up hockey in favour of joining the national speed-skating team.

Gaetan Boucher won more individual medals at the 1984 Olympics than any other Canadian. It would seem that Boucher's success came easily to him, but that is not the case. He had to overcome three important factors before his Olympic successes, and one of them was his perception of winning.

First, Gaetan Boucher's size—he is only 5'9" tall, which makes him smaller than most speed skaters who have longer strides and can cover the ice more quickly. His height was a clear disadvantage.

The second obstacle was his own personality—he suffered from what is often said to be the classic Canadian syndrome—being "too nice." Canadians have had the reputation of lacking toughness and a competitive edge when it comes to big events. Boucher explains: "My reputation was that I'd always panic in an important situation. I was fine when I had perfect conditions and the opposition was weak but I seemed to lack toughness for real competition. I'm not sure, but I do know that's how the speed skating world saw me."

Third, one year before the Olympics, he smashed his ankle in training so badly the doctors thought he might never skate again (Proudfoot, 1985: 127).

After a rest period to recover, Boucher realized that he really wanted to win at the Olympics. "The ability to win is something very special. You know I was a good skater for a long while before I got the knack of victory. I didn't believe, deep down, that I could be first. Only when that belief changed did those medals become possible. I went to Sarajevo expecting—not hoping—to win. It seems to me now that more and more Canadians are acquiring that feeling. And if that is in some way a result of what I did in Sarajevo, it might be my greatest reward."

Gaetan Boucher's successes include a bronze and a gold in the 1984 Olympics as well as a silver in the 1980 Olympics. He explains: "Sometimes it strikes me that in hockey I might have become a very rich guy, but even so, I'll always feel I made the right choice. I doubt that any hockey player has ever had the kind of feeling I experienced at Sarajevo during those days of the Olympics. I wouldn't trade it for anything." (ibid, 1985:125)

Athlete Information Bureau (O. Bierwagon).

Gaetan Boucher, winner of three medals in the Olympics.

In the balance of this chapter we will look briefly at three areas where individual and group ideology or beliefs affect sport and physical activity today. These issues will reappear, in various contexts, throughout the remainder of this book.

Women and sport

Many people feel that Canadian society is dominated by beliefs and practices that are patriarchal. A **patriarchy** exists when a society is organized in such a way as to perpetuate the privileges of men.

Those concerned about sport and physical activity want to change society so that more opportunities are available to women and girls. They argue that fairness and equality should be a greater part of society and that there should be more money, time and space spent on physical activities for girls in schools, in communities, in coaching programs, etc.

Women in Sports Leadership

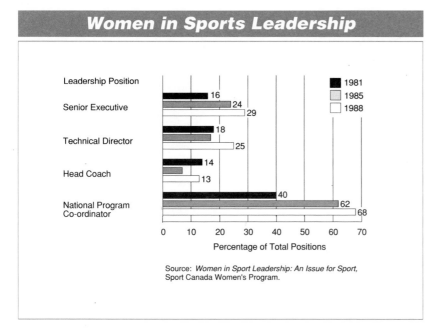

Leadership Position

Senior Executive
16
24
29

Technical Director
18
25

Head Coach
14
13

National Program Co-ordinator
40
62
68

0 10 20 30 40 50 60 70

Percentage of Total Positions

■ 1981
▨ 1985
☐ 1988

Source: *Women in Sport Leadership: An Issue for Sport*, Sport Canada Women's Program.

CHANGING VALUES

Yukon Erica is the professional wrestling name of Christina Dutkowski. She is one of the strongest women in the world—she can bench press 425 pounds.

Dutkowski is not well known in Canada—so far there have been few women's professional wrestling matches here. But in Japan she's a star.

Westerners often think of Japanese women as meek and submissive, but 60–70,000 Japanese women regularly pay to see Yukon Erica. The fans love to see her strength and power.

Sumo wrestling is part of Japanese tradition and, like the Sumo wrestlers, these professional women wrestlers train and dedicate themselves to competition from an early age. Christina Dutkowski brings Canadian expertise to this modern style wrestling that is respected and admired throughout Japan.

People of colour

At sporting events athletes are expected to stand at attention and listen quietly to national anthems. In a famous incident at the 1968 Olympic Games in Mexico City, two American athletes did not hold their hands over their hearts as is usual for American athletes. When they went to receive their medals, Tommie Smith and John Carlos stood on the podium with bare feet to symbolize the poverty of black people and raised their hands in a clenched fist salute. At that time black people in America were demonstrating in the streets to obtain equal opportunities in all aspects of social life. The bare feet and the clenched fists represented the ideology of equal opportunity, black power and the desire of black athletes to be heard. The American Olympic Committee felt it was inappropriate behaviour for these black athletes to bring "politics," (i.e. ideology) into the Games. The fact that racist, discriminatory ideology operated to prevent some athletes from participating in the games was conveniently forgotten!

Today black people are increasingly participating as equals in sports. Nevertheless, there is a long way to go before true equality can be said to exist in access, in the kinds of sports people of colour tend to participate in, and in coaching and management opportunities. Ideological beliefs and practices that segregate sports along racial lines are now under serious re-examination throughout North America and the rest of the world.

A wrestling star in Japan—Canada's Yukon Erica.

Christina Dutkowski.

Wheelchair Sport in Canada

Wheelchair sport began in 1944 as a form of treatment and rehabilitation for those with spinal cord injuries. Today, wheelchair sport has evolved from a recreational base to competitive sports excellence.

Officially organized in 1967, the Canadian Wheelchair Sports Association's (CWSA) mission is to promote and develop opportunities for Canadians to excel in wheelchair sport.

Structure

Nationally, CWSA has ten provincial offices responsible for developing recreational and competitive opportunities to meet the needs of wheechair athletes across the country. Internationally, CWSA is a leader in the development of wheelchair sport. Canada is one of over 70 countries who are members of the International Stoke Mandeville Wheelchair Sports Federation (ISMWSF), the world governing body for wheelchair sports.

Finances

CWSA is a volunteer, not-for-profit organization and operates on an annual budget of over one million dollars. Funding is derived from the following sources:

- Man in Motion Legacy Fund 40%
- Fitness & Amateur Sport 20%
- Sponsorship/Donations/ Fundraising 40%

Programs

CWSA governs the following ten wheelchair sports:

- Basketball
- Tennis
- Swimming
- Weightlifting
- Archery
- Track & Field
- Racquetball
- Shooting
- Table Tennis
- Wheelchair Rugby

On the competitive front, CWSA's technical programs develop athletes and teams who represent the country nationally and internationally against the best in the world. The Canadian team consistently ranks among the top five internationally.

Source: Canadian Wheelchair Sports Association, Ottawa.

Robert Kalthoff.

Logo for Gay Olympic Games, San Francisco 1982.

Disabled athletes

The sheer level of commitment and determination shown by athletes with disabilities has called into question their segregation within the world of sport. In the past, disabled athletes were shut out of competition. Increasingly, there are more and more organizations aimed at providing competition and participation for athletes with various kinds of challenges. These range from those with spinal injuries to those who are blind or deaf.

There is also an active movement spearheaded in Canada to include the disabled sports as part of the "regular" Olympics. The hope is that, by having everyone participate together, athletes who are additionally challenged will be included and receive their golds and laurels at the same time.

The outmoded idea that somehow these individuals cannot participate in sports or have little to offer in terms of ability to compete and excel is today undergoing a major challenge. We will probably

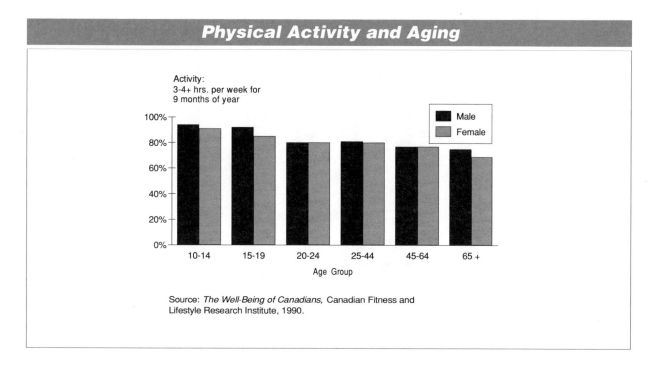

Physical Activity and Aging

Activity:
3-4+ hrs. per week for
9 months of year

Source: *The Well-Being of Canadians,* Canadian Fitness and
Lifestyle Research Institute, 1990.

find that not only will persons with disabilities increasingly participate in sporting activity but that they will help to define a new and improved notion of physical activity in the 1990s and beyond.

Gay athletes

The gay communities have also fought discrimination in all areas, including sport. In 1990, the Gay Games III and Cultural Festival was held in Vancouver, British Columbia. This event received support from many sectors of society.

The key elements of the philosophy of the Games are the opposite of conventional international competition—exclusion and ranking. The founder of the Games, a former Olympic athlete himself, Dr. Tom Waddell began the Games based on the premise:

To do one's personal best is the ultimate of all human achievement (Celebration '90, March 1989).

The aim was to create an open and supportive environment so that gay athletes did not experience the hostility and isolation they so often feel at "ordinary" or "regular" sporting events. Personal best is the central focus:

The Games were conceived as an opportunity for thousands of individuals with their athletic skills at various levels of development to have the thrill and joy of international competition. There was also

In the future more facilities will be needed to raise the fitness levels of older Canadians.

Athlete Information Bureau.

a definite attempt to avoid the ageism, sexism, racism, and nationalism that organizers believed were becoming dominant factors, sometimes overshadowing athletic achievement and international sports.

These Games are built on the principle of *Inclusion*—any person, of any age, race, ability or sex, may attempt any event. Whenever possible, women and men compete together, and each sport is available to the physically challenged (Celebration '90, March 1989:7).

The organizers at the Gay Games wanted to make the Games supportive and as positive an experience as possible. Karen Kiss, an announcer at one of the swimming competitions at the San Francisco Games described them in this way: "The events were competitive and at the same time supportive, exhilarating, loving and caring" (Kulicke & Califia 1982:29).

Seniors in sport

Increasingly, restrictions on athletic activity on the basis of age are also being questioned. Seniors are forming groups to compete at the international level and at the local level. Seniors increasingly engage in physical activities that range from power walking around malls to highly skilled gymnastic competition. The Masters Games attract older athletes from around the world to compete at the highest levels.

The idea that physical activity diminishes as we grow older is being abandoned in favour of seeing physical activity as part of an individual's entire lifespan.

REVIEW

Questions

1. What was the main period in which most of Canada's formal sport organizations were founded?
2. What are the key elements in defining the term "sport"?
3. What are the key differences in categorizing sport, play, recreation and leisure?
4. What is the difference between external/public rewards and personal rewards?
5. How do the general beliefs and practices of a society affect sport and physical activity?

Concepts

- organized sport
- urbanization
- industrialization
- rewards—public and personal
- informal sport—recreation, leisure, contest, play
- spectacle
- ideology
- patriarchal attitudes
- disabled sport
- gay sport

Discussion

1. What factors have changed in the last few decades to make sport and physical activities more available to the general population?
2. How can a person participate in soccer and, depending on the context, be participating in a sport, recreational activity or play?
3. Describe a physical activity you have seen that could be categorized as spectacle.

The Calgary Stampede, a uniquely
Canadian sporting event.

Chapter Three

CULTURE AND COMPETITION

"Winning isn't everything, it's the only thing."
Vince Lombardi, football coach of the Green Bay Packers

"Losing the Super Bowl is the ultimate loss, next to a death in the family."
Pat Bowlen, owner of the Denver Broncos football team

"Fair play is a Victorian concept, which, like many other concepts, is on the wane."
Cambridge social historian, Corelli Barnett

PROFILES IN THIS CHAPTER

• The Crazy Canucks

• Maurice Richard

• Ann Ottenbrite

• Ned Hanlan

Where we grow up greatly influences how we see the world and how we feel about it. Sometimes we take things so much for granted that we forget that not everyone has the same experiences.

Ken Dryden is a former Montreal Canadiens goalie and this is how he described his feelings, as he played in the backyard of his Toronto home:

> It was Maple Leaf Gardens filled to wildly cheering capacity, a tie game, seconds remaining. I was Frank Mahovolich, or Gordie Howe. I was anyone I wanted to be, and the voice in my head was that of Leafs broadcaster Foster Hewitt:
>
> There's ten seconds left, Mahovolich, winding up at his own line, at centre eight seconds, seven, over the blueline, six—he winds up, he shoots, he scores!
>
> … it was a glorious fantasy, and I always heard that voice (Dryden, 1984:56).

If Dryden had been born in Italy or Brazil, the images in his mind would have been of scoring goals on a soccer field. If he had been born in the Soviet Union, the ice hockey images might have been the same, but the heroes and the arenas would have been different.

Athlete Information Bureau (T. O'Lett).

Victory—Canada's women's hockey team celebrates world cup win.

ETHNOCENTRISM

When a person regards his or her own society and beliefs to be the only correct ones and is not interested or concerned about alternatives, that person may be described as having an *ethnocentric* view of the world.

In any analysis of the social world one should of course avoid *ethnocentrism*, try to be objective, and keep an open mind to alternative forms of social organization and behaviour.

Our definitions of winner and loser also vary with the context. In North America we are constantly bombarded with the idea that being Number One is all important. It makes people take risks that in other contexts they would not consider. Many athletes will do anything in order to win the gold or make the professional ranks. We saw Ben Johnson risk international embarrassment and exile from his sport by taking chances with banned drugs.

Culture and Society

Culture refers to the symbols, social institutions, values, language and technology that make up our world. It consists of those transmittable parts of our lives as humans that define who we are.

When a person says: "I am a Canadian," that person is saying he or she is a member of Canadian society. In this statement the person is identifying themselves by national boundaries. When an individual says: "I am an Italian-Canadian and I live in Little Italy" the focus is on one's own sub-culture, where there are shared values and expectations. A *sub-culture* is a smaller group of people who see themselves as having shared values, beliefs and behaviour. Food, clothing and language are among the identifiers that separate one group from others.

The scale of the society affects the degree of cultural integration. Small-scale societies tend to have shared values and economic integration, whereas in large-scale societies there is more specialization in the work force and differing values among various social groups. A large-scale society like Canada today consists of a variety of groups or sub-cultures. In smaller communities, like the traditional societies of the northern Arctic, all members tend to share the same heritage and have similar values. So, when a new technology such as the snowmobile is introduced to such a society, the affect is felt by all members of that society with respect to physical activity (Pelto, 1973). In the wider Canadian society, on the other hand, its introduction may touch only a few.

Elite athletes often perceive themselves as a sub-culture within the broader society. Their interests and concerns are different. They have special values of commitment to training, work-outs and to sport. They eat differently, wear different clothes and seem to speak a different language made up of special schedules and special words. They spend their time differently and with others who are similarly inclined.

J. Le Clair.

Boxing in Thailand, a popular martial art sport.

The Crazy Canucks—Canadian Ski Values

The Canadian men's downhill ski team in the 1970's was labelled the Crazy Canucks by a French sports writer. The composition of the team varied over the years but included Dave Murray, Dave Irwin, Ken Read, Gary Aiken, Rob Safrata and Steve Podborski. The team also included Jim Hunter, who was nicknamed Jungle Jim for doing such things as "breaking off tree branches with his bare hands" (Podborski, 1987: 41).

Part of the reason for the Crazy Canuck label was the athletes' willingness to attack downhill skiing in a manner that was quite different from the European teams. Canada had no history of successful competition in men's downhill skiing. In 1975, the decision was made to specialize in the manner of the Europeans because of limited resources. "Slalom and GS had something like 120 competitors and we'd be starting around 110th. Downhill in Europe usually had about 80 European racers, sometimes 50 on the more dangerous hills, so we would have a better chance starting with half-decent numbers" (Podborski, 1987: 70).

The Europeans were amazed by the competitive, seemingly fearless style of the Canadian team. Steve Podborski describes his understanding of their label in this way:

"We weren't bound by the perceived sane limits of the sport that confined the Europeans. We took wild chances on the courses because we didn't know any better. We had no pre-conceptions and convictions to hold us back and we were able to break new ground because of this. We tucked where others had feared to tread and flew to new heights because we wouldn't back off. It might have been mad, but it was also very fast, which tended to make our mistakes spectacular. We were a team of disparate personalities bound together in a common cause and we were as keen as hell. We used the 'crazy' approach to create a momentum, a driving force that's necessary to conquer a hill like Kitzbuhel (considered to be the most difficult and dangerous hill on the ski circuit)" (Podborski, 1987: 193).

The Components of Culture

1. Symbols

Objects nearly always have a significance over and beyond their mere existence. A traffic light is more than just a red light. Those who know its cultural significance know it means not to pass. A wedding ring is more than just a circle of metal on a person's finger. The referee's whistle is more than just a sound.

There are cultural symbols that signify being Canadian, like the flag and the national anthem. There are many elements that surround an individual item such as a flag: there is a history behind its creation; sometimes there is legislation protecting it; there are rituals around handling it—it is raised when an athlete wins, lowered when somebody dies. Similarly, in sport there are symbols that stand for excellence—like the Stanley Cup in hockey—and symbols that represent teams, such as the Canadiens' and Maple Leaf's logos.

Behaviour can have additional symbolic significance. The shaking of hands at the end of a tennis match does not just signify the end of

Paul Morrison.

Steve Podborski, one of the Crazy Canucks

THE ECONOMIC BASES OF SOCIETIES

Hunting and Gathering Societies
Food is collected by hunting and gathering; society is fairly egalitarian and not very complex.

Agricultural Societies
Food is grown and stored; social organization is more complex.

Industrialized Societies
Technological inventions permit the specialization of work and the introduction of mass production.

the match. It represents a tradition of fair play, respect for the opponent, the recognition of another player on the tennis circuit and an acceptance of the rules and the structure of the game itself. You have only to see what happens when a player refuses to shake hands with another athlete to see the emotional significance of this small ritual.

The anthropologist Ruth Benedict, in her book *Patterns of Culture*, now considered to be a classic work, compared the Zuni Indians of New Mexico and the Kwakiutl Indians of British Columbia. She outlined how each culture stressed very different elements. The Zuni stressed balance, restraint and harmony. The Kwakiutl emphasised competition, aggression and ranking (Murphy, 1989:31). In the same way, we can find general patterns of beliefs and symbols in all societies of a larger scale.

One of the symbols of athletic success, recognized internationally, is the gold medal of the Olympics. The medal is recognition for the feat of winning. The gold is recognition of the special nature of the event and its value.

2. Social and economic institutions

Within each culture there are social organizations and structures that facilitate the normal processes of human life: being born (hospitals), growing up (day care centres, schools and work), setting up households (families and communities), aging (extended families and homes for the aged) and dying (funeral homes).

In small-scale societies, the basis of the social life is kinship and the family. The analysis of kinship provides a framework for the understanding of such a society's operation. In larger, more complex societies there is a greater separation of activities. There are political and governmental organizations that make decisions for the society, as well as religious institutions, legal and judicial institutions, community structures, family and kinship networks and sport organizations.

Some social institutions are more important than others, depending on the society. In Canada, government and religion are fairly separate, whereas in other countries, such as Iran, religious and state structures are intertwined. Even attitudes towards physical and sport activities will be expressed in the society through these institutions. In some Islamic countries, for example, it is thought to be inappropriate for girls to participate in school games in skimpy gym attire, so the programs are not offered. It is also thought that boys and girls should have limited contact. In Great Britain, the more traditional members of the Moslem community have prohibited their daughters from participating in school games because they feel that the British athletic activities are unsuitable as feminine activities.

3. Normative behaviour

People live and work in a world of expectations—normally, people behave in accordance with how other people expect them to behave. **Normative behaviour** is behaviour that is defined as the usual or expected behaviour within a particular society or social group.

Murdering people, stealing property, or hurting people are, of course, not socially acceptable and are subject to various forms of disapproval by other members of society. **Sanctions** are actions taken to penalize individuals or groups for behaviour that is considered to be unacceptable. If the behaviour violates what are thought to be important norms, the individuals may be exiled, fined or even killed as punishment for these violations. For the Ancient Greeks it was Zeus who punished Olympic athletes and it was thought he had lightening and thunder at his command (Finley and Pleket, 1976:15).

A good example of different normative expectations is the contrast between typical southern Canadian sport and the Northern Games. In a typical southern Canadian athletic competition, winning is emphasized and participants have to show competence by eliminating rivals. But not all athletic events have the same focus in Canada:

> The Northern Games is an annual Native festival featuring traditional skills, crafts, games, dances, songs and legends. Non-native sports-minded people often do not understand the idea of the Northern Games, as they are used to thinking in terms of regimented athletic contests where winning appears to be the dominating aim. The Northern games, on the other hand is thought of as a festival in keeping with the traditional gatherings of northern peoples in days gone by (Fawcett, 1977:199–200).

> The emphasis is on participation of as many as possible in these Games and in the Arctic Winter Games the age ranges from 10 to 87 reflect this focus (Arctic Winter Games 1970:40).

In the Northern Games, the expected behaviour of the athletes is one of maximum participation, co-operation and enjoyment.

For a sports person who does not obey the norms, the punishment may be more or less severe depending on the seriousness of the improper behaviour. Tennis stars John McEnroe or Jimmy Connors are fined for inappropriate behaviour on the court. Ben Johnson lost his records and was banned. Baseball player Pete Rose was recently banned for life from baseball for placing bets on his own team at a time when he himself had direct influence on the team's performance.

4. Language

Language, the way in which we communicate, is an essential part of culture. Language constructs how we see the world. For example, someone cuts in front of a driver, a head sticks out and we hear "You

Street hockey is popular everywhere in the winter months.

Athlete Information Bureau.

The Language of Sport — Male in Orientation

The language used to define sport in our society is, for the most part, male in orientation. People talk of "sportsmanship" rather than of good sporting behaviour. We find that many aspects of non-sporting life are defined in masculine terms too. Women who represent their communities in local municipalities are often called aldermen. Women who chair committee meetings are called chairmen. There have been long campaigns to get the usages of these words changed.

Even the coverage of women's sport is different from that of men's sport.

Headlines and articles repeatedly mention the sex of the participants in athletic competitions. In *The Handbook of Non-Sexist Writing*, the authors Swift and Casey argue:

"In reporting women's and girls' athletics it is no more necessary to mention the players' sex in the headline and in every other paragraph than it is to refer to the sex of male players. (It's also not necessary to use social titles.)

"Finding pinpoint accuracy with her swift rival at net, Mrs. Lloyd continued to send shots whizzing past Miss Navratilova, finally evening the score

at 5–5. Miss Navratilova hit two sizzling overheads and an ace to save her next serve and she then took the set ..." (Swift and Casey, 1981:61).

When articles are written about Lendl and McEnroe, they mention their first names once and then refer to them by their last name's only. This is much more straightforward and practical. Calling Ivan Lendl Mr. Lendl does nothing to help the sport coverage.

If you change language you change perceptions about the world and confront the issues as well.

stupid—————." Assumptions of inferiority and superiority are encompassed in a single word of abuse. Each person who sees that blank fills in a word for age, sex, ethnic group membership, colour, religion, nationality, wealth, intelligence—whatever has an emotional component for that person.

When we examine the language around us we find that much of everyday living is permeated by sports images. Competition, team spirit, dedication, winning, and losing are reflections of sports images. In the same way as the Inuit have over thirty different words to describe snow, we have words to describe many aspects of sports competition. Each play in football has many sophisticated descriptions, as does competitive figure-skating.

Language is also a way of including and excluding individuals. If you do not know the jargon of a discipline, field or sport, you cannot understand what is going on. Different sports use different kinds of words to describe the movements, the scoring and the activities within the sport. Sports commentators describe baseball by reference to such things as home plate, the garden and on deck. The terms are not particularly hostile or aggressive. Football, by contrast, uses terms that are often aggressive and have a very military component. Table 3-1 lists some key terms in the sports of baseball and football. The first has more gentle language, the second more aggressive.

TABLE 3-1:
Sport Language in Baseball and Football

Baseball

banjo hit	an accidental ground ball, which "plunks" off the bat
home base	the last base to be touched by the batter before scoring
garden or orchard pasture	the outfield
get the thumb	to be ejected from the game by the umpire
spitball	an illegal pitch when saliva is put on the ball to make the ball perform unpredictably
infield	area inside homeplate and the three bases
load the bases	to have runners on all three bases
on deck	next to take a turn at bat (to play)
pinch hit	to replace another player at bat
sweetheart	the opposite of a "hotdogger"—a player who plays very well, quietly & consistently year-in-year-out, eg. Hank Aaron

Football (American)

birdcage	cage-like metal face mask
blitz	defensive backs rush the quarterback at the snap of the ball, to try to sack him or block or hurry his throw
blow dead	whistle so that ball is no longer in play
bomb	a long pass, especially a touchdown pass
box and chain crew	three workers who operate the down box and chain under the supervision of the linesman
butt-blocking	an illegal play where part of the mask is the main focus of contact
fieldgeneral	quarterback
nutcracker	a contact drill in which ball-carriers are subjected to game time hits by one or more players
shotgun offense	a spread formation primarily for passing when the quarterback is positioned several yards behind the centre to receive the ball with the other backs lined up as slotbacks and flankers
sledgehammer runner	a powerful and bruising runner who takes a physical toll on tackles through the game

SOURCE: Tim Considine, *The Language of Sport*. London: Angus and Roberton Publishers, 1982.

Maurice (The Rocket) Richard—A Cultural Hero in Quebec

b. 1921, Montreal, Quebec. Maurice Richard is one of hockey's all-time high scorers. He was born into a family that had little money. His father Onesime Richard was a semi-professional baseball player who worked for CP railway.

Richard played for the Montreal Canadiens and had 544 goals in 18 NHL seasons, 18 of which were play-off game winning goals, 6 of them in overtime. He also had 7 hat-tricks (three or more goals in a game).

Between 1942 and 1960, Maurice Richard played in 978 NHL games, spent 1,473 minutes in the penalty box and paid almost $3,000 in fines, which was a huge amount in those days. He was nicknamed "The Rocket" because of his explosive and dynamic style. The Montreal Canadiens goalie, Jacques Plante, said of him:

"He was not the greatest skater or the most efficient playmaker, but he had the biggest heart in the league ... The closer he came to the net, the faster he moved. Then all that you could see were those big black eyes staring down at you. It was like being mesmerized by a cobra; he had a hypnotic quality about him" (Goyens and Turowetz, 1987: 100–101).

People watching him in games felt they could not take their eyes off him.

As well as being known as a strong, aggressive, intimidating and skilful player, he was the centre of a controversial incident that took place on March 13, 1955. Many feel that this incident was central in the development of nationalism and a sense of French culture in Quebec. Unlike in the1940's, there were many French Quebecers on the team. Maurice Richard, Jean Beliveau, and Bernard "Boom Boom" Geoffrion were ranked 1–2–3 in the NHL. In a game against Boston, Richard was hit by former teammate Hal Laycoe and during the stick-swinging and punching incident, Richard also punched a linesman, Cliff Thompson, twice in the face.

Some like Frank Selke, the general manager of the Canadiens, said that "... certain people felt it was time to punish Richard for the way he acted on ice" (Goyens and Turowetz 1987: 94). The NHL President Clarence Campbell decided to suspend Richard and it is said that he was pressured by the other five teams to do so. (There were only six teams in the NHL then.)

Although Campbell was warned to stay away, he decided to attend the next game at the Forum. Emotion was intense; Montreal fans were furious. The Canadiens were losing and the crowd began to shout, "On veut Richard—à bas Campbell" (We want Richard—down with Campbell). Fans began throwing everything they could find at Campbell and suddenly a tear gas can exploded, so people were forced to leave. Fans poured out of the building and proceeded to break windows and set cars on fire all down the main street of Montreal, Ste. Catherine Street. The riots caused $100,000 in damage and more than one hundred people were arrested.

Sports writers for years explained the reason for the incident in this way: "The reason was simple. Richard was a fiery, hot tempered, unpredictable Frenchman" (Silverman, 1968: 155). However, "The Rocket" had important significance for French-speaking Quebecers and for many his suspension epitomized the controlling power of English Canadians in Quebec life.

Richard's view is personal, of course. He says: "Some nights, before I go to sleep, I still think about it, and I have trouble getting to sleep. I have no animosity toward anyone, but I can't forget what happened. I still believe what happened to me was unjust" (Scott, 1985: 36).

The very terms used to describe plays, movements, positions, strategies and officials are part of how each sport defines itself. Football defines itself in terms of two teams setting out to defeat each other in military formation. Strategies are very much influenced by the coach and the quarterback. "Orders" are given to the team members and these are followed out to the letter. Conrad Dobler, who

Words with Dignity

The following term guidelines are suggested/preferred by some 200 organizations that represent or are associated with Canadians with a disability.

Disabled	**Person with a disability**
Invalid	**Person with a disability**
Crippled by, afflicted with, suffers from …	**Person who has … or Person with …**
Lame	**Limited mobility**
Confined, bound, restricted or dependent on a wheelchair	**Wheelchair user**
Normal	**Able-bodied or non-disabled**
Victim, sufferer	**Person with a disability**
Cripple	**Person with a disability**
Deaf and dumb, deaf mute	**Person with hearing and/or speech impairment; or person who is deaf**
Retarded, mentally retarded	**Person with a mental handicap or person with an intellectual disability**
Spastic (as a noun)	**Person with Cerebral Palsy**
Deformed, congential defect	**A person born with …**
Physically challenged	**Person with a disability**

The terms paraplegic, quadraplegic and amputee are used and accepted by persons with those disabilities.

Source: Active Living Allowance for Canadians with a Disability, Gloucester, Ont .

Maurice Richard.

Maurice (The Rocket) Richard, scoring superstar throughout his career.

was known as one of the toughest and meanest offensive lineman in the NFL, describes playing football in this way:

> The truth is, you can't play a sport like football by going out there and thinking it's only a game or it's only a job. You genuinely have to believe that you're on a field of combat and that each one-on-one confrontation is a war. A war within a war (Dobler and Carucci,1989:18).

In baseball, on the other hand, the rhythm of the game is slower, there is opportunity for more individualism and the plays do not have a militaristic framework. There is almost a romance between lovers of baseball and the sport. In the book *Shoeless Joe*, the writer W.P. Kinsella captures that profound love of the game and the spirit of baseball. One of his characters says:

> ... I know that there are many who are troubled, anxious, worried, insecure. What is the cure? Is it to be found in doctors and pills and medicines? No. The answer is in the word, and baseball is the word. We must tell everyone we meet the true meaning of the word baseball, and if we do, those we speak to will be changed by the power of that living word" (Kinsella, 1982:229).

5. Technology

Culture also includes the technology available to the society. In sport, it includes the technology of aluminum bats and hockey sticks, video replays on television and the enlarged "sweet spots" of tennis racquets. The style of a game, for example, can change with the addition of different equipment. Some have argued that the introduction of helmets and high technology blades in hockey has lead to a rougher and more dangerous game.

Our current definition of sport is also influenced by television and other technology available to facilitate sports performance and viewing. Nowadays, it is possible for North Americans to have "Breakfast at Wimbledon" or watch high-performance sailing live from the coast of Australia. The technology that makes this popular affects every aspect of our life, whether we like it or not.

And, of course, the technology involves the invention and use of performance enhancing drugs, a subject we shall return to in a later chapter.

Sport in Japan

Baseball is one of the most popular sports in Japan. However, when we look at the game as it is played in Japan we find there are all kinds of differences with North American baseball. In order to gain a better understanding of the cultural influences on sport, it is useful to look at the differences between the same sports in these two parts of the world.

In Japan, there are racial restrictions as to who may be on the team and only two members of each team can be foreigners (*gaijin*). In Canada, on the other hand, there are no restrictions. Few members of the Toronto Blue Jays, for example, are born in Canada.

Ann Ottenbrite—A Canadian First and a Winner Across the Board

The Ancient Greeks would have liked Ann Ottenbrite. She was a winner by their standards. They only recognized first-place winners.

Ann Ottenbrite won the gold medal in the 200-metre breaststroke at the 1984 Olympics and the silver medal in the 100-metre. She was the first Canadian woman to win a gold in swimming since the beginning of the Games in 1896. To add to all this she won a bronze medal in the woman's 4 x 100-medley relay. Ottenbrite was also the first Canadian to win a gold, silver and bronze at the Olympic Games (Associated Press Sports Staff, 1986: 135).

Arguing with umpires' decisions is not allowed in Japan and coaches are never fired. Warren Cromartie, who played with the Tokyo Yomiuri Giants (formally of the Montreal Expos), explains:

> It's the same game here, but it's another world ... The differences are overwhelming ... They're so programmed, so structured, so traditionalize ... They do as they're told ... They never get mad—you make an error that costs a game, well, that's o.k. (Abel, 1984:53).

In North America baseball teams are given names that are different from those of the owners. In Toronto we speak of the Blue Jays, not of the John Labatt's team; in Japan the baseball teams are named after their corporate owners.

> The Nippon Ham Fighters are owned by a pork producer. The Taiyo Whales are owned by the Taiyo Fishery Company. And the Yakult Swallows are the property of a health drink manufacturer (Sneider, 1985).

In Japan, the team is not expected to be a money maker in and of itself. The public relations aspect is regarded as being beneficial to the corporate owner. Sometimes promotions are directly linked to the company that owns the team. The ball player's average salary is also much lower: in 1985, the average salary was $80,000 compared with $350,000 in the United States!

There are numerous ways in which the Japanese culture brings different expectations to the sport experience. Canadian ice-skating athletes, for example, have to adjust to different values while performing in Japan. Rob McCall competed in Tokyo ice-dancing events. He explained:

Athlete Information Bureau (Ted Grant).

Ann Ottenbrite—the first Canadian woman to win a gold in swimming.

We're usually the kind of skaters who feed off the crowd in our lively numbers. But you learn quickly that the crowd enjoys it but is silent. You make the mental adjustment and after a while you start to look for their smiles instead of listening for applause and you feed off that (Milton,1985:65).

It took the Canadian skaters a little time to become adjusted to the idea that the Japanese crowds expressed their interest and support in a different manner. They were used to noisy clapping and cheering. In the same way, American reporters who covered the Jays' games at Exhibition Stadium in the fall of 1985 wrote articles about how quiet, uninformed and unenthusiastic the Toronto fans were. The American media were not used to the Canadian style of appreciation.

Japanese hockey players are also expected to bow courteously to the referees regardless of the outcome of the game. The Finnair World Bantam Cup provided such a situation:

At the conclusion of each game all of the Japanese players would lineup on the ice and face the referees. And then with their helmets off, one of the players would give a cue to his team-mates. This cue was a signal for the entire team to bow in unison towards the referees. It was the Japanese method of saying "thank you" to the referees for officiating their game (Sigesmund, 1984:510).

By way of contrast, there is a tradition as commonplace in North America as it is unnoticed:

"There has not been one Canadian or American team that has come over before or after a game (in this tournament) to either Brian (Coles, referee #1) or me and said 'thank you' or 'good luck,'" explained Beamish. (Gary Beamish is the referee in the MTHL (Sigesmund, 1984:510).

To understand why games that are nominally the same can operate quite differently in different cultures, we have to understand the culture and history of the host country. Japan, to take the case under discussion, was determined to isolate itself from foreign influences until this century. Foreigners were not allowed to live within the boundaries of Japan, nor marry Japanese. The country was also feudal in structure—a few landowners held control and those who did not own land had few rights. Those without land were expected to be totally submissive to those who had power and money. In Japan, there also had not been the same political revolutions as in Britain, France and America, which were central to creating an ideology of individual autonomy and freedom. Japanese baseball reflects this—players are expected *not* to challenge the officials. Respect towards "superiors" is expected and control and deference are essential. Any players who violate Japanese codes of behaviour are heavily fined.

Athlete Information Bureau.

Mass sport in China—Chinese school children doing exercises.

The Need to Win

Part of the difference in behaviour between the Japanese and North American teams lies in their different attitudes towards competition and winning.

Competition is when people struggle against others for similar goals. But there are *different kinds of competition*. There is the competition inherent within society—people have to struggle to get to school, find a place on the bus, apply for jobs. It is so much a part of our Canadian society that we often do not notice it. There is also the competition within sport that directly links sport to financial rewards.

For many athletes, the competitive struggle is one to achieve personal goals. The search is for excellence and to be the very best one can be. The Olympic ideal encompasses that notion. The true Olympic spirit is not concerned with being Number One, but with giving one's best performance. In sport it is assumed that the competition will take place under similar conditions for all participants. This is what is meant by the term "a level playing field." Conditions should be fair. Each contestant or each team should be competing under the same conditions and with similar resources.

The drug question for track and field athletes has brought this issue of fair competition to the foreground. Many at the Dubin Inquiry into the use of performance-enhancing drugs in sport argued that Canada is at a disadvantage because some international athletes from other countries had "official" access to drugs and drug testing, so the playing field was definitely not level. Others have argued that all drugs should be permitted so that there will be no question about access—the playing field will be the same for all. Ben Johnson himself has said that he thought the only way he could win was to take drugs. He trusted the training program of his coach and he desperately wanted to be Number One.

Financial security is central to every individual's life in Canada. Naturally, it is an important issue in discussing Canadian athletes and Canadian sport. Athletes have to pay for accommodation, food and the things that everyone else does. For a typical Canadian athlete participating in a not very marketable sport, where there is no extensive sponsorship, government financial support is very important.

However, in order to get financial aid from Sport Canada a Canadian athlete must be ranked. Government aid is based on a carding system similar to that developed in West Germany. Athletes ranked in the first eight in the world are A-carded and obtain a grant of $650.00 per month. Athletes ranked 9th–16th in the world are B-carded, and those between 17th and 40th, C-carded. In addition, to

GOVERNMENT FUNDING FOR ATHLETES

Athletes Assistance Program—
Monthly payments, January 1989.

A-card 1 – 8th place	$650.00
B-card 9 –16th place	$550.00
C-card 17th–40th place	$450
C-1 Card	$350
D-card	$300
R-card	$250
J-card	$150

A-, B- and C-cards are isued to Canadian athletes who rank within the top 40 athletes in the world. In addition to the A-, B-, and C-carded athletes, there are four others.

"The C-1 card is a probationary type card for the first year an athlete satisfies the C-card criteria, while the D- or Development card is given to athletes with exceptional talent who have not yet obtained the C-card satus. ... R- and J- cards were established for team sport support. R-cards are for those athletes just below the national team level and J-cards are for junior team athletes" (Canada, 1989:22). In 1988, the total number of athletes supported was 856.

Zero-Sum Games—*Pok-Tat-Pok*

Zero-sum competition refers to certain competitive situations where you can only have one winner and one loser. Both competitors or teams cannot win.

An extreme example is the game of *pok-tat-pok* played in parts of Central America before the arrival of the Spanish (Coakley, 1982:10). A ball had to be passed through a hoop, without using hands or feet. The game sometimes took days. People placed bets in stadiums. The ball court was positioned beside the religious temples.

"Ritual sacrifices involving players were made at the end of some games. Some accounts report that the captain of the losing team was sacrificed to the gods to ensure fertility of the land and people, while other accounts indicate that the captain of the winning team was the one who was sacrificed" (Cordes, 1988:45).

The games were linked to the astronomical cycles of the moon and sun. The sport events were part of religious ritual. The human sacrifices were a way of propitiating the gods (Cordes, 1988:46). In this case, being a loser could mean the ultimate loss—death.

At the same period, in Europe, another form of zero-sum competition was taking place. Tournaments were originally military training sessions for knights in medieval Europe. However, by the fifteenth century it had become an organized sport. There were complicated rules and the tournaments provided entertainment for both nobility and commoners. But it was not common for men to die while participating in the events (Norman & Wilson, 1982:23). These men were competitors. The knights were competing to demonstrate who had the best riding and military skills. It seems that sporting events even in that period had elements of showmanship. Parts of the armour in these demonstrations were designed to fly off in a dramatic manner (Norman & Wilson, 1982:35).

the A-, B- and C-carded athletes, there are four others categories. In 1988 the total number of athletes supported was 856.

The pressure on athletes is to win not only in Canada but on the *international* scene. The national sport organizations and Sport Canada establish criteria. Athletes in non-Olympic sports are eligible if they:

1. Finish in the top six in the world championships or equivalent if twenty countries participate;

2. Finish in the top three with ten to nineteen countries participating (with a minimum of ten entries for team events or fifteen entries for individual events);

3. Finish first with five countries participating and ten entries in any event (Dubin, 1990:32).

In the arts community, it would be equivalent to asking all authors, actors and painters to rank within the best in the world at all times or there would be no funding of their talent, even though they might be the very best in Canada. Currently, artistic talent is supported because it is the best in Canada or reflects Canadian values. Clearly the expectations for the athletes are unrealistic in some sports, and can lead to a willingness to try anything to enhance performance.

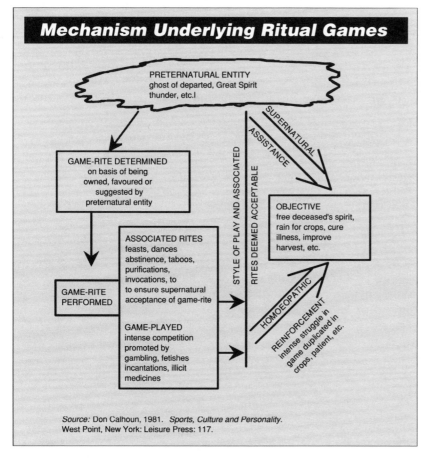

Mechanism Underlying Ritual Games

PRETERNATURAL ENTITY
ghost of departed, Great Spirit
thunder, etc.I

GAME-RITE DETERMINED
on basis of being
owned, favoured or
suggested by
preternatural entity

SUPERNATURAL ASSISTANCE

STYLE OF PLAY AND ASSOCIATED

RITES DEEMED ACCEPTABLE

OBJECTIVE
free deceased's spirit,
rain for crops, cure
illness, improve
harvest, etc.

ASSOCIATED RITES
feasts, dances
abstinence, taboos,
purifications,
invocations, to
to ensure supernatural
acceptance of game-rite

GAME-RITE
PERFORMED

GAME-PLAYED
intense competition
promoted by
gambling, fetishes
incantations, illicit
medicines

HOMOEOPATHIC REINFORCEMENT
intense struggle in
game duplicated in
crops, patient, etc.

Source: Don Calhoun, 1981. *Sports, Culture and Personality.*
West Point, New York: Leisure Press: 117.

In North America the assumption is made that only *winning* is important. It is important to place first—second, third, and fourth places do not count. Sometimes there may only be fractions of a second between these placements. In the past, such small time differences could not even have been measured.

In the 1970s the Olympic Games began using timers calibrated in hundredths of a second that were linked to automatic registers at start and finish. Then, in the Winter Olympics at Lake Placid in 1980, the inevitable occurred: the victor in an hours-long cross-country ski race was separated from the second-place finisher by a hundredth of a second. The observer may reasonably ask: Isn't this really a dead heat? Is the margin of error for two pairs of readings taken hours apart significantly smaller than a hundredth of a second? (Landes, 1983:5).

It is this excessive pressure to compete and *win* that shapes much of modern sport. It is a form of competition that is fostered by the existing carding and funding system. Until it is modified, this system puts unrealistic pressure on Canadian athletes.

SPORT IN ANCIENT GREECE

The Ancient Greeks were very competitive. Not only athletes but writers and singers competed as well. The Greeks used the word *agon* for any contest or struggle related to sport, war or the law. The English word agony finds its roots in agon (Pleket, 1976:21).

Athletic competition was directly connected to fearlessness and skill in warfare. The emphasis was always on coming first. There was no second or third place, however records in the sense of distances or times were never kept .

"Ancient Olympic competitors prayed for 'either the wreath or death'."
Historians M.I. Finley and H.W. Pleket

Ancient Olympic Schedule
Day One:
Opening Day—qualifications were checked, oath-taking and sight-seeing, entertainment and last minute practices.
Day Two:
Athletic competitions began.
Day Three:
Religious ceremonies including the sacrifice of one hundred oxen at the altar of Zeus.
Day Four:
Competition.
Day Five:
Celebrations and a banquet in the Magistrates' House for all winners as well as more sacrifices and offerings.

SOURCE: M.I. Finley and H.W. Pleket. 1976. *The Olympic Games: The First Thousand Years.* London: Chatto & Windus. p.15.

COMPETITION TO THE DEATH

Competition between Amber Heath and Shanna Holloway for a place on the school football cheerleading team in Houston, Texas, became a question of life and death in 1991.

Wanda Holloway, the mother of thirteen-year-old Shanna, was extremely ambitious and desperately wanted her daughter to succeed. Her competitive desire for Shanna was so strong that she arranged for her daughter's main competitor, Amber Heath, to be killed.

After being convicted in court Wanda Holloway claimed, unconvincingly, that she was not overly involved in her daughter's life. "I have never tried to live through my child." The competitor's mother Verna Heath was puzzled: "Why would a cheerleading position be so important?" (Hewitt, Maier & Howard, 1991: 94).

It was clear to all observers that this competition had gotten out of control. The burning desire to obtain a position on the team overrode all normal values.

In contrast to the forms of competition outlined above, there is also the kind of competitiveness that comes from within the individual, the desire to do one's very best. This form of competition has nothing to do with money or rewards—it has to do with an inner desire to do well, or to run faster, to jump higher or leap further. Often, a strong competitor can drive the athlete farther.

> One of the things which separates a champion from just another good player is the ability to win matches. This isn't as obvious as it sounds. The fact is that on match point against them—right at the moment the whole match is on the line—the absolute best players suddenly get about three times tougher (King with Chapin, 1974:56). Billie Jean King calls this inner drive in sports "the killer instinct."

Religion and Sport

As we have seen, there are countries where sport, like many other aspects of society, are completely dominated by religion and religious rituals. There are also situations where athletic competition can have religious or symbolic significance.

The North American indigenous peoples who lived near the Saint Lawrence River at the time Europeans began to settle in the area played competitive games as part of religious rituals. The games included:

> archery contests, pole-climbing, foot races, wrestling, handball, football, lacrosse, dice games, guessing games, hide-and-seek, tug-of-war. Each game was a contest symbolizing a struggle between elemental forces—good and bad weather, fertility and famine, illness and health, life and death. The successful playing out of the athletic contest was supposed to win the favour of, or give help to, supernatural forces or beings in these very life-important natural struggles—for the falling of needed rain, the fertility of crops or game, the healing of an illness, the freeing of a dead person's spirit (Calhoun, 1981:117).

The emphasis was not only on having fun but on serious competition in order to bring about a better world. In these small-scale societies, with people living in harsh environments and facing life and death problems, it is no wonder that these competitions were viewed so seriously.

Similarly, for the ancient Greeks, Olympia was a sacred site first and a place for the Games second. The Games covered five days and the events themselves did not start until the second day (Finley & Pleket, 1976:15). The focus of the festival was religious. There were many gods and goddesses and other divinities such as nymphs and heroes. Heroes were humans who had become divine. The head of the hierarchy was Zeus. People established specific relationships to

TABLE 3-2:

Religion and Sport Competition in West Germany

	Whole Population	Sport Club Members	Track Swimming	High Achievers
Protestants	52%	60%	67%	73%
Catholics	44%	37%	31%	26%
Others	4%	3%	2%	1%
TOTAL		1,880	366	111

Source: Gunther Luschen, *The Cross-Cultural Analysis of Sport and Games*. Champaign, Illinois: Stipes Publishing Co, 1970.

individual gods for particular areas of activity. For example, people would appeal to Aphrodite (Venus for the Romans) in matters of romance, Artemis if going hunting and to Poseidon if sailing.

At the Olympics there was no separation of the state and religion. The religious festivals were official public occasions and the government decided who participated. Women were totally excluded. Gifts were offered to the gods in the temples, but even if athletes set up statues declaring "I belong to Zeus," the focus was the athlete. "The gods, in other words, were patrons of success rather than its creators … Victory alone brought glory: participation, games-playing for its own sake was no virtue; defeat brought undying shame" (ibid:20).

Today sporting events are often taken very seriously yet the consequences are generally not life threatening. The emotionalism around sport in North America is secular, that is, non-religious. However, even today, religious values can affect attitudes about sport. A study done in West Germany in 1958, for example, found that there was a higher percentage of Protestants than members of other denominations participating in athletic competition and winning medals (Luschen, 1970).

Can There Be Neither Winners Nor Losers?

With the growing interest in sport as commercial entertainment, the emphasis on competing and winning has increased in order to provide more exciting entertainment and more marketing opportunities. If your team wins, if your media star wins, you have a more marketable product. It is hard to advertise your product by associating it with a runner up! For example, until 1986 the Americans had not

**CHRISTIANS IN SPORT—
Michael "Pinball" Clemons**

Michael Clemons is only five feet five inches tall but he is tough, determined and wily on the football field. He got his rather unusual nickname after being described by Bob O'Billovich as "bouncing around like a pinball" as he successfully avoided being tackled. The name stuck.

Clemons is part of a group of athletes called Christians in Sport who see their religious beliefs as an important part of their lives. Often athletes find the temptations associated with professional sport hard to resist—alcohol, drugs and a wild lifestyle. Some athletes decide that these things are not to be part of their lives and choose another route. Michael Clemons is one of them.

~ SPORT PROFILE ~

Ned Hanlan— "The Boy in Blue"

b. 1855, Toronto, Ontario; d. 1908. Ned Hanlan won the Canadian singles rowing title in 1877 and the US title in 1878. One of the few movies telling about the achievements of Canadian athletes is the one made about Hanlan. It is called "The Boy in Blue," which was Hanlan's nickname, derived from his rowing outfit.

Rowing was extremely popular during Hanlan's lifetime that thousands would come out to see his races. Hanlan was the first oarsman to master the sliding seat. This invention meant that, for the first time in history, rowers could more effectively use the full energy from their legs and move their boats more quickly in the water.

Hanlan retained the world rowing title for six years. In fact, he only lost six races out of over 350 races in which he competed in.

One end of Toronto Island is named after Ned Hanlan, so today many people know of Hanlan's Point, but few know the history of this famous Canadian rowing champion.

had a Tour de France winner and therefore the race was seen as a European event. During the Tour de France bicycle race in the summer of 1986, the commentators kept remarking that if Greg LeMond won it would certainly help market the Tour de France and bicycling in the United States.

According to some, the pressure to compete *and win* pervades the very nature of our self-realization.

> In North America … to be an individual—to realize himself to be unique and special and necessarily autonomous…this is measured by the subject's success through competition for domination. Indeed, it is through competition that the self is made and its value assessed. This is apparent in the everyday comment: 'What have you made of yourself?' To fail in competition is to fail as a person (Klein, 1987:53).

If you do not win, you are placed in the position of being defined as the opposite of a winner—a loser. In October 1989, the Toronto Blue Jays looked as though they might become the winners of the World Series. The moment they lost to Oakland, the media described them as weak, as losers, as failures, despite the fact that they almost made it! Again, in 1991, when they were ousted from the series finals, the media began to voice doubts their ability ever to win World Series.

This is not always the case in every culture, nor need it always be the case. In some cultures, the idea of defining players as winners or losers is regarded as inappropriate. Anthropologists who have done research among the Inuit in northern Canada and Alaska, for example, have found that the main emphasis in the society is on co-operation. This is carried over into their games as well. People are uncomfortable with the idea that one person would be the winner. They enjoy a "non-winning" game of marbles, a test of skill in which each player

Ned Hanlan, "The Boy in Blue"— Canada's famous rowing champion.

came with one marble and left with the same marble. The children tried the "winning" game in which one player takes all the marbles, but didn't seem to care for it (Calhoun, 1981:115). In this northern Canadian culture, the participants are not seeking to define who is the winner and loser but are learning the value of co-operation. In the harsh northern environment, it may be essential for survival.

China

An interesting national variation on the "winning at any cost" approach is the attitude China adopted as a national policy in the 1970s. The political climate of the country, after the communist revolution in 1948, was to challenge traditional values in all aspects of society. In sport the official policy was "Friendship First, Competition Second." The emphasis was on having friendly matches rather than on having competitions where the emphasis would be on winners and losers. At that time, as well, the government's focus was to encourage as many people as possible to be fit and healthy. The Chairman of the All China Sports Federation explained to foreign visitors that "Winning or losing is only temporary, friendship is everlasting" (Orlick, 1978:69). Competing was thought to be elitist and China did not compete in the Olympics or other international events.

Today, sport in China is very different. There is still a great emphasis on improving the health of the average citizen, and that remains an important aspect of national sport policy. But there is now an interest in developing world-class athletes who will compete successfully at international competitions. In order to succeed at the international level, they have imported coaches from the West to work with their coaches and athletes. There are Spare Time Sport Schools where potential elite athletes in the 6–17-year age bracket are trained. Also, there are Physical Culture Schools for training coaches, teachers and sport administrators. Chinese athletes have been successful in their first two Olympics (1984 and 1988) and did particularly well in sports such as diving and gymnastics that include the acrobatic elements, in which China has a history and tradition spanning thousands of years.

Eastern Europe

In many Eastern European countries the focus has been different from China. In these countries the governments have funded elite sports and it has been considered to be an important part of the country's development. Scholarships have been provided and jobs after retirement as well as special privileges have been made available to top-ranked athletes. Thus, the whole context and expectations of these athletes are quite different from those in North America.

SYNCHRONIZED SWIMMING

Competitors in synchronized swimming are fit and capable athletes.

Critics, however, feel that there is much more of an artistic element to this event and that this diminishes the athletic component. Nevertheless, the sport is increasingly getting the recognition it deserves.

The fixed smiles of the past are part of a somewhat stereotypical presentation of women in sport. Some athletes are pleased that this aspect will not be emphasized in the future.

The Soviet Sport System —GTO

Modern attitudes toward sport in the Soviet Union are based on the policies developed after the Russian Revolution in 1917. "In April 1918 the decree *On General Military Education* made military and physical training compulsory for all men aged between 16 and 40" (Louis & Louis, 1980:4). The aristocratic system had been overthrown and the new government wanted to abolish the privileges at birth. The old sports clubs, where membership had been based on wealth and family name, were closed. The new government also wanted to use sport as a means of education.

There was considerable disagreement between those who were opposed to sport and competition and those who favoured the physical culture approach. The Hygenists, as they were called, were against such sports as boxing, weightlifting, wrestling and gymnastics because of their individualistic and competitive nature. The Proletkultists did not want any fancy games from the past, when only the rich were well enough fed and had the time to participate in sports. So, throughout Russia in the 1920s men and women practised "sport" activities with their work tools. Using hammers and sickles, which they used to work with, they did exercises and practised "practical" movements (Riordan, 1980:28).

These pioneers in new physical activities had a vision of a democratic, non-competitive collectivist or co-operative society. The basis of these policies was a desire to create a society based on socialist principles with a workers' culture as the fundamental component.

In August 1928, the First International Workers Sportakiad took place. This was the first international competition where the old ideas of the Olympics (that only gentlemen could participate) were thrown out. In these new democratic games working women and men who had talent could compete and win medals. As fundamentally sensible and democratic as these ideas seem today, in 1928 it was a radical departure from accepted sport practice and it was not looked on favourably by the conservative sport bodies around the world. The participants and spectators thought these new games were wonderful, of course.

By the 1930s, the basis of the new Soviet sports system was in place and it has continued to the present day. The emphasis was on providing recreational programs for the general population and developing the talents of the specially gifted. A broad-based testing system was introduced and its motto was "*Gotov k trudu i oborone*," known as GTO,—"Ready for Labour and Defence." During this period Russia was moving from being an almost entirely agricultural country to a modern, urbanized one. In addition, the government wanted to use the sports activities as a tool to promote patriotism and nationalism.

The GTO program is structured in such a way that everyone is expected to participate in sporting activities in the same way that the Participaction program in Canada tries to encourage fitness and physical activity. There is one basic difference, however. In the Soviet Union there is a widespread organization to encourage that participation—through GTO testing. The target is not excellence in a single sport, nor even general skills, but all-round ability in many events and knowledge of hygiene, first aid and sports theory. The program has five stages, determined by age. All necessitate a certain minimum performance in running, jumping, throwing, shooting, skiing and gymnastics (Riordan, 1980:45). These aims are based on the premises developed in the 1930s: *massovost* (mass participation) and *masterstvo* (proficiency) (Riordan, 1980:45). The system is set up like a ladder whereby those with talent can feed into the system and work their way up, eventually to international competition.

For the individual Soviet or Eastern bloc athlete, success in competition might lead to additional benefits, but the assumption has been that the athlete would not market herself or himself in order to make individual profit. In the past this has been a basic difference between Eastern bloc and Western athletes. It has also been the reason some athletes have decided to live and work in the West. Tennis star Martina Navratilova is an example of an athlete who consciously made such a decision.

There are contradictory figures on exactly how many Soviet citizens do in fact participate in athletic programs. It should also be mentioned that the Soviet Union consists of many different cultural groups with their own folk and cultural traditions in the area of physical activity. It seems that many young people in the U.S.S.R. would rather listen to rock music than play sports, just like many youth in North America!

Unlike in Europe and North America, however, equal amounts of money and resources are spent on men's and women's sport. Almost equal numbers of boys and girls obtain their GTO badges (Riordan, 1980:131). Yet, just as in the West, there have been conflicting attitudes about the appropriate sports for women and the biological implications for women in competitive sport. Also, as in Canada, time constraints seem to play an important part in the reasons for the lower participation rates of women in physical activities. Women spend more time on cooking, cleaning and taking care of the children than do men. They therefore have less free time to spend on hobbies and recreational physical activities. Men in the Soviet Union on average spend about three times as much time on sport as do women (Riordan, 1980:135). But this is still more time than that spent by Western women, reflecting the different values about sport in the Soviet Union.

Women in the Soviet Union have played an important role in the economy of the country as workers and they have played a valuable role in the military history of the society. They have also obtained considerable recognition and prestige from winning medals in international competition, "proving" the superiority of the socialist way (Riordan, 1980:140–142). Therefore, the role of woman as athlete has been accepted and promoted more fully in the Soviet Union.

It is very clear that the sports system in the U.S.S.R. has put many resources and much energy into funding, coaching and providing support for talent. After the Soviet triumph at the Montreal Olympics an Italian newspaper even described the GTO as "the Soviet secret weapon" (Louis & Louis, 1980:17). As a result of these priorities, the Soviets have been successful in international competition and they have developed a large number of winners.

SPORTING BEHAVIOUR: IS WINNING EVERYTHING?

Sometimes, for extraordinarily generous athletes, winning comes second.

Fanny Rosenfeld was entered into the 1928 Amsterdam 800 metres in order to encourage a teammate, Jean Thompson. Rosenfeld had never completed in the 800 before. She broke the world record but instead of overtaking her teammate ... "she came from ninth position to close behind the seventeen-year-old Jeannie, and when she saw the latter falter coaxed the youngster to come on ... She refused to go ahead of the youngster. (She) let Jean finish fourth, taking a fifth for herself" (McDonald and Drewery, 1981: 12). Her concern was for her teammate, rather than with winning.

Education and Fitness in Canada

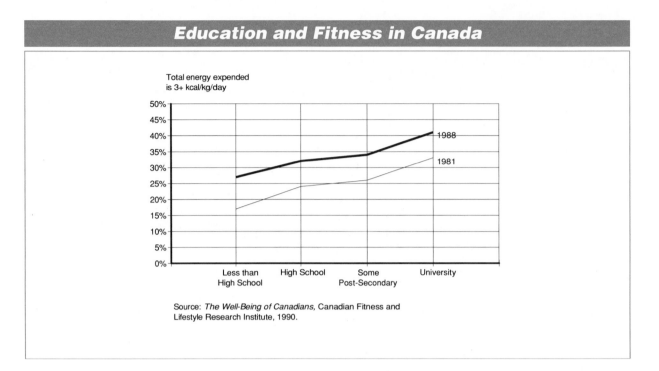

Total energy expended
is 3+ kcal/kg/day

Source: *The Well-Being of Canadians,* Canadian Fitness and
Lifestyle Research Institute, 1990.

Although today there is much emphasis on success in international competition, it is hard to predict what direction government funding of sport will take in the Soviet Union and Eastern Europe after the profound political changes in 1989. There has been a significant backlash against elite athletes in some Eastern bloc countries because of the special privileges and benefits given to them by the government as a result of their sporting successes. The extensive government-directed and financially supported sport systems have been dismantled. Athletes are now having to find funding and to search for sponsors themselves. Clearly, this will affect the sport performance of these athletes.

Canadian Sporting Values

Canada is a country made up of immigrants from many different countries. Each group of immigrants brings with them their own values, languages, foods and sport preferences. For this reason, our society is often described as being **culturally pluralist**. As we look around we see people playing sports that they have brought with them. These include *bacci*, soccer, the Highland Games, bullfighting, cricket, rugby, darts, and many others.

The Canadian Highland Games are held each summer in Nova Scotia and reflect the fact that there are many Maritimers who trace their roots to Scotland and Ireland. The traditional Highland sports of dancing, throwing and racing have been continued until the present. The images of strong men throwing huge cabers and women dancing in swinging skirts are familiar ones. In fact, Canadians often beat the competitors from the "homeland."

At the same time there are different athletic competitions in the other parts of the country. Fishing competitions are common in the Maritimes and in British Columbia. In the west, the ability to handle horses and cattle has been and often is an important aspect of everyday life. The important skills of controlling animals are show-cased at the Calgary Stampede. Competitions to determine who can ride uncooperative horses and rope cattle have long been held. Speed, courage and strength are all part of the events. Soccer and cricket are popular in the larger cities where immigrants from Europe, the Caribbean, India and Pakistan continue the sports they played at home.

Competitions related to forestry skills are seen less often nowadays. Previously trees were cut down by hand and the ability to climb, saw, and transport logs down rivers were valued talents. Someone who could climb trees, saw quickly and had good balance on rolling logs in the water was well respected.

Similarly, Canada's First Nations have long held summer gatherings called pow-wows where spiritual renewal and physical events take place. Athletic events, drumming and religious events are intertwined in a tradition that predates written history. Traditions old and new are retained and attract new followers.

Clearly, the values of a multi-cultural country such as Canada affect activities such as sport in complex ways. In attempting to understand sport and physical activity in Canada—and improve on it—this rich variety of cultural experience must be taken into account.

Canada's First Peoples, pow-wows are special celebrations where spiritual renewal, dancing and physical activities take place.

Athlete Information Bureau.

REVIEW

Questions

1. What are the main elements of "culture"?
2. Compare and contrast the attitudes towards competition and sport in Japan and North America.
3. Describe the current ranking system for Canadian athletes.
4. Give examples of how religion influences sports, past and present.
5. Compare and contrast the North American, Soviet and Chinese sports system.
6. Are attitudes towards competition and winning necessarily the same in all cultures? Give examples.

Concepts

- subculture
- symbols
- social institutions
- normative behaviour
- ethnocentrism
- language technology
- competition
- carding
- zero-sum competition
- GTO
- cultural pluralism

Discussion

1. Describe how cultural values have influenced your own sport choices and those of your friends.
2. Discuss how cultural values can influence sport programs, organization and attitudes towards winning.
3. Discuss whether the current ranking system for Canadian athletes puts unreasonable pressure on athletes.

Justine Blainey gives the "thumbs up" as she learns that the Human Rights Commission case was won.

Citius, Altius, Fortius—The Olympic ideals can be "serious" and "fun" in school team sport.

Athlete Information Bureau.

Chapter Four

HOW CHILDREN BECOME ATHLETES

"A lot of things got to me as a kid. I used to hate it when my mother had to patch our pants into the small hours of the morning or do the ironing after bringing the laundry in from outside, where it was thirty below and made the clothes like pieces of plywood."
Tiger Williams, NHL hockey player

"It was in order to put the pieces back together that I turned to my sport. Running was the easiest way to escape from the harsh reality of losing my sister because when I ran I didn't have to think about life and death."
Zola Budd, Olympic runner whose sister died suddenly when she was thirteen

From the moment of birth children are learning how the world works. Parents, family members, neighbours and friends all interact with the young child and give him or her cues about how to behave. Children learn to see themselves as winners or losers through the eyes of those around them. While the early learning experience is critical and greatly affects attitudes and behaviour in later years, this learning process does not end in early childhood but continues throughout one's life.

Often the fondest childhood memories are those moments separate from the influence of parents and "interfering" adults—those quiet times sitting on the dock, or those exciting times running up and down the back lanes, lying in the snow, rolling down the hill in the leaves, skipping rope or playing tag. Increasingly today these experiences are less common. As parents become more and more worried about the safety of their children, so the freedom for children to develop a world of their own shrinks further and further. This separate childhood world cannot develop in the same way when it is under the watchful eye of adults.

PROFILES IN THIS CHAPTER
- Wayne Gretzky
- Marilyn Bell
- Nancy Greene

Athlete Information Bureau.

Tobogganing—Canada's popular winter sport for families.

Socialization for Life

The first learning process is called *primary socialization* and takes place mainly within the family. Children are encouraged to play, be active and learn sports skills by their parents or caregivers.

Adult socialization takes place as adults learn how to function and operate in new environments such as in the workplace, college or university. The expectations and behaviour at college, for example, are quite different from high school; an athlete joins a sport club and learns how to behave at competitions and in work-outs.

Anticipatory socialization refers to learning new ways of behaving before you actually have to do them—you anticipate the roles you will have to play. Ken Dryden describes his experience in non-organized hockey in his book *The Game*. Hockey took place on an ice rink in the backyard of his house.

> My friends and I played (hockey) every day after school, sometimes during lunch and after dinner, but Saturday was always the big day… Each game would begin with a faceoff, then wouldn't stop again… It was here in the backyard that we learned hockey. It was here we got close to it, we got inside it, and it got inside us. It was here that our inextricable bond with the game was made (Dryden, 1983:56–58).

He describes playing against his older brother two weeks after joining the Canadiens. He did not feel any excitement at the novelty of playing against his brother in the NHL.

Resocialization is the learning of new ways of behaving and often entails completely abandoning old methods of doing things. Playing non-contact hockey means learning to play a new style of hockey for many adults. All through life new challenges and new environments mean new ways of behaving. For example, one of the most difficult times for professional athletes is the process of resocialization into the life of a non-athlete. The camaraderie, the team friendships, the fan attention and the highly structured life, organized and planned a year in advance, is very different from retirement. It is often much easier to adjust slowly to team membership than to life at the end of professional sport. This adjustment and trauma takes place for committed and dedicated amateur athletes alike.

Families from different socio-economic backgrounds and different cultural backgrounds often expect different things from their children. Some families expect children to be physically active and join teams. Others stress academic work. Some expect both. This influences how the family chooses to spend its time and its money.

As children begin to establish their independence from their mothers, they begin to develop a sense of who they are in the world. Charles H. Cooley used the term **looking-glass self** to describe how children begin to have a sense of self, as others view them and judge them. They evaluate others evaluating them. While playing physical activities children begin to keep score and compare themselves with other children. They also keep track of their own skills to see if they are improving.

Herbert Mead elaborated these ideas in a book called *Mind, Self and Society*. Children, once they develop language, begin to play roles (playing house and the role of Mummy and Daddy is the most common), reflecting the ideas and behaviour of the **significant others** in that child's life—Mum, Dad, Grandma, etc. Mead labelled this the *play* stage. Then as the child gets older, it becomes possible to enter the *game* stage. In the game stage the child can understand the different roles of people, the expectations of different positions and the needs of other children. The child in this stage has a sense of the *generalized other*, a recognition that there are values about what is right and wrong out there in the wider world. At this point the child can play games with other children and appreciate concepts of fair play, whereas very small children are unable to do this. They want to grab all the toys for themselves! Increasingly, the child becomes aware of the responsibilities and obligations involved in interacting with other children and adults. Children begin to develop a sense of where they fit into the society in relation to others and themselves.

The various groups and individuals who influence children are referred to as **agents of socialization**. They are called "agents" because they act as mediators between children and the wider community. Agents of socialization include the family, the mass media, peer groups, school, religious institutions and coaches. Today, many children are exposed to the television set before they begin to play with other small children. Frequently they can sing along to the Polka Dot Door or Sesame Street before they know their way to the park.

✷ Socialization into Sport ✷

Socialization is the process of linking each individual to the wider society. The young child is taught how to eat, how to talk and how to walk. From these fundamentals the child develops each day and continuously learns new ways of doing things.

Children learn what kinds of physical activities will receive praise. They get criticized for moving or behaving in specific ways ("be ladylike", "act like a man"). Through socialization children are linked to the cultural values of the world that they live in. They begin to learn the connections between themselves and the outside world. The emphasis on winning soon becomes apparent:

> You see them at all the arenas, faces red from the chilled air, or from all the yelling. "Jeez, ya rotten ref. Who're ya playing for?" "Shoot 'em hard. Let 'em die, *let 'em die.*" "Pe-e-e-ter. Score one for Mommy" (Dunphy, 1986:G1).

Parents play a crucial role for children with respect to sport and physical activity. Ken Griffey Sr., a baseball player for the Seattle Mariners, in 1989 became the first player in the major leagues to have a son play on the same team. Griffey Sr. "clearly remembers the day his son was born. Says that he knew even then that his son would be in the major leagues. But he didn't know he would be there with him. In fact, he didn't know which sport it would be" (Strachan, 1990). But the support was there from the start. Similarly, Gordie Howe claims that playing with his sons, Mark and Marty, was the biggest thrill of his career.

By means of radio and television small children get to hear and see sports, even if their parents are not very interested. If they have friends on the street who play hockey or skip rope, they will be encouraged to try too. When they go to school, depending on the school, they may be required to participate in physical activities. They may come in contact with teachers or coaches whom they admire and these individuals may encourage them to join a team. Religious institutions can also affect sport in a number of ways, and some religions encourage participation in sport more than others. Churches and synagogues also teach values about ethics and cheating.

Coaches also play an important part in the introduction of children to the roles they, as athletes, are expected to play. Children become socialized into the roles of a team player and committed competitor. They learn the expectations of the athletic community and the obligations and expectations that accompany the role of an athlete or team member. Through encouragement, corrections, punishments and rewards children learn what is expected of them while they play games and engage in physical activity.

Canadian champion racewalker Ann Peel, with son Michael.

TABLE 4-1:

Agents of Sport Socialization

1. The Family	learning to compete; learning to be a good sport; learning skills
2. The Mass Media	learning expectations from the role models of successful athletes; learning what sports are considered important; learning values around competition
3. The Peer Group	learning values about physical activity and competition
4. The School	learning about competition, status in sport
5. Religious Institutions	learning about ethical and moral values
6. Coaches	learning specific sport skills; learning values about training, competition, winning and losing
7. Sports Clubs and Community Groups	learning skills and roles within teams and sports with other athletc teams

K. Thompson.

Fun in the snow—children on climbing bars at playschool.

Walter Gretzky has described the early years of his son Wayne. Wayne wanted to spend every moment on the ice, so his father made a backyard rink. However, Walter Gretzky's initial problem was that his son was only five and desperate to play on a hockey team. "In those days minor hockey in Brantford started with ten-year olds. There was no place for Wayne to play. Boy, was he disappointed" (Gretzky & Taylor, 1984:47). Gretzky was socialized into the life of a dedicated athlete and, as everyone knows, became one of the most successful professional hockey players of all time.

Often parents have a great deal invested in their children's hockey, both financially and emotionally. Sometimes, the parents can become more emotionally involved than the children. They want the things for their children they were unable to have, or look to the sporting successes of their children to provide a better future than would be obtainable by other means. The games stop being fun for the kids and come to reflect the parents' aspirations and what they want for their children. Parents can be overheard saying such things as: "I'm spending a lot of money on you. You're not supposed to be out there having fun." They feel that because they are spending money, the child should be working hard at the sport.

Parents pressure the coaches as well. John Hope, the former coach for the MTHL Marlboro Major Midgets, feels that the competition in hockey is ruining the team aspect of the game. "There were parents who instructed me to play their son when he was injured. I refused. All they thought about was exposure to the scouts and the people who were drafting. Exposure, exposure, exposure" (Dunphy, 1986:G1).

How the sport experience is defined for children reflects the values of the wider society. If parents see sport as a potential route towards financial success or prestige, then there will be pressures on children to do well. If the sports experience is seen to be a recreational one, the attitudes of parents will be different.

Winning has increasingly become the focus for children's organized sport activities, as it has for adult sports:

> As the importance of winning is increasingly emphasized, the competitive process—how one plays the game—becomes further de-emphasized. The worth of the inner rewards declines in comparison with the magnificence of the prizes distributed. Raising the material stakes in contests tends to move competition out of the traditional realm of sport—safe excitement and imaginary risk—and into the real world that frequently seems so scary and so stressful that we invented games as a means of escaping it (Gilbert, 1988:97).

Of course if the parents' values are different from the values and orientation of the league, it can be hard for the parent to encourage those values that lead to success.

Today, fewer and fewer children play informal sports in urban centres. Children are driven off to hockey games and tennis lessons; their timetables look like those of junior executives with every minute accounted for. Gone are the days when most children spent hours playing on their own or with other children in an unstructured environment. They learn very quickly that they are either winners or losers, depending on whether or not they are chosen by the coach.

> ... kids indicate that what they dislike most about sports including such things as: getting yelled at for doing something wrong, getting hit or kicked, dirty play, sitting on the bench, feeling like a failure. Community leagues and school teams often make reinforcement (social approval, praise, encouragement) dependent upon successful performance before children have had adequate preparation (Orlick in Martens, 1978:149).

For average players the pressure to win can be terrible. If the pressure to perform becomes too great, then the pleasure and enjoyment turns to unhappiness and sadness.

The children themselves, of course, are usually very highly motivated to play and win. " ... kids who played organized sports revealed that 'fun' and 'action' were the things they liked best about sports" (Orlick in Martens, 1978:149). This is true in both western and

PARENTS' COMMITMENT—FINANCES, EMOTIONS AND TIME

Parents can invest considerable amounts of money in their child's sport. Registration fees for the amateur hockey association are in the $350-dollar range, with an average cost for a child playing a season of organized hockey being approximately $1,500. Many parents spend additional funds on coaching, extra ice time, tournaments and hockey camps.

The competition for teams is intense and demands a larger commitment from the parents. Hockey, for example, is often highly organized . Although, ideally, hockey should be played for fun, parent's desire to have a future Guy Lafleur or Wayne Gretzky in their family can put pressure on their child.

The pressures are real, as are the rewards, because there are hopes of the "big time" or the possibility of a university scholarship in the United States.

INTERPRETING THE DATA

These data suggest that persons with post-secondary education are more active both in low intensity activity (eg, walking) and, to a slightly lesser extent, in activities requiring a moderate or greater level of intensity (eg, any organized sport).

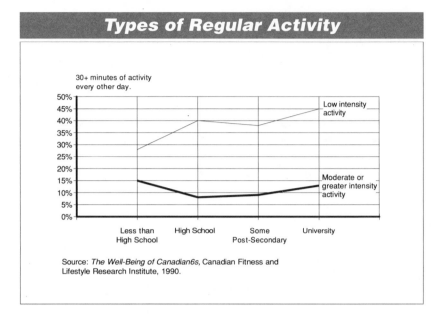

Types of Regular Activity

30+ minutes of activity every other day.

Low intensity activity

Moderate or greater intensity activity

Less than High School | High School | Some Post-Secondary | University

Source: *The Well-Being of Canadian6s,* Canadian Fitness and Lifestyle Research Institute, 1990.

non-western societies. Vladislav Tretiak, the Soviet hockey goal-tender, tried out for the Central Red Army Children's Sports School and made the team. Like Gretzky, Tretiak was an all-round athlete. He had participated in all kinds of sports earlier, including running, ping-pong, volleyball, track and field, basketball and skiing, but he became absolutely dedicated to hockey as his favourite sport.

> When I was twelve, I received my first serious injury. The puck hit me squarely in the forehead. I didn't cry only because I was afraid that I'd be kicked off the team. Hockey was no longer just a hobby to me by then. I had fallen in love with the game so much that I was selflessly devoted to it as only a young boy can be (Tretiak, 1987:6).

Both Tretiak and Gretzky loved hockey and put all their waking time into training for hockey and in developing all-round athletic skills. Sometimes parents in these situations feel defensive because they are accused of orchestrating their children's lives, but the love for the sport is often in the children themselves.

The Importance of Informal Games for Children

The focus of informal games is quite different from organized or formal games. Obviously, one of the main differences is that children themselves usually organize informal games. The adults are not there determining who will play and when. The politics of who has bought the uniforms or whose Dad knows the coach do not apply. Scoring is less important because the rewards for winning are not the same.

Athlete Information Bureau.

More fun in the snow—group instruction in cross-country skiing.

~ SPORT PROFILE ~

Wayne Gretzky ("The Great One")—Having Fun as a Kid while the Whole World Watches

b. 1961 Brantford, Ontario. Wayne Gretzky's parents, Walter and Phyllis Gretzky, provided a great deal of support for Wayne's interest in sports. Walter Gretzky describes the family in this way: "Kids and sports. Life has sort of centred around the two for as long as I can remember. Maybe it's because Phyllis and I both come form large families and sport was always a part of both of them" (Gretzky and Taylor, 1984: 50).

But the love for hockey, the drive to play and the dedication came from Wayne himself. "You see, once we got him on skates the tough part was getting him off the ice. He loved it. He'd bug us to go to the farm or take him to the park every night so he could skate. He couldn't get enough of it" (Gretzky and Taylor, 1984: 46). And this was when he was *three years old!*

Because of his extraordinary hockey talent as a child, Wayne Gretzky often was the centre of attention and sometimes faced a good deal of hostility and got picked on. When he was twelve, his father bought him a particularly light-weight pair of hockey gloves, but they were white. Walter hesitated to buy them because he was worried the white gloves might mean more "talk," but Wayne wanted the gloves because he was sure they would mean he could stickhandle better. So, he wore the gloves. Many people commented on the white gloves, but Wayne continued to use them because they were good gloves. Later, he was even nicknamed "The White Tornado."

His father explains: "He was learning a lesson he'd need through his career: do what you think is right and never mind what they think up in the stands" (Gretzky and Taylor, 1984: 70).

One difficulty for any young person with extraordinary talent is that adults forget that this talented person is a child. Things were no different for Wayne Gretzky. Gretzky was in zone playoffs in Welland and word got out that some older teenagers were going to beat him up. Therefore, Wayne was provided with police protection. This time he was nine years old ... "when this ordinary boy with ordinary boys' likes and dislikes laced on skates, it was as though people suddenly considered him an adult" (Gretzky and Taylor, 1984: 77–78). Fortunately for him, and for hockey fans too, Wayne Gretzky continued to ignore all the off-ice goings on and went on to even greater successes as an adult.

Even team membership and size vary from day to day or even from the beginning of the game to the end. A typical street hockey game slows down or stops when cars go by. A team member will go home when supper is ready. Usually there is no team captain. Punishments (sanctions) for inappropriate behaviour are informal too. There is no such thing as being benched. Rules are enforced by group agreement or the disagreeing participant gets fed-up and leaves. Prestige comes from the group itself, not from trophies or pennants. The ranking in terms of status for the players derives from the athletic ability—the better players always receive a certain amount of respect, even if they are considered to be jerks outside the games.

Prestige in informal games can also come from other kinds of skills. The sociologist Jay Coakley did research on children's games and found these key elements: action (preferably leading to scoring), personal involvement in the action, a close score so each team has a

Toronto Argonauts.

Wayne Gretzky (right), extraordinary hockey talent.

Blacks and Whites: "Kids could always work things out."

The experiences of children vary, of course. Those who have grown up in the context of ethnic, religious, gender or socio-economic (class) conflict often have negative experiences of street play. The battles between the larger social groups continue between the players. Bullying, cruelty, teasing, verbal abuse, obscenities and even violence can take place. The strongest and the meanest take the opportunity to victimize the weakest. In this unsafe environment it is impossible for children to enjoy themselves. Fear dominates. In this kind of situation the presence of supervising adults provides safety and refuge. The child who is small, clumsy, the "wrong sex," inarticulate, dressed differently, or somehow defined as "other" can often suffer miserably.

The extraordinarily gifted black baseball player Willie Mays faced considerable difficulty as a young athlete. He was born in 1931 in Alabama in the southern United States. "Birmingham even had a city law that banned blacks and whites from competing" (Mays, 1989:22). Because blacks were not allowed to play in the Major Leagues, Mays played with the Birmingham Black Barons in the last Negro League World Series in 1948 (Mays, 1989:50).

Interestingly, however, Willy Mays' description of his childhood is not filled with a sense of racial conflict or exclusion.

… I always enjoyed playing ball, and it didn't matter to me whether I played with white kids or black … But see, I never recall trouble. I believe I had a happy childhood. Besides playing

school sports, we'd play football with the white kids. And we thought nothing of it, neither the blacks nor the whites. It was the grown-ups who got upset. If they saw black kids playing on the same team with white kids, they'd call the cops, and the cops would make us stop. I never got into a fight that was started because of racism. To me, it was the adults who caused the problems. I still believe that. Kids could always work things out and find a way to get along (Mays, 1989:11).

Mays had a special athletic talent from an early age. He loved baseball and he viewed the world through the opportunities he had to play baseball. His passion for the game, and that of his young friends, overshadowed racial differences. It was only when adults came into the picture that problems arose.

chance to win, and opportunities to reaffirm friendships in the games (Coakley, 1980). The excitement of playing and the fun of being with friends can be more important than winning. "Rules" are bent in order to maintain these criteria. Each neighbourhood or street has an individual who might not be the best player but is respected for other skills. These may lie in the ability to resolve conflicts, get hold of equipment, tell jokes or whatever. These skills would be classified under social skills, which may or may not be directly related to athletic ability.

There are also considerable differences between girls' games and boys' games. Every evening when people go home from work or school, it is very obvious that many streets and parks are almost entirely sex segregated. The boys are "hanging out," playing hockey or gathered on their bicycles, depending on the time of year. Occasionally the odd girl is seen here or there, but it is as if 50% of the population is invisible. Socialization into different roles based on sex encourages different kinds of behaviour.

Studies on girls and boys playing sporting games show clear differences. The boys play outside more and are more competitive.

Cultural Expectations: Girls and Boys

We have different cultural expectations about what girls and boys can do. In a typical neighbourhood there are areas usually defined as "safe" for the girls, including the front yard, the backyard, possibly part of the lane and going to the corner store. As a result, girls under the age of twelve have a very small circle of friends to play with, often only three of four, i.e. those children who live immediately adjacent to the child's house. Their brothers, on the other hand, are usually to be found playing hockey on the street or "hanging out" with their buddies on the corner of the street. As they get a little older, the park becomes part of the scene as well. Again, as they get into their teens, the more distant facilities become more interesting, whether they are arenas or swimming pool facilities.

Because the brother can play in the same "safe" area as his sister, plus the length of the street and the two additional lanes, it means that he has a larger number of kids to play with and has a greater possibility of playing team games or sports. It should also be mentioned that many parents often feel that boys are more fidgety and active and need to go outside and that it is important that their daughters learn the household tasks, like laundry and washing dishes. They frequently put less pressure on their sons to do these things, which means that the boys have more free time to play outdoors.

In all these situations, of course, children break the rules. Mum says only go to the end of the street and the kids go to the park anyway. Girls sneak around the corner to see their friends in spite of being told it is dangerous. Many girls love sports so much that they participate with the boys and end up being called "tomboys," for doing what they like to do. When no one is around to see, boys try "double dutch" and find out it is much harder than they thought.

LEVER'S DIFFERENCES IN GIRLS' AND BOYS' GAMES

Boys played outdoors more than girls

- Boys played in larger groups than girls

- Boys played with boys with a greater age range

- Boys played competitive games more often

- Boys' games had more specific goals and involved teams more often

- Boys' games were more complex, had more rules, more positions (roles) and more teamwork

- Girls more often played with groups dominated by boys than vice-versa

SOURCE: Janet Lever. "The Differences in Games Children Play" *Social Problems* 23(4): 471-483.

They usually have more complex rules and regulations. The reasons for this lie in the wider community, socialization and our culture. We have different cultural expectations about what girls and boys do in our society. Little girls are constantly warned about the dangerous strangers in the streets. Somehow parents think that boys are more self-reliant and in less danger.

An American study examined the physical activities that children participated in within community settings and found many common interests among boys and girls in the lower grades. The community organizations were part of parks and recreation departments, sport leagues and teams, church groups, YMCAs and YWCAs, clubs and spas, scouts and farm clubs. The five top-ranked activities for boys in Grades 1–4 were: running, swimming, soccer, baseball, and bicycling. The top-ranked activities for girls were: swimming, running, playing on the playground, bicycling and baseball (Ross, Pate, et al., 1987:88).

THE OTHER SIDE

It can also be argued:

- girls learn to relate in small groups, one-on-one

- girls learn how to be co-operative

- girls learn how to have reasonable rules

- girls learn to play with boys more often than *vice versa*

TABLE 4-2:

Most Frequent Physical Activities by Grade for Girls

Grade	1		2		3		4	
	Rank	*%*	*Rank*	*%*	*Rank*	*%*	*Rank*	*%*
Baseball		*		*		*	4	.14
Bicycling	4	.13	3	.16	3	.14	3	.17
Playing on playground	3	.18	4	.15	4	.13	8	.09
Racing/sprinting	2	.34	2	.35	2	.30	2	.28
Swimming	1	.35	1	.39	1	.39	1	.43

Source: James G. Ross, Russell R. Pate, et al. 1987. "Home and Community in Children's Exercise Habits." *JOPERD* November-December:89.

Mary Usher-Jones.

Children identify with their favourite team (Michael and Timothy Usher-Jones).

(See Table 4–2; 4–3.) Girls ranked playing on the playground higher than the boys and the boys ranked soccer higher. These American results are similar in Canada.

Unfortunately, the attitudes about what is appropriate—or normal—influence children as they are growing up into adults. Often it means that some girls are uncomfortable with larger groups and the idea of hanging out with a gang. It has not been part of their experience. Some researchers maintain that women are at a disadvantage in business because they have not had the same experience in team participation. They have not learned how to compete in groups and when to play the role of a good team member.

Mary Cunningham of Bendix Corporation has said that her situation as a senior director was affected in this way. Although she was bright, hard-working and ambitious, she was a loner who did not know how to joke "with the boys," accumulate information (including gossip), and lobby for support on the issues she thought were important.

> I wasn't very savvy when I first went to work for Bendix. Oh, I was intelligent, and like most of my classmates at the (Harvard) Business School, ambitious, but I lacked any real know-how about how the corporate world operates (Cunningham, 1984:353).

She had been an excellent student and could evaluate and design long-range planning projects extremely well as a member of the senior board at Bendix Corporation. However, she did not have the experience of working as a team member with a group of men.

TABLE 4-3:

Most Frequent Physical Activities by Grade for Boys

Grade	1		2		3		4	
	Rank	*%*	*Rank*	*%*	*Rank*	*%*	*Rank*	*%*
Baseball	7	.11	4	.20	3	.29	3	.32
Bicycling	5	.15	5	.13	5	.17	5	.17
Racing/sprinting	1	.34	2	.31	2	.33	2	.33
Swimming	2	.32	1	.39	1	.34	1	.38
Soccer	4	.16	3	.24	4	.21	4	.26

Source: James G. Ross, Russell R. Pate, et al. 1987. "Home and Community In Children's Exercise Habits." *JOPERD*. November-December:88.

This is not to argue that business skills are learned while playing basketball and hockey but rather that cultural patterns are learned from an early age and influence how individuals see the world and behave in it. Operating as a member of a sports team, no matter what the context, would have been useful to Mary Cunningham and others.

Edward Devereux, a developmental psychologist, has concerns about the kinds of things that formal or organized sport does not teach children. In a paper called "Backyard Versus Little League Baseball: The Impoverishment of Children's Games" he argues that in backyard sport children learn many things about social interaction.

The game was so structured that it required us to use our utmost ingenuity to discover and understand the hidden rules behind the rules—the general principles which make games fair, fun, and interesting, and which had to govern our complex relationships with each other; the recognition of the subtle differences in skills, including social skills, which gave added respect and informal authority to some; the ability to handle poor sports, incompetents, cry-babies, little kids, and *girls*, when the easy way out of excluding them from the game was somehow impractical (Devereux in Martens, 1978:123) (emphasis added).

In contrast, Devereux feels that in games such as Little League baseball, everything is too structured and too competitive.

It is all so carefully supervised by adults, who are the teachers, coaches, rule-enforcers, decision-makers, and principal rewarders and punishers, that there's almost nothing left for the children to do but play the game (Devereux in Martens, 1978:124).

Integrated Sport: Justine Blainey

Integrated sport for girls and boys or women and men always seems to arouse controversy. Even raising the issue gets many people upset. The reasons for this are obvious. With such exceptions as riding, yachting, figure skating and tennis, few competitive sports are integrated. If all sport were integrated, it would lead to a re-definition of sport. It might mean that sport would be promoted and recognized as an appropriate activity for both sexes. Sport would no longer be defined as primarily a male activity.

An eleven-year-old girl, Justine Blainey, wanted to play hockey on a boy's team as there was no equivalent girls' team near her. During her three-year struggle through the courts many articles were written about her and the issue. The opposition she faced would certainly have discouraged most young girls who would not have had the time or determination to continue to fight.

Much of the media's coverage was unsympathetic or even hostile:

- "Toronto girl is barred from school team play."
- "Hockey ban violates girl's rights, court told"
- "Girl's battle over hockey stalled again"
- "All-female teams offer best chance for women in hockey, inquiry told"

- "Women's hockey much improved but still gets less money, ice time"
- "Girls should leave boys' teams at puberty"
- "Playing boys' hockey distorts girls' personality: coach"

But in spite of these headlines there are many who supported Justine Blainey and feel that girls should be able to play at any athletic level for which they are capable.

The Human Rights Commission in December 1987 decided in her favour so the Justine Blainey's of the world can now play hockey where they want—as long as they make the team.

In order for children to become interested in physical activity or sport, the activities must be fun. That is the starting point. If the child does not enjoy the activity there will be little interest in pursuing it. Is it important for children to set their own agenda for play? Possibly providing all the structures does not allow for individual growth outside the official structure of sport.

Child's Play or Apprenticeship

Sport can be a means whereby a child matures, develops friends and increases self-confidence. These can be very positive aspects of a child's personal development. However, sport can also emphasize competition and performance at the expense of fun. Depending on the sport, this can happen at an early age. In gymnastics, for example, coaches are looking for talent as young as four and five years of age.

The emphasis given to sport will remain with the child into early adulthood and beyond. Canada's Victor Davis, ranked number one in the 200-metre breaststroke, came in second at the Australian Commonwealth Games. Adrian Moorhouse was first with a time of 2 minutes 16.35 seconds and Davis was second with 2 minutes 16.70 seconds. Davis was quoted after the race as saying:

Marilyn Bell, conqueror of Lake Ontario, 1954.

~ SPORT PROFILE ~

Marilyn Bell—A School Girl Proud to Be Canadian

b. 1937, Toronto, Ontario. In 1954, the Toronto Exhibition had arranged for the American swimming marathon champion Florence Chadwick and three other swimmers to compete in a swim across Lake Ontario from Youngstown, New York, to the Exhibition Grounds in Toronto, Ontario—a distance of thirty-two miles. No swimmer had made it across the lake ever before.

The prize was a huge amount for those times, $10,000 dollars. However, no Canadian was invited to compete. Two Canadians, Marilyn Bell and Winnie Roach Leuzler, wanted to prove that "if Lake Ontario could be conquered, it could be conquered by Canadian swimmers" (Wise, 1974: 95).

Marilyn Bell explains: "We were definitely unwelcome guests at the party! The sports director at the CNE did not want me to swim. They viewed us as troublemakers. I can understand now why they did, but we felt very strongly that Canadian swimmers had been overlooked by the organizers.

We had a lot of good swimmers and it should have been a Canadian-promoted event ... The challenge for me was to go one stroke further than the American. As corny as it sounds twenty-five years later, I did it for Canada." (McDonald & Drewery, 1981:87). Both Marilyn Bell and Winnie Roach entered the race, supported financially by the *Toronto Star* newspaper.

The swim covered 40 wandering miles, much of it at night in the dark with little light, while the water was cold and rough with lamprey eels attacking Marilyn Bell's body. Her coach, Gus Ryder, accompanied her by boat using signs to communicate. Her good friend Joan Cooke at one point jumped into the water to encourage her along. All across Canada people were eagerly listening and waiting to see if this young Canadian could beat the lake. She had captured the imagination of the whole country.

Marilyn Bell was a five-foot-one sixteen-year-old school girl, who only weighed 110 pounds. Ryder described Bell as having "a sort of deep well, a kind of reservoir ... But it wasn't courage so much, or even will or tenacity, as a kind of response, a natural generosity that kept her swimming—swimming on strongly long after she'd lost track of time and place" (Wise, 1974: 94).

After 20 hours and 59 minutes Marilyn Bell arrived at the shores of the Toronto Exhibition Grounds to a crowd of 250,000 (Jensen, 1985: 36). Bell proved to everyone that a slight, Canadian girl, still in school, could conquer Lake Ontario. It had a tremendous impact on the Canadian consciousness.

A year later, in 1955, she became the youngest person ever to swim across the English Channel, and in 1956 she became the first woman to cross Juan de Fuca Strait from the United States to Vancouver Island. In fact, no one equalled that achievement until thirty-three years later, when Canadian Vicki Keith swam the Strait in 1989.

Second is for losers. When you're No. 1 in the world, second is for losers. And this one time I'm a loser ... I don't mind losing but I don't like losing to someone I know I can beat ("Davis Loses," 1986).

Clearly, Davis did not like to lose. In fact, he had already won the event sixteen times in a row! Here the focus is very different from your neighbourhood informal game. In such a context, one might wonder if the sport continues to be a source of enjoyment.

In children's formal or organized sport, it is the adults who organize the activities. They are very much concerned with teaching the rules and regulations of the game. There is ranking of the players by skill

The Quebec Hockey Battle: Fun or Competition

Many have felt that hockey has been and always will be Canada's premier sport. However, a great debate has developed in the last few years over the issue of violence and competition in hockey, putting a question mark over the future of this sport. Should there be less emphasis on competition in hockey?

In 1986, the CAHA (Canadian Amateur Hockey Association) sought to address this problem by introducing its Initiation Program for 5–10 year olds. The program stresses basic hockey skills—skating, puck handling, passing and shooting—to bring the fun back to hockey (Christie, 1986:D1). Howie Meeker has been arguing for years that hockey should try to keep as many players in the system as possible. He feels the Canadian Hockey Association should not focus on the 6-, 7-, 8-, and 9-year olds. He maintains that players are being driven from the game:

"The rules sanctioned by the CAHA and the Ontario Hockey Association, and everybody else involved, are purposely designed to drive the kid who has average size and average skills and who isn't mentally tough out of the game by the time he's 13.

"Size and strength and mental toughness totally dominate the game from the age of 13 on. We drive the little guy out because of the size of the rinks. Our rinks are designed to keep the big tough guy, the slow-moving guy, in the game" (Strachan, 1986:C1).

The declining participation figures in Quebec led to the re-examination of this issue. Participation fell 24% in a four-year period, while the birth rate only fell 6%. In Atoms, Peewees, Bantams and Midget hockey there were 29,000 drop-outs, a loss of 56%. Francois Bilodeau, a physical education specialist, has done research on this decline and feels one of the solutions would be to hire specialized hockey advisors to work with teaching and training volunteers and to facilitate promotional work. He found that the decline in hockey interest was attributable to the following causes: other sport choices, the high costs of participation, a preference for family activities, a dislike for violence and a sense that participants were not improving (Smith, 1989:A16). Bilodeau found that players had 15 minutes of learning time during each hour of training and that the focus was on what he called the NHL "star-system" model. (Smith, 1989:A16). If the hockey system is a "feeder system" for the professional NHL teams, then clearly the system is geared to the minority of exceptional athletes.

Changes may be in the wind. There has been increasing support for a reduction of fighting in hockey. In the past, fighting was viewed as a "natural" part of hockey and a safety valve for the emotions of players. Now it is thought that fighting may hinder the marketing and development of hockey in the American television market. In 1991, Wayne Gretzky came out in support of new ways to address the question of fighting in the NHL. This is an important direction.

If the focus is to develop and encourage children to learn hockey skills, have fun, learn good sporting behaviour, and, most importantly of all, to learn to strive to do their best and have a real sense of achievement, then the present system is *not* serving those ends.

Ontario has decided not to change its organization, but in Quebec the authorities have decided to do away with competition for children under the age of twelve and they hope to include hockey in the physical education programs in the schools (Kalcham, 1988:A23).

DECLINING PARTICIPATION IN QUEBEC MINOR HOCKEY 1983-88

Birthrate drop

Males 10–19,	6%

Reduction in Minor League players

1983–88,	24%

Reductions by team group:

Atom (10–11),	10.4%
Pewee (12–13),	18.5%
Bantam (14–15),	27.5%
Midget (16–17),	40.9%
Junior (18–20)	63.4%

and by the players' willingness to do what they are told. The consequence of not doing what you are told is sitting on the bench. The goals of both players and coach are the same—to score and to win.

The rewards are public and are known to everyone. Variation from the rules is punishment—by being thrown out of the game or being benched. The composition of the group is quite stable because the rules are followed and because there are all kinds of pressures outside the game to ensure enforcement takes place (parents might file complaints, officials from the provincial organizations might object, etc.). When the focus is on performance, records and winning, support for a child's personal growth may be put on the back-burner. The emphasis is on guiding talented children through the apprenticeship system to become stars provincially, nationally or internationally. The characteristics of fair play, respect for others and good sporting behaviour are less important than "the killer instinct" and the will to win.

Summer fun—coaches dedicate hours to tennis lessons for young children.

Physical characteristics that match the needs of the professional system become more important than simply ensuring maximum involvement. A very good basketball player who is merely 5' 7" or a gymnast who is "too tall" will be overlooked if the aim is to develop champions. It has been argued, for example, that the requirements of the NHL have influenced the focus and direction of children's hockey.

There is no reason why sport cannot do two things simultaneously—provide an opportunity for youngsters to have fun and learn hockey skills as well as provide an opportunity for those with exceptional talent to go further to an elite level. As very few children will ever make it into professional teams, it makes sense to put the most energy into encouraging each and every child to develop his or her full potential, rather than sending the message to the child that he or she is not one of the chosen few. The small, the slow, the quiet and the clumsy should all have a chance to play and excel.

The Special Olympics and Disabled Sport

The Special Olympics were created to allow mentally handicapped children to participate in sport. It was recognized that in "regular" sport the emphasis is always on finding the best in a particular event and there is no place for children who do not excel. What place was there for children who do their best, but whose best was not recognized by the wider society? There was none. So, a group of people in the 1970s decided to create events where each child would receive an award just for participating. The intention was that each child would attempt to do his or her best. Being able to complete the course was, in some cases, a major achievement.

~ SPORT PROFILE ~

Nancy Greene—The Tiger of the Slopes

b. 1943, Ottawa, Ontario. Nancy Greene was a member of the Olympic teams in 1960, 1964 and 1968. She won the gold in the Grand Slalom and a silver medal in slalom in the 1968 Olympics. She also won a gold at the world championships.

She redefined Canada's image of sport. To the public Nancy Greene seemed sweet, pleasant and gentle. To those who knew her in the ski world, she was "tough, aggressive, and highly ambitious ... her team mates ... called her "Tiger"— (a) nickname for the skier who was determined to be number one in the world" (McDonald & Lawton, 1981:127).

She was tough, she was strong, and she won against the best in the world. Greene was also a pretty young woman, who, it was said, had stronger legs than any hockey player in Canada.

In recent years, there has been a major change in attitude towards those who do not fall into the category of children who can take part in "regular" sports. In the past, people spoke of the crippled or handicapped. On July 1, 1983 the Canadian Human Rights Code substituted the term "disability" for "physical handicap." **Disability** refers to "any previous or existing mental or physical disability, disfigurement and previous or existing dependence on alcohol or a drug." Sports organizations, however, do distinguish between physical and mental "disabilities."

Increasingly, the media and the public are paying greater attention to the achievements of those athletes who have a disability. Terry Fox ran half way across Canada after he had lost a leg to cancer; Steve Fonyo completed the task that Fox was unable to finish; and Rick Hansen travelled around the world in a wheel chair—these are just three examples of major achievements. All these athletes re-defined the image of the disabled, both in Canada and around the world.

More and more events are being staged for persons with disabilities. Wheelchair basketball, skiing, highjumping and many others all field disabled competitors. Finally, these athletes are getting the opportunity to enter competitions and receive the recognition that is their due. Parents of the disabled find their children as eager and as competitive as non-disabled children and opportunities are being provided for them. Bill C–62, passed by the federal government in 1986, requires federally regulated companies with 100 employees or more to promote the hiring of the disabled. Just as we see more ramps being built to allow persons with disabilities to become more independent, so more sport events are becoming available to them. These changes have come about as a result of the efforts of disabled adults and other interested groups.

Athlete Information Bureau.

Nancy Greene, gold and silver winner in 1968.

Roger Bannister's Personal Search for Excellence

For many athletes it is the personal search for excellence that provides the drive to do well. That feeling can be enhanced in competition against an excellent athlete or team—there is nothing like the thrill of "beating" a strong opponent. Before the Johnson drug incident in Seoul, for example, track and field saw some of its best competitions between Ben Johnson and Carl Lewis. Each brought out the most in the other.

Roger Bannister, the first athlete to cover a mile in less than four minutes, says that one of the most significant races for him was not the race where he ran under four minutes (a feat that was considered a physical impossibility at that time) but another race in Helsinki in 1952. The British press had been severely criticizing his training methods and there was a great deal of pressure on him to come first in the 1500 m. Bannister had the unexpected misfortune of having to run three days in a row (heats, semi-final and final), and the pressure meant that he had not slept well. Nevertheless, he ran his best and he, along with eight out of the other twelve runners, broke the Olympic record of 3 minutes 47.8 seconds set by John Lovelock in 1936 (Bannister, 1989: 162-176).

Everyone criticized his fourth place finish but Bannister saw competition in a new light.

> I had found new meaning in the Olympic words that the important thing was not the winning but the taking part—not the conquering but the fighting well. All week I had seen the interplay of success and failure and felt no bitterness at the outcome of my race. My only chance to win an Olympic title was over. I had seen some who had been beaten when a luckier position might have won. Others had won and I had been happy for them (ibid, 1989:177-178).

Toronto's Dan Leonard provides an example of the kind of determination found among disabled athletes to participate in non-disabled athletic events. He lost his left arm while learning to operate a punch press in 1977. In 1987, Leonard was a participant in the famous Hawaii Ironman Triathlon. Having found sponsors, he had a specially designed bike made with customized brakes, gears and pedals. He swims using a stroke that is a combination of front crawl and butterfly.

Motivation is directly linked to opportunity. If a person thinks that he or she has no chance, he or she will tend not to be motivated to try to complete the task. The creation of sporting events and competition for the disabled has opened up new opportunities for disabled persons. A great many are experiencing physical activity in ways that simply did not exist a quarter of a century ago.

To Be the Best You Can

Competition can be individualistic, where each individual is encouraged to do his or her best, or the focus can be on a team approach, where the emphasis is on the group or team as a whole doing well. The Tour de France is an interesting example of a team approach to competition. The coverage of bicycle racing in the media has traditionally focused on the stars, with the camera following an individual,

F.A.M.E.—ROLE MODELS

Female Athletes Motivating Excellence (FAME) is an organization comprised of high-performance athletes who visit schools to speak about their sport experiences.

These female athletes provide role models for school students, male and female, encouraging them get involved and to be the best they can be in sport.

Kim Gretzky—Keeping Options Open

Wayne Gretzky has a sister, Kim, who was an exceptional junior athlete just like her brother. However, while Wayne Gretzky has been very lucky in terms of serious injuries, his sister has been less fortunate.

Kim Gretzky excelled in track and field. After slipping on a patch of ice, however, her competitive days were over because of "demolished" tendons. Kim Gretzky was only fifteen years old when this happened (Gretzky, 1984:55).

Wayne Gretzky's sister is an example of what can happen to even the most talented athlete. It is this danger of injury and the fact that so few people do succeed professionally that should give strong warnings to parents who have sport dreams for their children. Other options should be kept open.

such as Connie Carpenter-Phinney or Greg Lemond. It is only recently that the strategies of the competition have been outlined. The racers are part of a team and individual team members take turns leading attacks. Team members head the front of the pack, which is tiring, to try to put pressure on other team members to keep up. Cyclist Steve Bauer, for example, tried to make things easier for the "stars" like Hinault and Lemond by taking the lead and creating a "draught." So we have a situation of individual effort in the context of team effort. In 1985 and 1986, there was considerable publicity over the disagreements between the cyclists and team-mates Lemond and Hinault. Hinault wanted his fifth and sixth wins in the Tour de France, Lemond wanted his first. A great deal of pressure was put on Lemond to function as a "good" team member and help Hinault win by sacrificing his own chances.

Some cultures are uncomfortable with the idea of competition, so sharing and minimizing competition is stressed. The traditional Inuit, mentioned in a previous chapter, are an example of this approach. Some argue that competition can even have a negative effect on the majority of children who are not of exceptional ability.

Orlick and Botterill (1975) studied children and competition and in their now classic study, *Every Kid Can Win*, describe how the usual approach to sports programs (competition encourages excellence) did not seem to work when the behaviour of children was examined. They found that 100% of elementary school children gave competition as *the reason they dropped out of organized sport*. In high school the figure was 60%. The fiercely competitive nature of the organized sports programs was turning children off rather than encouraging

Athlete Information Bureau.

First Peoples children in the north playing baseball.

them to try harder. Children were dropping out of sport because of the competition, because so few were defined as winners—because it was the only way to avoid being labelled losers.

A study of the motivating factors in participating in gymnastics provides insight into children's choices. In an article entitled "Perceived Competence and Motives for Participating in Youth Sports," researchers Klint and Weiss (1987) found the top ten motivators were:

1. Desire to learn new skills
2. Desire to get in shape or get stronger
3. Desire to improve skills
4. To have fun
5. Desire to stay in shape
6. The challenge
7. Using the equipment
8. Desire to compete at higher levels
9. Desire to be physically active
10. The teamwork

These are the elements children are searching for. They want to have fun, develop skills and enjoy physical movement.

Terry Orlick, in his book *The Second Cooperative Sports and Games Book,* outlines what he thinks sport and games should be. He is very concerned about the kinds of values children learn through the games that most of them play at school and in the community. He feels that children learn much about the world, and how to deal with it, through sport. But he sees many children learning what he thinks are somewhat anti-social values.

> ... if you distort children's play by rewarding excessive competition, physical aggression against others, cheating, and unfair play, you distort children's lives (Orlick, 1982:3).

Orlick is convinced that children should be allowed to make decisions while playing games and sport activities, and that this increases motivation (Orlick, 1982:6). He also thinks that if aggression is encouraged in sports children learn that this is an appropriate way to treat other people in other contexts as well. He is sure that this is the message of such sports as boxing, tackle football and full-contact hockey (Orlick, 1982:7). Although coaches who are committed to their win-loss record would probably argue against this position, Orlick feels that better values can be learned from co-operative games. He argues for the setting of multiple goals, so that even a team loss has winning elements.

ORLICK'S COOPERATIVE GAME RULES

- Everyone plays.
- No one is left out (on the sidelines).
- No physical contact of a destructive nature (for example, hitting or tackling) is allowed.
- The smiles in the game become the priority.

SOURCE: Terry Orlick, 1982. *The Second Cooperative Sports and Games Book*, New York: Pantheon Books: 232.

A High School for Skiers

Burke Mountain Academy in Northern Vermont is a high school for skiers. The idea behind the school is that students get an excellent training in competitive skiing and go to school at the same time. Usually skiers have to miss school for months at a time in order to compete. One obstacle is that there are only 15 to 20 openings every year and the fees are in the region of $15,000 (US) a year (Davidson,

1985:c4). If the money is not available, it is impossible for a child to attend Burke, although the school does have some scholarships. In addition, some children find it difficult to adjust to being away from home and to the discipline within the school.

Students at Burke sign a code of honour that pledges them not to drink, smoke or take drugs. Television is allowed only on Friday and Saturday

nights. The day starts at 6:45 am. with a three-mile jog or a run down the slopes. Most are asleep by 10:0 pm. Their day includes a regular high-school curriculum for about six hours and a training schedule of equal length (Davidson, 1985). As in any elite pursuit, only those who have the necessary dedication can make it through.

COOPERATIVE COMPETITION IN TEAM EVENTS

- The focus is on the fastest time of a specific group; e.g. 100m., 200m., etc.

- The groups are divided according to age or grade, etc.

- Each runner is timed and must run as fast as possible.

- The individual times for each race are put together and averaged for a group time.

- Averages for groups of very different abilities are included.

- No one is eliminated.

SOURCE: Co-operative Games.

An alternate approach to competing and winning increasingly being used successfully by coaches is the personal-goal approach. Each athlete sets his or her own goals based on the particular sport. The aim is to achieve the goals you set for yourself. This is quite different from trying to "beat" the opponent. In some ways, it is harder too because the opposition is always tough!

There are numerous personal goals that can be set and achieved that have nothing to do with winning. Among these are: completed skills (such as new moves, plays, sequences, routines, formations, etc.), improvements in self-control, mood control and relaxation, as well as improvements in interpersonal relations with teammates, coaches and referees. (Orlick, 1982:103). Good coaches already set these goals, but Orlick would like more to do so.

Many children like to compete. These children love their sport and enjoy the thrill of getting better. They even enjoy the training and the repetition that bring about improved performance. Often parents are in awe of their children's dedication. A typical parent, Hank Whittemore, describes his daughter's dedication to figure skating:

It is dark and cold as we climb into the car. Three times a week, she has lessons from 6 to 8 in the morning before her fourth-grade classes begin. She also skates in the afternoons and on the weekends.

It is a kind of obsession I have come to feel. A pursuit such as figure skating simply has no bounds in terms of the effort required. Not even for a world champion (Whittemore, 1985:7).

A parent in this situation has a choice—to help the child compete or not. Many parents end up making great sacrifices to facilitate their children's participation in sport.

Children often make the decision to train and compete when they are very small. Many gymnasts start before the age of five, as do many swimmers. Brad Creelman, holder of ten Canadian records in the 11–12 age group and six in the 13–14 division, began swimming competitively when he was six years old (Sokol, 1985:c7). His father has driven him to the pool at 4 in the morning for years and paid the $1,500 annual travel and club fees (Sokol, 1985:c7).

Some sports analysts feel that very young children cannot really evaluate their choices. They are often not even aware of what they are giving up. This is a complex question, but it does seem that parents should try to achieve a reasonable balance in the early years between sport and friends and school. If a child lacks the talent or inclination to pursue sport as a career, there will be then other options available. So too, if the sports training comes to an end due to injury, the child will have already developed other interests to pursue.

Education for Fitness and for Life

Many educators in Canada feel that there needs to be more consistency in the physical education curriculum across the country. Of course, all schools are involved in extensive physical education instruction, but there is a case for more consistency in the approach to physical education across Canada. Except in Quebec, for example, students can drop physical education in Grade 9, 10 or 11 (Trottier, 1987:9).

Research on children's fitness seems to indicate that children and teenagers are less fit than twenty years ago:

- 60% of Canadian children and 65% of American children do not meet minimal cardiovascular fitness standards.
- A recent study of U.S. elementary schools found that 76% of the girls and 26% of the boys could not do one chin-up.
- Twelve-year-old children drink an average of 680 millilitres (2½ cans) of pop daily and the average child eats one of three meals away from home (Lapointe, 1986:E2).

In 1981 a national survey was done in Canada entitled "The Canada Fitness Survey." People were asked to do the "stepping test," which involves walking up and down steps over three, three-minute periods. It was found that only 36% of girls and 60% of boys between 15 and 19 could be designated fit (Clark, 1987).

Blake Ferris of the Canadian Fitness and Lifestyles Research Institute feels that television is a major obstacle in encouraging children to become active and fit. "I think the average kid is watching about

Getting an early start—Thai schoolboy playing at recess.

Fatness, Thinness and Weight Control

The average amount of calories needed by women and men are as follows:

- Male office workers, 2520
- Male university students, 2930
- Male building workers, 3000
- Female assistants in stores, 2250
- Female university students, 2290
- Female factory workers, 2320

(Bucher & Prentice, 1985: 163)

Each person uses energy every day even if the body is not active. The term used to describe this is the basal metabolic rate.

Basal Metabolic Rate (BMR) is the rate at which your body uses energy when resting (*The Measure of Energy*, 1985: 6). The higher the percentage of fat that a person has in their body, the lower is that person's BMR. Because women usually have a higher percentage of body fat, their BMR is usually lower. However, if a person is active the BMR will remain elevated for up to eight hours after the exercise.

Weight Control

The key aspect in weight control is caloric balance. Two people may consume the same amount of calories, but one of them will gain weight because the energy expenditure of the one person is less than the other.

To calculate your caloric balance you must first estimate how many calories you have consumed (ie. how much food you ate). Then subtract the number of calories you expended during activities.

Caloric Balance Formula:
Number of calories consumed *less* the number of calories expended

Clearly, if your intake is higher than your output, you are going to gain weight. If your caloric balance is negative, you will lose weight (Bucher & Prentice, 1985: 163). It is easier to lose fat tissue through exercise than through dieting only, but it is difficult for people to lower their caloric intake.

The meal listed below has 715 calories, almost half the total for an 1850 calorie daily diet. Many of us would think of it as a snack! It is listed however, as dinner in a sample meal pattern.

- 1 Hamburger patty (4 oz.) on 1 hamburger bun
- 1 cup of tossed green salad with 1 tablespoon of dressing
- 4 oz. low fat milk
- 1/2 cup ice cream
- Total kcal. 715
  (Bucher & Prentice, 1985: 164)

It is easy to see that if a chocolate bar or a couple of beverages are added in, the inevitable will occur—the individual will gain weight.

Women usually stop growing at about 18 years of age, and men at about 21. If you have gained weight since you stopped growing, you can work out your daily energy imbalance by filling in the formula.

CALCULATE YOUR DAILY ENERGY IMBALANCE

WEIGHT GAIN:
Present weight (kg.)   _____
***Minus* former weight (kg.)**_____
Equals
Weight Difference (kg.)   _____

Subtract 18 for women and 21 for men from your current age.

Present age (yrs.)   _____
Minus former age (yrs.)   _____
Equals
Age Difference (yrs.)   _____

To obtain your daily energy imbalance, divide the two figures.

Weight Difference (kg.)   _____

Divided by Age Difference (yrs.)   _____

Equals   _____

Multiply by 100

Daily Energy Imbalance (kj.)   _____

Source: Measure of Energy, Fitness Canada: Participaction,1985: 9.

Cutbacks and the Future of Physical Education

The 1990s appear to be a decade of financial difficulties. Everywhere there are economic cutbacks and job layoffs. Physical education programmes in the schools are at greater risk than ever.

One consequence of economic restraint may be the introduction of user fees. When the Tuscon school district, for example, implemented a $105 per-activity user's fee for sports and other activities, 30% fewer children went out for school sports (Swift, 1991: 66). Educators are very concerned because this may mean that school activities and sports become limited to those who can afford to pay fees.

In response to the financial pressures, the San Francisco city government recently passed a sports ticket tax.

Every ticket bought at Candlestick Park in 1992 has a tax on it—25¢ on a Giant's ticket and 75¢ on a Forty-Niners ticket will go to high school and middle school taxes (Swift, 1991: 67) . This proposal passed city council unanimously!

Schools are also looking for corporate sponsorships, and coaches and athletic directors are adding fund raising to their duties.

Many question the economic sense of the cutbacks in education spending. The American National Federation of State High School Associations argues that extra-curricular activity costs are not high for the numbers who participate. Brice Durbin the executive director says that: "The net cost of funding school activities is between one and three percent of the total school budget ... and 60 to 70 percent of the students participate in some activity, whether it's a sport, the band, the student council, the debate team or whatever" (Swift, 1991: 64).

The direction for children's physical activity is undergoing change. There is considerable concern that play, recreation, games and sport be available to all children regardless of physical ability, income, ethnicity or sex. This means a commitment on the part of schools, the community and business to support these activities. The programmes need to encourage both individual and team excellence *and* an enjoyment of life-long health and fitness.

The hope is that all children will be winners in terms of athletic participation and their self-definition.

21 hours a week of TV in Canada" (Clark, 1987). An American researcher, Guy Reiss, who has done work in this area over the past twenty years, describes the television viewing of a typical American child: "He's sitting in front of the television with his hand in the fast-food box and his other hand around a quart bottle of Coke." Reiss found that "about 50 per cent of girls aged 6–17 and 30 per cent of boys aged 6-12 could not run a mile in less than 10 minutes" (Clark, 1987). Other American researchers have reported that children in Grade 4 watch an average of 2 hours of television on school days. At the weekend these figures rise to an average of 3 hours. Generally, the more the child watches television, the less active a child is (Ross, Pate, et al., 1987:88). Canadian children are little different: "In 1987, children watched 3.1 hours of television a day, while the figure was 2.7 hours for those aged 12-17" (McKie and Thompson, 1990: 232).

On the basis of this evidence, it appears that fitness and sport are not an important part of the typical North American family. No longer do most children play outside until it gets dark or it's time for supper. The list of non-physical activities available to children after school are quite different now from the 1970s or even 1980s—a typical bedroom

Pull in your tongue!—a stable of fun for
Kirsty and Zoe

J. Le Clair

might offer a sound system for CDS, a tape deck, a television with
regular programming and cable stations, a video machine for previously taped programs or rented movies and a computer with computer games like Nintendo (in addition to traditional resources such
as books, newspapers and magazines). Certainly, there are many
entertainment options that compete with going out to play games or
run about. All across Canada little "couch potatoes" are growing up
into big, overweight "couch potatoes." In fact, Chicago holds a "Spud
Potato Olympics" where there are events like "who can make an
onion dip the fastest," or do the best flip onto a sofa—and these
people are serious!

Public awareness about the importance of physical education is
perhaps at the same stage as public awareness about the value of not
smoking in the 1950s and 1960s. It is necessary to confront the lack
of physical activity in the same way as smoking. There needs to be
more education through the media, at the workplace and in the
schools and many more opportunities for everyone to be physically
active. Physical activities have to be seen as part of every child's life
instead of being the preserve of specially talented children. At the
same time, more facilities have to be made available for physical
activities and sport where parents can feel sure that the children are
safe. Physical activities should be offered in many different forms—
competitive activities for those who want them and non-competitive
for those who don't. Even such practices as choosing teams in order
of ability should be changed.

Good physical education programs include praise for students and
a supportive learning environment. Learning a physical skill may be
easy for one child and hard for the next as the learning involves social,
emotional and intellectual factors (Bryant & Oliver, 1974:26–27).

REVIEW

Questions

1. Who are the six main agents of socialization?
2. What role does socialization play in the different informal games that girls and boys play?
3. What were the reasons for the creation of the Special Olympics?
4. Why should equal opportunity for sport participation be available to all?
5. What should be the key elements to encourage children to remain involved in organized sport?
6. What are some of the factors that explain why children appear to be less fit today?

Concepts

- socialization (primary, adult, anticipatory, resocialization)
- agents of socialization
- athletes with disabilities
- Special Olympics
- individual competition
- team competition
- co-operative sport
- sexual differentiation
- integrated sport
- fitness for life

Discussion

1. Outline how the "segregation of the sexes" affected your sport participation as a child, with reference to opportunities, games and attitudes?
2. Describe how attitudes toward disabilities have changed in the last ten years and discuss how they might develop in the next ten years.
3. Outline why educators are concerned about the health and fitness of children in Canada and discuss what changes might be made to improve the fitness of children in Canada.

Tom Glesby gets some ringside advice from his coach.

Chapter Five

COACHING AND COACHES

"The sad thing is, the really qualified guy isn't always the best for kids. Can't always relate. ... He reduced the kids to tears daily. I've seen him, and others, too, manhandle kids, pick them up and throw them around. ... The kids were eight-year-olds. They'd just turn to jelly, walk off the field crying."
Bob Cupp, golf course designer and children's coach
and advocate

"I had to learn to live with pain. I often wanted to jump out of the pool and choke Sherm (the coach). He treated us like mechanical robots but it was the only way to win."
Debbie Meyer, American Olympic swimmer

"The secret to managing a baseball club is to keep the five guys who hate you away from the five guys who are undecided."
Casey Stengel, Yankee manager

Coaches are everywhere. They, too, are usually described as winners or losers. There are strong images—Vince Lombardi "the winning coach" at the Super Bowl; Reggie Dunlop, the fictional "losing coach" in the film *Slap Shot*; and Ronald Reagan's famous portrayal of "Win one for the Gipper."

Coaching is central to the development of sports talent at the local and high-performance level. So what are coaches and what do they do?

What is a Coach?

A **coach** is a person who helps others achieve their goal of a better performance. This is done by demonstration, support, criticism and teaching both mental and physical skills.

A coach has two main areas of responsibilities—the first responsibility is to the individual athlete and the second is in the field of sports administration. A 1978 study of 423 volunteer children's

PROFILES IN THIS CHAPTER
* Edmonton Grads
* Ted Nolan
* Debbie Brill
* Don Cherry
* Sue Holloway

Angela Issajenko and Charlie Francis, athlete and coach.

~ SPORT PROFILE ~

Edmonton Grads—The Most Winning Canadian Team

The Edmonton Grads were a team of women who played basketball from 1915–1940. They are the most winning team in Canadian history. James Naismith, the creator of basketball, described the Edmonton Grads this way: "The Grads are the greatest team that ever stepped out on a basketball court."

The Edmonton Grads were such a powerhouse and talented group of athletes that of 522 games played all over the world, they lost only 20. They competed in 13 Canadian Ladies Championships and won every one. They played 27 games at four different Olympics and 24 more games on three European tours and were never beaten. During this whole period they only had one coach—Percy Page.

They were enormously popular and huge crowds came to see them play wherever they played. The Edmonton Grads' style of play emphasized precision and relentless teamwork—short on flash and long on execution (Batten, 1971).

Every one of these athletes were amateurs. Noel MacDonald was the highest scoring player and team captain from 1936-39. She, like the others, worked full time in offices and schools and trained after work. Competition tours took place during vacations. So closely did they follow the amateur guidelines that there was concern that their status might be threatened when their coach, Perry, gave them each a dollar so they could enjoy an evening in San Francisco!

coaches found that they saw the socialization of young athletes through sport as a major goal and hoped the athletes would have fun and develop interpersonal skills (Hansen, 1988:147). The images of coaches in films and in the media tend to focus on this special interpersonal component, but the other aspect is equally important. The larger the number of athletes handled, the greater the need to have excellent organizational skills as well.

A central aspect of coaching is, of course, obtaining a better performance. That performance can be in many different areas. It can be athletic—a person might want to throw the discus further, improve a golf swing, or swim the English channel or Lake Ontario in the fastest time. The performance could also be completely non-sport related—many actors and singers, for example, have voice coaches to help them achieve the volume, tone or timbre they need. The performance could also be a fairly private affair, as in the situation of a person helping a mother to give birth. In each and every one of these situations the coach is there to help the person do whatever it is that they want to do, better.

In the sport context, performance has two aspects—the physical and the mental. The specific skills of throwing, handling the bat, positioning the feet, following the ball, etc. are formed under instruction from the coach. Part of the instruction, and central to the performance itself, is the mental attitude or psychological component. The coach gives instruction on attitudes and behaviour, which are part

Canada's Sports Hall of Fame.

Percy Page coached the most winning team for 25 years.

Cricket for All Ages

Imran Khan, the Pakistani cricketer, developed his cricket skills in an unusual learning environment. Generally, athletes develop their skills with children their own age and, as their skills progress, they are allowed to compete with others at a similar skill level. Khan, however, grew up in a small, wealthy community in the city of Lahore, Pakistan, where his family and neighbours all loved cricket. Cricket players of all ages and abilities competed together.

"The games were quite remarkable, in that the players were between ten and thirty years old: first class cricketers played with and against youngsters who could only just hold a full-size cricket bat. Yet children and grown-ups alike were extremely serious and competitive in their approach to the game. The cricket was of a high standard, with the result that the youngsters' development was extremely rapid" (Khan, 1989:3–4).

In Canada, it is hard to imagine a similar situation with an adult hockey player competing seriously in a mixed age team. Here, competitive sport is segregated by age, sex and ability. Sometimes there is a mixture of ages, sexes and skills within a sports competition, but usually the focus of the sport then switches from competition to recreation.

Perhaps one example of such a mixture of fun and competition is exemplified by the long standing tradition held by the Brown family of Toronto. Every Thanksgiving weekend an official "Turkey Bowl" is held. Anyone can join in and play touch football, at any ability level. The focus is a mixture of fun and competition. Marilyn Brown supports "the fun is number one" philosophy but Philip Brown's philosophy has a strong undercurrent of "Woe betide anyone who fumbles and drops the ball!"

and parcel of the athletic performance. The diver cannot perform his or her best dive if fear of injury or failure are impeding the execution. Athletes cannot achieve optimum performance if they are too anxious to win:

> The main purpose of the American Coaching Effectiveness Program, of which (Rainer) Martens is the founder, is described by its name … A good coach, in terms of influence and, generally of won-lost records, too, concentrates on the details of *how* to win rather than on what his charges already are thinking too much about—what happens if they win or lose … focusing on smaller, more solvable technical problems increases physical efficiency and reduces anxiety and stress. Also these methods increase, in a sense, the number of potential winners (Gilbert 1988:98).

The coach helps the athlete learn the best ways of maximizing performance physically and, at the same time, teaches mental skills as well. In the context of the neighbourhood T-ball league, the coach may be teaching children to do their best *and* the principles of good sporting behaviour. Just as schools and parents teach children to be on time for classes, respect their elders, do their homework, tell the truth, etc., so the coach socializes the child or adult into the expected roles of an athlete. Coaches also help athletes anticipate success and prepare for it.

Ted (Teddy) Nolan— "My Culture and My Heritage"

b. 1959,Sault Ste Marie, Ontario. Ted Nolan is an Ojibwa, a member of the Asuishabec Nations, who grew up on the Garden River Reserve just outside Sault Ste. Marie. He was born into a family of twelve and, like many in Nolan's family, had a love of hockey from the start. But, he had no access to formal coaching to improve his skating and other hockey skills. He was only able to play by arriving on the ice and sharing the gloves and sticks that others had.

Like Wayne Gretzky who was a teammate on the Soo Greyhounds, Noland had a backyard skating rink as a young boy. Unlike Gretzky, it was created by carrying heavy buckets of water because there was no running water in his house. Nolan says "If I was born in this age there is no way that I'd be able to play. Hockey's too expensive. We had to borrow everything including cars."

Nolan kept trying out for teams in Sault Ste Marie but without proper training and second-hand equipment, he was continually turned away. "I always believed in myself. What I lacked in skill I made up for in heart. I hate to lose. Some say that native people play sport for fun, rather than for winning, but I hate to lose. I never give up. I always believe I can win."

Eventually, at fifteen through the Elks Club, he got a chance to play house league and then Tier II hockey in Kenora. His Elks' manager, Bill Le Clair, says he always knew that Nolan would make it, but Nolan himself says that the first months were very hard.

Like many members of Canada's First Nations, he suffered from culture shock. He missed the intimacy and support from his friends and family on the reserve and faced hostility and racism from the unfamiliar community and even from his teammates. "I got into a lot of fights. I fought a lot in school, on the ice, in school classes, gym class—they were a rough bunch. The major issue was my heritage— they gave it to me all the time. I got a lot of my strength from my parents, the idea that you have to fight. I understood that there is a difference between starting fights and standing up for yourself. This helped me in life … I stood my ground and once I made a few friends it worked out pretty well."

Teddy Nolan is tough and tenacious. "Everybody has a centre of strength. Mine is my culture and my heritage. It's something that makes me feel good and gives me extra strength. I look back to the way it used to be, and to the future and the way I want it to be."

Nolan has a quiet, soft spoken, almost gentle manner. But there is a determined glimmer in his eye when he talks about what he wants to do—he wanted to play hockey then, and now he has a vision for First Nations athletes today.

Nolan returned to the Sault and spent two years with the Soo Greyhounds. He was drafted to Detroit and the NHL. He was recognized as a hard-working player who was tough in the corners. A hard "clean check," he says, forced him to retire from hockey in 1986. He blames no one and says that it was his fault because "my head wasn't up." He wanted to stay in hockey and took the job as assistant coach in 1987 of his former Junior-A team, the Soo Greyhounds. In 1989, he was promoted to head coach, and in 1991 won the Memorial Cup by leading the team to win the Ontario championship in the finals against the Oshawa Generals.

Nolan strongly feels that anything is possible and he imparts that same way of thinking to his players. "If you want to do something you can." He defines himself as a players' coach and insists coaches have to earn respect —they cannot demand it. Before coaches used to threaten players, today he explains "kids have so many options—hockey isn't the only way out." He wants the athletes he coaches to stay in school as well as play hockey and is part of a programme with the theme "Education can keep you in the game."

The film *Slap Shot* irritates Ted Nolan. He feels that it creates a violent perception of hockey. In his coaching he tries to look at the hockey player as a complete person. The coach has to know when a player is mentally prepared, needs a rest or is ready to be brought up. "The time in Junior A is a period of apprenticeship—a time to teach how to become great athletes as well as to develop young gentlemen to be polite, kind, and the best person possible, not just the best hockey player."

Nolan has also been instrumental in creating hockey schools to encourage and develop the skills of native athletes in Alberta in 1991 and in Ontario in 1992.

Quotations from a personal interview by the author, May 1991.

Coaching takes place in different contexts and the goals and aims vary accordingly. Coaching can take place informally in the context of the family or with neighbours and friends, where there are no organizations involved and the coaching is informal and one-on-one. Coaching can also take place in the context of recreational activities on a volunteer basis—this constitutes the largest numbers of coaches in Canada. Tens of thousands of parents are involved in this type of coaching at the local level. Another area is the educational context at schools, colleges and universities. Finally, there is professional coaching of both individual and team sports.

Clearly, coaches in a recreational program have very different aims to those of coaches working in an educational setting or with professional players. The intimacy and intensity will vary according to the personalities of those involved, the sport itself, the success or failures of performances and whether competition is individual or team oriented.

As we discussed in an earlier chapter, the sports world forms a sub-culture, in some ways sheltered and isolated from the outside world. At the Dubin inquiry, some observers were surprised at the trust, faith and dedication that many athletes had for coach Charlie Francis. In the case of Ben Johnson, Charlie Francis had worked with him from the time he was a young, skinny fourteen-year-old without enough money to go to track meets. Initially, Francis supported Johnson as well as other team members financially and after years of working together they achieved international standing.

Outsiders to athletic competition are often struck by the intensity of this relationship between the coach and the athlete. The coach in some ways knows the athlete better than family or close friends. The coach pushes, cajoles, nags, threatens, encourages, and scares the athlete in the struggle to improve. Olympic swimming star Debbie Meyer, quoted in Sherm Chavoor's book, *The Fifty Meter Jungle,* puts it this way:

> I had to learn to live with pain. I often wanted to jump out of the pool and choke Sherm. He treated us like mechanical robots but it was the only way to win (Tutko & Bruns, 1976:132–133).

For this reason, many athletes feel that the coach has played an essential part in creating who they are.

In a team, the dynamics become a little more complicated because the coach must juggle the concerns of each individual and the needs of the team as a whole. Sometimes these are not the same. Also, with more complex team structures, there are often several coaches involved with a division of labour between the coaches.

DO COACHES MAKE A DIFFERENCE?

The media often minimize the importance of the organization and history of a team, implying that one specific coach or manager makes *all* the difference. Consider these statistics, for example:

- Poor teams will probably improve their records with or without a coaching change.
- In studies of professional baseball teams, the more often the teams changed managers, the further behind the leading team they were on average.
- In college football rankings, 5 out of the top 10 teams repeat from one year to the next (Curry & Jiobu, 1984:116).

This would suggest that the key to a successful coaching career is to get a job with an already winning team. In football in the U.S.A. you would want to coach the Chicago Bears and in Canadian hockey, you would want to avoid the Leafs!

Soo Greyhounds (James Brawley).

Ted (Teddy) Nolan, former NHL player and coach of the Soo Greyhounds.

COACHES: MACHIALVELLIANS OR NICE GUYS.

One of the stereotypes about coaches has been that they are people who have warped personalities, usually in the dictatorial mould. Studies done on coaches using a scale called a Machiavellian scale (usually abbreviated to the Mach V scale) found evidence to the contrary. The test attempts to find out if people have a tendency to try to exploit people and gain control of groups.

Other studies, using Polyphasic Values Inventory (PVI) tests to see if coaches were more conservative than the general population, found that coaches were no different from those in the Mach V test and fell between businessmen and students on conservative values. It should be added that all these particular tests were done on men (Coakley, 1982:192–193).

In other words coaches, as far as their personalities are concerned, are probably very little different from other people.

Debbie Brill, using her innovative high-jump technique.

An important aspect of the coach's role is to provide the athlete with an outsider's view. Regardless of the context, it is often very difficult to see what you are doing wrong, where you are making errors. It is virtually impossible to step back and criticize yourself, except for the most obvious kinds of things. A knowledgeable person watching a golfer, on the other hand, can advise changes in stance to prevent hooking or slicing or ensure a more complete follow-through. Such advice may lead to improved performance.

The advice a coach or advisor gives may not simply be technical in nature. When US cyclist Connie Carpenter Phinney spoke at the "Women in Motion" Conference, held in Toronto, a number of competitive racers asked her what piece of advice could she give to those whose aim was to get to the Olympics and win a medal, as she had in 1984. She thought for a moment and then said: "Know yourself." The audience was quite taken aback. They had expected all kinds of hints about hill work, diet, lengths of runs, etc. Instead, she said it is most important to figure out what motivates you and how you feel. Between March and the end of July, when Connie Carpenter Phinney won her medal, she had only taken two days off. She even said that she was sure the turning point was one particular day in June when she did hill work with the American Olympic team. She had reached a plateau in her training and that particular day made the physical and psychological difference.

Coaching is all about giving tips, advice, encouragement, support, and criticism to help the individual do whatever he or she is doing more effectively and more efficiently. In elite level competition, everyone is concerned about getting an edge in every aspect of the competition and coaches provide this edge. The classic movie scene is the coach or trainer telling the boxer how to conduct the fight. In other sports, coaches may include information about the speed of the track, the attitudes of the judges, the appropriate costumes or music, and even how to "psyche out" the competition.

In local or neighbourhood sport the focus is a little different. These coaches are usually trying to help athletes achieve their best performance. The coach might also want to ensure that as many children as possible play and that everyone has as much fun as they can. The agenda also may include a number of non-athletic goals that would not exist in a high performance coaching.

Organization and Personal Skills

In North America we tend to have a romantic view of the coach—standing at the bench, chewing gum and encouraging the team during the game itself. The time put into other aspects of coaching gets

Athlete Information Bureau (J. Merrithew).

~ SPORT PROFILE ~

Debbie Brill—High Jump Innovator

b. 1953, Mission, British Columbia. Until the 1960s, high jumpers ran up to the bar and scissor-kicked their way over. Everyone did it and it was considered natural. Then, along came a revolutionary method independently developed by Debbie Brill and Dick Fosbury. The new technique involved approaching the bar backwards.

In 1968, at her first international meet, fans laughed at her—"I could hear peals of laughter ringing around the big stadium" (in Stockholm, Sweden) (Brill & Lawton, 1986: 21). Surgeons warned athletes against using this new technique and coaches were unimpressed. Brill thinks that it is no accident that the techniques evolved in North America with two athletes who both had a high level of natural talent. "The Eastern countries were already deeply into the science of sport, with heavily regimented coaching. I don't think individual instinct flourishes in that kind of atmosphere" (Brill & Lawton, 1986: 20).

Brill explains: "For three years I used the scissors style, and I could see how I was benefiting. But then, quite naturally, without any theoretically input, my technique evolved into the backward style. This had a great deal to do with the fact that foam rubber pits were being introduced and that, subconsciously, I began to realize that I could go over backward without any serious prospect of breaking my neck" (Brill & Lawton, 1986:19).

The coach Lionel Pugh entered Debbie Brill's life without the somewhat critical view of other coaches. Brill says he took the position; "This is something unusual, but it is working for Fosbury, and it could work for this girl. Let's do some work and some thinking. Let's explore this a little" (Brill & Lawton, 1986: 25).

Often non-athletes forget that much of athletic competition is linked to the physics of performance: the positioning of the feet, the legs, the body as well as the mental attitude. Pugh worked with Brill to maximize her natural skill with improvements of her technique. The approaches used by Dick Fosbury or Dwight Stones were not necessarily the best approaches for Debbie Brill.

"What Lionel (Pugh) recognized right away was that running from the side (like Fosbury) is not a strong position for my kind of backward jump. It means that you have to produce a dramatic amount of torque off the ground ... The trick is to have a runup with the momentum that naturally takes you across the bar. You have to take your hips straight into the air. The hips are your centre of gravity, the essential point to get over the bar" (Brill & Lawton, 1986: 42).

Good coaches let the athlete keep control over their own approach and use their own view of what is right. They can make suggestions that athletes can adopt, modify or reject in their own way. It worked for Brill. She jumped nine inches higher than the famed gold leap of Ethel Catherwood in the 1928 Amsterdam Olympics and won her own Olympic gold medal.

overlooked: the hours spent talking to scouts, discussing plays and players with management, making decisions about appropriate programs, and planning practice sessions with assistant coaches and team managers. John Wooden the former UCLA basketball coach has said:

> I can go back twenty-four years and tell you what we did at 3:30 p.m. on a given afternoon ... My assistant and I spend two hours every morning closeted away planning a practice that may not last that long. Every entry is made on a white 3 x 5 card that I carry in my pocket (Curry & Jiobu, 1984:125–126).

Nothing is left to chance. Everything is evaluated and re-evaluated. What appears to happen naturally is the result of years of experience and dedication.

The Fear Factor in Sport

One important aspect of coaching is to encourage athletes to push themselves to their farthermost limit. In many sports, the sport performance encompasses danger and can cause permanent injury or even death. Coach Currie Chapman spent many years developing the skills of some of the best women skiers in the world.

"What you have to do as a downhill racer is to try and control ... fear. ... you can tell by the results which skiers can handle it. It comes down to two things. First, they have to be mentally strong enough to put it in the back of their minds on race day. Second, they

have to recognize that fear and deal with it when it becomes predominant. They have to deal with what's causing the fear, whether it be a difficult bump or a certain corner, put it in perspective and then go after the course.

There are some people who are able to put their anxieties behind them, but they don't have the necessary technical skills. Sheer guts will take you only so far, and the final destiny is usually the infirmary. But the skier who has the technical skills and the mental makeup—plus that ability to control fear—is the one who will end up on

the podium" (Chapman, 1988:87).

Chapman feels that the Crazy Canucks were successful because of their ability to control fear: "The key for downhill racers is being able to ski outside their comfort zone" (Chapman, 1988:90). He argues that skiers must feel in control and dominate the course and the hill (Chapman, 1988:93). But, according to Chapman, "Even the best skiers eventually fall prey to the fear factor." It is at that point that the athletes have no choice— they have to retire.

In many respects, coaches are managers in the same way that business managers are managers. They have to make decisions about who can do what, where, when and how. The dates, times, places and statistics of performance are all recorded. The computer record follows the athlete at all times.

Middle-level managers and coaches are subject to evaluation and can be fired by their employer in turn. To add to their problems they operate in an extremely public context. Whereas a typical sales manager may have to justify the sales figures every quarter, the coach is under the gun every game. What is more, they must deal with the fans as well as the media reporters and camera people who are sometimes so close they are able to record every drop of sweat or curl of the lip.

Coaches spend a great deal of time encouraging their athletes to improve their performance, but they focus on all aspects of the athlete's training. Currie Chapman, the coach of the Canadian women's ski team for a decade, explains that sport is not just the physical skills and technique.

The mental approach is critical in skiing. Breaking the sport down, I'd say it's probably 10 percent physical preparation, 20 percent technical and the rest psychological (Chapman, 1988:94).

The Canadian ski team also worked with Terry Orlick, a sport psychologist, to improve performance by developing planning strategies and using imagery and visualization (Chapman, 1988:98). The need to feel confident and capable and to be able to imagine winning are as important as being injury free and well-prepared physically.

The methods and programs for coaching range from the relatively unsophisticated, at the volunteer level, to the highly complex at the national level. Martin and Lumsden outline six important stages for coaches to follow in order to maximize the work they do with their athletes (Martin & Lumsden, 1987: 120-30).

1. *Identify behaviours you want to motivate*. First, explain what behaviour you want to improve (laps, jumps, blocks, serves, etc.).

2. *Arrange for the behaviours to be recorded*. Often detailed records are overlooked because the focus is on the performance at the moment.

3. *Display the results in a way that provides meaningful feedback*. With records both the coach and the athlete can immediately see what is happening with each run, jump, lap, etc. Sometimes posting results can help all teams members. For example, Dayna Daniels, coach and professor at the University of Lethbridge, developed a posting system for gymnasts that let everyone know the stage an athlete had reached in reference to a specific skill (Daniels quoted in Martin & Lumsden, 1987:126-127).

4. *Make sure that the coach's praise or feedback is immediate and frequent*. No one can remember what happened a week before and few can remember in detail even a half an hour earlier.

5. *Set performance goals*. Specific goals need to be presented and it is useful to include an evaluation of effort as well.

6. *Reward goal attainment on an individual and team basis*.

It is only when both the coach and athlete are clear as to where each workout fits into the overall scheme that maximum benefit can be obtained. Coaches are also constantly looking for improvements in their training programs. They continually re-evaluate their approaches and methods of training. Every day the athlete has to struggle with injuries and fatigue and keep on going. The coach tries to help in these areas as well.

COACHES: DEALING WITH POTENTIAL ABUSES OF POWER

Some coaches are very clear and deal quickly with any potential abuse of power.

Currie Chapman asked any staff member who became romantically involved with a skier to leave. For him, a person having a love affair with an athlete disrupted the relationship of the coach with the other team members. "When I hire people, I tell them as casually as I can over a beer that if they fall in love, they're gone. It's unfortunate, but if a coach is emotionally involved with someone on the team, it's just unworkable" (Chapman, 1988:72).

Other coaches are not so public in their position or are ambiguous about the situation. Usually, lack of clarity on the part of coaches will lead to major problems later on.

THE ROLE OF THE COACH AND MANAGER

- Educator
- Advisor
- Financial consultant
- Disciplinarian
- Travel arranger
- Spokesman
- Consultant
- Training supervisor
- Health adviser
- Friend

Don Cherry.

Don Cherry, lively and provocative on and off the ice.

The Special Relationship: Trust and Betrayal

Coaches push athletes to the limit and in the process often develop an intense personal and emotional relationship. Charlie Francis, Ben Johnson's coach, describes Johnson's race at the 1988 Olympics in an almost poetic manner. It is obvious his love for sprinting is immense, as is his respect for Ben Johnson as a runner.

In his book *Speed Trap*, Francis describes Johnson's determination and tenacity. He also outlines some of the elements he developed to help bring about Johnson's success—the immediate reaction to the starter's pistol; the fast, powerful start, pushing off with both feet so that at ten metres he was more than a foot ahead of his nearest rival; and the changeover from sprint position to erect running position in five strides (others needed seven or eight strides). He describes in detail the time and energy put into shaving minute fractions of seconds to improve performance—the positioning of the feet, the raising of the leg, the workouts and the weight training. All this coaching effort and experience gained have been largely ignored in the context of a positive drug test.

This special position that coaches are accorded by athletes is of concern to some sports analysts. As with doctors, dentists, teachers and priests, there is a special position of trust between the two individuals. Obviously, this trust can be abused. The coach often has a dominance emotionally as well as power to control many opportunities that may lead to the chance for future successes.

When the coach acts in the interest of the athlete, it is positive for the athlete; when the coach acts in the interests of himself or herself, it can be destructive for the athlete. Sometimes the coach may be caught in the middle—trying to protect the athletes' interests, while being pressured to act on behalf of owners or promoters. Some of the concerns that have been raised in this regard are as follows:

1. Because the athlete is constantly encouraged to stretch the limits of "the comfort zone," athletes sometimes lose sight of what is their comfort zone in performance. Often safety is the central issue. Promoters or owners sometimes want events, competitions, matches or games to go ahead even if conditions may appear hazardous for the athletes. At issue may be weather, safety equipment or playing surfaces. Sometimes the coach has to fight on behalf of his athletes against these financial interests.

2. Athletes are often children and cannot make decisions for themselves—they may be only ten, fifteen or eighteen years of age.

~ SPORT PROFILE ~

Don Cherry—More Popular than Hockey?

Don Cherry, the former NHL hockey coach, is so popular that in Quebec more people tune in to watch him between periods than watch the games during *Hockey Night in Canada*.

Cherry describes himself in this way: "I'm a beer hall kind of a guy and I know those are the guys watching me … The proudest thing in my life is that I got up at 5.30 am. on the coldest winter mornings facing a jackhammer. That builds character. They're my guys" (Slater, 1989: B1).

Some people are offended by Cherry's "roughneck" style. He explains: "I'm like bagpipes. Either you like them or you hate them." (Stock, 1990: F2). "I'm not a diplomat. I still think and talk like a coach. When I watch a game, I don't see it as a fan or as a TV commentator; just as a coach" (Slater, 1989: B4).

Cherry certainly says what he thinks about news events and foreign players. In 1989, he was even accused of racism over his jokes about Alpo Suhonen (the newly appointed coach for the Jets' Moncton, New Brunswick, team. At the time he said: "Look, Alpo is the name of a dog food, isn't it? Sure I made fun of his name but he didn't take offence to it. And (Shenkarow, the Jets president) calls me a racist. Who maligned who here?" (Cherry threatens: 1989: E1).

His hockey credentials include the fact that he spent many years in the minors as a player and a coach. Then he coached the Boston Bruins for six years winning four division championships and reaching two Stanley Cup finals, losing both times to Montreal (Slater, 1989: B4).

Cherry is extremely popular, has numerous television and radio spots and has expanded his efforts into a restaurant chain called Don Cherry's Grapevine. His nickname is Grapes. It originated from the time he was arguing over money with the late Eddie Shore who said to Cherry: "That's just sour grapes." The name stuck with his teammates as Grapesy, and eventually was shortened to Grapes.

Cherry certainly creates interest and controversy wherever he goes.

---

3. Athletes may be encouraged to make decisions that they would not otherwise make because of the desire to please their coach or their parents— to continue to compete even if they do not really want to; to take drugs when they are not clear as to what the substances are or what the long-term consequences might be; or, to agree to enter a personal or sexual relationship with the coach where the power and the experience of the coach puts that coach in a position that might be labelled sexual harassment in another context.

4. Coaches make final choices as to who will be on a team or attend a competition. Usually the decision is made by the coach unilaterally and sometimes the decisions may appear to be unfair or the reasons for the decision might be unclear. Rarely does the athlete have the opportunity or the right to challenge a decision of a coach that seems unfair—there is no "athletes rights commission" to appeal to; it is the coach who holds the power even though it is the athlete who is the "performer."

PLAYER/COACHES

Coaches or managers of professional teams can be either career coaches or players who have become managers after being professional athletes themselves. The percentage of coaches with a player background varies from sport to sport.

- 73% in baseball; 19 of 26 team managers are former players

- 67% in basketball (NBA); 18 of 27 head coaches are ex-players

- 59% in hockey (NHL); 13 of 22 coaches

- 39% in football (NFL); 11 of 28 head coaches were players

(Houston, 1991: C11)

GASTON VS. ROBINSON

It is interesting to note that in spite of all the talented black athletes in professional baseball, it was only in 1989 that two teams played against each other while under black managers. The game took place between Cito Gaston's Toronto Blue Jays and the Baltimore Orioles, managed by Frank Robinson.

TABLE 5-1:

*Career Changes of Baseball Manager Bobby Cox**

Year	Club	League	Position
1985	Toronto Blue Jays	American	First (E)
1984	Toronto Blue Jays	American	Second (E)
1983	Toronto Blue Jays	American	Fourth (E)
1982	Toronto Blue Jays	American	Sixth (E)
1981	Atlanta Braves	National	Fourth/Fifth (W)
1980	Atlanta Braves	National	Fourth (W)
1979	Atlanta Braves	National	Sixth (W)
1978	Atlanta Braves	National	Sixth (W)
1976	Syracuse Chiefs	International	Second
1975	Syracuse Chiefs	International	Third
1974	Syracuse Cheifs	International	Second
1973	Syracuse Chiefs	International	Third
1972	West Haven	Eastern	First
1971	Ft. Lauderdale	Florida St.	Fourth

Source: Trent Frayne. 1985 *The Globe and Mail.*
* Since 1986 Cox has worked for Atlanta.

Coaches and Their Tenure

What, then, makes coaches so interesting to the rest of us? Movie stars, writers, and athletes are seen to be glamorous; coaches operate in a similar environment. Much of the glamour is generated by the industry itself. The hard work, the travelling and the hassles are easily forgotten. The press writes stories about the coaches; the athletes talk about them. TV shows interview coaches' wives before big games. The very jobs and the media hype make them appear glamorous, and to some extent they are.

On the other hand, coaches come and go, and everyone knows that is the name of the game, particularly in North America. This may even be part of the glamour! Owners or governing bodies constantly judge the coach's performance. Team owners often play an active part in what they feel should be done in the coaching area, and frequently they directly intervene. George Steinbrenner, owner of the New York Yankees baseball team, was an interesting example, as was the late Harold Ballard, owner of the Toronto Maple Leafs. In Toronto, many

Coaching: Insecurity the Norm, Longevity a Luxury

Field Hockey: Marina Van der Merwe was the coach of Canada's national field hockey team. Although she had taken the team from 16th place internationally to 5th at the Los Angeles Olympics, her coaching abilities were questioned (Ormsby, 1985b). She was fired and then rehired for a one-year appointment in 1985.

The Olympic goalie Zoe MacKinnon said that "Marina is knowledgeable about field hockey but coaching isn't just knowledge. It's also knowing how to interact between players..." (Ormsby, 1985:44). However, another team member, Sharon Bayes, has said: "I honestly believe if we had won a medal at the Olympics, any medal, none of this would have arisen. Maybe we were looking for excuses" (Ormsby, 1985:53).

Women's Basketball: The co-coach of the Manitoba women's basketball team, Jeff Gosman, was dismissed because the rules for the Canada Summer Games maintain that one of the two officials who coach must be of the same sex as the team. The reason for this is that the coaches are there to look after the teenagers in other ways and to enusre teams have people who can chaperone and enter the dressing rooms (*Manitoba Cage*, 1985:53)

Highschool Hockey: Sometimes school coaches have different philosophies about the nature and organization of sport. At Father Henry Carr Secondary School in Toronto approximately 10% of the school's students pay an additional fee of $800 to play in the hockey program. The school has done well—nearly fifty students have gone on to play major U.S. college hockey. Some criticized Peter Miller, the athletic director, for stressing hockey when there are Junior-A teams available (Campbell, 1982).

Cycling: Eddie Borysewicz, the coach of the American National Cycling Team, used his Polish style training methods and was criticized. The term "Polish mafia" became a popular term of abuse for his administration. There were allegations that he did not understand America's youth and that his regimented training program would discourage young racers. As one Board member put it, "The coach is supposed to be controlled by the board, but he was making his own policies. What we had was the tail wagging the dog" (Searchinger, 1985). As a result, he has had a struggle to obtain funds. He was given only $500,000 for 1986, less than in 1984, and in spite of the fact that the United

States Cycling Federation received $700,000 from the Los Angeles Olympic Organizing Committee (Searchinger, 1985). Team U.S.A. won five out of six golds in the Pan Am Games and nine medals at the Olympics. Rumours of blood doping however led to an investigation. Eddie B. was suspended for a month without pay. At a press conference the Board said: "The USCF Board of Directors condemns the incident and considers the involvement of the USCF representatives a serious error in judgement by individuals who were charged with solemn responsibilities" (Searchinger, 1985). Eddie B. went from being seen as a hero to disgrace in a few short months.

Baseball: Ted Turner, the owner of the Atlanta Braves, said of Bobby Cox in 1981, "If I hadn't just fired Cox, he's the guy I'd hire," and sure enough he re-hired him in 1985 (Frayne, 1985:132). Cox had only a one-year contract with the Jays and commuted from Atlanta where his family lived. Table 5–1 lists the places Cox has worked and the placing of the teams he worked with, from 1971 to the present.

people are now anxiously watching to see what changes will take place with the new management of the Maple Leafs following Ballard's death.

While the coach may have priorities that he or she feels are essential for the good of the team and its members, often financial considerations are of primary importance to senior management and the owners. When Bob O'Billovich offered his resignation as coach of the

Sex Tests—Accurate in Labelling Women?

So much controversy and so much debate takes place over the issue of sex testing. Before a woman can compete, for all sports except open shooting and equestrian events, she must have a sex test to ensure she really is female.

The reason for the testing is that "in most sports, the average man's muscular strength allows him an advantage over the average female athlete" (Turnbull, 1988: 61). It is important to remember that many elite women athletes beat the records of the "top" men of a decade ago, but in international competition it is the "top" men against the "top" women in sports that are primarily based on muscular strength. Some feel that the solution lies in an historical approach. "At the Ancient Olympics in Greece, sex testing was a simple procedure. Athletes and their coaches walked naked through the gates. No penis, no admittance" (Turnbull, 1988: 61).

The first sex tests were introduced in 1966 and were gynaecological examinations. "Mary Peters, pentathlon gold medallist in the Munich Olympics of 1972, describes them frankly as the most crude and disgusting experience I have ever known in my life. ... I was ordered to lie on the couch and pull my knees up. The doctors then proceeded to undertake an examination which, in modern parlance, amounted to a grope. Presumably they were searching for hidden testes. They found none and I left" (Turnbull, 1988:61).

At the 1968 Mexico Olympics, the sex test was completed by using the "sex chromatin" test to ensure that the athlete has two X-chromosomes. Men have an X-chromosome and a Y-chromosome. The test is completed by scraping cells from the inside of the mouth—a buccal smear—and then examining the cells under a microscope (Turnbull, 1988: 61). It appears quite simple and straightforward, but it is not.

"Deviations from typical patterns can occur in up to one out of every 1000 births" (Carlson, 1991: 26). Sometimes women fail the sex-test because they have chromosome abnormalities. At the same time, there are women with chromosome abnormalities (resulting in muscle-building advantages) who do pass the sex test. How an individual is biologically labelled female or male is not so simple. All normal women and men have both female and male hormones within their body structures.

Many women athletes find the whole issue of sex tests irritating. Often women athletes are severely judged for how they look as well as how they perform. They feel the emphasis should be on their sport performance rather than on how "feminine" they appear to be. For their classification to be based on an inaccurate and "unscientific" tests seems unfair.

Toronto Argonaut football team, he said "Winning's the name of the game and from that standpoint I wasn't happy." (King, 1985).

Nowadays coaches rarely stay long periods with the same team. In examining the 1990 coaching changes in American college football it is easy to see why coaching is a "fragile profession where insecurity is the norm and longevity is a luxury" (Rhoden, 1990:17). Some feel that the job creates so much stress that it causes heart attacks and even suicides, as in the case of Rick Carter, a coach for the Holy Cross Crusaders football team. Carter committed suicide after having one losing season, even though it followed three winning seasons.

In many sports in North America, caoches are not well known or praised. In Europe, the situation of coaches is somewhat different. Coaches for national ski teams, for example, are stars in their own right. They are well known and well respected. Skiing is viewed as

Personalities and Coaching

Coaches and managers have many different styles and personalities. Sometimes, the cities which they represent themselves help shape the coaching "persona." "Martin of their Yankees is scrappy and abrasive, mirroring the aura that most New Yorkers radiate" (Strachan, 1985). Whitey Herzog of the St. Louis Cardinals is a midwesterner, "... where people still feel that hard work should be rewarded, that public decency should be expected and that a man ain't a man unless he hunts and fishes... When Herzog is faced with a baseball difficulty, he doesn't consult a computer—'he goes fishing'" (Strachan, 1985).

Vince Lombardi is known as one of the "winningest" coaches of all times because of his record coaching the Green Bay Packers. He set high standards for himself and all those associated with his football team. He believed in dedication and excellence. It will be interesting to see how his ideas will be received in the 1990s, in the days of steroid use and cocaine.

Lombardi said that in order to win, a person must follow five principles. He also thought that these principles were applicable to the non-sporting world—in business and school.

- *First,* Lombardi felt that in order to win athletes must commit

themselves to a dedicated life of excellence. This meant that the athlete must be mentally prepared at all times to achieve the goals of the individual and the team. He described this aspect as mental toughness. He thought that success in football was 75% mental and 25% physical. Lombardi thought that each person should give a full effort and be totally committed. He was not interested in a football player who only put in a half-hearted attempt.

- *Second,* he thought part of being prepared was to be on time. He felt it was important to be fully prepared and in order to be prepared an individual has to be ready to go. For Lombardi this meant being early; for Lombardi, on time meant being fifteen minutes early!

- *Third,* and not surprisingly, he insisted on his players being physically ready. He argued that many football games were won or lost in the last two minutes and often the key was the fitness levels that allowed a player to perform effectively at the end of a tough game. He felt that when athletes were fatigued they lost

courage and the strength to go on. The teams who were in the best shape would do best.

- *Fourth,* Lombardi lectured on the importance of dominating the plays. He used the term "control the ball." This one is obvious. The person who controls the ball, controls the play. He wanted athletes to concentrate on the central issue of the game.

- *Fifth,* Lombardi stressed the importance of making "the second effort." Lombardi thought the difference between winners and losers lay with those athletes who make a second try even when it seems that success is impossible.

Lombardi felt that these five principles could also be used in any walk of life. He thought that it was important for people to be in shape and to try as hard as they can to achieve their goals.

All of us know someone who dropped out of school. They gave up, sometimes when it was clear to their friends that they could have made it. They were not prepared to make that second effort. Lombardi would have been disappointed in them!

---

an important national sport and the coaches are expected to win. "The European coaches are under tremendous pressure. When their teams are slumping, they get everybody from the prime minister on down phoning them to say they'd better start doing something" (Chapman, 1988:20). The pressure is the same, perhaps, but there is greater respect and latitude for the coach to make decisions and build a team.

The attractions of the security of a longer-term contract and more money can lure coaches, managers and players from one team to

TEAMWORK WORKS WHEN YOU KNOW YOUR ROLE

As the basketball coach for the Knicks in 1991 Pat Riley had a clear coaching philosophy. Each player had to submit to the discipline and needs of the team.

"I'm very easy to get along with as long as you accept the spirit of the team. The most difficult thing to teach players is how to get away from being themselves and get with the program ... Teamwork multiplies the potential of everyone on it. The key to teamwork is to learn a role, accept that role, and strive to become excellent playing it.

The Lakers understood the importance of their roles: floor leaders to guide the team strategically, wingmen and trailers to make our fast break click, aggressive rebounders to deliver the ball to our best shooters, and solid patient reserves to keep control of the game when the starters need a rest" (Anderson, 1991: 27).

another. Obviously, this makes coaching an even more unstable profession. A successful coach is sought after by competing teams. All these factors also have a bearing on the coach's ability to encourage, motivate and make the right decisions for his or her team.

The reality for a coach is that there is always pressure. No matter how good you are, in a sense you are only as good as your last win. Even at secondary schools where academic matters are supposed to be most important, the win-loss framework is there. Part of the problem for coaches lies in their attempt to meet many different, and sometimes conflicting, goals. Particularly in high schools, coaches want their athletes to develop as people but they also are under a great deal of pressure to produce winners.

Part of the stress of coaching involves helping athletes deal with various difficulties they are experiencing. For example, sometimes coaches have to coach athletes who are from another country or speak a different language. This can cause difficulties, even though the team may be strengthened because of the athlete's skills. Athletes who speak only Spanish have become part of professional baseball teams and it has been difficult for some of these Latin players to adjust to an English-speaking environment. Skaters from Eastern Europe and the Soviet Union have joined NHL teams and have found playing hockey in North America to be somewhat harder than in their dreams. Quebecers who speak French have also had adjustment problems where coaches and most team-mates speak only English. Sport Canada has made bilingualism part of its coaching programs to try to address this particular problem.

A consequence of these pressures and the ones listed above is burnout. **Burnout** is when a person has been under so much stress they can no longer effectively do their job. Increasingly coaches are quitting high school coaching in the United States because of low pay and stress. Researchers have suggested a number of solutions to burnout: (1) warn coaches what the job is really like, so the coach does not have unrealistic (television version) expectations; (2) provide a better education for coaches in sport techniques and methods and in the social and philosophical foundations of physical education; (3) educate the coach in the areas of ethics and human relationships; and (4) train coaches to have positive relationships with players, other students, and the community (Wishnietsky & Felder, 1989:71).

Many coaches obtain a great deal of satisfaction working with young people. For some coaches, working with young people adds meaning to their lives. Sometimes there is no money to be gained and very little prestige. There is only the joy of helping others develop their skills and their love of sport. For such people it is not always easy to evaluate their performance in terms of win-loss ratios.

~ SPORT PROFILE ~

Sue Holloway—A Champion in Two Sports

b. 1955, Halifax, Nova Scotia. Sue Holloway grew up in Ottawa, Ontario. Sue Holloway is the only Canadian woman to compete in both the Summer and Winter Olympics in the same year. In 1976, she competed in cross-country skiing and in kayaking. Realizing it was impossible to excel in both, she decided to focus full-time on kayaking.

"I felt I had my best chance to excel in kayacking. I liked the people in the sport and I loved being on the water. Between these two things it was a lot of fun. For our hot Canadian summers it's cool on the water and it's the best."

Like many athletes in 1980 she was bitterly disappointed when the Canadian government decided to boycott the Moscow Olympics. She had spent ten years of her life to peak in 1980 and suddenly all this work ended in the nightmare of a boycott that prevented athletes like herself from competing. The athletes were victims of a political debate in which they had no input.

Initially devastated by this terrible blow, Holloway became determined to press on with her training and renewed her commitment to sport and competition. This dedication paid off and at Los Angeles in 1984 she won an Olympic silver medal in the 500-metre doubles event, with Alexandra Barré, and a bronze medal in the 500 metre kayak four events (Bryden, 1987: 162).

After retirement, Sue Holloway headed up the Olympic Athlete Career Centre that provides assistance to athletes with their career development outside sport. She coaches athletes in a very different context from the athletes' regular coaches, but with the same aims—helping athletes achieve their best. Holloway explains: "It's really important, when it takes so much for athletes to be the best, that we support their development in all areas of their lives—to develop socially as well as physically. The Canadian Olympic Association is a leader internationally in providing such services to Canadian athletes." The Bureau has helped nearly 800 athletes over the six years between 1986–91 to make the difficult transition from full-time competition to a very different way of life after retirement.

Quotations from a personal interview by the author, May 1991.

Careers in Coaching

It is difficult to attract people to a career in coaching if the salaries are inadequate and the job itself is not respected. Geoff Gowan, President of the Coaching Association of Canada, feels that Canadian athletes, both amateur and professional, will not reach their full potential "unless the sports system solves its main weakness: a lack of paid full-time, well-qualified coaches" (Smith, 1989:A19).

Coaching salaries vary from sport to sport depending on the number of participants in the sport, public interest in the sport, how the sport is defined and the nature of the sport. Figure skating in Canada and the United States provides an interesting contrast. Coaches charge higher fees in the United States—with the result that most figure-skating students come from wealthier families and belong to private clubs. On the other hand, figure skating is much more accessible in Canada—it is cheaper to participate and, consequently,

Athlete Information Bureau (T. O'Lett).

Sue Holloway, a winner in both winter and summer sports.

TRAINING TOGETHER

When the Canadian wrester Yukon Erica (Christina Dutkowsi) first began training at Mack's Gym in 1982, trouble started.

Mack's is a "serious" gym, its members do not see themselves as members of a social club. A number of men threatened to boycott the gym. Mack Miya, the owner and trainer explains: "Most of them had been training in my gym for more than ten years. When a girl was lifting more weight than them, they resented it. It hurt their ego ...They were pretty upset, but a few months later they were asking her how to train. Everything was reversed." They stayed and she now coaches there.

Quotations from a personal interview by the author, October 1991.

Sexual Harassment

In the context of sport, the coaches and administrative staff often hold considerable power over the athlete. They are able to advance the athlete's career, include or exclude the athlete from teams, and label an athlete "uncoachable." If you add in an intense emotional involvement and youth, the boundaries of appropriate behaviour can be violated.

Today many campuses and workplaces discuss sexual harassment in the context of employment and social dating. Employment guidelines apply equally in the sport context. Here is a typical guideline taken from an employment contract:

"Harassment means engaging in a course of vexatious comment or conduct that is known or ought reasonably to be known to be unwelcome. Every employee (or athlete) has a right to be free from: a) a sexual solicitation or advance made by a person in a position to confer, grant or deny a benefit or advancement, the employee where the person making the solicitation or advance knows or ought reasonably to know that it is unwelcome; or b) a reprisal or a threat of reprisal for the rejection of a sexual solicitation or advance where the reprisal is made or threatened by a person in a position to confer, grant or deny a benefit or advancement to the employee."

there are more figure skaters in proportion to the size of the population. In Canada, the Canadian Figure Skating Association includes both recreational and elite skaters. In the U.S., there is a split between the United States Figure Skating Association, which caters to elite athletes and has approximately 450 member rinks, and the Ice Skating Institute of America, which has 400 rinks, although the two associations often skate at the same rink or club (Smith, 1988:D1).

In the United States there are about 3.5 million recreational and professional coaches, but less than 20% receive formal training to become coaches. There is no nationally certified system for training coaches. In Canada, anyone can enrol in the coaching program to obtain a certificate. There are many who take Level One (the beginning level), which is part of the developmental program (as are Levels Two and Three), but few take Level Four or Five, which qualify coaches to direct high-performance athletes (Smith, 1989:A19).

Individual sports are increasingly trying to develop more formal training structures for their coaches and players. The Canadian Amateur Hockey Association (CAHA) and the Coaching Association of Canada put on clinics all across the country to develop children's skills (Hansen, 1988:147). Coaches hope that the result of training programs will be fewer injuries, fewer law suits and better first-aid training (Kimieckik, 1988:124).

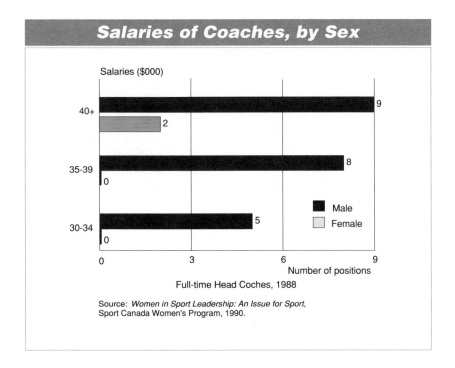

Salaries of Coaches, by Sex

Salaries ($000)

Full-time Head Coaches, 1988

Source: *Women in Sport Leadership: An Issue for Sport,*
Sport Canada Women's Program, 1990.

Minorities and Women in Coaching

One concern of sport experts, as well as those who want to make careers in sport, is that the opportunities to enter the field of coaching are greater for athletes who are male and white. There are more male-dominated sports and there are stereotyped expectations about women and visible minorities.

An important aspect of the path to a coaching career is the position an athlete plays on a team before becoming a coach. In baseball "three-fourths of all baseball managers are former infielders or catchers. One-fourth played just one position—catcher" (Grusky, 1963:346). Very few athletes from the outfield become coaches. The experience of working in the infield, in close interaction with other players, helps prepare the athlete for a coaching role. Since very few pitchers and catchers are non-white, we find very few non-white coaches. In football, there are similar stereotypes about black athletes and their performances: very few quarterbacks in the United States are black, and few become coaches or managers.

In 1979–80, there were two black head coaches or managers in the NBA (out of 22). By 1991, there were six black head coaches in the NBA. In 1981, in the NFL there were none; and in baseball in 1979–80, none. There were a few who were assistant coaches: 4 out of 26 in

Marina Van der Merwe, Canadian women's field hockey coach.

Athlete Information Bureau.

Gender Segregation in Coaching

In a study of students in coaching programs in the United States, women and men answered questions somewhat differently.

Male students expected to coach at a higher level and more planned to use coaching as a stepping stone to higher teaching or administration positions. They expected to reach more senior positions and felt that marriage and children would have little affect on their coaching career (Pease & Drabelle, 1988:30–32).

The typical problems faced by women coaches were:

- There was an emphasis on the fact that women were women rather than coaches. "Other male coaches were saying to their teams, 'Guys, you've got to beat that team because you can't lose to a woman'."
- There were problems with male coaches and officials—the

authority of women coaches was not recognized … "a basketball coach reported that when she stood in the coaches' box, an official said, 'Lady, sit down and shut up.'"

- A small minority of fathers interfered and thought women should not be coaches. Some mothers were quite supportive .
- It was important to establish that you were tough and, like male coaches, were willing to fight to keep your power base.

The different attitudes reflect differences in socialization and values in our society.

In the report prepared for Sport Canada, entitled "The Gender Structure of National Sport Organizations," the first problem encountered was that many within sport organizations do not see any obstacles to the participation of

women. Men in sport often think that it is merely individual women who are unable to "put the time in" to pursue successful roles in sport. Women and men viewed this differently (Hall, Cullen & Slack, 1990:11).

Clearly, there are women who have been successful in pursuing careers in sport, but they are in a minority. However, there was no disagreement that women are under-represented within national sport organizations. The researchers concluded that it is necessary to examine the structures of sport themselves.

The problems women face within sport organizations are similar to those in corporate structures: lack of role models, exclusion from important informal networks, limited participation in decision-making at the higher levels and negative attitudes towards the participation of women.

the NBA; 16 out of 235 in the NFL; and 11 out of 102 in baseball (Simons, 1980:50). So, in spite of the fact that there are many black players in these three main sports in the United States, we find that retired black athletes are not moving into coaching and managing positions proportionate to their numbers.

In sports organizations and in coaching positions we also find few women. Although women have participated in the Olympics since the beginning of the century, it was not until 1981 that there were any women on the International Olympic Committee (IOC). This is perhaps indicative of the problems that exist.

While sport has become more integrated in the colleges and universities, there seem to be fewer women becoming heads of athletics and coaching. There has been a decline in the number of women coaching women's teams in the United States in the last ten years.

When we list six of the ten most popular sports in the United States, we find that the percentage of women coaches has declined in all of them. It seems that, in spite of affirmative action programs, various legal cases and the Title IX legislation to ensure equal federal funding for women, sport is still very much a male preserve when it comes to administration and coaching. The same pattern is found in Canada. "… the Ontario Commission on Inter-University Athletics (OCIA) carried out a study in the spring of 1987 and found that only 45 percent of the persons who coached women's intercollegiate teams in Ontario were female" (MacIntosh, 1989:8).

If sport as a whole is examined, it is clear that the differences in the career paths of women and men cannot be understood merely by examining the individual women themselves. The same problems exist for women in sport administration as for women trying to break into high managerial positions in business. There are three factors that keep women out of male-dominated, sport occupations—there are fewer opportunities for women in sport; women have less power in terms of the industry and in the professions; and, women are a minority within sport (Knoppers, 1989:40).

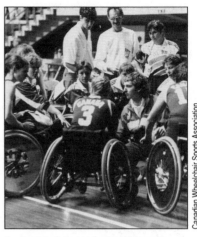

A wheelchair basketball huddle.

Canadian Wheelchair Sports Association.

The Future of Coaching

The future direction of Canadian coaching will be affected just as much by developments outside the immediate world of sport as within sport itself. The public's expectations of coaches has increased enormously in the aftermath of the revelations of wide-spread drug use by athletes. Nowadays coaches operate under much greater public scrutiny and increasingly will need to be aware of the moral and ethical issues in sport and society.

A coach's priorities can range from a focus on fun to a preoccupation with winning and financial concerns. Coaches have a very special, often quite intimate, relationship with their athletes. The coach is not only responsible for the actual performance but also for the values and outlook of the individual athletes.

For Canadian sport in general, coaching will require more attention and more financial resources. This will be essential if Canada is to reach a higher level of general fitness for its population and achieve a higher international showing in elite competition. In large part this will involve a more open policy that encourages athletes to go into coaching following their athletic careers. In the past opportunities in coaching have been fewer for women and minorities. This too will have to change if the pool of coaching talent in Canada is to be tapped.

The essential role they play ensures coaches a prominent place in the future of sport in Canada.

REVIEW

Questions

1. What are the essential aspects of a coach's role?
2. What are the factors that make the job of a coach so insecure?
3. What are the conflicting role pressures on professional coaches?
4. What are the five principles Lombardi feels are essential to being successful?
5. Why are there few female coaches and administrators in sport programs? Why is this also the case for persons of colour and those with disabilities?

Concepts

- coach
- coaching stress
- sexual harassment
- discrimination

Discussion

1. Explain the influence a particular coach has had on your sport experience in relationship to training or competition.
2. What are the central factors that explain the low number of athletes of colour in management and coaching positions?
3. What changes would you recommend to bring about the greater participation of women at all levels of sport management?

The Old Orchard Skating Club poses for a
photograph in the 1920s.

Jocelyn Lovell, Canada's cycling star at the head of the pack.

Chapter Six

CAN ONLY THE RICH PLAY

"Money was always an issue in our life. There were six kids and we just didn't have enough."
Larry Bird, basketball MVP player with the Boston Celtics

"I estimate my parents spent between $30,000 and $50,000 per year for five or six years when we were in serious competition and I mean in 1960 dollars."
Otto Jelinek, former Canadian Minister of Sport and 1960 Olympic pairs figure skater, with his sister Maria

"Face it. You don't see people outside on Sunday afternoon polishing their refrigerators."
Ron Hill, former Detroit automobile designer on North America's fixation with cars

PROFILES IN THIS CHAPTER

- Silken Laumann
- Vicki Keith
- Arnold (Arnie) Boldt
- Ann Peel

How often do you hear "I can't go to the game, I don't have the money"? To participate in sports activities is often quite expensive. Having enough money allows an individual to participate in physical activities and obtain the training and coaching needed to develop skills. Children or young adults may be quite keen to go horseback riding or downhill skiing but the funds may not be available. The financial background of an individual defines and limits opportunities, whether we like it or not. Even those with exceptional athletic talent may be excluded from a particular sport and never have the chance to be called winners because of limited financial resources.

The Roulette Chips of Life

Each child is born with a certain number of opportunity chips to start out in life. The child is totally unaware yet people speak of a child being born with a silver spoon in its mouth. There are various factors that directly affect a child's sport opportunity:

- financial resources—what can parents afford to spend on equipment, time to help, coaching fees, etc.?

Youthful lacrosse players around the turn of the century.

Ontario Public Archives.

Social Ranking: Class, Status, Power

Sociologists and political scientists who have examined Canadian society find that it is not just a collection of middle class people. They have found that there are rankings in the society based on power, authority and economic influence.

If we examine who owns and controls economic institutions in Canada, we find that a relatively small number of people control the businesses, the media and service industries in this country. Wallace Clement found that about 1,000 families controlled approximately 80% of Canada's wealth (1975). He also found that there were direct connections between large corporations, the government and the media. Therefore, it should come as no surprise that these same connections are found in the world of corporate sport.

Sociologists Peter Pineo and John Porter gathered information about how people rank individuals in Canada. Not surprisingly, doctors and lawyers are ranked higher than garbage collectors or letter carriers. This study was done some years ago, so it would be interesting to consider what differences we might find today. Where would professional athletes fit in? Where would television personalities rank?

Pat and Hugh Armstrong, authors of *The Double Ghetto*, have done considerable work in the area of the separation of women's and men's work in Canada. Women and men for the most part do different work in Canada. Most of the jobs done primarily by women are less well paid and have less prestige. The fields dominated by women are listed in the adjacent table . **Ghettoization** is the

term used to describe the separation of women and men into separate areas of work. Between 1985 and 1991 there was a considerable growth in the number of women attending university and joining the ranks of lawyers, doctors, dentists and other professionals. Unfortunately, there is still a separation by employment, even if the wage gap between women and men is narrowing.

Single parents are financially in even worse shape. Women earn less money than men on average (.64 cents for each $1.00 earned) and often take responsibility for child care which restricts their career options. The **feminization of poverty** refers to the increasing number of women, some with families, some without, who are poor or are becoming poorer. The "double load" carried by many women, of work in the home and in the

workplace (in certain job areas) is sometimes referred to as **the double ghetto** (Armstrong and Armstrong, 1984). Of course, this double responsibility in turn directly affects the opportunity and time that women have to participate in and to follow sport. .

Increasingly Canadian families are finding it harder to maintain a middle-class "lifestyle"—with a home, a car or two, vacations, university education for children and various consumer possessions. Economists are talking about income polarization or the grouping of people at both ends of the income scale—those who earn a lot and those who earn little (Chisholm, et al., 1989:57). Statistics Canada found that the average family income in 1980 was $42,879. In 1987 this figure had only increased to $43,604 (Chisholm, 1989:57).

Dominating Female Occupations in Canada, 1981

Occupation	Female % in occupation	% of all female workers
Stenographers	98.7	10.1
Salespersons	56.3	6.4
Personal Service Workers	92.5	2.3
Teachers	63.5	4.2
Fabricators, assemblers & repair of textiles, fur and leather products	81.2	2.7
Graduate nurses	94.9	4.0
Waiters and bartenders	81.5	4.7
Nursing assistants, aides and orderlies	83.4	2.3
Telephone operators	94.8	0.7
Janitors, charworkers & cleaners	72.2	2.1
Total	72.2	39.5

SOURCE: Pat and HughArmstrong, *The Double Ghetto Canadian Women and Their Segregated Work* (revised edition). Toronto: MacClelland and Stewart, 1984. pp. 36–37.

- **family support**—is the rest of the family interested in physical activity?

- **geographic location**—are there varied climatic conditions and what facilities and coaching is available (a town far away from large sport centres reduces development opportunities)?

- **cultural, religious or moral values**—what are the attitudes toward physical activity and what sports are considered suitable?

- **gender of the child**—if the child is female are there reduced opportunities in physical activities?

- **colour or ethnic group membership of the child**—will the skin colour of the child or ethnic group membership reduce athletic opportunities because of discrimination?

- **genetic background**—does the child have a healthy, fully-abled body?

All these factors may enhance or reduce a child's ability to engage in sport and physical activity. Many very gifted children overcome incredible odds and succeed anyway, but they are the exceptional children.

Social Stratification and Sport

Having fewer resources than others sometimes makes people feel victimized or ashamed. Seeing other athletes with fancy, new equipment and unquestioned confidence can make a person feel less worthy and somehow vulnerable. Studies have shown that children have a pretty clear idea of their social standing by the time they are eight or nine years of age.

The **socio-economic status** of an individual refers to their social and economic position or ranking within society. John Porter, a Canadian sociologist, described Canada as a **vertical mosaic**. He found that, although Canada is made up of many different cultures, the percentages of members of different cultural groups represented in dominant positions are not equal. There is, for example, no correlation between the numbers of Italians, Greeks and West Indians in the general population and their numbers in parliament. According to Porter, Canada was not a "melting pot" of different cultures so much as a mosaic—and an unequal one at that. (Porter, 1965). He found that white, anglo-saxon, protestant (WASP) males dominated the important positions in Canadian society.

~ SPORT PROFILE ~

Silken Laumann—A Sculler for the Laurels, not the Money

b. 1964, Toronto, Ontario. Silken Laumann competes in a sport that has a long Canadian history stretching back to Ned Hanlan. At one time many male university students expected rowing to be part of their post-secondary education. The Oxford-Cambridge boatrace, which occurs in London, England, each year, is a well-known public competition reflecting that tradition. It is only in recent years that women's rowing has had the opportunity to flourish.

Rowing is not one of television's glamour sports and, in spite of her A-card rating by Sport Canada, Laumann is not well-known. Photogenic and articulate, she is a sponsor's dream, but her sport receives little attention.

Laumann has experienced two quite typical aspects of the life of a Canadian high-performance athlete. Fractions of a second divide winners from losers. When she is racing she sees nothing around her. "Whenever I race I don't look at anybody. I'm so focused I never really see anything. It's like having tunnel vision." In spite of winning a medal with her sister Daniele at the 1984 Olympics, she felt frustrated. After the race her response was not delight but disappointment. "I felt I hadn't achieved my potential. 6/10ths of a second came between second and third place. Six tenths of a second had meant a bronze."

Struggling with limited funds is another aspect of competitive life. Sport clothing and shoe manufacturers have not yet lined up to provide lucrative contracts. The Laumann sisters were not dressed in expensive clothing with promotion labels attached everywhere, like in downhill skiing. In August 1984, Silken Laumann wore her sister's shorts which kept falling down and a quick knot in the back had to solve the problem.

After the 1984 Olympics, Laumann registered at the University of Victoria and received both an academic scholarship of $1,000 and a second scholarship of $1,000 as a member of the Varsity rowing team. As a B-carded athlete at that time, and one of the top 16 athletes in the world, she was paid $450.00 a month by Sport Canada. But even that small amount of money would sometimes be three or four months late. At this point, her father Hans Laumann, like many sport parents, had to help out. In the summer, she worked part time for her father's firm "Sparkle Window Cleaners." She heaved heavy window frames up and down ladders while working with a team of men. Her East German and Romanian competitors focused on rowing and received massages, special diets, and rigorous training schedules, while Silken Laumann had to worry about paying the bills.

Regardless, Silken Laumann has continued training and improving her competitive skills. After a disappointing Olympic year in 1988, Laumann almost quit. In 1990, she decided to commit to training full-time. With a new coach and a move to Victoria, B.C., where she could train all year, success followed. Laumann was the 1991 Ontario Athlete of the Year. At Amsterdam, in the summer of 1991, she set a world record of 7 minutes 22.41 seconds in the 2,000-metre single sculls event. In Lausanne she won the World Cup gold medal and a $5,700 prize, and she won a gold medal in the World Championships in Vienna.

Quotations from a personal interviews by the author in 1989 and 1991.

WARNER'S SOCIAL CLASSIFICATION SYSTEM

Upper-upper class
Upper class
Upper-middle class
Middle class
Lower-middle class
Lower class
Lower-lower class

People's socio-economic status affects the sports they play, the leisure time activities they enjoy, and the activities in which they encourage their children to engage. Some people, for example, join clubs which are considered "exclusive," are expensive or restrict membership to certain groups of people.

Housing, transportation, food and clothing must all be covered before money is available for activities like sport participation or training. It is easy to understand why participation in some sports is limited to those who come from higher socio-economic backgrounds.

Many families have difficulties making ends meet. The situation can be even worse for certain low-income groups. If a person is disabled, for example, his or her financial resources are likely to be extremely limited. Little money is available for spending on physical activities and sport after regular expenses are met and often extra expenses, made necessary by their disability, are required.

There are many costs involved in participating in athletic activities, even at the recreational level. Some of these items of expenditure include the following:

1. Specialized clothing—shoes, shorts, tights, rain gear, special coloured clothes, specifically designed clothes (eg. cycling tights have a chamois for comfort, rowing tights do not).

2. Specialized equipment—a racing shell, special racquets, boats, canoes, clubs, horses, etc.

3. Specialized coaching or training—specific training programs, diets, how to use equipment, how to compete, etc.

4. Other costs—associated with fees for club membership, travelling, entry fees, etc.

If a person does not have the money to pay for these requirements, he or she is automatically excluded and does not get the chance to be a winner.

Some sports also cost more money than others. To play golf the athlete must spend a considerable amount of money on clubs and clothing and, if he or she wants to play regularly, green fees or a club membership. On the other hand, if the athlete is interested in participating in a team sport, such as basketball, the costs are quite low. The school provides the coaching and transportation, so the only direct costs are such things as running shoes. It is for this reason that across the United States you find many students playing basketball. It is accessible and cheap.

Costs for competitive figure skating, however, are much higher. The Canadian Figure Skating Association says the costs are between $5,000 and $30,000 a year. Obviously, the top contenders spend more. Brian Orser, the Olympic silver medallist, left high school at sixteen to concentrate on skating.

"It was getting to the point where I was putting sort of half effort into skating and half effort into school. I decided to put a full effort into skating" (Brian Orser, 1980:10).

He was lucky in that his parents were very supportive of this decision. Brian's father, Hal Orser, spent about $100,000 on his son's skating from aged six to eighteen (ibid:10).

CANADIAN HOUSEHOLD INCOME PATTERNS

Under $30,000	22%
Between $30– $70,000	52.2%
Over $70,000	25.8%

SOURCE: Statistics Canada quoted in Patricia Chisholm, et al. 1989. "Destroying the middle class" in *Maclean's*. November 6:56–62.

Athlete Information Bureau (C. McNeill).

Silken Laumann, gold winner on the water.

Vicki Keith—"I don't believe in the word 'impossible'."

b. 1961, Winnipeg, Manitoba. Vicki Keith is the holder of fifteen world swimming records. She achieved all this without a coach and without connections to the sport world.

Keith is now retired and explains: "Throughout my career I tried to accomplish what people claimed to be impossible. When I decided to do a double crossing of Lake Ontario they said it was impossible. When I said I'd swim the Great Lakes, they said it couldn't be done. Three men before me tried to cross the English Channel using the butterfly—one man made it for one mile and the second made two miles. It was deemed impossible also. In covering the swim all the writers said that this swim can't be done and after 23 and a half hours they said this is unbelievable. I like to turn people's minds around. I don't believe in the word impossible."

Vicki Keith holds many long-distance swimming records: the longest butterfly swim at 47.06 miles in 1989; the longest non-stop swim for a female at 129 hours and 45 minutes in 1986; and the longest non-stop distance swim of 33 miles in 24 hours in 1987. She has also completed a two-way swim across Lake Ontario (Page, July 28,1988: A20). Her attempt to complete a *three-way crossing* of Lake Ontario was only stopped because of the terrible pollution. The sewage and garbage present in the lake in the summer of 1990 made the swim a physical impossibility.

Keith's list of achievements is a long one: she has done the butterfly on a double crossing of the Sydney Harbour in Australia, the 34-kilometre English Channel, the 30-kilometre Lake Winnipeg and the 37-kilometre Juan de Fuca straits between Washington State's Olympic Peninsula and Vancouver Island (Page, 1989: A4). Vicki Keith also was the first person to swim across all five great lakes, Lake Erie, Huron, Michigan, Superior and Ontario. The purpose of the swim was to raise money for the aquatic wing at the Variety Village Training and Fitness Centre in Scarborough (Page, June 25,1988: A21).

Marathon swimmers usually only do one long-distance swim every two months, preferably one every four months but Vicki Keith had "either one week or two weeks between swims and during the Butterfly Summer I had on average two weeks between swims."

While Keith was swimming the marathons, she focused on catching up to the boat accompanying her and learned to accept the hallucinations and passing out that comes after hours in the water. Through the fifty hours or more she concentrated on making two more strokes and built up the miles by adding one stroke at a time. She knew she must not be tempted to swim down to look at what appeared to be tile on the bottom of the lake. Throughout the swims she was supported by a crew of teenage boys that included Craig Williams and her brother. No one could believe they could do the job, but they did, swim after swim.

When she was ten-years old, Keith taught a disabled child to swim. The delight on the child's face resulting from the sense of freedom from the wheelchair made a deep impression. It was at this time that she decided she would eradicate the word "impossible" from her vocabulary. She saw, time after time, children achieve the impossible and she decided she wouldn't accept limits presented by others and would make a contribution to the lives of these children.

It is disappointing that Keith has not been able to raise the millions of dollars she hoped from her incredibly difficult feats. Possibly it is because her swimming is not as easily covered and marketable with photo opportunities and media events. Often she is miles out in distant water. But her achievements over-shadow all this.

Quotations from a personal interview by the author, September 1991.

Expenses related to skating competition are not new. Otto Jelinek, who was Canada's Minister of Sport in the 1980s, and his sister Maria Jelinek were figure skating pairs in the late fifties and early 1960s. They competed in the 1960 Winter Olympics at Squaw Valley, California. He said that when he competed there was no financial help for athletes and his parents paid all the bills.

> I estimate my parents spent between $30,000 and $50,000 per year for five or six years when we were in serious competition. And I mean in 1960 dollars (Schiller, 1988:B1).

A skating costume by one of the top designers alone may cost as much as $2,000.

Sometimes competitors receive assistance and it can come from a number of sources. The Canadian Figure Skating Association has an Athletes' Fund from which it dispenses money to assist athletes. Often the amounts are small ($500) but serve to recognize an athlete's talent. Private sponsors also help athletes. However, even taking into account sponsors, when we examine the socio-economic background of competitors we find that figure skating has been dominated by athletes whose families had considerable resources to support their children's sport interest. Because visible minority groups tend to have fewer economic resources, we find that there are very few visible minority participants in this sport; in this respect, figure skating is the opposite of basketball.

The High Cost of Participating

Competing in sport has unavoidable participation costs. For many parents this money is simply not available to spend. The three examples that follow indicate the costs of participating in bicycling, hockey and skiing.

Cycling: If a recreational athlete decides to participate in cycling, he or she faces the purchase of a bike, clothing and cycling gear. If a person wants to cycle seriously then there are additional costs tied to racing. Repair expenses are higher because of the wear and tear on the bike. Bike performance is very important, so the bike has to be maintained properly. At the same time, participation in races means fees for association memberships. There are transportation costs to the competitions and, if these are outside the city, there are further costs for accommodation. This does not include the costs involved in coaching, going to a training camp in the United States or improving the quality of one's equipment.

Hockey: Adults who want to play recreational hockey must buy good quality protective gear. This is important if they wish to avoid injury and therefore loss of income if they cannot work. In fact, people

CONSPICUOUS CONSUMPTION

The term **conspicuous consumption** is sometimes used to describe the behaviour of individuals who make it clear to everyone that they can afford to engage in expensive activities or own certain kinds of costly things. Such people go out of their way to show others that they can afford to buy expensive things; that is, they consume goods or services obviously (conspicuously). A non-player wearing $180 basketball shoes might be an example of conspicuous consumption.

Vicki Keith, world-record holder in long-distance swimming.

COSTS OF COMPETITION IN VARIOUS SPORTS

The United States Olympic Job Opportunities Program collected data related to the costs of competition in various sports in 1989. The most expensive sports as regards costs to the athletes are:

Equestrian	$81,065
Bobsled (Drivers)	$36,364
Figure Skating	$29,893
Fencing	$24,438
Yachting	$22,900

Source: Personal correspondence with Sheryl McSherry, Manager, Olympic Job Opportunity Program, United States Olympic Committee. June 1990.

Sport as a Means of Upward Mobility

Sport is sometimes a means of upward mobility to a better life. One such story in the world of basketball is that of Larry Bird of the Boston Celtics. As a child he preferred playing other sports to basketball. His family had very limited resources.

"Money was always an issue in our life. There were six kids and we just didn't have enough. Dad always worked, but he was lucky if he made $120 a week. Mom worked all the time as a waitress or a cook, sometimes working two jobs—but the best she'd wind up with would be a $100. I can remember that whatever she made, she always needed an extra $20 or $30 for groceries" (Once) I did get a basketball for Christmas and when I unwrapped it I thought it was the greatest thing I had ever seen in my life. It was better than a football, a bicycle or anything.

Remember those potbellied stoves? I got that basketball out and played in the snow. It lost air and I couldn't dribble it. I brought it in and put it next to the stove to get it heated and then I brought it back out. It would last two or three hours that way. One night I left the ball by the stove by accident. I got up in the morning and discovered a basketball with bumps all over it. I kept that ball for two years because I couldn't afford a new one and when I would dribble the ball it would go this way or that" (Bird, 1989:11-22).

Larry Bird was certainly not from a wealthy family. He was not able to pick and choose his sport nor buy new equipment when he felt like it.

are often surprised by exactly how much money they have to tie up in their favourite sport. If a child wishes to play hockey, there are annual expenses for parents in new hockey gear simply because the child is still growing and needs larger sizes. Additional expenses for parents who wish to encourage their child's development might include fees for hockey school in the summer. These schools, which are aimed specifically at developing hockey skills, are not cheap. Residential fees range from three hundred to over four hundred dollars *a week*, and that does not include extras. If the child wants to develop hockey skills seriously, it will probably cost thousands of dollars a year.

Skiing: The cost of skiing, like most sports, varies according to the level of competition. As a child gets more seriously involved in competition, so the costs rise. But even initially the costs involved in obtaining skis, boots and proper clothing are high. In order to participate one must travel to ski locations and pay fees there as well. For many these costs are prohibitive.

In order to participate in any sport in a serious fashion, money must be spent on special schools. In the past, children had to leave Canada and travel to the United States. Carling Bassett is an example of

Athlete Information Bureau.

Otto and Maria Jelinek competing in the 1960 Winter Olympics

~ SPORT PROFILE ~

Arnold (Arnie) Boldt—International Spokesperson

b. Manitoba. Arnie Boldt lost his right leg at the age of three, but this has not stopped his athletic activities at all.

Although it sometimes surprises abled athletes, Boldt holds international records in both the high jump and the long jump.

In 1989, he brought back gold medals from both the Australian and Icelandic

nationals. He also participates in other track and field events, volleyball, racquetball and soccer.

Boldt has worked very hard in promoting sport for persons with disabilities. He has become known around the world for both his athletic prowess and his promotional work.

In 1990 he was one of the recipients

of the King Clancy Award, which is presented by the Canadian Foundation for the Physically Disabled.

---

someone who left Toronto to train at a residential tennis school in Florida. Only a few Canadian schools offer such facilities. An important exception is Seneca College in Toronto, which has programs for gymnasts, tennis players and figure skaters. The purpose of these programs is to train top athletes who will end up competing internationally. Entry to the programs is very competitive and children are only accepted on a year-to-year basis.

> Parents pay an annual coaching fee varying between $1,050 and $2,400, depending on the sport … if the parents are public school supporters living in Metropolitan Toronto, their taxes can be directed to cover the basic educational costs. Otherwise they must work something out with their local board of education or pay for the schooling themselves. They also cover the cost of travel and uniforms (Brunt, 1986).

Certainly these fees are a great deal lower than the residential schools, but even so they too are not cheap.

American prep schools are often used to help talented athletes stay in both the academic system and the sport system. These schools provide support for academically weak students so that they can continue to play sport. Fees range "from $4,600 at a day-school like Flint Hill in Oakton, Vermont, to $11,200 at Maine Central Institute and $13,000 at Culver Military Academy in Culver, Indiana, both of which are boarding schools" (Alfano, 1989:49). Culver's hockey team is coached by a Canadian, Al Clark, and some students are attracted there because the hockey team is better than most high schools and there is support for academic study.

COSTS OF COMPETITIVE SKIING

Alpine club team	$4,500
Regional/distance level	$14,000
Ontario team level	$24,000
National team level	$55,000

Source: Bill Bennet. November 1989. Ontario Ski Council.

Canada's Sports Hall of Fame.

Arnold (Arnie) Boldt, gold medallist in long jump and high jump.

First Peoples in Canada

Some important facts.

- 3% of the Canadian population is made up of aboriginal peoples. According to the 1986 census of Canada the proportions are as follows: N.A. Indian, 286,225 (40.2%); N.A.Indian and non-aboriginal, 239,400 (33.6%); Métis, 59,745 (8.4%); Métis and non-aboriginal, 68,695 (9.7%); Inuit, 27,290 (3.8%); Inuit and non-aboriginal, 6,175 (0.9%); other multiple responses with aboriginal origins, 23,995 (3.4%). Total population with aboriginal origins, 711,720 (100%).

- 65% of the population live in rural or remote areas.

- 35% live in urban or semi-urban areas.

- Aboriginal people die on average *eight years* earlier than non-aboriginals.

- More babies die: infant mortality rate is 17.2 babies per 1,000 born compared to 7.9 per 1,000 babies for non-aboriginal people.

- The average annual personal income of an aboriginal person on the reserve is only $9,300 compared to Canadian average of $18,200.

- Functional illiteracy is 45% or two and a half times the overall Canadian rate of 17%.

- Aboriginal people are not receiving the health, educational and physical or recreational services most Canadians are getting.

Why Are Treaty Rights And Land Claims So Important To First Peoples?

The First Peoples of Canada, those people who lived here thousands of years before the arrival of the Europeans, signed treaties with the British government. The First Peoples were never defeated in war—these were not conventional peace treaties—they were documents of co-existence.

Today the land claims are tied to much more than the issue of financial compensation. The Assembly of First Nations wants recognition of the traditional rights of self-government and independence recognized in Canada's Constitution. (In the 1982 Constitution Act neither women's rights nor aboriginal rights were recognized.) These are some of the reasons the negotiations with the Federal Government are so important to the First Peoples.

Source: J. Rick Pointing. 1990. "Public Opinion on aboriginal peoples issues," in *Canadian Social Trends,* Thompson Eucational Publishing, Inc. Toronto: 21.

Athlete Information Bureau.

Ann Peel, winner in racewalking and lobbyist for women in sport.

In the United States, **Proposition 42** prohibits giving university scholarships to students who do not meet minimum academic requirements. However, it is thought that this might tend to attract such students to the junior colleges which have no such restrictions on their entrance requirements. Once there, an athlete can then make the jump directly to professional teams (Alfano, 1989:50).

~ SPORT PROFILE ~

Ann Peel—Lean and Mean in Two Successful Battles

b. 1961, Ottawa, Ontario. Ann Peel is a determined competitor in sport and a fighter for the issues that she believes in. She is tall and has the build of most long distance runners—as Peel describes it—"lean and mean".

Peel spent many years lobbying, persuading and informing people about the need to include women's racewalking in the Olympics. While male racewalkers were able to concentrate on training and competition, Peel was forced to divide her energies—she put time into training and winning races (with the unique rolling gait that racewalkers use, keeping one foot on the ground at all times) *and* pressing for the event included in the Olympics.

"A men's racewalk has been in the Olympic Games since 1908. With the women's racewalk well-developed internationally (over 30 countries compete annually in the world championships), I couldn't understand why women were shut out of the event around which amateur sport revolves—it seemed contrary to the Olympic ideals of equity and fairness. Finally we succeeded at the IOC meetings in Seoul, in 1988, in convincing the IOC that the event should be added to the programme."

Because of these efforts women are no longer struggling for the right to compete, but can fully concentrate their efforts on training and obtaining places on the Canadian National Team going to the Olympics.

As many people have been told "life is not easy." After Ann Peel won the battle to have women's racewalking recognized by the IOC, another surprise was in store for her. The Canadian Athletes' Assistance Program supports athletes who get injuries while training and competing. In 1990, while pregnant with her son Michael, Ann Peel discovered that Sport Canada would be reducing her benefits because of her pregnancy. In fact, funding even varied depending on whether the athlete was pregnant with the first, second or third child!

A champion of fairness, with a clear understanding of the legal issues (she is a lawyer), Peel argued with Sport Canada and talked to the media about the position of pregnant athletes.

"I was troubled by Sport Canada's assumption that pregnancy jeopardized high performance. The majority of high performance athlete-mothers find, in fact, that their performance levels improve following pregnancy. In addition, the policy seemed clearly discriminatory since all other reasons for which an athlete might reduce training, such as injury or illness, did not result in a reduction in AAP benefits on the reasonable premise that a meritorious athlete should be assisted through the inevitable ups and downs of an athlete's career. In my mind, pregnancy may also be part of a female athlete's life cycle. It seemed to me that Sport Canada had to recognize the athlete as a whole human being, not just a performance machine."

Finally, thanks to the pressure brought to bear by Ann Peel and others, in 1991 Sport Canada changed its position. Peel explains "now women athletes will continue to receive funding while pregnant as long as the athlete undertakes to train at a level which minimizes risk to the athlete's health and ensures a return to full training and competition at the earliest possible date." The focus of the female athlete can remain on sport rather than on the fear that funds will come to an end.

Ann Peel's concerted efforts concluded with two major benefits for women athletes.

Quotations from a personal interview by author, July 1991.

Schools which offer non-competitive physical training are developing in Canada. The École National de Cirque, the only professional circus school in Canada, trains young athletes in juggling, acrobatics, the high wire, trampoline, trick-cycling, rope climbing, the trapeze, mime, dance and acting (Black, 1989:L1). It is loosely linked with the famous Cirque du Soleil and has thirty full-time students who train in Montreal. Previously, students had to travel to the United States, Europe, China or the Soviet Union to join a circus school.

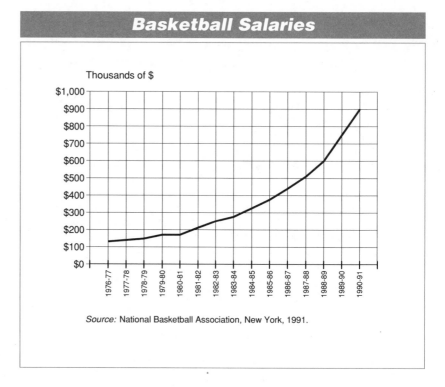

Basketball Salaries

Thousands of $

Source: National Basketball Association, New York, 1991.

Sport and Social Inequality

A study completed by the Ontario Medical Association for the Social Assistance Review Committee found that poor children were two and a half times more likely to die of infectious diseases and twice as likely to die from accidents (Stefaniuk, 1987:135). According to Statistics Canada, in 1984 there were 363,000 children under fourteen years of age living below the poverty line (Stefaniuk, 1987:85). A sizeable number of children, therefore, do not receive the nutrition and health care which are the prerequisites for active participation in sport activity. The downturn in the Canadian economy in the early 1990s has only made this situation worse.

A few athletes overcome all social obstacles in their path and acquire "fame and fortune" in their chosen sport. Raghib (Rocket) Ismail, the Toronto Argonauts' new acquisition from Notre Dame in the United States, is a case in point. He comes from a poor, African-American family in the United States. Because of sheer talent, however, he has been able to negotiate a multi-million dollar contract with Argonauts owners, Bruce McNall (owner of the Los Angeles Kings hockey team), hockey star Wayne Gretzky ("The Great One" himself), and John Candy (movie star).

Toronto Argonauts (John Sokolowski).

Raghib (Rocket) Ismail, scholarships made the difference.

Ismail's "rags to riches" story is not an isolated case, but it is certainly not typical by any means. The chances of making the "big time" are slim and, if by circumstances of birth you are poor or belong to a minority group, the chances are even more remote.

Some individuals are born with better chances than others of becoming "winners," by virtue of the opportunities they have before them at birth. The country or culture they are born into helps to define these opportunities. In Canada and the United States today, a person's socio-economic background and other factors directly affect the athletic opportunities available to that person.

REVIEW

Questions

1. What is meant by "the socio-economic background of a person"?
2. What are some of the costs that affect sport opportunity?
3. What are the differences between competing in basketball and figure-skating in terms of expense?

Concepts

- socio-economic status
- feminization of poverty
- job ghettoization
- vertical mosaic
- social stratification/class

Discussion

1. Describe how socio-economic factors influenced your sport opportunities or those of your friends.
2. How would you describe your own socio-economic background?
3. How do economic factors affect sport participation in Canada?
4. What economic investment do you and your family have in sports equipment, club memberships, training, etc.?

Vicki Keith.

Vicki Keith crossing Lake Ontario in front of
the Toronto skyline.

Angella Issajenko running in the Olympic relay race.

Chapter Seven

WOMEN AND MINORITIES

"Women have but one task, that of crowning the men with garlands."
Baron Pierre de Coubertin, 1902

"History is being made. The world champion is a woman."
Television commentator when Gail Greenhough won the 1986 integrated world showjumping championship

"It is ironical that America, supposedly the cradle of democracy, is forced to send the first two Negroes in baseball to Canada in order for them to be accepted."
Chicago Defender editorial, April 13, 1946

PROFILES IN THIS CHAPTER

- Tom Longboat
- Ethel Catherwood
- Dorothea Beale
- Justine Blainey
- Jackie Robinson
- Jocelyn Lovell

In addition to differentiation based on income, there are social rankings based on other criteria: sex, colour of skin, ethnic group membership, physical skills, sexual orientation and age. All have an effect on the individual's experience of the world and of sport.

The issue for any society is how these differences are handled. Will the society make a commitment to *equal* access to sport? Will the society encourage fitness and health for *all* of its members? Too often, certain members of society have not had the opportunity to obtain the status of winner because of their sex, colour of their skin, age or physical disabilities.

Equality in Sport—What Is It?

In 1982, Ann Hall and Dorothy Richardson evaluated the state of sport in Canada and wrote the classic study *Fair Ball: Towards Sex Equality in Canadian Sport*. For Hall and Richardson, "The word 'equal' means having the *same* rights, privileges, ability, rank, etc.," and "equality" is the "state of or instance of being equal." **Equity** is "fairness, impartiality, justice"; equal chance to participate and equal recognition of achievements for major social groups. Hall and

Cross-country skiing at the turn of the century.

~ SPORT PROFILE ~

Tom Longboat—An Unknown Legend

b. 1884 on the Six Nations Reserve, near Brantford, Ontario; d. 1949. In 1907, Tom Longboat shocked North America by winning the Boston Marathon under terrible conditions of rain, snow and slush in a time that was a full five minutes faster than the 1901 record. He ran the race in 2 hours and 24 minutes (Batten, 1971: 118). He became Canada's national sport hero. He became a legend.

Longboat was a racer with a huge stride, over six feet in length. He won many races in North America. In those days, however, Olympic athletes were supposed to be amateurs and not receive money for competition. This meant that mainly well-to-do athletes competed. There was considerable controversy over how Tom Longboat supported himself.

After he turned professional, he was one-half of "the race of the century" on February 5, 1909. Longboat ran against an Englishman called Alfie Shrubb in front of 12,000 people in Madison Square Gardens. Shrubb led by nearly two-thirds of a mile after fifteen miles, but during the twenty-fourth mile Longboat surged past Shrubb to win (Wise & Fisher, 1974: 245).

At this time, he was considered the best distance runner in the world. However, his promoter-trainer, Tom Flanagan, decided to maximize his profits and sold Longboat's contract to an American for $2,000. The contract was sold a few month's later for $700 (Wise & Fisher, 1974: 245). Longboat had found himself in the position of not being able to control, market or

benefit from his very special skills. As with many athletes, he found others benefited financially much more than he did. He did not make a great deal of money from racing.

After retiring from running, he worked for the City of Toronto and explained that the reason he liked working for the Parks and Recreation Department was that he could not bear to be indoors. Some people thought it was inappropriate for such a "star" to work in this way, but it was what he liked to do.

Although he was a gifted runner, sadly, many Canadians today hardly know his name.

Canada's Sports Hall of Fame.

Tom Longboat, best distance runner at the beginning of the century.

Richardson argue that if competition were on the basis of such things as weight and age, integrated sport would be feasible in most sports. But, because there are some physiological differences between women and men, they argue that sex equality in sport should focus on equal opportunity (Hall & Richardson, 1982:10–11).

In reading the material on the history and present situation of women, minorities, the disabled and gays in sport, it is necessary to keep in mind this issue of equity. Does equity exist for the various individuals and groups who are not part of the so-called majority?

Equality of opportunity encompasses all aspects of sport. It includes: access to facilities; numbers of events; jobs in coaching, teaching and managing; leadership roles; professional opportunities; media coverage; promotion; positions in sports organizations; and respect for accomplishments. If any aspect is excluded, equality of opportunity does not exist. If athletes of colour are allowed to play on professional team but do not progress to management positions, that is not equity. If girls do not get access to arenas at reasonable times, this constitutes inequality.

Legal Discrimination—Repealed, 1986

Until December 1986, the *Ontario Human Rights Code* had a specific section that prohibited discrimination in the areas of housing and employment *but* excluded sport. Section 19(2) specifically stated that sport was excluded from the Human Rights Charter.

It was on this basis that the Ontario Hockey Association (OHA) went to court in order to exclude Justine Blainey from a boy's hockey team. She had applied to play on a boy's team because there was no girls' team in her area with players at her ability level. She tried out for the team and was eighth out of 64. The coach wanted her on the team, the other players wanted her, but the OHA did not want her to play, so she was

prohibited. In the summer of 1986, the court decided that she had the right to appeal to the Human Rights Commission. For two years she had not been allowed to play. The issue was not her talent—she had the ability. The only reason she had not been allowed to play on the team was because she was a girl.

After the Standing Committee on Justice heard representations from many members of the public and sport organizations, it decided that Section 19(2), the section of the *Ontario Human Rights Code* which permitted discrimination, should be repealed. This meant that sport organizations could no longer exclude talented girls and women on the basis of their sex.

Employment Equity and Equal Pay in Sport

Much discussion is taking place today over *pay equity* and *employment equity*. Issues of pay equity and employment equity also arise in the world of sport. Sport Canada and some sectors of the sport world are currently addressing the differential opportunities, training and rewards in sport.

Employment equity refers to the recruiting, hiring, training and promoting of women, the disabled, visible minorities and native persons to ensure that these groups are fairly represented at all levels of responsibility. Historically, it was considered appropriate that women hold only such jobs as nurses, teachers and secretaries and receive quite modest salaries for this work. It was assumed that fathers or husbands would take care of the family and be the breadwinners, even if the reality was often different. In sport, employment equity means that a coach or manager would be hired on the basis of skill, not on the basis that men have always done the job or that there never has been a non-white manager, and so on.

BILLIE JEAN KING
Billie Jean King is an example of a leading athlete who pushed for better prize money for professional women tennis players. King was a driving force behind the creation of a professional women's tennis circuit.

OLYMPIC EVENTS FOR MEN AND WOMEN

	Women	Men
1932	14	87
1964	32	115
1980	50	146
1984	73	153

SOURCE: Jay Coakley, *Sport and Society:Issues and Controversies*. (St. Louis: Times Mirror/Mosby, 1986) p. 124.

Canada's Sports Hall of Fame.

Ethel Catherwood, gold winner in the high jump at the 1928 Olympics.

~ SPORT PROFILE ~

Ethel Catherwood—"Saskatoon Lily"

Canadian women did extremely well in the 1928 Olympic Games. The track and field team won four medals and the women's team title. Ethel Catherwood, the "Saskatoon Lily," won the high jump event and the attitudes of the time are represented by the following poem:

The equal of her brother she has proved
Her worth and holds her solid place unmoved
In letters, art and every kind of lore
And calmly waits new kingdoms to explore;

In mental fitness she has well excelled,
And now, a record makes in track and field
Proving her mettle for the stronger role,
Where man had thought he held complete control.
  (Cook, quoted in Lenskyj, 1987:223)

These successes helped redefine the role of women. A number of attractive women (and this was considered important) were very successful at the Olympics and had proved they could succeed in a "man's world."

Pay equity is the attempt to rectify or change "the wage gap"—the fact that men on average earn more money than women. *Equal pay for equal work* is when all bus drivers, tennis players, bank clerks, mechanics, and others, doing the same or equivalent job, get the same pay regardless of their sex or ethnic background, etc. Comparisons are based on skill, effort, responsibility and working conditions. For example, in down-hill skiing women competitors train and compete just as conscientiously and with the same desire to win as men, but the financial rewards have been greater for male competitors.

Until recently these pay and employment differences were ignored or accepted. However, as more and more women and minorities have taken their rightful place in the world of sport and other sectors of society, the pressure for equality in employment and pay has increased accordingly.

The Fair Sex and Sport

One hundred years ago, women around the world were unable to vote, own property, control their own children, get the educational or vocational training they wanted or work in their chosen field. In the nineteenth century, a woman's role was defined exclusively by her biology as a reproducing organism.

Physicians saw the body as a closed system possessing only a limited amount of vital force; energy expended in one area was necessarily

Maria Patino—When is a Woman not a Woman?

Maria Patino, the Spanish national record holder in the 60-metre hurdles, competed for 24 years without ever thinking about being female. She had passed her sex test and focused on her training.

In 1985, at an international competition in Japan, Patino was asked to report to "Sex Control" to be re-tested because she had left her "certificate of femininity" at home. Subsequently, she was informed that she had failed the test and would not be allowed to compete. Her life was in ruins. She lost her scholarship, she was banned from sport and many of her friends abandoned her.

John Money, a psychologist who has spent many years studying questions of gender identification is very blunt about the question of fairness in sport based on gender classification. "The difference between male and female is not black and white—it's a biological continuum. Any dividing line is a matter of context" (Carlson, 1991: 29).

Money doubts the possibility of defining fair competition as well. "If some women are extra strong, others are taller or smarter. Some have higher oxygenation capacities. All these traits are programmed genetically. "Who gets excluded? Sports are not democratic; they're elitist. The tallest play basketball, the shortest are jockeys. You might as well break the Olympics into biological classes and run them like the Westminster Dog Show" (Carlson, 1991: 29).

Patino challenged her sex-test failure and in 1989 was re-instated and allowed to compete once again. She made it to the finals of the National Championships in Oviedo, Spain. Maria Patino explains; "I was nervous in a way I had never been before. To run there again signified something special. I went out a winner and wanted to come back one" (Carlson, 1991: 29).

But she was a winner off the track as well. She was the first woman to go public, protest her disqualification and be re-instated. Because she spoke out and put pressure on the International Amateur Athletic Federation (IAAF), the Federation is coming up with better testing methods for the IOC (Carlson, 1991).

---

removed from another ... A young women, however, who consumed her vital force in intellectual activities was necessarily diverting these energies from the achievement of true womanhood ... The brain and ovary could not develop at the same time (Smith-Rosenberg & Rosenberg, 1987:19).

Women were portrayed as weak and frail and were terrorized into thinking that active physical exercise would destroy their potential to bear children! Although contraceptive methods, such as the condom and diaphragm, were available from the middle of the nineteenth century, scare tactics were used by suggesting sterility would follow their use (Smith-Rosenberg & Rosenberg, 1987:25).

The repression of female sexuality also played a part in the attitudes toward physical activity. Bicycling was seen as an "indecent practice," swimming "smacked of depravity" and "athletics was viewed more seriously as synonymous with indecency—a corrupting influence for 'a properly brought up girl'" (Hargreaves, 1987:141). Specially gifted women were labelled "Amazons." Ella Hattan, for example, who was born in 1864 and took the stage name of Jaguarina, fought sword

LADYLIKE BEHAVIOUR

The expectation of women athletes has been that they be "lady-like" and feminine. The very pursuit of so-called "unfeminine" goals has meant that women who loved physical activity and did not meet the conventional expectations of looking "pretty" at all times (even on the hockey or soccer fields) have been accused of being "weird" or unfeminine.

Legal Discrimination—Redefined

In the U.S.A., Title IX of the Education Amendments of 1972 was passed to ensure on the equal funding of women's sports by any organization or educational institution receiving money from the federal government. The law began to be enforced and it was hoped that overt discrimination would end.

However, the U.S. Supreme Court decided in the case of *Grove City College v. Bell* that restrictions on discrimination and equal funding only applied if an institution or organization was receiving *direct* funds from the federal government.

So, all the institution had to do was opt out of a specific program and that was the end of any legal right of appeal.

fights and had mounted combat with a broadsword against men *and* defeated them. Women who were athletically talented and challenged the role of men as athletes came under severe criticism. Mildred "Babe" Didrikson Zaharias, the American athlete, was always being described as a "tomboy" as she succeeded in a variety of sports in the 1930s and '40s (Mrozek, 1987:290–293).

Those pressing for the rights of women to get an education had also to fight for the opportunity for girls to participate in physical activities. The small group of women who were educated at universities brought their view of competitive games to the girls' educational system. As women lobbied and fought for the right to vote and fully participate in society, so they argued for women's right to be active in sport. Cheltenham Ladies' College was founded in 1853 in Britain and the pioneering Dorothea Beale fought to be able to "furnish girls with a sound and balanced religious, intellectual and physical training that would magnify rather than threaten their womanhood" (McCrone, 1987:107). At that time, to include calisthenics was a radical step; even Dorothea Beale opposed the inclusion of competition for girls and team sports like tennis and field hockey right into the twentieth century (McCrone, 1987:108).)

Helen Lenskyj, one of Canada's foremost researchers in the area of women and sport, has outlined the history of attitudes towards women in sport in Canada in her book *Out of Bounds: Women, Sport and Sexuality*. She documents the domination of male authority figures who used moral and biological rationales to support a view of women as passive, nurturing and dependent (Lenskyj, 1986:13). Jennifer Hargreaves, a well-known English sport sociologist, argues that the sports that did develop in the latter part of the nineteenth century—"golf, tennis, badminton, skating, hockey, netball, lacrosse,

TABLE 7-1:

Participation Rates of Men and Women in Olympic Games

Year	Place	Countries	Men	Women	% Female
1896	Athens	13	311	0	0
1908	London	22	1,999	36	1.8
1920	Antwerp	29	2,543	64	2.5
1928	Amsterdam	46	2,724	290	9.6
1936	Berlin	49	3,738	328	8.1
1948	London	59	3,714	385	9.4
1960	Rome	83	4,738	610	11.4
1968	Mexico City	112	4,750	781	14.1
1976	Montreal	88	4,915	1,274	20.6
1984	Los Angeles	140	5,458	1,620	22.8

SOURCE: Mary A. Boutilier and Lucinda SanGiovanni. 1984. *The Sporting Woman*. Champaign, Illinois: Human Kinetics Publishers, Inc. (modified).

rounders, cricket, gymnastics, swimming and athletics—became possible because they did not constitute a challenge in their relationship to men" (1987:141). Young women began to participate in physical activities but separately from men and in a totally non-threatening manner.

Throughout the nineteenth and early part of this century women were fighting against the expectation that they wear corsets, long dresses, long sleeves and stockings while playing sports. Of course, the supporters of "rational dress" knew it was impossible to run, jump and cycle in long, tight clothing. Bloomers, the divided skirts of the nineteenth century, created such a stir that some women even had rotten vegetables thrown at them as they wore them on the streets. The wider use of the bicycle certainly helped in the fight, because it was impossible to ride a bike in heavily restricted clothing. However, even in the 1920s women were still fighting to have "sensible clothing" to allow full freedom of movement. Tennis stars, like Helen Wills and Suzanne Lenglen, "advocated shortened skirts, sleeveless blouses and *bare legs* as imperative in improving the women's game" (Mrozek, 1987:294). Imagine trying to play tennis with a long skirt, long sleeves and stockings!

This is not to say that women did not run, jump, throw and compete. It was just that most often these feats were not generally on public record. We do find snippets of information about the local athletic endeavours of women. Depictions of races where the prizes

FLEX SOME MUSCLE

Even in the 1990s women athletes feel social pressure to conform to media-created images of women.

Athletes such as Canadian rower Silken Laumann help to demolish artificial media images. She is tall, well-muscled and attractive in the traditional sense.

Lauman tells young women to discard "the cardboard image ... and go out and flex some muscle" (Robinson, 1991).

Female Journalists—Olsen v. Kiam

Under Title VII of the Civil Rights Law in the United States, women are supposed to have equal access to the locker room.

In September 1990, Lisa Olsen, a reporter with *The Boston Herald*, was interviewing some New England Patriots in the locker room. Apparently some of the players, while naked, surrounded her and made rude gestures and verbal comments. Olsen felt it was sexual harassment yet wanted to keep things just between herself and the Patriots. A rival paper, however, *The Boston Globe* ran a story on it and the incident hit the front pages across the country.

Probably the whole thing would have died there, except the Patriots' owner Victor Kiam did not take the issue seriously. Various NFL players objected. The Bengals quarterback said: "This is 1990. This is ridiculous. This stuff shouldn't be going on."

(*Echoes from the Cave, 1990:38-39*).

The result was that the Patriots and some of the players were fined and Kiam issued public apologies.

There are two issues here. First, should reporters be allowed in locker rooms at all? In tennis the players are interviewed after they have showered and are fully dressed. Second, is nakedness a special issue for women reporters?

CHEERLEADERS

Cheerleading provides an interesting example of changing gender roles. Cheerleading in the late 1800s was an exclusively male activity but by the 1940s it was increasingly viewed as being for women only (Davis, 1990:153). Certainly, women cheerleaders today are athletic and fit, but the emphasis is more on physical beauty. The women are expected to be pretty and decorative.

would be smocks (dresses) were completed by artists like John Collet and Thomas Rowlandson in the 18th century. The events often took place at local fairs, usually in bare feet. Occasionally a women's cricket match would take place as well (Goldman, 1983:21,23,51).

The history of women's participation in the Olympic Games underlines both the move towards greater equality in sport and the persistence of inequality. The Olympics is committed to fairness, and therefore one would expect to find an equal number of female and male athletes participating, and certainly the same number of events for both sexes. In fact, this is not the case.

The impression from television coverage of the Olympics is that there is an almost equal coverage of women's and men's sporting events. In fact, we find that there is a much greater emphasis on male sports. Women have increasingly participated in the Olympics but the rate of increase has been slow. In 1928, only 9.6% of the competitors were women. In 1960, the figure had only risen to 11.4% and, by 1984, it was 22% (Boutilier & SanGiovanni, 1984).

There are also fewer events for women than men in the Olympics. While various international sport organizations have been requesting the addition of their sport, women's events in a number of the already existing sports do not exist. In 1984, there were 153 events for men and only 73 for women (Coakley, 1986:124). Mary Decker-Slaney, for example, went to court to be able to run the 3,000-metre race in the 1984 Olympics. For certain sports there are no events for women to enter. The message women athletes are receiving is that sport does not treat them in the same way as men are treated. There is concern that if new sports are added it might mean continued inequality of events on the basis of sex.

Me Tarzan, You Jane

The prestige and glamour attached to being an athlete has a sexual component as well. The "Me Tarzan, You Jane" stereotype abounds. Jim Brown, the former NFL player, describes providing various friends and hangers-on with introductions to women who were part of his entourage. The women were regarded as a commodity, provided in the same way as a swimming pool, drinks and something to eat. Jim Brown says being an athlete has given him an advantage with women.

"I can't speak for track men or golfers, but women love those football players. Guys who play football have that manly, physical image—the gladiator—and women go crazy for it. Talk all you want about brain power, but the intellectual gets the secondary women. It's the physical giant who gets the premium women. You see a guy in the NFL, even a big ugly-ass lineman, with his woman at a party, it doesn't fit. The dude is 300 pounds, 45-inch neck, he's with the head majorette from USC. But he bumps into people for a living so she's fascinated. He leaves the NFL, her ass is gone. I've seen it a hundred times, and it goes for all sports" (1989:133).

There have been a number of incidents in the last few years where girlfriends of married ball players have gone public about the superstars, off-field activities. Generally, though, the press has been quite "discreet" about these matters, in the same way politicians' private lives are tacitly off-limits to journalists.

Access to Sport for Women

The founder of the Olympic movement, Baron Pierre de Coubertin, was very clear in 1902 when he declared that: " Women have but one task, that of crowning the men with garlands." He did not see a role for women in athletic activities, and certainly some of those ideas continue today. Women athletes who participate in sports that seem to stress "traditional views of femininity," such as figure skating or gymnastics, tend to get positive press coverage. Women athletes who participate in team sports like ice hockey or strength sports, such as rowing or weight lifting, often receive less positive coverage.

In the early 1980s, pressure from women's groups led to demands for an investigation of sport opportunities. John Sopinka completed a major study on equal opportunity in athletics in 1984 and found that funding, opportunities and facilities were not the same for women and men in Ontario universities and colleges. Even though women provided funds out of their own pockets, they were not getting the same services. Below is a summary of some of the findings:

"To play the piano, the harp or some other ladylike instrument, to sing, to dance: these were the accomplishments which would make a young lady universally admired and lead her into matrimony."
The 19th century view of women, quoted by Josephine Kamm

~ SPORT PROFILE ~

Dorothea Beale—Girls and Physical Education

Christian Socialists in Europe began to argue in the 1840s that "women had rights as well as men" (Kamm, 1958: 13). By 1848, in London, England, after a great deal of argument and pressure, women were allowed to attend their own Bedford College, initially in order to be better trained as governesses. Among the first students was a young woman named Dorothea Beale.

Shortly after graduation, Dorothea Beale became the headmistress of Cheltenham Ladies College, committed to the then radical idea of providing an education for girls. Girls who had wealthy parents might have a

tutor, but most girls had little formal education. She saw the College as playing an important role in providing girls with opportunities. She herself felt that teaching was a vocation and spent her life dedicated to the College and improving opportunities for girls and women.

One aspect of education that Beale felt was important was physical activity. She had been exposed to the ideas of a Swiss reformer Pestalozzi who argued that girls should be active. Therefore, she encouraged students to walk and do calisthenics in the school gym. She opposed competitive games until the turn of the century

when she realized that they could be fun for girls too.

Dorothea Beale provided a strong leadership role. Realizing it was imperative that women be trained as teachers, she started St. Hilda's College at Oxford University, after the university kept rejecting women students. In later years, a number of her students came to Canada and brought their ideas of physical education for girls with them to Canadian schools.

St. Hilda's College, Oxford, England.

Dorothea Beale, pioneer in physical education for girls.

- *At most colleges intramural activities were offered on a male only, female only and co-ed basis.* "At most colleges there were more activities offered to males only than females only" (Sopinka, 1984:88).

- *The participation statistics in intramural activities showed a greater participation of males than females.* "In most colleges women were allowed to participate on men's teams if the same activity was not offered for women (for example hockey). However males were not generally allowed to play on female teams" (Sopinka, 1984:91).

- *Greater resources are dedicated to male sporting activities.* "An unequal portion of the intramural budget (in colleges) is allocated to male activities" (Sopinka, 1984:92). The explanation often given for this is that fewer women participate in sport and that "male" sports are more expensive, eg. football and hockey.

- *In intercollegiate sports more programs are available to males at the indoor level.* "In 1982/83, approximately twice as many males as females were participating in inter-college sports" (Sopinka, 1984:94).

~ SPORT PROFILE ~

Justine Blainey—"I just want to play hockey"

b. Toronto, 1973. Justine Blainey was a little girl who decided she wanted to play hockey. Suddenly the adult world made the world of children's sport a very hostile place.

Catcalls, insults, equipment thrown out of the locker room — sadly, the list of incidents is a long one. Journalists were condescending, calling her "sweetheart" and asking if she knew about the birds and bees. Mothers made irrelevant comments like "The poor coach will have to carry sanitary napkins in his first aid kit." Girlfriends at school stopped talking to her. And all of this came about because she wanted to play hockey at the best level she could.

Blainey was clear throughout it all: "I was doing what I wanted to do." The lawyer Anna Fraser went to court five times. Initially Section 19(2) of the Ontario Human Rights Code excluded sport. No one could discriminate in housing or employment — but sport was exempted. Until the section was repealed, there seemed to be few grounds even to challenge discrimination on the basis of sex. Year after year, Justine and her supporters continued the battle. Finally, after great public pressure, the law was changed and and in 1986 they succeeded.

Justine Blainey secured a place on the team of her choice.

Quotations based on a personal inteview by the author, March 1991.

In 1984, Sopinka found that 64% of all inter-university athletes were male (Sopinka, 1984). Three years later, the survey conducted by the Ontario Commission on Inter-university Athletics (OCIA) in the spring of 1987 revealed that the comparable figure for 1986–1987 was also 64 percent! (MacIntosh, 1989:7)

Today there are many prominent women athletes and coverage of women's events is more common than in the past. However, women are still seriously under-represented in the sports world. Many sports, and in many ways the very idea of sport itself in our society, is associated with males. Early access to sport opportunities is not as great for young women. The sports in which women excel are not usually promoted as mass sports. On the whole, the financial rewards are less for women athletes, even for those women at the top of their sport.

Would more women students come out for physical activities if more were offered? Many suspect that this is the case. Some even feel that sport itself has to be re-defined to allow more people to feel comfortable with participating in physical activity. Perhaps both *equal access* and *a re-definition of sport* is required to encourage a wider range of athletic expression.

Justine Blainey outside the Ontario Human Rights Commission hearings.

Looking Back, Looking Forward: Justine Blainey

By JUSTINE BLAINEY

At nine years old I was like all young girls. I did gymnastics and ballet, needle work, art and figure skating. I cheered loudly at my brother's hockey games. I was a perfectly normal little girl, until I stunned my mother with the question "Can I play hockey too?" My mother didn't think girls played hockey, so I pestered her continually with "Why not?" "Why can David play and not me?" and "Why can't girls play hockey?" Finally my mother found me a girls' league. With the clear uncompromising eyes of a ten year old, I quickly noticed that elite boys got more ice time, better equipment and uniforms, more games and practices, a longer season, summer practices, and body checking—the most fun of all. David's coaches kept on saying that they would happily sign me if I would pretend I were a boy or if I could get "legal." I refused to pretend to be a boy, but with the help and support of my family and lawyer, Anna Fraser, and through five court cases, I finally got "legal."

At the time, I wanted a better calibre hockey and that meant hockey with the guys. I also wanted other girls to be able to play top calibre sport and, even if I never succeeded in time for myself, I wanted my daughter (if I have one) to have the chance at top calibre sport. It was only fair, I thought, if girls are good enough to do something, why not?

By the time I finally stepped on the ice with the East Enders, MTHL (Metro Toronto Hockey League) boy's team, my thinking had evolved into a philosophy. I wasn't just a little girl who wanted to play hockey with the guys; I was a girl with a dream. With the support of my family and Anne Fraser, I ran with my dream. As in the game of hockey, sometimes I faltered, fell down and lost a game, but I still got up and got ready for the next shot, the next game. In my public speeches to teenagers, I generalized my experiences and encouraged others to follow their dreams, never give up, get help, keep pushing, keep trying, even if your dream takes years. Mine did.

During the summer of 1988 my thinking developed greater depth. I worked in Toronto's Red Door Family Shelter where abused women shivered behind locked and guarded doors and where most faced a life of poverty when they left those protective doors because their traditionally female homemaking, secretarial skills would not earn nearly enough for daycare, food and shelter. That summer I grew to understand that poverty is a "feminine word" in Canada and that Canadian violence is overwhelmingly against women.

Hockey players push, shove and race for a puck, and regularly fall down or get knocked down, all in fun. Perhaps a female hockey player who has gloried in the development of her own personal strength, and especially a female hockey player who has played with and against males, will be less likely to cower in terror or accept violence in her personal life. Women need some of those learning experiences of rough and tumble games with males and females when they are young in order to be better prepared for their adult lives. It is certainly reasonable to assume that a young woman who has competed with males in fun will turn her eyes with equanimity to a range of careers including well-paid jobs traditionally considered male. Surely a woman who has competed for a puck with men will have the developmental background needed to consider her place as an electrician, plumber, construction worker, firefighter or police officer. There are a host of traditionally male jobs that pay more than daycare, cashiering or secretarial work and will allow a woman to support her family in reasonable comfort.

Have I placed too much emphasis on equal opportunity in sports, on the need for mixed sport? A seed can become a tree. If we want fit, strong, competitive capable female athletes, we must socialize our female children to be fit, strong and competitive. Mixed sport is one such socializing vehicle, and legislated equal opportunity in sport is an open door though which can be viewed the possibility of a future Canadian society where men and women work and play as equals.

Racism in Sports—Alabama, 1967

In his autobiography, the baseball player Reggie Jackson describes his days after being signed in the major leagues.

He went from being a scholarship student at Arizona State University to play for the Kansas City A's in Birmingham. His white roommates were threatened with eviction when he stayed in their apartment, so he moved to an apartment hotel which accepted "coloureds" and just went straight from the baseball field to his hotel. At first he tried eating out but soon gave up (Jackson, 1984:58–59).

The waiter came back with the steak quickly. Too quickly. As he held it in front of my face, I could see that it had barely been cooked.

Then the waiter just dropped the plate on the table, from a height of about three feet. Just dropped it. The steak flopped onto the tablecloth. The silverware went flying, water glass tipped over. Big racket. Loud——racket.

'Nigger,' the waiter said, 'don't you *ever* come back here.'

"I said, 'Yes sir,' hotfooted it out of the Red Lion Inn, *ran* the five or six blocks back to the Bankhead (hotel), and ordered room service.

"It was fear, pure and simple. I wasn't going to force any social change—that never even *occurred* to me—I was just going to survive, keep my nose clean and survive. When you'd been raised the way I'd been, all you needed were the essentials to survive … So I made a very conscious decision to lay low, take myself out of the line of fire of the racism as much as possible. And survive.

Thank God Martin Luther King didn't feel that way. But I sure did" (Jackson, 1984:60).

This is the athlete who had the courage to face anything, But in Birmingham, Alabama, life playing baseball was dangerous. And this was not the America of Jackie Robinson in 1946. The year was 1967.

Minorities and Sport

Racism in sports

Today, when we look at American professional baseball, football and basketball teams we see many non-white athletes. Until quite recently, this was not the case. In the United States, only white athletes were allowed to play on major league baseball teams. Black athletes had to play in what were called the Negro Leagues, where there were fewer jobs, lower pay and sometimes even dangerous situations. In other words, it was not illegal to discriminate *on the basis of colour*. Even the famous "Satchel" Paige suffered in the Southern Negro League. "The Tigers made money by passing the hat among the spectators at their games. Reputedly, Paige sometimes received lemonade in return for his stint on the mound" (Rogosin, 1987:44).

Discrimination took place in all aspects of black people's lives. Black men and women were not allowed to enter certain restaurants, ride in the front of the bus, go to college, vote, or walk where they liked on the sidewalk. The list of prohibited things goes on and on. Black people knew that the laws would not protect them. Lynchings continued right up to the 1950s, and as a result black people often lived in fear of their lives.

The Fight Goes On—Shoal Creek, Alabama, 1990

In 1990 not just the ball was white in the world of golf. Hall Thompson of the Shoal Creek Country Club in Birmingham, Alabama, refused to allow black golfers to join. Civil rights leaders said they would picket the 67th PGA Championship and sponsors like IBM, American Honda, Toyota, Spalding, Sharp Electronics, Lincoln Mercury, and Anheuser-Busch withdrew from the television coverage .

Suddenly black athletes like former footballer O.J. Simpson were being asked to join clubs across America, as it became clear there were many clubs, scheduled for PGA events, that had no black members—these included Hazeltine, Baltusrol, Oakmont, and Shinnecock Hills, Crooked Stick, Bellerive, and Aronomink.

Angry Associated Press sports editors sent a letter to the various heads of the golf associations, the PGA, US Golf Association and LPGA. They stated: "Private clubs do have the legal right to choose their own members, but our nations's major golf organizations should not subtly endorse discriminatory policies by continuing to award major championships to clubs that discriminate."

The threat of financial disaster seemed to encourage the immediate "honourary" membership of a black insurance executive at Shoal Creek. Unlike Reggie Jackson's experience in 1967, the issue was public and the outcome of the confrontation was that the PGA declared: "Those courses selected for the PGA Championship beginning in 1995 will have minorities, including women and blacks, as members." A month later Butler National, with no women members, said "I would rather lose the tournament than admit women," but most clubs began to open their doors. (Showdown, 1991: 28)

The first black baseball player to play in the major leagues worked first in Montreal on the minor league team, the Montreal Royals, and then went on to play for the Brooklyn Dodgers. This was in 1946, and his name was Jackie Robinson. Players like Jackie Robinson, along with their wives, had to put up with having to stay in hotels separate from their team mates because many hotels barred blacks. Robinson suffered the embarrassment of eating behind screens in some restaurants (so as not to offend white customers). "Nothing humiliated veteran stars like Robinson and Campanella more than waiting on a bus while their teammates ate in a restaurant" (Tygiel, 1983:315). He also roomed alone. Right until the end of the 1960s, black and white players did not room together.

Jackie Robinson came from a talented athletic family. His older brother came second after Jesse Owens in the 200 metres, and won the silver medal at the 1936 Olympics. He himself was unusually talented. He had all-round athletic ability and participated in a variety of sports while at university in Southern California (UCLA). He was the first black athlete signed up to play baseball in the major leagues— he was signed up by Branch Rickey, the manager of the Brooklyn Dodgers. For years black writers had been pressing the baseball teams to hire the extremely talented players of the Negro Leagues. Rickey decided to choose an athlete who was exceptionally talented and whom he felt could handle the terrible abuse he would face from fans, the media and other baseball players.

TABLE 7-2:

Players Positions of Black and White Athletes in Professional American Sport

Sport	Positions	Black	White
NFL Football	Linebacker, quarterback, offensive guard, centre	31	69
	Defensive line, offensive tackles, tight end	46	54
	Defensive safety & halfback, offensive running back, flanker split end	82	18
Baseball (Majors)	Pitcher, catcher	5	95
	Shortstop, second and third base	17	83
	First base	43	57
	Outfielder	56	44
Basketball	Center	56	44
	Guard	84	16
	Forward	76	24

SOURCE: Source: Jay Coakley. 1986 *Sport and Society: Issues and Controversies,* St Louis: Times Mirror/Mosby:145.

There were no enforceable laws to protect Jackie Robinson. Racist attitudes were so widespread that only an exceptional person could tolerate the situation. Robinson was accepted by his teammates—they recognized his great ability. However, he received verbal abuse from fans and opposing team alike. "Sometimes players would yell from the dugout, 'Nigger, what are you doing up here?', wrote Hank Thompson of his early years in the majors" (Tygiel, 1983:308).

The racism also spilled over into the game itself.

… Statistics reveal that pitchers hit blacks with startling frequency. Robinson continually ranked among the league leaders in the hit-by-pitch category. In 1947 he set a National League record for rookies when pitchers found him nine times, seven during the first half of the season. The following year Robinson led the league. In 1952 he established a new Dodger record with twelve "hits." The next season he broke the record. Through the 1954 campaign pitchers had victimized Robinson *sixty-five* times … Other players received similar treatment (Tygiel, 1983:309). (emphasis added)

Pitchers threw balls at his head constantly. Robinson himself, however, presented it this way: "Those guys were trying to test me, … They were trying to see what I was made of … It had nothing to do with what colour I was" (Tygiel, 1983:309). However, the statistics tell a different story. Frank Robinson, the 1989 manager of the year, joined the Reds in 1956. He "immediately became a popular target, absorbing twenty poundings in his rookie year" (Tygiel, 1983:309). Of course, the black players tried to avoid confrontations.

The Importance of the South Africa Sports Boycott

By BRUCE KIDD

It is sometimes said that sports boycotts have little effect. Critics of the 1980 stayaway of the Moscow Olympics point out that it made no difference to the Soviet intervention in Afghanistan, the intended target. But the international boycott of South African sport, now in its 30th year, has been extremely effective in dramatizing the world's repugnance of apartheid, the savage system of racial separation legally in force in South Africa, and pushing the apartheid government toward change.

The international campaign was launched in the 1950s by the victims of South African racism in sport—non-white athletes, coaches, and administrators. Unable to work publicly for integration because of the viciousness of state repression, they sought to create pressure from outside the country by having the all-white South African sports bodies excluded from international competition. They formed a new organization, the South African Non-Racial Olympic Committee (SANROC), for this purpose. In 1963, SANROC persuaded the International Olympic Committee to suspend South Africa from the Olympic Games. SANROC's arguments were based on the ideals of sport. How could the Olympic Movement preach fair play and opposition to discrimination and extend the handshake of sport to those who denied it to others on the basis of race?

In 1970, after South Africa refused to make any changes, the IOC expelled it altogether. Since then, virtually every government and sports body in the world undertakes to restrict sporting contacts with South Africa. The Canadian Government, for example, will not allow any South African to enter Canada for the purposes of sport. (That's why well-known South African golfer, David Frost, no longer competes in the Canadian Open at Glenn Abby.) Sport Canada asks Canadian athletes not to compete against South Africans anywhere in the world, and will withdraw federal funds from any sports body whose athletes do so.

The Commonwealth, which expelled South Africa from membership in 1961, has been another important bulwark of the international campaign. Under the Gleneagles Agreement, adopted in 1977, member countries undertake to "take every practical step to discourage contact or competition by their nationals with sporting organizations, teams or sportspersons from South Africa."

South Africa is a sports-loving country, so its growing isolation has become a front-page story, and a growing source of anger and tension. Can you imagine the censure Canadians would feel if no one would play us in hockey, our best athletes were barred from the Olympics, and those few Canadians who did manage to sneak into international competitions were met with massive demonstrations? That's the message—and the pressure for change—the sports boycott has achieved.

In response, the apartheid government has recently relaxed some of the laws affecting apartheid in sport. It is now possible for blacks and whites to play a game together on the same field without ending up in jail. But the allocation of facilities is still unequal. In Natal, for example, 330,000 blacks in the townships of Umlazi and Lamontville shared six soccer fields and two swimming pools. The 212,000 whites living in nearby Durban shared 146 soccer fields and 15 pools. Not surprisingly, SANROC and other anti-apartheid organizations (such as the African National Congress (ANC) and Mass Democratic Movement (MDM)) pushed for the boycott.

The extreme racism during spring training in Florida hindered the development of team skills and good baseball. There were constant incidents of harassment and even a lynching threat in 1948. Branch Rickey and the Dodgers decided to lease a former naval station with its own air strip at Vero Beach just to avoid all the local problems. Inside these boundaries the emphasis was on good baseball to the exclusion of all else. Life outside was a different matter. "White players could visit beaches, go on fishing trips, play golf at the country clubs and shop in the better stores of Vero Beach. Blacks could do none of these things" (Tygiel, 1983:317).

Victory for the Sports Boycott

By BRUCE KIDD

The 30-year old sports boycott of South Africa is rapidly being brought to an orderly and successful conclusion.

In recent months, the De Klerk Government and the white sports establishment have agreed to the minimal conditions set by the African National Congress (ANC) and the coalition of forces which have kept South Africa out of international sport for so long:

- the abolition of apartheid policies related to the Group Areas Act, the Population Control Act, the Land Acts and discriminatory legislation
- the creation of single, democratic, non-racial sports organizations for individual sports
- the creation of anti-discriminatory by-laws in every sport
- the obligation to create a major campaign of sports development for black athletes and communities

The recent progress has been far more rapid than anyone dared to imagine. The Association of National Olympic Committees (ANOCA) obtained agreement to these terms from the anti-apartheid sport groups such as the South African Non-racial Olympic Committee (SANROC) and the South African Council on Sports (SACOS) with the two white South African sports organizations, the old South African Olympic Committee (SANOC) and the Confederation of South African Sport (COSAS). Sam Ramsamy of SANROC will oversee the implementation of the new policies and the IOC has recognized Ramsamy's coordinating committee as the Interim South African Olympic Committee with technical assistance from its office of Olympic Solidarity.

It is expected that the South African government will continue its commitment to the dismantling of apartheid. Evaluation on a sport-by-sport basis will take place. If the requirements are met sports organizations like the International Amateur Athletics Federation (IAAF) will invite a South African team to compete.

Not everyone is pleased with this approach. Groups such as SACOS previously argued "No normal sport in an abnormal society." They wanted each and every black person in South Africa to have the vote (universal suffrage) before the boycott of South Africa ended. However many boycott leaders like Ramsamy feel that the promise of international competition will give an enormous boost to black efforts in soccer, track and field, boxing and those other sports where participation is strong. Certainly that is how the prospect is being taken in the black South African townships, where the changes are regarded as a major victory for the African National Congress (ANC). *There have almost never been any black South African representatives in international competition.* White South Africans who held power prevented this from happening.

Many also felt that the boycott could not be maintained because international politics have changed. In the past the Soviet bloc would automatically threaten to withdraw from events if South Africans were included. This is no longer the case.

The agreement is a good one. Both practically and symbolically, it constitutes a major advance. It promises to end racial discrimination in South African sport, open up new opportunities for those black athletes already competing, and turn the symbolism of South African teams into a powerful argument for non-racial meritocracy. Organizations like NSC have clearly linked political issues in the wider society with sport. The participation of black South Africans in international sport is an exciting prospect for those anti-apartheid sportspersons like Sam Ramsamy who have spent decades of heroic agitation and self-denial to bring about change in South African sport.

To be sure whites still dominate most of the new sports bodies. Very little change will occur unless there is substantial redistribution, not only in sports but in education, employment, health and housing. There are only ten sports (out of some 60 nationally organized) where there is any significant degree of black participation. This is why the Interim Committee will not send its first team to the Winter Olympics next year—black athletes are not involved in any of the winter sports.

The sports boycott has been extremely successful in achieving what it set out to do—combat legal racism in sports. In the process, it has forced the international sports leadership and the South African sports establishment to embrace the anti-apartheid cause, which includes not only the fight against racism but the advancement of third-world interests across the board.

This is a remarkable achievement.

Bruce Kidd is currently Director of the School of Health and Physical Education at the University of Toronto.

TABLE 7-3:

Black Athletes in Professional Sport: Baseball, Football and Basketball

Baseball		Football		Basketball	
Year	*%*	*Year*	*%*	*Year*	*%*
1954	7	1956	14	1954	5
1967	11	1968	28	1962	30
1978	17	1975	42	1970	56
1980	22	1982	49	1980	75
1985	20	1985	54	1985	75

SOURCE: Jay Coakley. 1986. *Sport in Society.* Toronto: Times Mirror/Mosely College Publishing:145

STACKING THE DECKS

Most fans could tell you that there are few black pitchers in baseball, but few probably have a clear idea as to the extent of the differentiation in the various sports. Table 7–3 clearly outlines the patterns within baseball, football and basketball. The material was taken from the Media Guides and did not include the Latin Americans who make up approximately 10% of Major League baseball players.

On top of all this, Robinson received death threats in the mail. But Robinson never lost courage. He was very aware he was pioneering opportunities for other black players to follow. He constantly pressed for better conditions and better pay for black athletes.

Canada was not entirely different from the United States. Black Canadians like Burnley (Rocky) Jones in Nova Scotia have been working for the last twenty years to bring about changes in Canada. Towns in Nova Scotia had specially designated areas for black people. Some places like barber shops and theatres and even schools were segregated (Story, 1987:B5).

Although there are many highly visible black athletes in football, basketball and baseball, athletes of colour in sport are in fact under-represented in proportion to the population. There are few black cyclists, equestrians, golfers or swimmers.

In those few sports where black athletes are found in larger numbers, we find that significant changes have taken place in the past few years. In part, these changes are rooted in changes in the law in the United States in the 1950s and 1960s. Before this time, there was an official system of separate schools, churches and places of residence, called **segregation.** The successful de-segregation campaign in the 1950s and 1960s aimed to break down these official barriers to blacks participating equally in their society. Martin Luther King, the black civil rights leader, and thousands of others, both black and white, marched on Washington, held sit-ins in restaurants and buildings that excluded black people, and spearheaded voter registration campaigns. In 1954, the U.S. Supreme Court in *Brown vs. Board of Education of Topika, Kansas* declared segregation unconstitutional. In 1964, the enactment of the *Civil Rights Act* meant that, for the first time, blacks could legally assert the right to participate fully in sporting and recreational activities because discrimination on the basis of colour, race, religion or national origin was prohibited in public places.

An even more extreme form of segregation—one that has shaken up the sport world—is the **apartheid** policy of the South African government. Black South Africans cannot vote, and until recently could not live permanently in the cities. They had to carry passbooks at all times, drink from separate water fountains and use separate public washrooms. This apartheid system has been kept in place by the most brutal violence.

Mark Mathabane, a South African tennis player, described a typical violent police scene in his own home and what happened to him as a little boy of four.

> As (the door) swung wide open, with tremendous force, two tall black policemen in stiff brown uniforms rushed in and immediately blinded me with the glare from their flashlights. Before I knew what was happening one of them kicked me savagely on the side, sending me crashing into a crate on the far corner. I hit the crate with such force that I nearly passed out. With stars in my eyes I grabbed the edges of the crate and tried to rise, but I couldn't; my knees had turned to Jell-O, my eyes were cloudy and my head pounded as if it were being split with an axe. As I tried to gather my senses, another kick sent me back to the floor, flat on my face. As I went down, my jaw struck the blunt side of the blade of an axe jutting from the side of the crate. My head burned with pain. Blood began oozing from my nostrils and lips... (Mathabane, 1989:33).

Unfortunately, Mathabane's experiences as a little boy are similar to those of many other children in South Africa. After seeing Arthur Ashe (the African-American Wimbledon champion) at a tennis clinic in Soweto, he decided to develop his tennis skills. Unlike many others who do not escape the inhuman conditions of poverty and apartheid, Mathabane was able, because of his tennis abilities, to attend Princeton University in the United States.

Apartheid has been a dominant feature of South African society. Recently, however, major changes are taking place and the apartheid system is slowly being dismantled. Blacks are the overwhelming majority of the population in South Africa and their determination, and that of black leaders such as Nelson Mandela, to dismember apartheid is unparalleled. The full effect of these political changes on South African sport is still unclear. In July 1991 the IOC decided to allow South Africa to participate in Olympic sport. The participation of black South Africans in international sport will have considerable emotional and political significance for many athletes around the world.

First Black Quarterback—What Did I Change, Nothing

Doug Williams was the first black quarterback to play in the Super Bowl. He played for the Washington Redskins in January, 1988. At the time he was irritated about the media's emphasis on that fact he was the first black quarterback in the Super Bowl. He wanted the reporters to focus on his ability as the Redskin quarterback.

Williams was concerned also about the effect this issue would have on the rest of his teammates but the tackle, Joe Jacoby, who is white, said, "White, black, green or yellow. You're our quarterback. ... We're going to win with you." I knew then, it wasn't an individual thing, and it wasn't a black thing. It was a team thing" (Lieber, 1990:88). He was called "the Jackie Robinson of football" by his former coach Eddie Robinson, of Grambling State University.

Three years later Williams questioned the impact of his participation in the Super Bowl. "What did I change? Nothing. If there were now 10 or 12 black quarterbacks in the NFL, some black backups and third-teamers, then I'd think I had changed something. The NFL would still rather draft a (white) guy from Slippery Rock than give a black quarterback a chance"(ibid:88-89).

Williams wants faster change in football. "Things won't be on an equitable basis until there are proportionate numbers of black NFL quarterbacks to the population of blacks in this country (the USA). That means that 20 percent of the quarterbacks in the league should be black" (Willliams, 1990: 188). As for his role, Williams explains: "I hope people will always think of Doug Williams as a guy who gave everything he had whenever he put on that helmet—and kept giving it all to the very end. I felt like I never lost, regardless of the score, because when you give it your all, that's all you can give. I don't want to be remembered as the great black quarterback. That's putting me in one category. I'd like to be remembered as a true competitor in the National Football League (Williams, 1990: 188).

Discrimination today—Stacking

When professional team sports are examined, we find that white and black players are not equally distributed in various playing positions. **Stacking** is the term used to refer to this phenomenon. It refers to the over- or under-representation of athletes who are white or non-white in specific team positions.

Stacking is a form of discrimination against athletes on the basis of colour. These patterns would not take place if there were a random filling of the positions. In the past, black quarterbacks would have to take other positions on football teams simply because they were not given a chance at the quarterback positions.

> Historically, college teams have taken good black high school quarterbacks and switched them to the production line—running back, defensive backfield or wide receiver. And black collegians, looking to play as pros, opted for positions of opportunity, where blacks were already established (McDermott, 1987:45).

Gwendolyn Allen, the mother of footballers Marcus Allen of the L.A. Raiders and Edmonton Eskimo quarterback Damon Allen, points to what she sees as discrimination. "Society doesn't look at a black athlete and perceive him to be a quarterback because people don't expect blacks to be the team leader" (ibid:45).

~ SPORT PROFILE ~

Jackie Robinson—First Black Player in Baseball's Hall of Fame

b. 1919, Cairo, Georgia (USA)., d. 1972. Jackie Robinson began playing baseball in the days when black and white baseball players were segregated. Talented black players were excluded from the major leagues and were forced to play for what were called the Negro Leagues. Robinson was the first black athlete to play modern day major league baseball.

Robinson has a Canadian connection. In 1946, he played baseball in Canada with the Montreal Royals. He was very popular and an outstanding player.

With the increasing pressure on baseball to include black athletes, in 1947, the manager, Branch Rickey, moved Robinson to the major leagues to play with the Brooklyn Dodgers.

He was a courageous and self-controlled man who faced incredible racism and hostility that seems more like life for blacks in South Africa than anything else. "It did cost him: he is the only baseball player in history whose hair turned white in his rookie season" (Jones and Washington, 1972: 98).

He was the National League's All Star second baseman in 1950, 1951, and 1952. He helped the Dodgers to win pennants in 1952, 1953, 1955 and 1956. His lifetime batting average was an incredible .311.

Five years after his retirement, in 1961, he became the first black baseball player to be admitted to the Hall of Fame in Cooperstown, New York. Until his death at 53 years of age, Robinson continued to work to improve the opportunities for black youth in their communities.

In analyzing the performances of black athletes it appears that black athletes also have to be better than whites in order to get a chance to play major or minor league sport. Their statistics are higher—black pitchers "won an average 2.7 more games a year" (Tygiel, 1989:338), but there are fewer black pitchers. There have been few umpires and few jobs in front offices.

Sociologist Harry Edwards (1973) argues that where the positions on a team are central and are decision-making positions, whites will usually fill them. If the positions are less central and do not involve making key decisions, then those positions will be filled by black athletes. Interestingly, coaches often explain the assignment of athletes in terms of personality—they describe black athletes as being quick and white athletes as "thinkers." Such stereotypical assessments are reminiscent of the ways in which "experts" used to describe the basic characteristics of women. Women were seen as passive, dependent and dominated by their physical characteristics.

Perceptions about the competence and ability of black players seem to be changing slowly. In the summer of 1989, for the first time, two opposing baseball teams met and both of them had black managers—Frank Robinson of the Baltimore Orioles and Cito Gaston of the Blue Jays. Frank Robinson won the Manager-of-the-Year Award for 1989.

SPORT CANADA'S "WOMEN IN SPORT" POLICY

Sport Canada's policy on *Women in Sport* is based on the *Canadian Charter of Rights and Freedoms,* which guarantees certain basic rights to all Canadians. The aim of the sports program is to address the inequities of the past through the Woman's Program of Fitness and Amateur Sport.

The following areas are included:

- policies and programs
- sport organizations
- leadership development
- high performance competition
- resource allocation
- research
- education
- promotion
- advocacy
- monitoring
- and evaluation.

Source: Sport Canada policy on Women in Sport, 1986:15–18.

Sport and Canada's First Nations

In Canada, native people have been overlooked in most aspects of our society. Land claims and the terrible conditions relating to health and education have been conveniently ignored. It is hard to discuss athletics when fundamental issues about self-government, land ownership, poor health and discrimination are outstanding.

In the days before and after the arrival of Europeans, sport, physical activities and games of chance were an important part of North American life. Visitors from Europe recorded their occurrences frequently. Historian Michael Salter has found that native sports were associated with four main activities:

a) *mortuary practices*—designed to honour the dead, comfort the living relatives, honour those surviving and promote tribal unity;

b) *sickness*—games were associated with healing and epidemics for individual and group help. Shamans (or priests) played a central role here. Different games were played but the most important game associated with healing was lacrosse;

c) *climatic conditions*—the most well known of these are of course the rain dances, often portrayed in Hollywood movies. However other conditions such as cold, heat, snow, hail or winds could be the focus too;

d) *fertility*—games were played at Thanksgiving to celebrate births and good harvests (Oxendine, 1988: 7-8).

The main sporting activities were foot racing, swimming, archery and ball games, but ball games were viewed as the most important. Their importance was considerable in early North American life. "One well-known Cherokee legend held that the moon is actually a ball that in ancient times was thrown against the sky." Players were not supposed to touch the ball with their hands. "The ball was usually propelled by being kicked, batted, or thrown with a racket or a stick."

The most popular game in North America was lacrosse. It was called various names, including game of ball or ball game and *baggataway*. In the nineteenth century it was called racket or racket-ball in the south and lacrosse in the north. It is thought it was given the name of "lacrosse" by French missionaries because "souls" was a French game similar to the North American game, but it was played with a "crosse"; hence, the two words were put together. "It contained many of the components necessary for early Indian warfare (e.g. courage, ruggedness, skill, speed, and endurance). It has been described as being halfway between sport and deadly combat."

~ SPORT PROFILE ~

Jocelyn Lovell—Wheelchair Sports, a Critical View

b. 1950, England. Jocelyn Lovell dominated men's cycling in Canada for twenty years. He was known for his tough competitive attitude and his love of winning. In 1983, a dumptruck knocked him off his bike, his spinal cord was crushed and he found himself a quadriplegic.

The Spinal Cord Society has as its motto "cure not care." Lovell agrees that the thrust of the Society's concern should be towards a cure rather then spending money on wheelchairs or rehabilitation centres (Bird, 1987: A3). There are "35 million neural-injured individuals in the United States (one-sixth of the population), 500,000 of those who suffered severe spinal conditions averaged nineteen years of age. Between 10,000 and 20,000 new spinal injuries occur each year ... and more than 85% of the injured suffer permanent paralysis, according to the Spinal Cord Society" (Sokol, 1985: L9).

Lovell agrees with the Society's position that there is too much glamour attached to wheelchair sports. The disabled are "kept titillated and diverted from sensible priorities by handicapped sports spectacles and media romanticizing of paralysis, equating it with heroism and, worst of all, with far less disabling conditions such as missing a limb". Lovell says: "I would give my eyeteeth to have no legs, or be deaf and dumb. Of course it's wrong to compare disabilities, but you do anyway" (ibid, 1985).

There are not many recorded documents from the participants' point of view, but in spite of the prejudice of the newcomers the skill and beauty of the players impressed many European travellers.

> Of all the Indian social sports the finest and grandest is the ball play. I might call it a noble game, and I am surprised how these savages attain such perfection in it. Nowhere in the world, excepting, perhaps, among the English and the Italian races, is the graceful and manly game of ball played so passionately and on so large a scale. They often play village against village, or tribe against tribe. Hundreds of players assemble, and the wares and goods offered as prizes often reach a value of a thousand dollars or more (Kohl quoted in Oxendine, 1988:39).

The size of the field varied depending on the number of players. The shape and style of the lacrosse stick varied too. The stick most commonly used today was developed by the Iroquois and is used with both hands. Originally balls were often made of wood. The game was tough, injuries were common (no protective gear) and fights between players were usual. However there was a great emphasis on fairness and friendship (ibid:47).

Lacrosse is unofficially Canada's national sport and has been since 1859, although it is often overlooked because hockey is so well-marketed and popular. Today, lacrosse is making something of a comeback and is becoming increasingly popular both among native peoples and in the non-native population.

Athlete Information Bureau.

Jocelyn Lovell dominated cycling for 20 years until his road accident in 1983.

Women in Senior Leadership Positions in Sport

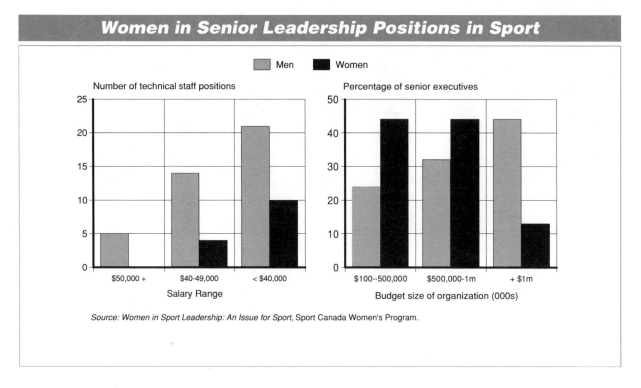

Source: *Women in Sport Leadership: An Issue for Sport,* Sport Canada Women's Program.

Shinny was also practised across North America but it was played mainly by women and children, although mixed games did take place. It, in fact, was very much like modern-day field hockey (ibid:51).

Today, the concerns of native people in Canada with regard to sport, fitness and recreation are twofold: *cultural concerns* and *equity concerns.*

There are special *cultural concerns* about the traditions and values of native society and that sport should reflect these values. Special events, such as snow snake or lacrosse, and the values of inclusion and sharing rather than competing are important concerns. Sometimes the context of religious and spiritual values have to be included with the physical activities as well.

The second area is *equity concerns* in the support of sport and physical activities for native peoples. By most social indicators—income, health, housing, education, etc.—native people in Canada are at the bottom of the social ladder. Isolation from sports events, lack of financial resources or sports facilities, limited coaching opportunities and the absence of support and encouragement are central to this discussion. The fact that there are many native hockey players but few in the NHL is one concern of First Nations sportspeople.

Although the values and needs of Canada's native communities with regard to sport and recreation have largely been forgotten, there is some indication that this will be addressed in the future planning of Sport Canada.

Other victims of discrimination

Equality refers to the principle that everyone should have the same opportunity. This does not mean that everyone necessarily wants to choose the same kinds of physical activities. It means simply that everyone should have the opportunity to participate fully in the manner they choose. Two groups greatly affected by present inequalities in sport are disabled and gay athletes.

Until recently, the persons with disabilities often were hidden by their families. Parents were ashamed of these children. Today, however, there are many organizations that have worked hard to enable disabled athletes to compete with the same opportunities as able-bodied athletes.

Gradually, those who participate in sport and physical activities are becoming more sensitive to the concerns of disabled people. However, it is hard to see yourself as an equal when sport structures and organizations do not recognize you as such. Disabled athletes feel that if the determination and skill of disabled athletes is to be fully recognized, they should be an official part of the Olympic Games. In the fall of 1989 a campaign was initiated to have the Disabled Games included as part of the Olympic Games.

Increasingly, guidelines are being prepared for coaches and participants in a variety of sports for the disabled, including skiing and water sports.

Members of the gay community also face discrimination. Because a person's livelihood, rental accommodation, job and family's affection could be at risk, it has been a step of great courage for gay people to identify themselves publicly. For the most part professional sport has defined itself as being male, heterosexual and homophobic, i.e. antagonistic and hostile towards homosexuals. The first North American gay athlete to say publicly that he was gay was NHL football player Dave Kopay, in 1976.

Researcher Brian Pronger has interviewed a number of high performance gay athletes. He found one of the issues for gay men was hiding their sexual orientation.

> You did everything you could to hang on to your seat, to make the crew, that you would never jeopardize—you wouldn't even tell the coach you had a cold. You could be *crippled* and you'd hide it from the coach, because if there's any perceived weakness, they'll put somebody else in the boat. So to hint that I was gay was to kiss rowing goodbye (Pronger, 1990:147).

Jeff Adams and Marc Quessy, wheelchair athletes.

Athlete Information Bureau (T. O'Lett).

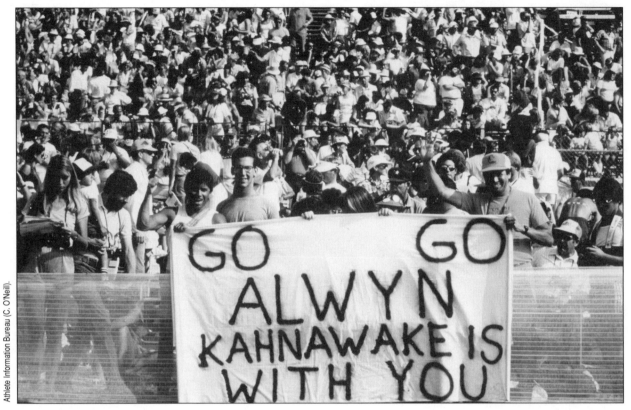

Athlete Information Bureau (C. O'Neill).

Alwyn Morris supporters show
solidarity with their hero.

Sexual orientation is not a public aspect of professional sport.
While certain individual athletes have been singled out, for the most
part there has been little discussion of this issue in the athletic
community.

Humanist Approach to Sport and Physical Activity

Women, racial minorities, native peoples, the disabled and gays
face enormous difficulties in obtaining equality in sport. Their
legitimate struggle for equal access and treatment in sport has raised
fundamental issues about sport in society. Our society must find ways
to remove all obstacles in the way of equity in sport as well as other
aspects of society.

The sociologist Harry Edwards, who was directly involved in the
1968 Smith-Carlos Olympic incident in Mexico City, argues that we
need a new sport ideology. He is particularly concerned about discrimination and the abuses associated with high performance competitive sport.

Some of the key elements in the "humanitarian" approach that he advocates in order to bring about a more open sports system are:

1. A system of sports participation which would be open to all regardless of sex, innate physical capabilities, political philosophy, or life style ...

2. There is nothing wrong with the essence of competitive sport ... agonistic struggle in sport...is a healthy, valuable human activity. [But] there is a vital interplay between competition and cooperation in healthy sports activity. Competitive sport is in trouble when the balance is tipped toward competition, as it is today, or toward cooperation as the counter-culture would prefer.

3. There is nothing wrong or dehumanizing about a person taking pride in accomplishment. But his *(or her)* quest for excellence should not be accomplished at the expense of himself *(or herself)* or others. When a humanistic process replaces the present dehumanizing system the sport experience will be [all the] richer ...

4. Perhaps the most fundamental aspect of the [Humanitarian Creed] is how the competitor sees his or her *opponent* ...The champion athlete will share his knowledge and skill with lesser athletes in the hope that they will rise to his level. His pride in victory comes when he struggles courageously in the face of real challenge (Edwards, 1973:337–338) (italics added).

The humanitarian perspective seeks to make the sports experience more open and fair for as many people as possible while retaining a dedication to excellence and good competition.

Because of discrimination, women and minority groups have had to rethink the entire direction of sport in our society. These discussions and debates may help our society to redefine the true meaning of sport in the 1990s and beyond.

REVIEW

Questions

1. What is meant by the terms: *employment equity* and *pay equity*? Why are these issues important in sport?

2. Why have court cases played a significant role for women and minorities in sport?

3. Has women's participation been equal to that of men in the Olympics?

4. What were the attitudes towards black athletes in the earlier part of this century?

5. What is *apartheid*?

6. What are some of the concerns of disabled and gay athletes?

7. What are the components of a humanitarian approach to sport?

Concepts

- equality
- racism
- segregation
- apartheid
- sexism
- stacking
- stereotype

Discussion

1. Discuss the attitudes towards women's involvement with sport in the past and how have they changed in the past twenty years?

2. Describe and discuss discrimination that you, your friends, or acquaintances might have experienced in relation to sport.

3. List the essential factors you think are crucial to more equal access and treatment in sport for all. Be sure to include an analysis of the organization and structures of sport, as well as attitudes.

First Nations lacrosse team in the
nineteenth century.

J. Le Clair.

The Georgia-Florida college football game in Jacksonville, Florida, 1991. Many Canadian athletes attend university in the United States on athletic scholarships.

Chapter Eight

WHO BENEFITS FROM SPORT SCHOLARSHIPS

"We are dealing with a 16 year old, an infant in the eyes of the law. We do not want them to be dealt with as commercial commodities or a side of beef. (But) I am also of the view that, where possible, the court should not interfere with internal rules and regulations of clubs. If someone has joined a club, he ought to abide by its rules."
Justice Robert Montgomery of the Supreme Court of Canada on the draft of Junior A hockey players

"I took my high school career as a job. I knew I had to be there every day, practising, even when I didn't really feel like it. ... I knew damn well that if I didn't get a scholarship, I wasn't going to college."
Kenny Anderson, high school basketball player in New York City

"Less than two percent of the athletes who participate in collegiate football or basketball ever make a payday as professional athletes ... "
Harry Edwards, American sport sociologist

PROFILES IN THIS CHAPTER

- Bruce Kidd
- Raghib "The Rocket" Ismail
- Harry Jerome
- Barron Pierre de Coubertin
- Alice Milliat

Sport scholarships provide educational opportunities for those who otherwise would not be able to obtain a university education. Many are concerned, however, that the focus of the sports programs in these educational institutions has been to create elite international competitors and winning teams for the television markets. There have been a number of scandals about holders of athletic scholarships who are barely able to read or write, let alone pass exams and get degrees. One highly-publicized incident in the United States involved a basketball player at Creighton University called Kevin Ross who never learned to read or write properly or do simple arithmetic. He was finally sent to an elementary school to learn the basics he had never been taught (Simon, 1985:137).

Youth on the track—wheelchair sport in Canada.

~ SPORT PROFILE ~

Bruce Kidd—From "Golden Boy" Runner to Sport Critic

b. 1943 Ottawa, Ontario. Bruce Kidd is often viewed as the person who was a focal point for the re-entry of Canadian track and field athletes into North American competition in the 1960s. Both he and Bill Crothers trained at the East York Track Club with coach Fred Foot. His hard work and commitment to training earned him the admiration of many.

During his last year at high school his day was very busy, and this was in the days before the super training of pre-teens. At 5:30 am. he got up to deliver newspapers and then studied between 7:00–7:45 am. He had breakfast and went off to school. After school he studied another forty-five minutes and then took a streetcar to train with his coach Fred Foot for a couple of hours. After that he would do another hour of homework and then be in bed by 9:30 pm. He wanted to be both an honours student and a long-distance runner (Wise, 1974:243). Fans also liked the same determination Kidd brought to competition. He was a middle-distance runner, winning medals at the 1962 Commonwealth Games in the 3-mile and 6-mile events.

After running one of the fastest ever indoor two miles he was offered a scholarship at Harvard University in the United States. He found out immediately that the coach's interests might not be his own.

"The Harvard coach told me: 'With your strength I can use you in dual meets in the two-mile, the one-mile and the two-mile and one-mile relays.' I wanted to run three and six miles, so I decided to stay in Toronto where I could pick my own races and train for the Olympics."

Another aspect of the decision was Canadian nationalism. The Americans implied Toronto was a backwater and the "real" opportunities lay south of the border. Kidd wanted to show them that he and Canada could do just fine.

Kidd was chosen as the Canadian athlete of the year in 1962 and 1963 and received the *Toronto Telegram's* Citizen of the Year Award in 1963. He made a speech at a major sports banquet outlining a number of problems he thought athletes faced — hockey fights, financial problems and cheating. Perhaps naive, he was surprised when, as he puts it, he went from being the "golden-haired boy" to "juvenile" and "immature." Suddenly he found that people shouted insults at him and were unfriendly.

"Success in sports elevates you to act as a representative, a spokesperson for certain values … People were happy to exploit me ideologically, but were not prepared to let me have my say. I realized there were certain kinds of things that could not be said and that made me even angrier."

The about-face of sports writers and the public shook him up, forced him to evaluate the political context of sport. So began his life-long evaluation of the role of athletes in a highly commercialized sport world. In spite of his love of running, at one point he became so discouraged he almost gave up sport entirely.

Fortunately for Canadians, Bruce Kidd stayed to contribute. He is known as an advocate for athletes' rights and for more equitable sport systems (coaching, access to facilities, funding and competition) for women, minorities and the disabled. Kidd is now Director of the School of Health and Physical Education at the University of Toronto and remains a committed supporter of the Olympic movement .

Bruce Kidd feels that every talented person should have the opportunity to go to community college or university. "If a student is a talented athlete they should have the opportunity to be there too. It should not be a system where students sell their athletic labour in order to gain access to university. After adequate physical education and recreation programs are provided to the community, then the special needs of athletes can be provided. Attempts should be made to lower the barriers (that prevent young people from going to institutions of higher learning) and not to give the athletically gifted special entrance, routes or ways of getting in."

Kidd explains: "I spend a good deal of time trying to talk athletes out of going to the United States. Ultimately it's a student's choice. It is a free world. I ask them why they want to do it? I suggest they ask the following questions of the sport program they are thinking of joining (these are part of a questionnaire developed by friends in the States).

- What can you tell me to assure me that my education will come before training and competition?
- What guaranties are there that I can attend the courses I need?
- What happens if there are conflicts between training times and my courses?"

Quotations from a personal interview by the author, June 1991.

"Education Can Keep You in the Game"

Education and Hockey Do Mix—the Ontario Hockey Association

In years past hockey players often left school as early as Grade 10 in order to learn the skills of their sport. The need to be free to train and play conflicted with the demands of high school and college. Many players found themselves at a distinct disadvantage when it came to the time when they had to step off the ice and retire.

Today it is recognized that many young hockey players will not make it into professional sport and, even if they do, it is important for players to have a sound educational base. Also there is the reality that some young players are choosing to accept sport scholarships to American universities so they can study and play without the gruelling Canadian schedules.

Coaches like Ted Nolan of the Soo Greyhounds (in Sault Ste Marie) stress the importance of school attendance equally as much as they emphasise the development of hockey skills. He has actively promoted the educational program entitled "Education can keep you in the game."

Players for the Greyhounds are hoping to "make it" into the NHL and therefore are eager to learn hockey skills. But Nolan and his staff stress education as well. Players are required to attend school and obtain good grades. There is an educational consultant who checks with all the schools. The preference is to have the players in regular classes with the other students. There are also study halls while the team is on the road. Attendance is kept at school and if any member of the team misses one class without a legitimate excuse, *the whole team* is required to show up at the arena for a practice at five o'clock in the morning. The team members therefore put pressure on each other to attend classes. Sceptical that they really did this, the author asked how many times this had happened? The answer was once in the 1990–91 season and twice in the 1989–90 season! There is no question of skipping school.

Nolan and the OHL are well aware that many of the young hockey athletes who play on Junior A teams will never make it to the NHL. They feel it is essential to prepare these players for alternatives in case their hockey dreams do not come true.

Bruce Kidd, runner and sport analyst.

A study at North Texas State University found that over 56% of freshmen players dropped out of school during or immediately following the school year. Fewer than 20% of all athletes received degrees and of those who did, 90% took more than four years to graduate (Coakley, 1982:100).

What has been happening in many colleges and universities, of course, is that students are promoted for their athletic ability while their educational needs remain un-met. Because the media glorify sport so much, many young people are willing to do almost anything,

~ SPORT PROFILE ~

Raghib "The Rocket" Ismail—Scholarship Made A Difference

b. 1970, Newark, New Jersey. Raghib "The Rocket" Ismail seems to have it all. Everywhere he goes people ask for his autograph and envy his $18 million contract with the Toronto Argonauts Football Team. But appearances are sometimes deceptive.

Ismail grew up in a family where there were restricted resources and limited choices. A football scholarship provided opportunities that would have otherwise been unavailable. He explains:

"Football was the only thing that would enable me to get a scholarship to university and continue my education as well. Anything that would enable me to get a scholarship right away would help. Nine out of ten academic scholarships are not full scholarships, but the football scholarships cover everything. Universities with track scholarships, unless it's at a top program, don't have the funds to give full scholarships to one person. Whereas in football it's such a high revenue sport where income is steadily coming in, they can afford to give people money to pay for everything. It was definitely one of the factors, or I'd probably have ended up going to a community college."

In school Raghib Ismail was clear what he enjoyed studying—Anthropology and Afro-American studies. "I liked those classes because they were very interesting to me and I learned a lot. When something interests me and I'm really focused on it I do really well."

In 1991 opportunity knocked. Bruce McNall, the owner of the Toronto Argonauts, and Ismail signed a regular CFL contract and a sizeable personal services contract to help him and his co-owners, John Candy and Wayne Gretzky, promote the team and the Canadian league.

"People were saying that I wouldn't be able to handle the pressure—I wasn't used to it—when they knew I was going to play for the Argos. But I just told them that they haven't known attention or pressure or anything like that, as far as I'm concerned, until they've been in the position of a high-profile person at the University of Notre Dame. You are constantly in the public eye. Regardless of whether you do good or bad it'll always be blown up to make it look like you're either the best person or the worst person. You're on national television every week. I was kind of surprised how people who follow sports in Canada knew who I was. When I was a freshman and I'd go to New York or Los Angeles, people wouldn't know who I was. But when I became a Junior, people would point me out and it made me realize how big Notre Dame's exposure was. Their audience is so vast."

Some critics argued that Ismail should have stayed in school, rather than leaving before completing his final year. "The Rocket" explains that he felt that he had to seize the offer presented.

"In society today, if you're in school and some top law firm comes to you and offers you a job for a lot of money, you'd be stupid not to take it. You still have the opportunity to go back and get your education. When the money is there at hand and you don't know if you're going to be around next year, you've got to take advantage of it. You've still got the opportunity to go back. People who say 'I'd never do that, I'd stay in school,' those people are hypocrites, because they know don't know what they'd do in the same situation."

Ismail is also very clear about the role of athletes in professional sport. "In any sport today the athletes basically are just like property of the team and you're treated as such. However some owners, some franchises, treat you a lot better than others. McNall and his people treated me a lot better and showed me more respect as far as sport is concerned. They approached me and said they wanted me to come up to Canada. They wanted to bring more publicity to the team and to the entire league and to bring more people to the stands. This is where Notre Dame comes in. They said everyone knows me and wants to see what I'm all about ... But at the end of the conversation they didn't say 'We're going to pay you two dollars to do all that.' They said 'we're going to pay you accordingly. We know it's a lot.' The NFL were asking me to do all that but here's some change to buy a soda ... I was treated better, I was treated like a man instead of a boy."

Quotations from a personal interview by the author, June 1991.

U.S. College Sports: A Feeder System to the BigTime

Roger Rollocks is a 6-foot 7-inch basketball guard who went to the University of Texas at San Antonio. However, he soon returned to Canada. Rollocks explained:

"My problem was adjusting to the American attitude toward sport and getting along with players who believed in that attitude. In political science (his major) you learn that there is a Canadian attitude and an American attitude and character. Down there, the ideology of sport is different too. Their attitude is to win at all costs. My attitude has always been to do what I can to win, but the main reason I play is because I enjoy it" (Parrish, 1986).

What made Rollocks finally decide to leave was the incident described below.

Rollocks had a wisdom tooth pulled on a Thursday. On Saturday, his mouth was still bleeding and he felt nauseous but was told to report for practice Sunday morning. Not having had anything to eat for three days and feeling weak and dizzy from a recurring headache, he asked the trainer for something to settle his stomach, was refused, threw up, went back on the floor, still felt sick, returned to the training room and was advised by an assistant coach that he'd better quit dogging it and get back on the floor. Later, his

teammates began getting on his case. "It wasn't like in high school where the other guys all back you up no matter what. You feel like you're all alone, that you can't trust anyone. Your confidence starts to slip away" (Parrish).

Perhaps what Rollocks and others like him did not fully understand was that American college sports act as a feeder system to the "big time" and the American students know it. They are out to win because many of them hope to become professional players. They are not in college just to get an education or to have fun playing basketball.

including skip school, to become superstars in their favourite sport. In the hope of becoming winners in professional sport, many students fail in their academic pursuits.

Scholarships and Canadian Athletes

Unlike in the United States, sport scholarships have not been an important part of Canadian colleges and universities.

> The Canadian Inter-University Athletic Union does not permit schools to offer sport scholarships as they exist in the United States. There is a feeling in the CIAU that to do so would hurt the academic integrity of the physical education programs at Canadian schools (Christie, 1989:A21).

Grants for Canadian university students are $1,500 a year, *but* only for returning students. The money cannot be used to entice high school students to a specific institution. There is some variation among the provinces—funds are available for students in the Atlantic provinces; Western Canadian provinces receive provincial funding; in Alberta and British Columbia students can receive up to $2,000; in Quebec, a university sports federation raised one million dollars and the interest from that fund goes towards student athletes; and in Ontario athletes only receive federal funding (Ormsby & Zwolinski, 1989:F1).

Toronto Argonauts.

Raghib "The Rocket" Ismail, from sport scholarship to million-dollar player.

Income, Ethnicity and Educational Attainment

Canadian studies show that the economic resources of a family have a direct affect on the likelihood of a child going on to post-secondary education.

In a study of over 8,000 students in Grades 8-12 in Ontario, Porter and Blishen (1979) found that students from higher socio-economic families are much more likely to *expect to enrol* in university. In contrast, among the students with high mental ability, more from lower socio-economic expect to work after high school (Li, 1988:75).

Clearly, it is not a question of ability and grades but social expectations and family finances.

Those who complete university or a college education in Canada are in a minority.

… For Canadians fifteen years old or older and in the labour force about 10 per cent have completed university and another 10 per cent have some university training. The majority has either completed a secondary education (18%) or has obtained less than secondary education (39%). Among ethnic groups, Jews have the highest percentage of persons with university training, and Chinese the second highest. For example, 32% of the Jews and 21% of the Chinese have completed university (Li, 1988:77). Ethnic groups value education differently, some valuing it more than others.

Due to the selective immigration and recruitment policies of the Canadian government, some ethnic groups have a high percentage of members who received their professional or technical training *before* coming to Canada. (ibid: 79). These families generally want their children to acquire post-secondary education.

The costs involved for putting an athlete through the first year of university are considerable. In 1986, *Sports Illustrated* calculated that a good linebacker at Southern Methodist University cost about $25,000 (Wilson, 1988:5). Another consideration is academic standards. To be accepted at a university such as McGill in Montreal, students must have an above 75% average, so this often excludes many talented athletes. Once at McGill, students must maintain a C-average and the Canadian Inter-University Athletic Union (CIAU) insists on the completion of three courses a term (Wilson, 1988:5).

The fear of losing talented Canadian athletes to American colleges leads some athletic directors to think it might be better if Canadian universities offered first-year scholarships similar to those in the United States. Certainly, some Canadian athletes have decided to accept American sport scholarships so that they could train at the elite level or prepare for a career in professional sport. The hockey player Craig Simpson, for example, decided to go to Michigan State University on a hockey scholarship rather than play Junior-A hockey in Canada. This was a different route to that of his brother, Dave Simpson, who chose to play Junior-A hockey while attending the University of Western Ontario. This he found extremely difficult and his family felt that it was virtually impossible for him to get an education and play Junior-A hockey at the same time (Christie, 1989:A21).

Soaring Sport Budgets at Colleges

Despite cutbacks in many schools due to the recession of the early 1980s, American sport budgets continued to grow during the decade.

In 1981, Ohio State University spent $9 million, the University of Michigan $8 million, the University of Missouri $7 million, and Arizona State $6 million dollars (Curry and Jiobu, 1984:125). These figures seem high, but running sport programs is expensive. For a football team, a typical breakdown is as follows: 100 full scholarships $100,000; salaries for 10 coaches $250,000; equipment $50,000; publicity $75,000; recruiting $60,000; training table $30,000; travel $30,000; trainers $40,000 and various other things like film, laundry, scouting reports, janitorial services, etc. (Coakley 1982:152).

Revenue can be generated by television coverage and by donations from alumni. A winning team helps bring in the donations. At the University of Michigan only two out of twenty-one varsity sports are money makers: football and men's basketball. Of a $20 million annual budget, those two sports bring in about $16 million with football providing the lion's share (Cormsby & Zwolinski, 1989:F11). In ten years, an average of 47% of the Notre Dame alumni contributed on average $150.00 (Coakley, 1982:153). Clearly, the wealthier and larger universities have an advantage.

An interesting comparison can be made between the budget of the University of Toronto Blues football team, which is one of Canada's best college sides, and the University of Michigan's Wolverines. The Michigan team had a 1989 budget of $20 million, compared to a budget of $300,000 at the University of Toronto.

Source: Mary Ormsky and Mark Zwolinski. 1989. "Money, crowds: the american grid dream." *The Toronto Star.* October 25,.

SCHOLARSHIP UNLIMITED

Talented high school athletes are often overwhelmed by the scholarship choices available to them in the United States.

A company called Sports Recruits International charges $449 to help students evaluate the various possibilities. The company will put together a resumé for the student and provide information about available scholarships. Because of new NCAA rules and financial cut-backs, this kind of service has become increasingly popular, according to the NCAA legislative assistant Amy Privette (Kalchman, 1991:F11).

Canadians are often surprised to find out that "748 NCAA schools offer financial aid to female basketball players, 695 for volleyball ... 537 for softball; and on the men's side, 536 schools seek soccer players while 579 offer golf scholarships."

It is hard enough for many students to maintain good grades when they are concentrating exclusively on their studies. When travelling, training and competing are added, it becomes much harder. It has been proposed that high performance athletes who are competing at the national and international level should be allowed to take a reduced academic load. These athletes are often competing against full-time athletes in other countries, and therefore the days of casual or part-time training are over. Rather than put unreasonable demands on student-athletes, one solution might be to give direct financial support for courses and allow them to be taken at a later date.

Increasingly, talented Canadian hockey players are choosing to take U.S. scholarships rather than play Junior-A hockey in Canada.

In the past National Hockey League amateur draft, 48 U.S. college players were chosen, more players than were drafted from any of the three major-junior hockey leagues in Canada. Of that 48, 34 were

~ SPORT PROFILE ~

Harry Jerome—Unconventional and a Winner

b. 1940, Prince Albert, Saskatchewan; d. 1982. Harry Jerome liked playing baseball and was spotted as a sprinter as he flew between the bases. At eighteen, he broke Percy Williams' thirty-one year old record in the 220 yards. He also ran the 100 yards in 9.5 seconds.

Jerome's family had limited resources as his father was a pullman attendant on the CN railway (Wise, 1974: 241). Fortunately, he was able to study at the University of Oregon on a sport scholarship.

Jerome ran the 100 m. in 10 seconds and won a bronze medal at Tokyo in 1964. However, he was often criticized by the press in spite of the fact that for four years in the 1960s he was co-holder of the world record in both the 100 metres (10 seconds flat) and the 100 yards (9.1 seconds) — these

records stood until Ben Johnson. In the 1964 Olympic trials at St. Lambert, Quebec, Jerome had the nerve to run in sunglasses and sweatpants! Other more serious charges of being a quitter were laid at his feet, when in fact he suffered from serious injuries. At the 1962 British Commonwealth Games he was pressured to run when he had tonsillitis. The Canadian track and field officials wanted a Canadian win, and when Jerome did not perform exactly when and as they wanted, he was criticized. His University of Oregan coach said at the time: "Greedy! More interested in medals than in an athlete's health" (Batten, 1971: 110).

When Jerome won a bronze medal in the 1964 Olympics, placed fourth in the 200 metres and won a gold in the Commonwealth Games in 1966, he

suddenly became a hero for Canadian officials and the press. The attitude toward Jerome reflected the undeveloped approach of the organizers of Canadian track and field at the time (Batten, 1971: 110–113).

Harry Jerome was not able to translate his achievements as Canada's greatest sprinter into the kinds of financial rewards available to great athletes of 1990s. Through his own experiences, he knew that Canadians needed better training and facilities. After retirement from competition, he worked hard to encourage elementary school children to participate in sport through a program he organized called The Premier's Sports Awards. Everyone was shocked when he died suddenly at the early age of forty-two (Kearney, 1985: 113).

Canadian Olympic Association.

Harry Jerome, as fast as Ben Johnson on the track.

Canadians who opted to take a scholarship from a U.S. school, rather than tackle the rigours of life in the junior ranks (Christie, 1989:D4).

The scholarships provided at such schools as Michigan State "are worth about $10,000 a year and include accommodation, tuition. books and extra required charges such as laboratory fees" (Christie, 1989:D4). Canadians, like Jason Muzzatti of Woodbridge, Ontario and Joby Messier of Mercier, Saskatchewan (cousin of Edmonton Oilers Mark Messier), prefer playing at Michigan State because they only play two games a week, there is not much travelling and the games are in front of sizeable crowds. This contrasts with playing up to 72 league games in major-junior hockey, which makes it very difficult to complete a college education in a regular time frame.

Another side to the story is the number of Canadians who accept scholarships and then decide to return to Canada before the end of the four-year period. Some return because they discover that the small print in the scholarships states that if they become injured, or get

Baron Pierre de Coubertin—Founder of the Olympic Games

b. 1863, France; d. 1937. Baron Pierre de Coubertin was born into the French aristocracy and very much wanted to make a new kind of contribution to the changing world. He decided that his work would be in the field of education.

The research he conducted in England led him to the conclusion that the British public school model of academic studies and physical activity would help France evolve in more positive ways, especially after the recent humiliating defeat by the German army. He greatly admired the work of British writer Thomas Arnold who wrote *Tom Brown's Schooldays* based on the English school called Rugby. It was because of these interests he began to develop the ideas of recreating the Ancient Olympic Games.

After two years of work he held an international sports meeting in 1894 and obtained support from nine countries—Belgium, England, France, Greece, Italy, Russia, Spain, Sweden and the United States. Although he wanted the Games held in France it was agreed the first Olympics would take place in Athens and move to other cities every four years. Nine sports were included—cycling, fencing, gymnastics, lawn tennis, shooting, swimming, track and field, weightlifting and wrestling—with 311 athletes participating. Today, some of their ideas seem very narrow—no women were included, no non-European or Asian countries were included and only gentlemen could participate (meaning those who did not make a living by their physical prowess, such as sailors who rowed or stevedores who lifted heavy weights etc.). However, the principles—personal excellence, competing with the best, focusing on the process of competition rather then the end goal of winning the gold—have had a wide and profound influence on many young people around the world in ways Coubertin probably could never have imagined. Children and young people in schools and communities around the world aspire to do their best according to the Olympic ideals Coubertin revived.

---

dropped from the team, the scholarship ends too. Others find that the expenses are greater in the U.S. schools and that they have to spend money out of their own pockets. Still others decide to return home because they find the competition and pressure-cooker pace difficult to take. American high school students often find themselves caught up in recruiting drives and many find the ceaseless vigilance of the recruiters quite stressful. They have to weigh each offer and attempt to evaluate which sport, coaching and educational program is the best. The money and opportunities involved are considerable.

Colour, Sport and Upward Social Mobility

What are the chances of "making it" in professional sports? Many educators and professional athletes express serious concern about the effect that the dream of making it to the "big time" has on high school students. Many educators also feel that athletes who play on American university teams are drawn disproportionally from less-privileged families. Students from better-off families often are encouraged to get their academic qualifications and may be discouraged

Pierre de Coubertin, educator, rower, and creator of the modern Olympics.

International Olympic Committee Photographic Archives (Switzerland).

PRESSURE ON SCHOLARSHIP HOLDERS

The pressures on holders of athletic scholarships to devote their time to sport is very real. Len Bias, the university basketball star, who died tragically the day after signing his first professional contract, had failed every one of his courses the term before.

Staying in School: A Better Bet

Sport provides the dream of rags to riches. The statistical reality, however, is quite different.

Wilbert M. Leonard and Jonathan E. Reyman did research on two aspects of upward mobility and sport. They asked: (1) What is the probability of becoming a professional athlete in a specific sport? and (2) How do race, ethnicity, and gender affect the general odds? The study calculated the odds of different categories of athletes (male, female, white, black, Hispanic, Native American, and Asian/Pacific Islander) attaining professional status in the major U.S. sports of football, baseball, hockey, basketball, golf, tennis, and auto racing.

"The opportunities for upward social mobility in sport are highly restricted—for females 4/1,000,000 (.0004%); for males 7/100,000 (.007%)" (Leonard & Reyman, 1988:165). In fact the odds are even worse because there are athletes on American teams who come from other countries, such as the Canadians who play hockey and Hispanics who are not American, who play on baseball teams (more than half are not) (Leonard and Reyman, 1988:163–64).

Obviously playing collegiate sports is not going to provide a realistic career opportunity for 98% of those students who do have considerable athletic talent. It might provide an interest and some recognition at college, but it will not provide a short-term career, let alone a long-term one. The success of an athlete like runner Ben Johnson is the exception not the rule.

Statistics Canada contrasted levels of schooling and income for 1987. "A male with eight years or less of schooling earned $25,454 compared with to $44,891 for a university graduate. Corresponding data for females were $15,077 (grade eight or less) and $31,259 (university degree)" (Earnings of Men and Women, *Statistics Canada* 1988). Clearly an individual's earning capacity increases with education.

A slightly older Canadian study on graduates from various kinds of post-secondary institutions showed the relationship between further education diplomas and income. A 1984 study was done on annual median incomes of 1982 graduates. The more education the higher the salaries. For the 99% of the student population who will never become super-stars, staying in school as long as possible is the best bet. Earning capacities rise with each additional qualification.

from over-emphasizing sport whereas young black athletes, in particular, may cling to the dream that sport will provide them with an opportunity to improve their economic position. As a result, the situation often arises where the student body is primarily local, white and middle class while team membership is made up of non-local, poorer, visible minority students.

Black families in the United States, on average, make only 59 cents for each dollar a white family makes. This income differential has remained almost the same for twenty years, in spite of the vast changes in American society. Being a member of a visible minority in the United States generally means poor-paying jobs, poor housing and poor schools. These students are disadvantaged compared with the average white student.

Research, in fact, shows that children in families that are financially better off are more likely to be encouraged to pursue excellence in their studies and use sport as a leisure-time activity. Parents who see the chances of their children succeeding through professional careers are less likely to think upward mobility will take place through sport. On the other hand, those who are less well off and have no professional careers in sight tend to see sport as possibly providing a way up the social ladder.

Researcher Melvin Oliver studied the attitudes of "upper white collar" and "lower blue collar" white and black families in order to compare their attitude towards their children participating in community baseball programs (in the United States). He wanted to see what percentage thought that community baseball activity might lead to a career in professional sports. The standard terms used to label individuals and families by their incomes and the kind of work they do are: *upper white collar, lower white collar, upper blue collar* and *lower blue collar.* Upper white collar refers to those individuals who have professional or managerial jobs (and usually wear a white collar). Upper blue collar individuals are those who have training and skills and most probably are unionized.

In this study, a sizeable number of black families thought that participation in community sports was "A very important benefit" (23% of upper white collar families, 32% of lower white collar, 37% of upper blue collar families and 27% of lower blue collar families). Of the white families (upper white collar, lower white collar and upper blue collar), 0% thought the participation was "A very important benefit." However, 50% of the lower blue collar white families said that they thought that it would be "A very important benefit" (Oliver, 1980:79). So, for both black and white families with limited financial resources, athletic ability was seen to provide the possibility of a future successful and financially rewarding career.

I.Q. TESTS SUPPOSEDLY MEASURE INTELLIGENCE.

Many students on athletic scholarships in the US do not do well on I.Q. tests. Does this mean they should not have the chance to go to university?

Today, educators feel there are many kinds of intelligence—social skills, mathematical skills, spatial skills, artistic skills, leadership skills, interpretive skills, language skills, physical skills and creative skills. Rarely does a person do well on all of these.

A typical test such as the Wechsler Intelligence Scale for Children-Revised (WISC-R) is made up of various subtests. They include vocabulary tests of such words as "obliterate," "imminent" and "dilatory." A sub-test on "Similarities" and another on "Comprehension" include the need to have specific language and knowledge skills.

In the "Information" sub-test children are asked questions like; "Who invented the electric light bulb?" The "Arithmetic" sub-test includes arithmetic skills, calculation skills and short-term memory (Siegal,1989:A15). The tests are very specific in nature.

Specific knowledge, vocabulary, expressive language, and memory skills are required in varying degrees by each subtest. A low I.Q. score means a problem in one or more of those areas, *not* lower intelligence (Siegel, 1989:A15).

Alice Milliat—Founder of the Women's Olympics

b. 1884, France. Today, the participation of women in the Olympics is taken for granted. The sport world of Canadian women and Alice Milliat, a French athlete, in the early part of the century was very different.

Pierre de Coubertin, the founder of the Olympics, was opposed to women participating in public sporting events, as were many sport federations including track and field, swimming, basketball, soccer and cycling (Leigh & Bonin, 1988: 72). Women were forced to form their own sport clubs, so Femina-Sport organized the first French national championships in track and field in 1917. Later in that year, a national sports federation was created (by men)—the Federation des Societies Feminines de France (FSFF).

Because of her dynamic and determined personality Milliat became the first woman elected president to a national sport body in 1919, at a time when women had little voice in any public matters. In 1934 Milliat was quoted as saying in the magazine *Independent Woman*: "Women's sports of all kinds are handicapped in my country by the lack of playing space. As we have no vote, we can not make our need publicly felt, or bring pressure to bear in the right quarters."

The IOC refused to include women in track and field events, so in 1921 Alice Milliat founded the Federation Sportive Feminine International (FSFI). The organisation decided that if the IOC refused to include women then women would create their own

Olympics! The first Women's Olympic Games were held in Paris in 1922 and continued until 1936. The first Games attracted 20,000 fans, five nations took part and there were eleven events in the one day competition.

The International Amateur Athletic Foundation (IAAF) which controlled track and field felt very threatened by these separate games. They insisted that the second Women's Olympic Games (held in Sweden) be merely called the Second International Ladies' Games and agreed that by 1928 a limited program of five events could be included in the 1928 Amsterdam Olympic Games as "an experiment." Canadian women decided to participate, but British women were so angry at the shabby treatment of women athletes they boycotted the 1928 Olympics entirely, even though they were expected to win many events.

Using the explanation that women athletes had "suffered" in competing in the 800 metres at Amsterdam, the IOC decided to cancel all the track and field events for women in the next Olympics. The American representatives then threatened that all American male athletes would boycott the 1932 Olympics unless women were admitted. Meanwhile women's sport flourished. The Third Women's World Games were held in Prague, Czechoslovakia with 200 athletes from seventeen countries competing over three days.

The IOC finally realized it would have to change its position. Negotiations between the IAAF and the FSFI concluded with the inclusion of

women's track and field within the Olympics and the end of the FSFI which had grown from a membership of five nations in 1921 to thirty nations in 1936. At last, instead of opposing and trying to slow down women's sport internationally, the IAAF had taken it over and women's track and field events were recognized as a legitimate part of the Olympic movement.

It was clear that these changes had only become a reality because of the energy and tenacity of Alice Milliat in the creation of an independent Women's Olympic Movement that put direct pressure on the hostile IOC.

Academic Achievement

At the high school level, and even at the grade school level, there is a fear among educators that the increasing pressure on students is leading to an imbalance between the requirements for academic and sporting excellence. Richard Lapchick, the Director for the Institute for Sports in Society at Northeastern University in Boston, found that "of the 30 million children participating in youth sports in this country (the United States), only 198 will become professionals in any given year. It is the same as trying to win the lottery" (Alfano, 1989). Further, he found that less than *two percent* of those who participate in collegiate football or basketball ever make a payday as professional athletes and the careers of those who do make it into the professional ranks are over within three to four years (Edwards, 1985:11). As Edwards points out "…70–75% of all black scholarship athletes *never* graduate from the colleges that they represent in sports."

Nevertheless, companies already promote high school events such as high-profile media events and the elements present in varsity sport are filtering down to the high schools. The Dapper Dan Classic, sponsored by Nike, brings 13,000 fans to Pittsburgh's Civic Arena. SportsChannel America, MSG and ESPN produce weekly "magazine" shows of high school basketball games (March 5 *New York Times*, 1988:18). Dave Krider, the sports editor of the LaPorte (Indiana) Herald-Argus, ranks high school basketball players across the United States as does Doug Huff, the sports editor of *The Intelligencer* in Wheeling West Virginia.

After many scandals in the early 1980s, the NCAA decided that it would deal with the problem of academic requirements for athletic students. The NCAA has nearly 800 member institutions and is the largest of the athletic associations. Two aspects were considered:

Curriculum—In the past students could take scattered courses on such things as the "History and Theory of Basketball," "Weightlifting," etc., without meeting the requirements to get a specific degree or diploma. A core curriculum for all students is now mandatory.

Entrance requirements—High school students in the United States who want to go to college now have to take country-wide multiple choice tests, which are called SAT (Scholastic Aptitude Tests) or the ACT (American College Test). Like I.Q. tests, however, these have been criticised as being a very poor evaluator of those students who are neither white nor middle-class because the tests assume that the students have an Anglo-American background.

The NCAA makes clear to all students that they are students first, not athletes who happen to be at university (Simon 1985:148). In 1986 the NCAA decided to insist that only students who scored either a GPA

Education and Physical Activity

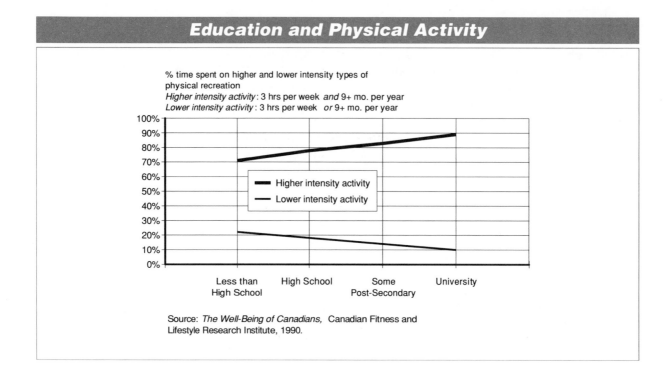

% time spent on higher and lower intensity types of
physical recreation
Higher intensity activity: 3 hrs per week *and* 9+ mo. per year
Lower intensity activity: 3 hrs per week *or* 9+ mo. per year

Source: *The Well-Being of Canadians,* Canadian Fitness and
Lifestyle Research Institute, 1990.

TENNIS SUCCESS AT AN EARLY AGE

Jennifer Capriati is the youngest tennis player to reach the semi-finals of a Grand Slam and the youngest to advance to the second round at Wimbledon. She is also the youngest to win a U.S. Open match. Billie Jean King is impressed by her talent.

> She's the most powerful person of her age I have ever seen without any question. Chris (Evert) proved that if you're going to be a great player by the time you're 14, 15, you're there. And she's there, believe me, with bells on. For her, the sky is the limit (Carter, 1991:55).

Capriati entered the Virginia Slims rankings at 25, the highest any player has ever entered since records began in 1986 (Carter, 1991:55). She achieved all this at *fourteen.*

of 2.0 in a college-preparatory core curriculum and 700 on the verbal and mathematical sections of the SAT or 15 out of 36 on the ACT could compete in first-year intercollegiate athletics (Simon 1985:145). However, as black students tend to score lower on these tests, the NCAA was accused of discrimination against black students, and a loophole was created for those who met some of the academic requirements for admission: "these players could enrol in a university and receive full financial aid, but they could not play or practice with the team as freshmen" (Reed, 1989:16).

Many scholarships have specific stipulations about who should receive them—Roman Catholics, Jews, francophones, etc. Scholarships themselves have been under scrutiny since some of the foundations that distribute funds are discriminatory. The most famous of these probably is the Rhodes scholarships, which in the past were for men only, although today both women and men are eligible. Recently, the Supreme Court of Canada heard a case concerning Colonel Reuben Leonard who left scholarship money for white Protestants of British ancestry. This particular scholarship fund has $1.9 million in assets and distributes about $175,000 a year to students (Makin, 1987:A14).

Many professional athletes are developed and promoted initially at the college level in the United States. As student athletes, they attract loyal fan followings that increase when they turn professional. Anywhere from ten to thirty thousand fans will turn out for college games, which means that the schools can also generate substantial amounts of money. The athletes are scouted carefully by the professional teams. Characteristics other than their physical skills are evaluated as well—does the athlete function as a team member; can he or she handle the press; what is his or her scholastic record.

For baseball and hockey the route to professional sport is somewhat different. Most baseball players still go directly from high school into professional baseball. Until recently, the same has been true of hockey players. Today, that is changing somewhat as more and more athletes are studying in the United States on hockey scholarships and then joining the NHL at an older age. Some experts feel this is good. First, it gives the athlete a chance to gain experience and mature; second, the fact that the players are older means that they are bigger physically and the chance of injury is reduced. The collective agreement signed in July 1986 between the NHL and the NHL Players Association included revisions in the entry draft of college players, and as a result fewer 18-year-olds will be drafted in the future.

Self-Financing Model

Increasingly, sports organizations are being asked to generate their own revenues. This is known as the *self-financing model.* Under this model, the emphasis will be given to sports that are or have the potential to be self-supporting.

Donald MacIntosh, a professor in the School of Physical and Health Education at Queen's University, is very concerned about the pressure on universities to develop self-supporting, high-performance, high-profile sports. Like many others, he is afraid the emphasis will be even more on the athletic component rather than on the educational aspect of university life. "These athletes will typically enrol in the minimum number of courses that are required by CIAU regulations" (MacIntosh, 1987:A13). Some American educators, including Timothy Healey, the President of Georgetown University, are opposed to freshmen students participating in varsity teams at all, especially football and basketball which feed into professional teams. They want students to focus on the adjustment to academic life first. Georgetown University even refused to allow photographers to follow student Patrick Ewing into classes and his dormitory, so that he would be left alone to participate in athletics and his studies (Healey, 1988:142)!

SUCCESS RECORD

There are important instances where a coach has also been able to ensure athletes complete their studies. For example, basketball coach George Morrison, at the University of Prince Edward Island, has attracted black players from far away Toronto to play on his successful team.

Morrison "sells" the positive attributes of small-scale, friendly P.E.I. and uses the 60% average entrance requirement to his advantage. Morrison stresses that even where such "imported" players have not made the team all have stayed to complete their studies (with one exception) (Brunt, 1989:18). The educational success of Morrison's athletes contrasts favourably with the record of most American athletic programs.

EVERYONE HOPES,
BUT FEW WIN

What percentage of American high school students do in fact end up with sport scholarships? Unfortunately, it's rather like the lotteries.

Seven percent of the more than half a million high school football players in the US go on to play at college, and only half of these receive financial aid (3.5%); for basketball it's approximately three percent, with 1.5% of the students getting financial aid (Curry and Jiobu, 1984:77–78).

Another concern with self-financing sport is the question of access for women. The main self-supporting sports in the United States are those that feed into professional sport. They attract the crowds, are promoted well on television and generate television revenues. However, in the past these sports have not included many women. Therefore, it is thought that under a system of self-supporting sports there will be even fewer sports opportunities for women in the future. The few women's sports that are promoted, like tennis and golf, are not team sports and do not bring in large numbers of fans.

Dr. Earle Zeigler, a professor of physical education at the University of Western Ontario, is concerned about creeping "semi-professionalism" at Canadian universities. He argues that sport should follow the example of the music world in its definition of professionalism. A person who plays the trumpet in a high school band is an **amateur**, as there are no financial rewards. If he or she is good enough to play with some group regularly on weekends for fifty dollars a night, then a degree of semi-professionalism has been achieved. Finally, this person may become a professional musician or music teacher as a lifetime occupation. At this point the individual really is a professional because his or her entire living will come from this source (Zeigler, 1989:2–3).

Zeigler also feels the trust funds set up by the various associations on behalf of young athletes are not taken seriously. A-carded athletes have to try to survive on limited funding as their main source of income. On the other hand, the fact that Ben Johnson did receive government funding is regarded as inappropriate because of his other sources of income. Other A-carded athletes had to try to survive on that funding as their main source of income.

Senator Ernie Chambers of Omaha has taken a very different approach in the United States. He thinks that football players should receive direct salaries. In Chambers view, the athletes bring in huge revenues for their institutions while they "… are denied compensation and forced to live with the fiction that they, like flowers, exist in air, sunshine and water." Because the NCAA rules prohibit the payment of any extra money above the scholarship maximums, Chambers supports athlete payments (Neff, 1988:21). The College Players Association was founded in 1984. Many felt that student athletes should be offered more than just four-year scholarships and that they should get a bigger share of the profits. There may eventually be a student players' association along the same lines in all major sports.

TABLE 8-1:

***The Age of Starting, Specializing, and Reaching High Performance
in Different Sports***

Sport	Age to Start Practicing	Age of Specialization	Age to Reach High Performance
Track & Field	10-12	13-14	18-23
Basketball	7-8	10-12	20-25
Boxing	13-14	15-16	20-25
Cycling	14-15	16-17	21-24
Diving	6-7	8-10	18-22
Fencing	7-8	10-12	20-25
Figure Skating	5-6	8-10	16-20
Gymnastics (women)	6-7	10-11	14-18
Gymnastics (men)	6-7	12-14	18-24
Rowing	12-14	16-18	22-24
Skiing	6-7	10-11	20-24
Soccer	10-12	11-13	18-24
Swimming	3-7	10-12	16-18
Tennis	6-8	12-14	22-25
Volleyball	11-12	14-15	20-25
Weightlifting	11-13	15-16	21-28
Wrestling	13-14	15-16	24-28

SOURCE: Bompa, quoted in Sandy Straw, 1990. *Women in Sports and Physical Recreation Project (WISPER) Report.* City of Toronto, Parks and Recreation.

Children's Rights: Hockey Contracts

If a child wants to play competitive hockey in Canada, that child must sign a Canadian Amateur Hockey Association Certificate. The Minor League Hockey Association argues that "it needs the stability the no-release contracts afford. Officials say it would be chaos if kids were free to jump from one team to another" (Kalchman, 1989:C4). To obtain a release, there must be a legitimate grievance.

Some parents have gone to court over these contracts. For example, as a sixteen-year-old, Eric Lindros, rated number one for the junior draft in May 1989, was drafted by the Junior-A hockey club in Sault Ste. Marie. However, Lindros's parents argued that they wanted their son to be in a city near a large university. Their reaction greatly offended the residents of Sault Ste. Marie. When drafted by the Soo Greyhounds, Lindros decided to go to Detroit instead, so that he could go on to university afterwards (Kalchman, 1989:C4). Lindros stood his ground and the OHL passed the "Lindros Rule" that allowed him to be traded by the Greyhounds to the Oshawa Generals. There he lead his team to two Ontario finals and a championship.

Hockey players with disabilities, in Alberta.

Athlete Information Bureau.

FIELD OF DREAMS: GIRLS IN BASEBALL

Girls were excluded from Little League Baseball until 1972 when a 12-year-old called Maria Pepe from Essex County, New Jersey, wanted to play and a civil rights legal suit was laid (Rounds, 1991: 44). In 1973, after fifty years of existence, the Little League suddenly came up with a softball program for girls, just before the decision that the Little League Baseball *had* to open its doors to girls.

Many girls even today, twenty years later, do not feel welcome. Julie Croteau, who played high school and college baseball in the United States, describes her experiences, which are similar to other girls who love the game. Her talent was not recognized. "When I was younger I was so obsessed with the game I blocked out the things I heard." She suffered name calling of all kinds, ranging from "pussy" to "dyke" (Rounds, 1991: 45).

At the professional level women umpires have had a difficult time as well. Pam Postema graduated from umpire school seventeenth out of 130 in 1977 but then faced sexual harassment on the job: "One manager actually took Postema's mask off her face at home plate and kissed her" (Rounds, 1991: 45).

Postema has seen fellow male trainees make it to the majors as umpires. Postema has now filed a discrimination suit against the American League, the National League and the Major League's Baseball Umpire Development League. Like others she feels baseball has betrayed and abandoned all those girls who love the sport.

In another case, Jeff Greenlaw of St. Catharines, Ontario, did not want to move to North Bay and the court decided against him.

> Justice Robert Montgomery of the Ontario Supreme Court concluded: We are dealing with a 16-year-old, an infant in the eyes of the law. We do not want them to be dealt with as commercial commodities or a side of beef. (But) I am also of the view that, where possible, the court should not interfere with internal rules and regulations of clubs. If someone has joined a club, he ought to abide by its rules" (Kalchman, 1989:C4).

Clearly, sports associations need to be able to enforce regulations if chaos is to be avoided. However, the question remains whether children are competent to make evaluations and major decisions with regard to their future careers. We do not allow children at this age to enter legal contracts on other issues. Children do not sign leases or vote, but they can be obliged to move away from home if they want to play hockey.

The age at which children begin to take their sport seriously varies from sport to sport. Table 8-1 outlines the different ages at which children start practising their sport, specializing and reaching high performance competitive levels. In gymnastics and swimming children are spotted when they are little more than toddlers. In other sports such as rowing, cycling and boxing, children start to specialize at an older age.

The issue of age is one that concerns sports educators. The entry age for some sports is very young and children have often to make the decision to compete at a very early age. They also have to make choices that may affect their whole lives, and they may not always be aware of the consequences of these choices. The young athlete only feels the love for the sport and the pride in doing well and may not understand what it means to spend a childhood training and not playing or going to school with other children.

Today, when there is so much money to be made from the well-marketed sports, children become entertainers in the world of sport at a young age. However, just because a basketball player is 6 feet 7 inches tall and is a powerhouse on the court does not change the fact that the young athlete is only fifteen.

There are two focuses in the world of sport for young people—that of the development of the young person as learner and athlete and that of their apprenticeship into the world of sport entertainment. Often these two clash, sometimes with great anguish for the athlete. Increasingly we see the dominance of the business of sport because of the large amount of money to be made. Teenage athletes choosing the college of their choice may not have advisers to help and protect them. One solution might be the introduction of a system of child or

How Muscles Work

Everyone has had the frustration of trying to do something and then having difficulty in completing the task because the strength just wasn't there. It is interesting to see just why this is.

Endurance is important for any athlete because it links directly with the athlete's ability to work at a high level. The body draws on different energy sources to do work. We obtain our energy from food. Carbohydrates are the most important and are made up of carbon, hydrogen and oxygen. Enzymes in the body serve as catalysts to allow the chemical changes to take place in the body to provide muscular energy. Glycogen stored in the liver and muscles is broken down by the enzymes to permit energy expenditure for short-, medium- and long-term basis (Watson, 1983: 30).

Short-term energy requirements. This source of energy is used in about ten seconds, in explosive events. Ben Johnson's performance in sprints is one example. Here, oxygen is not needed for energy requirements, and this is called anaerobic exercise.

Medium-term energy requirements. In 800–1000 metre track events and 200-metre swimming events, over a two- or three- minute period. pain starts from the build up of lactic acid (when the glycogen in the body is broken down in the absence of oxygen) (Dyer, 1982: 19). Often high school students are told "no pain no gain," which is not a good basis for training, as pain is always an indicator that the body is "in trouble." But, obviously part of obtaining improvement is the pushing beyond your present limits.

Long-term requirements. So long as the athlete does not push too hard, he or she can continue for long periods because there is not the build up of lactic acid.

Just so that it is clear what are the differences in the consumption of energy by an athlete who is competing, it is interesting to compare the kilojoules (the metric equivalent of calories) used: a sedentary person—8,500 kilojoules in 24 hours; long-distance cyclists—42,000 kilojoules or more (Dyer, 1982: 20).

Therefore it is important that the athlete train appropriately for the event. At the same time, for the recreational athlete, it is important that all-round fitness be achieved in order to have the three kinds of energy sources available.

RINGERS: THE ISSUE OF HIGH SCHOOL ELIGIBILITY

In some Canadian districts there have been conflicts over the eligibility of players on high school teams. There have been complaints that parents have filed false addresses to meet residential qualifications to enable their children to play in better hockey leagues.

youth advocates to protect the interests of those under twenty-one. Knowledge and information gives power to those who have it. Those young athletes who have information and informed advisers can maximize their skills and secure their futures.

The cold reality that few young athletes actually "make it" in the professional sport world should encourage a re-evaluation of what the emphasis ought to be.

REVIEW

Questions

1. Why is there a good deal of controversy over athletic scholarships in the universities and colleges?
2. Why do Canadian students accept American sport scholarships?
3. What are some of the differences between American and Canadian university sports programs?
4. How does socio-economic background affect a family's attitude towards their children's sport participation?
5. What effect does staying in school have on future income levels?
6. What is the debate over I.Q. tests?
7. Why have some hockey contracts with junior athletes resulted in court cases?

Concepts

- upward mobility
- Proposition 48
- scholarship
- I.Q. tests

Discussion

1. Describe, compare and contrast the sports scholarships system in Canada and the United States.
2. Describe and discuss the debate over the effect of first-year scholarship on academic achievement.
3. Discuss why age is such an important issue in athletics today.

Soo Greyhounds.

Teddy Nolan in his characteristic pose behind the Soo Greyhounds' bench.

Canada's sport structures—as complex as a children's climbing gym.

Chapter Nine

SPORT STRUCTURES IN CANADA

"The system is unbelievably complex because of the multitude of organizations responsible for sport and the various ways the system is glued together."
Carol Anne Letheren, President of the Canadian Olympic Association and IOC

"We know that volunteers are always going to be the lifeblood of our sport. We need to involve good people, and to run sport in such a way that good people want to stay involved."
Unidentified Executive Director quoted in The Game Planners

In small-scale communities, individuals come into contact with each other on a regular basis and it is relatively easy to organize things such as physical activities. When societies grow in size, however, greater specialization is required and complex, sometimes even vast, organizations develop to carry out the work of society.

Increasingly, the administration of sport is taking place through highly complex organizational structures at the federal, provincial and even the local level. The term **bureaucracy** is sometimes used to describe this modern phenomenon of complex organization. The term "bureaucracy" is a difficult one, because often it is used simply as a term of disapproval—"There is too much bureaucracy"; "The bureaucracy is slowing things down"; "Sports today is run by bureaucracy"; etc. Strictly speaking, a bureaucracy simply refers to the development of an organization with many "bureaus" (or offices), all of which are necessary to carry out a given task. However, the difficulty with complex, specialized organizations—and this is the reason the term is often a term of abuse—is that people in them can become more concerned with servicing their own needs and preserving their own position than getting the work done. To make matters worse, the various "bureaus" in any complex organization develop

Canadian Sport and Fitness Administration Centre, Ottawa.

Carol Anne Letheren—No New Upstart in the Complex Sport Structures

You can't believe everything you read. In 1990 when Carol Anne Letheren was appointed as the Canadian replacement for Jim Worrall on the International Olympic Committee, she was described as "relatively unknown" (Christie, 1990: C14). As the President of the Canadian Olympic Association, she is in fact well known in both Canadian and international sport circles.

Letheren explains: "Sport has always been a part of my life. I started in sport when I was a kid. After completing degrees in physical and health education and anthropology and psychology, she decided an MBA from York University would better equip her with a business background as sport was moving from its volunteer base to a more business orientation.

She taught at the University of Toronto and coached archery and volleyball. Letheren started the gymnastics program within the university system. The sport was very new in 1964 and the only other person working in the sport at the national level was Marilyn Savage. She also became involved with judging. "As I developed the sport within the university system then by natural evolution I began coaching and we worked our way into the system such that the University of Toronto had the national championship team and I went on and coached the Canadian team at the World Student Games." She was the founder of the Women's Technical Committee in Ontario and then worked administratively at the national and later the international level.

As someone who has worked in many different areas of the Canadian sport system, she has some clear ideas about its organization. "Many people don't understand the sport system. The Dubin Inquiry got an A-plus on Seoul and the specificities of the Seoul incident but the Dubin Inquiry failed to understand how sport functions in this country and internationally. The system is unbelievably complex because of the multitude of organizations responsible for sport and the various ways the system is glued together."

Letheren, with an insider's view as an IOC member, explains the unique nature of the Olympic Movement that alternately infuriates and fascinates outsiders. "The Olympic movement is one of the most high profile movements in the world. There isn't an event that is as widely watched as the Olympic Games, or as closely followed. It's a natural target and people are going to take potshots. Also, it's one of the few organizations that appoints its members and its members are not answerable to any national institutions, although they do, by the Charter of the IOC, have seats on their national Olympic committees.

As an IOC member you take an oath and swear that you won't be influenced by your own government or any other body and that you'll be ruled entirely by the charter of the Olympic Movement. But in some ways it is very important to the organization because it allows it to be independent of political pressure."

Carol Anne Letheren's presence on the IOC is a reflection of the changing composition of the IOC itself. She has been described as part of the youth movement.

She explains: "The last two groups that went into the IOC, one in Tokyo (September 1991) when I did, and the group in Birmingham (in June,1991) lowered the average age. The tenure is until you are 75, so unless there is fresh blood coming in pretty constantly, you're going to get a swing to an older age. The average age has been brought down. Many countries are putting in younger members."

Her participation in sport structures has been based on a very democratic perception of organizations. "I go into these organizations with the idea that no one owns sports. This is not a private business or association. This is not your association. You're given an opportunity to further the aims and ideals and aspirations of this organization and the people it represents ... When you leave the organization you should be leaving something better than it was before you went in and the legacy should be that the organization is achieving what it wants to achieve."

Quotations based on a personal interview by the author, June 1991.

Founding Dates for Canadian Sports

Organization	Date Founded
National Lacrosse Association	1867
became National Amateur Lacrosse Association	1880
Canadian Association of Amateur Oarsmen	1880
Canadian Wheelman's Association (bicycling)	1882
Amateur Athletic Association of Canada	1884
became Canadian Amateur Athletic Association	1898
became Athletic Union of Canada	1909
Canadian Lawn Tennis Association	1884
Canadian Rugby Football Union	1884
Canadian Lacrosse Association	1887
Canadian Cricket Association	1892
Royal Canadian Golf Association	1895
Canadian Canoe Association	1900
Canadian Amateur Swimming Association	1909
Dominion Football Association (soccer)	1912
Canadian Amateur Lacrosse Association	1914
Canadian Amateur Hockey Association	1914

SOURCE: Alan Metcalfe. 1987. *Canada Learns to Play: The Emergence of Organizaed Sport 1807–1914.* Toronto:McClelland & Stewart: 101.

WORK AREAS ON COMPLETION OF SPORTS ADMINISTRATION PROGRAMS

- Physical Education Departments
- Athletic Departments
- Recreation Departments
- Fitness Centres
- Private Health and Sports Clubs
- Sports Associations
- Professional Teams
- Camp and Sport Schools
- Sport and Facilities
- Consultant Services
- Government Agencies

SOURCE:*Graduate Diploma in Sports Administration,* Concordia University 1989.

very specialized skills and knowledge, and therefore it is often difficult for an outsider to know whether inefficiency and self-preservation exists or not!

Today, in Canada and throughout the world, organized sport is administered by vast bureaucracies. To be sure, much of this bureaucracy is essential in order for sport in our society to run well. Nevertheless, in the administration of sport, there is also a great deal of bureaucracy in the bad sense, with the purpose of sport and the interests of the individual athletes overlooked in the interest of self-preservation, duplication and simple inefficiency. Bureaucracy should help individuals achieve success and become winners in their chosen fields. Sometimes it seems the athlete loses *because* of the overwhelming organizational structures.

Carol Anne Letheren, educator, coach and Canadian IOC member.

Matthieu Letheran Associates.

WOMEN AND THE IOC

IOC member Carol Anne Letheren has a very personal view of the role of women in organizations.

"I think women operate a little differently from the way men do, although you can't generalize. Women tend to be more people oriented and concerned with how the group is going to get along while they do the task ... We have grown up more with compromise—related to organizing the family. It's often women who are patching up differences and getting the groups together. We are quite happy to deal with compromise, rather than dealing with every situation where there is conflict with almost head-on confrontation. We are quite capable of confronting, but we will look at a situation and, if compromise is going to be better for the group, we're prepared to put the time in to do that. Women tend more to consensus management. But often people mistake consensus management for *laissez-faire*. We're just prepared to take more time to ensure that people understand the issues. When they're debated, we get the viewpoints out there so that when the vote is taken and the final decision is made, it probably is a consensus."

Quotation from a personal interview by the author, June 1991.

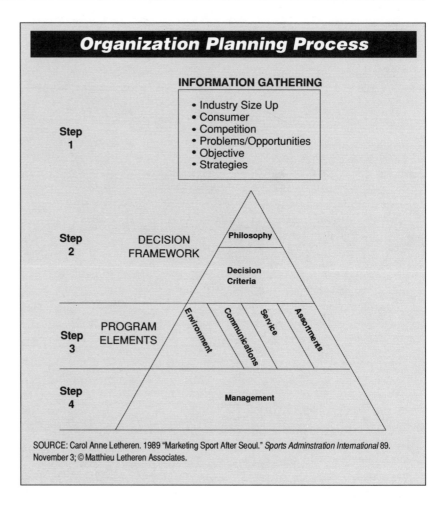

SOURCE: Carol Anne Letheren. 1989 "Marketing Sport After Seoul." *Sports Adminstration International* 89. November 3; © Matthieu Letheren Associates.

Classifying and Managing Sports Organizations

As might be expected "who benefits" permeates the whole nature and structure of an organization. For example, an organization whose aim is to encourage as many people as possible to participate in a sport program and to maximize usage of community and recreational parks has a *totally different focus* from an organization primarily geared to maximizing profit.

Organizations can be classified according to this "who benefits" criteria:

1. *Mutual-benefit associations*—the members all benefit.

2. *Business concerns*—owners and managers benefit primarily, although it may appear that all benefit, including athletes.

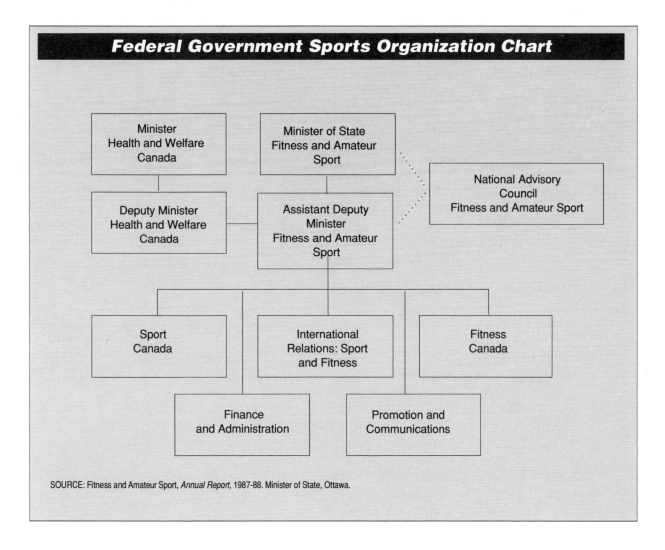

Federal Government Sports Organization Chart

SOURCE: Fitness and Amateur Sport, *Annual Report*, 1987-88. Minister of State, Ottawa.

3. *Service organizations*—provide services to the members as well as to the larger community (community recreation programs), where financial gain is not the prime focus.

4. *Commonwealth organizations*—the public at large benefits; such activities as national fitness programs or the Olympic Games fall into this category
(Quoted in Snider & Spreitzer, 1989:224).

This is a useful classification scheme not only for looking at sports organizations but practically any organization in society.

Whatever interests they represent, all organizations also need to be managed. If the framework is a corporate one, then the organization

Canadian Sports Continuum

It is important to see the connection between the child who goes to skate at the local arena and the competitor at the Olympic Games.

The whole system starts with the child who loves to run, jump or skate. That child enjoys physical activity and slowly begins to develop specific sport skills. As these skills improve, the child will often want to join a club to compete at the appropriate skill level.

Then as the child further develops his or her physical skills the child may be identified as having special talent. At this stage, in addition to other children with similar sport interests, coaches, trainers, judges and volunteer club members become part of the circle in which the young athlete operates.

When we look at the diagram below it becomes clear that each athlete who stands on the winners' podium has years of training and work behind him or her. There is no such thing in the 1990s as instant stardom. Each athlete works his or her way through the system—there is no overnight success story.

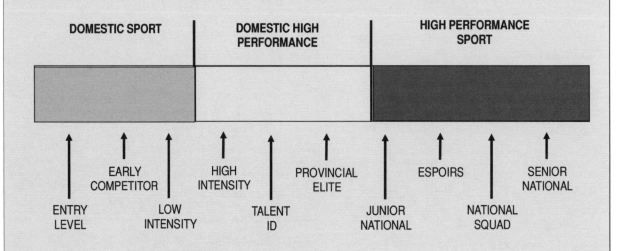

SOURCE: Committee of the Inter-Provincial Sport and Recreation Council. 1989.

will have a board of directors which will act in the financial interests of the shareholders. The board will seek to ensure that the company is efficient and well run in order to maximize productivity and profits for the shareholders. On the other hand, if the organization is a non-profit organization, in addition to ensuring a well-balanced budget, the board of directors will focus its efforts on advancing the basic aims for which the organization was established.

Volunteer organizations in Canada are based on a different premise. Volunteers are those who work in an organization without being paid. In the case of sports organizations, they participate

Athlete Assistance Program, 1985-1988

Year	Number of Athletes	A	B	C	C-1	D	J	R
1985-86	745	124	70	551				
1986-87	793	107	80	384	148	74		
1987-88	856	103	92	415	121	70	35	20

Payment Categories	1985-86	1986-87	1987-88
Living Allowance	$4,430,403	$4,481,876	$4,474,655
Tuition	310,194	338,680	270,155
Special Needs	19,922	8,165	9,079
Extended Assistance	124,200	107,532	61,942
Totals	**$4,884,719**	**$4,936,253**	**$4,815,831**

SOURCE: Canada. 1989. *Fitness and Amateur Sport Annual Report, 1987–1988*. Ottawa: Fitness and Amateur Sport. p.22.

because they love the sport, have children who participate in the sport or simply want the sport organization itself to grow. An interesting aspect of Canadian sport is that it is the volunteers who provide the foundation on which the national sports organizations are based.

As sport or any other activity develops, it becomes necessary to formalize activity. As a result, rules and regulations are codified for various sports and regulatory bodies are set up to enforce them. In the case of sport, guidelines are put in place for the required size of the area to be used, the kinds of equipment allowed, the surfaces permitted, and the involvement of fans. Sanctions exist to ensure that these guidelines are met. A well-known example of the creation of a formal sport is basketball. James Naismith, a McGill university graduate, developed a game that would allow indoor facilities to be used during winter. After the creation of this game for the Y.M.C.A., a handbook was developed and it became a formalized sport.

Good management is also essential in organizations. Regardless of who benefits, an organization must have good lines of communication, well-trained personnel and clearly outlined goals. Carol Ann Letheren, Canada's Chef de Mission at the Seoul Olympics, argues that regardless of the nature of an organization, be it voluntary or profit oriented, it must clearly outline its goals and aims in order to survive and grow. There are four steps in this organization planning process (see chart on page 198).

GROWTH IN FEDERAL EXPENDITURES ON SPORT

Expenditures of the Department of Health and Welfare (Fitness and Amateur Sport), 1961–1968

1961–62	$ 29,641
1962–63	$ 981,270
1963–64	$1,549,824
1964–65	$1,996,603
1965–66	$2,508,493
1966–67	$4,665,769
1967–68	$3,655,413

SOURCE: Charles L. Dubin 1990 *Commission of Inquiry into the Use of Drugs and Banned Practices Intended to Increase Athletic Performance.* Ottawa: Minister of Supply and Services:p.9

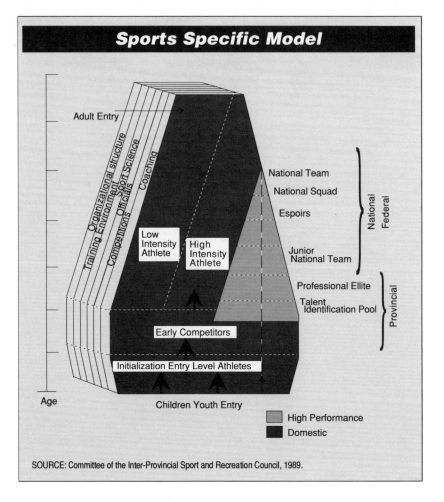

SOURCE: Committee of the Inter-Provincial Sport and Recreation Council, 1989.

1. *Information gathering.* At this stage the members of the organization must outline where their sports fits into the sport system. Who is interested in their sport? What are the characteristics of this group? What is their competition? What is the financial picture? What are the objectives to be achieved and what are the strategies to achieve them?

2. *Setting up a decision-making framework.* This involves outlining the philosophy of the organization and deciding on the criteria and method for making decisions.

3. *Evaluating the program.* The various program elements must be evaluated and it must be clear what the organization is offering—understand the environment the organization is operating within (the office, the sites of competition, all locations); outline a communications program (the advocates, the public relation personnel and the promotional

Sport Canada Funding

Sport Canada funds many different areas of sport, including:

- the National Sport and Recreation Centre which houses 64 national sports and fitness organizations in Ottawa ($4.8 million)

- the Coaching Association of Canada which operates the five-level National Coaching Certification Program (NCCP) and various training programs ($2.4 million)

- Sport Medicine Council of Canada (SMCC) which provides medical, paramedical and scientific services as do the four "provider" organizations of specialist doctors, sports scientists, therapists and physiotherapists (1.2 million and $211,000 to the provider organizations); the SMCC also helps to administer the Drug Use and Doping Control Program.

- the Athlete Information Bureau (AIB) which produces and distributes information and audio-visual material on athletes ($1.09 million)

- the Sports Information Resource Centre (SIRC) which operates a computerized documentation centre for sport, physical education, fitness and recreation ($.5 million)

- financial assistance required for costs of the Olympics, Pan American, Commonwealth and World University Games

- the Canadian Interuniversity Athletic Union (CIAU) the coordinating body for university sport and for Canadian participation in the World University Games (FISU) ($1.3 million)

- the Canadian Olympic Association ($1 million)

- the Commonwealth Games Association of Canada ($39,000)

- various other programs that deal with the health of athletes and sports research

- the Fair Play program, which was developed to encourage honesty and fairness in sport through educational programs in schools (Canada, 1989:21).

All the programs sponsored by Sports Canada are designed to encourage the development of sport skills. At the centre of the whole system are, of course, the athletes, and the Athlete Assistance Program provides financial support to athletes to allow them to focus on their training at the high performance level.

---

activities system); decide on the nature and kind of service to be offered (who are the sponsors, and what message is to be communicated); and evaluate the programs and services offered, (the technical package, the educational program and the kind of competition).

4. *Evaluating and giving direction to the management team.* (Letheren, 1989b).

By following such a program, short-term and long-term goals can be carried out efficiently and effectively.

These criteria were used by Letheren and her colleagues in planning Canada's role at the Seoul Olympics. The Canadian mission's approach included: embracing the Korean hosts; providing a home away from home for the Olympic team; administering quietly and effectively; and exposing the Canadian team to a variety of cultural experiences (Letheren, 1989). This meticulous planning, which so

Sport Canada Organization Chart

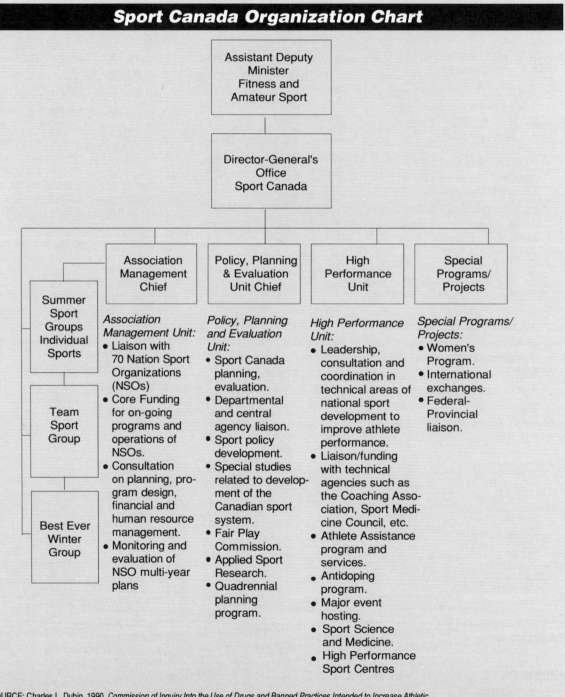

Assistant Deputy Minister Fitness and Amateur Sport

Director-General's Office Sport Canada

Association Management Chief

Policy, Planning & Evaluation Unit Chief

High Performance Unit

Special Programs/ Projects

Summer Sport Groups Individual Sports

Team Sport Group

Best Ever Winter Group

Association Management Unit:
- Liaison with 70 Nation Sport Organizations (NSOs)
- Core Funding for on-going programs and operations of NSOs.
- Consultation on planning, program design, financial and human resource management.
- Monitoring and evaluation of NSO multi-year plans

Policy, Planning and Evaluation Unit:
- Sport Canada planning, evaluation.
- Departmental and central agency liaison.
- Sport policy development.
- Special studies related to development of the Canadian sport system.
- Fair Play Commission.
- Applied Sport Research.
- Quadrennial planning program.

High Performance Unit:
- Leadership, consultation and coordination in technical areas of national sport development to improve athlete performance.
- Liaison/funding with technical agencies such as the Coaching Association, Sport Medicine Council, etc.
- Athlete Assistance program and services.
- Antidoping program.
- Major event hosting.
- Sport Science and Medicine.
- High Performance Sport Centres

Special Programs/ Projects:
- Women's Program.
- International exchanges.
- Federal-Provincial liaison.

SOURCE: Charles L. Dubin. 1990. *Commission of Inquiry Into the Use of Drugs and Banned Practices Intended to Increase Athletic Performance.* Ottawa: Minister of Supply and Services. p.26.

~ SPORT PROFILE ~

Abigail (Abby) Hoffman—Many "Firsts" in Sport

b. 1947 Toronto, Ontario. There were few opportunities for girls to play competitive ice hockey when Abby Hoffman was a child in the fifties, so she played on a boys' team. She became the centre of a great deal of publicity when it became known that the all-star hockey player "A. Hoffman" was a girl. At that time the League decided her sex alone was grounds for excluding her from the team.

Contrasting with the negative attitudes of adults around her, Hoffman did have some impressive female athletes as role models. She admired and met Fanny Rosenfeld, Canada's Woman Athlete of the Half-Century (1900–1950) and also became aware of many great Canadian women athletes on teams like the Edmonton Grads. She was able to dismiss the negative biological myths about girls,

women and sport and focus on her enjoyment and training.

Continuing from her pioneer steps as a little girl, Hoffman later fought the exclusion of women from the only indoor track at the University of Toronto. Overcoming these overtly discriminatory attitudes towards girls and women in sport, she went on to succeed at the international level competing in four Olympic Games, four Commonwealth Games and four Pan American Games, winning medals in the 800 and 1500 meters.

She then continued to have a significant impact on the structure and organization of sport itself. Abby Hoffman was the first woman ever elected to the Executive of the Canadian Olympic Association. In July 1981 she was appointed to the top

position of Director of Sport Canada, which overseas the entire Canadian sport system and distributes funds in the excess of $65 million dollars. She held that position for ten years, until October 1991.

She has been and continues to be a committed promoter of sport and an outspoken critic of South Africa's apartheid sport policies.

"In view of my belief in the provision of equal opportunity for men and women in both sport and work roles. I have had a long standing interest in exploring the history of Canadian women in sports and in debunking many of the myths that have limited their participation" (Cochrane, Hoffman, Kincaid 1977: 5).

impressed the world audience, also allowed Letheren and her staff to deal with the crisis over Ben Johnson's positive drug test. Because the priorities of the Olympic team had been well thought out, Johnson was treated with respect, the general public was properly informed, and the other Canadian team members were supported through a difficult time.

Sport Organizations in Canada

Today, sports organizations take many different forms in Canada. They range from small volunteer groups, to government sports structures, to incorporated businesses. The level of organizational complexity is staggering. To service this network, universities such as Concordia University in Montreal offer a graduate diploma in sports administration to provide a graduate level education that prepares students to work in all areas of sport administration. Community colleges across Canada also provide training in various aspects of sport services—recreational leadership, medical and technical training, etc.

Canadian Olympic Association (Carl Bigras).

Abigail (Abby) Hoffman, competitor and administrator.

THE SPORT COMMUNITY

Canada's federal sports structures interconnect with international sport organizations as well as local and provincial sport bodies.

Abbreviations

ANOC—Association of National Olympic Committees

CASM—Canadian Association of Sport Medicine

CASS—Canadian Association of Sports Scientists

CATA—Canadian Athletic Therapists Association

CCAA—Canadian College Athletic Association

CGAC—Commonwealth Games Association of Canada

CGF—Commonwealth Games Federation

CIAU—Canadian Inter-University Athletic Union

COA—Canadian Olympic Association

CPA-SPD—Sports Physiotherapist Division of the Canadian Physiotherapists Association

CIJF—Comité internationale des jeux de la francophonie

FISU—Fédération internationale du sport universitaire

GAISF—General Assembly of International Sport Federations

IOC—International Olympic Committee

PASO—Pan-American Sports Organization

In Canada, the formalization of sporting organizations began to take place at the end of the nineteenth century. Increasingly the athletes interested in a given sport established themselves as associations with management boards and regulations. These boards determined the rules and regulations of their sports, in conjunction with provincial and federal bodies.

Today, most sports associations are concerned with a single sport, such as hockey or tennis. Those involved in disabled sport are, however, presently working to form sports organizations based on the nature of a disability rather than on individual sports. This can get quite complicated due to the variety of disabilities.

Unlike in the United States, where most sports activities tend to be privately funded, in Canada there is a strong commitment to sport at the various government levels. Sport, fitness and recreational programs in the public schools are heavily supported with funds from municipal taxes, as are the parks and recreation departments. The maintenance of facilities such as arenas, playing fields, stadiums, etc. is also administered at the local level. High-performance training centres at universities are supported by provincial governments through the educational system. The federal government supports such programs as Sport Canada and the funding of the carding system for high performance athletes. At the present time there is considerable overlapping of the various areas of responsibility.

If we examine what happens within a specific sport, it is clear that there are really two groups participating—the high-intensity athletes competing on a "full-time" basis and those who compete at a low-intensity or recreational level. For high-intensity athletes, funding from the provincial and federal bodies is important. For recreational athletes the support provided by local municipalities is important—taxes provide money for parks, running tracks and bicycle paths, as well as facilities such as public swimming pools and tennis courts which might otherwise be unavailable except through private clubs.

Many children develop their love of sport through local, freely-accessible activities and facilities. Municipal parks and recreation departments spend considerable amounts of money providing sports services to the local communities. These expenditure items include the park grounds, the actual sport facilities (ie. ice rinks, swimming pools, baseball and soccer fields, etc.) as well as salaries for staff (instructors, groundskeepers and many others). Most Canadian children and adults use such facilities at some point during the year.

At the provincial and federal levels, the organization of sports overlaps and becomes quite complex. There is an inter-linking of age and skill levels within the provincially and federally funded sports systems.

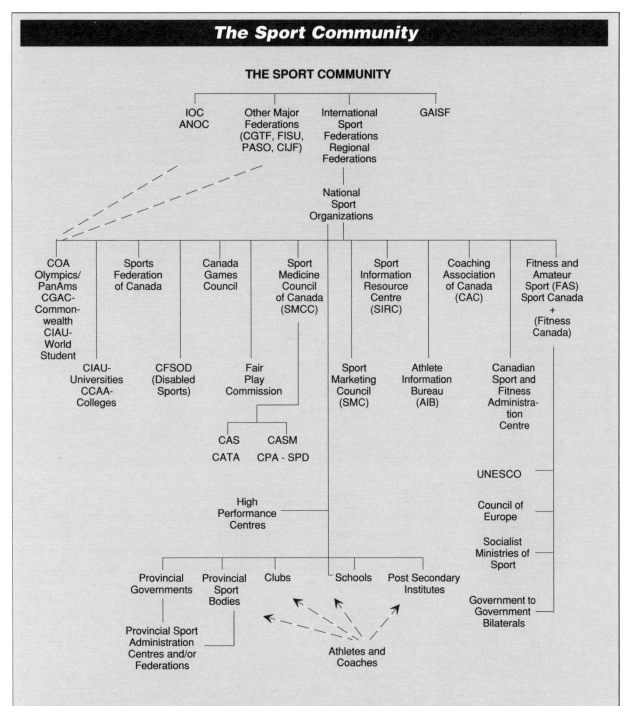

The Sport Community

SOURCE: Charles L. Dubin 1990 *Commission of Inquiry into the Use of Drugs and Banned Practices Intended to Increase Athletic Performance.* Ottawa: Minister of Supply and Services:p.18–19.

~ SPORT PROFILE ~

Sam Ramsamy—Fighter Against Apartheid in Sport

b. South Africa. Sam Ramsamy played sports in South Africa until 1972 when he was forced to leave the country. Since that time he has waged a battle against the South African government's apartheid policies.

South Africa was the only country in the world where "sports facilities (were) built specifically for the exclusive use of one particular racial group" (Ramsamy, 1982:7). Also black athletes were excluded by the "official" South African white sport organizations and until 1976 most international sport organizations accepted these "South African rules."

Knowing how important sport is to South Africa Ramsamy has spoken out, lobbied and organized to bring about an end to apartheid. He pressured the South African government and in doing so exposed

the roles of athletes, companies and sport bodies that have supported South African participation in international sport.

Canada has been one of the supporters of the South African boycott (see Bruce Kidd "The Importance of the South Africa Boycott" in Chapter 7).

Although forced into exile he has never faltered in his commitment to the struggle. Surprisingly he is not bitter. He continues to travel around the world and keeps in contact with sports people everywhere, including Canada. He speaks quietly, almost gently, about the issues of discrimination, but there is a tenacity that no one can mistake. As Chairperson of San-Roc, the South African Non-Racial Olympic Committee, he spent long hours in a

small, modest office in London, England. From there he worked to keep the world informed of what is happening with South African sport.

After an information-gathering trip to South Africa in 1991, Ramsamy supported the proposal to allow South Africa to participate in international sport *so long as specific guidelines were met on a sport-by-sport basis.* Finally, he will be able to see opportunities open up for black South African athletes and the beginning of the end of the great inequities faced in every aspect of daily life.

Ramsamy is now head of the racially integrated South African Olympic Committee and, for the first time in almost twenty years, will be able to live in his homeland.

Sam Ramsamy.

Sam Ramsamy, lobbyist for fairness in sport.

In the 1990s, it is taken for granted that we have a highly developed sports system. However this was not always the case. *The Fitness and Amateur Sport Act* was passed in 1961 "to encourage, promote and develop fitness and amateur sport," with amateur sport being defined as "any athletic activity engaged in solely for recreation, fitness or pleasure and not as a means of livelihood." This marked the first time the federal government was officially committed to the promotion and development of fitness and amateur sport (Dubin, 1990:6–7). Funding was administered by the Department of National Health and Welfare.

Initially, the aim was to encourage fitness among the general population, but gradually this focus changed. The expenditures were quite small by today's standards, even taking inflation into account. In 1961-61, $29,641 was spent; but by 1967–68 the amount had risen to $3,655,413.

Provincial Sport Programs

The Ontario Ministry of Tourism and Recreation also supports a wide range of programs in the area of sports and fitness:

Assessment— standardized fitness testing across the province

Athletic Achievement Awards—the Ontario Athlete of the Year Award, and funding for talent identification and training

"Best Ever Ontario" Program—this program aimed to encourage the best ever olympic performances at Calgary and at Seoul in 1988; to encourage a greater participation in sport and maximize economic benefits of athletic successes

Corporate Challenge— encourages increased fitness of the employees of private companies

Development— consultation and funding provided to encourage recreational and elite sport activity by providing funding to 76 provincial sport governing bodies

Elite Athletic Program—encourages and increases Ontario representation at the Commonwealth, Pan American, and Olympic Games and increases the number of Ontario athletes on the National and Federal Athlete Assistance Programs by assisting them in training and competition to achieve carded status within the

Federal Assistance Program

Programs cover the development of high performance athletes and the encouragement of fitness and recreational programs at the local and community level. The main thrust of these various programs is to support and develop sport and fitness in Ontario at the community and elite level. Awards are given for outstanding contributions and scientific testing is done on high performance athletes. The "Best Ever Program" was discontinued but did provide support to athletes prior to the 1988 summer and winter Olympics.

In 1987–1988, the combined expenditures of Fitness and Amateur Sport and Sport Canada was over $67 million dollars according to the Annual Report (Canada, 1989:35). This represents an enormous growth in thirty years.

Fitness Canada and Sport Canada

Sports programs are managed federally by the Minister of State for Fitness and Amateur Sport. The federal government's sports programs are divided into two main areas: *Fitness Canada* and *Sport Canada*.

The federal government links provincial and national sports organizations across the country. Their Federal Government Sports organizational chart outlines the relationships between the various ministries (see page 199).

In the 1990s, Fitness Canada has the same mandate as in the 1960s: "to promote, encourage and develop fitness and amateur sport in Canada" (Canada, 1989:8). However, its specific objectives have evolved through time to develop greater access to fitness and recreational programs. The objectives of Fitness Canada are:

1. To increase the motivation of Canadians to become and remain active, thereby leading toward fitness and a healthy lifestyle;

THE OLYMPIC ATHLETE CAREER CENTRE—MORE THAN JUST ATHLETES

The Olympic Athlete Career Centre provides assistance to athletes with their career development outside sport. This Canadian Olympic Association organization helped nearly 800 athletes between 1986-1991. It is headed by former athlete Sue Holloway. Canada is a pioneer in providing such a service to athletes.

The Variety of Sports Programs, Ontario

- *Employee Fitness*: encourages firms to develop employee fitness

- *FitFive Program*: promotes a more active lifestyle for Ontario residents and has an award program for individuals and families

- *Fitness Grants*: assists provincial fitness programs at the community level and coordinates the delivery of fitness training programs

- *Fitness Leadership*: standardizes the basic level of fitness leaders and provides professional development

- *Fitness Resource Services*: assists local agencies in the design and delivery of effective and appropriate fitness and physical activity programs

- *Francophone Initiative*: assists sport governing bodies in the provision of services to Franco-Ontarians

- *Grants to Sports Governing Bodies*: assists sport organizations in a variety of ways such as encouraging higher levels of competition and training to help strengthen sports programs and through including the development of volunteer support

- *Junior Olympics*: this is a ready made program to encourage a grass-roots participation program involving Olympic and Pan-American games

- *National Coaching Certification Program*

- *Community Coaching Development*

- *Ontario Sports Centre*

- *Ontario Sports Heritage Display*

- *Ontario Sport Medicine and Safety Advisory Board*

- *Participation Development*: aims to increase the participation of Ontarians in sports and fitness activities at all levels, including introducing new sport activities and expanding existing ones

- *Promotion*: encourages participation and performance

- *Regional Development*: encourages the development of regional affiliates

- *Regional Fitness Grants*: promotes regional fitness programs

- *Regional Sports Councils/Advisory Committee*: improves the coordination of delivery of sports programs to regional and community levels and assesses needs

- *Sports Awards Programs*: recognizes achievement, participation and contribution to fitness and amateur sport by individuals or groups

- *Sport Sciences and Testing*: scientific testing is provided to enhance high performance development and training

- *Sports Travelcade*: mobile resource centre which includes audio-visual materials

- *Training Institutes*: to assist in training volunteers at all levels

- *Youth and Special Populations*: promotes and encourages physical fitness programs for children and other target groups such as seniors

The Ontario Sports Centre in Toronto allows small sports organizations to operate with the support of the Ministry of Tourism and Recreation. The range of sport and fitness activities included at the Ontario Sports Centre is considerable with organizations ranging from tennis and volleyball, to hang gliding, jiu-jitsu, the rifle association and wheel chair sports.

Source: Bell, George and Andrew Pascoe, *Ontario Government: Structure and Functions*. 1988. Thompson Educational Publishing, Inc., Toronto.

A Case Study: The Mazda Optimist Club

Unlike tennis and hockey, track and field athletes cannot work professionally all year round and then enter the Olympics. There is a strict dividing line between *amateur* and *professional*. With this distinction in mind the story of the Mazda Optimists track club, of which Ben Johnson was a member, provides important insights into the world of sport today.

In the early 1980s, there were attempts to merge the Scarborough Optimists Club with a high-performance training centre at York University in Toronto. This is similar to the approach used in Eastern bloc countries to use all the skills and resources available within the university and research context in order to develop strong international competitors. In 1985, the IAAF agreed that multinational companies like Mazda could sponsor sports teams. Mazda used the International Management Group (IMG), the major sponsor of sports events in North America, as its chief sponsor (Dewar, 1990:60).

The Optimists received support from a number of sources: Sport Canada, Mazda, paid attendance and performance fees and the CTFA (which paid salaries to coaches like Charlie Francis). The Optimists Club also raised considerable sums of money through bingo, although the bingo operation has since come under investigation.

Coach Charlie Francis was also able to attract private sponsors because of Ben Johnson's enormous talent. The potential sources of money seemed overwhelming. Johnson was doing so well in international competitions perhaps few wanted to ask many questions.

In these circumstances it is easy to understand the pressures on everyone to come up with winners. The athletes themselves, the club, the sponsors, the coaches, the sport administrators and the government officials all wanted Johnson to succeed. The benefits were obvious—international standing, prestige and financial rewards.

The temptation to cut corners or take advantage of performance-enhancing drugs is very real in a situation like this.

---

2. To improve the general environment, organizational infrastructure, and program delivery system nationwide; and

3. To increase the availability and accessibility of quality programs which will make it easier for Canadians to become active and healthy (Canada, 1989:9).

Because it has limited resources, Fitness Canada tries to focus on those groups that have "been traditionally neglected or restricted in their opportunities to become active," and these are the "youth, seniors and the disabled," with particular concern for fitness in the workplace. Fitness Canada also works in conjunction with other organizations— "national, voluntary, non-profit organizations, sport governing bodies and Participaction—to provide increased opportunities for Canadians to become physically active" (ibid, 1989:10).

Sport Canada, on the other hand, provides financial support to amateur sport across the country and works closely with some 85 national sport organizations (NSOs) as well as a number of specialized agencies to encourage both high performance sport and opportunities for all Canadians.

Ben Johnson, coached by Charlie Francis at the Mazda Optimists Club.

Athlete Information Bureau (Ted Grant).

Amateurs and "Shamateurs"

The root of the problem for many sports is the question of **amateur** standing—under sport regulations, amateurs are not permitted to receive financial rewards from their performance in their sport.

How are athletes to live if they cannot receive direct salaries from sports? This is particularly important when you consider that most athletic careers are very brief. The level of competition is such that, today, it is almost impossible for an elite athlete to train part-time. Yet, everyone wants winning teams and winning athletes.

By the early 1980s, it was recognized that the long-standing amateur status of athletes had to be revised. Amateur athletes were being called *shamateur* because under-the-table payments made genuine amateur status a sham. Track and field was becoming ever more popular and event holders offered significant prize money to athletes. However, the athletes could not accept these payments or they would risk losing their amateur status.

In 1981, the International Amateur Athletics Federation (IAAF) decided that amateur athletes could earn over $250.00 (U.S) but that the money had to go to the athlete's National Sport Organization (NSO). The NSOs had to create a reserve fund to hold this money until the athlete's retirement. In 1983, the Canadian Track and Field Association (CTFA) created the Athlete Reserve Fund (ARF) to administer athletes' earnings. Athletes could receive money for "housing, training and transportation" but all endorsements and sponsorships had to pass through the NCOs (Dewar, 1990:41).

WHERE WILL THE MONEY COME FROM?

One of the central problems for sports organizations, of course, is finding sources of funding.

Skiing gets substantial support from ski manufacturers, for example, but it is much more difficult for sports which do not have links with specific sponsors. Sports like the luge or the javelin do not have a large group of participants following their sport and buying specific products.

This means that these sports have much less money to support the development of their athletes.

The goals of Sport Canada are:

1. To coordinate, promote and develop high performance sport in Canada in conjunction with recognized national sport organizations;

2. To assist in the development of domestic sport in Canada in those areas that require coordination at the national level;

3. To provide administrative and technical leadership, policy direction, consultative services and financial resources for the development and maintenance of an effective delivery system for sport at the national level; and

4. To develop federal government policies for sport (ibid, 1989:17).

Within Sport Canada, various areas of responsibility exist to provide better development of sport and to evaluate the effectiveness of funding. The Sport Canada Organization Chart presents the different areas for which the Director General of Sport Canada is responsible (see chart on page 204). These activities include cooperating with National Sport Organizations (NSOs) to plan and fund coaching, health, high performance centres and special projects such as the Women's Program and the 1994 Commonwealth Games.

There has been a significant increase in the number of athletes supported by Sport Canada. In 1987–88, 856 athletes were aided by this program for a total budget of almost $5 million dollars.

IOC Commissions

- Commission of the Internal Olympic Academy
- Eligibility Commission
- Apartheid and Olympism Commission
- Athletes Commission
- Cultural Commission
- Finance Commission
- Medical Commission
- Commission of the Olympic Movement
- Commission of New Sources of Financing
- Commission of Preparation of the XII Olympic Congress
- Commission for the Olympic Programme
    "Summer" sub-commission
    "Winter" sub-commission
- Press Commission

- IOC Radio and Television Commission
- Olympic Solidarity Commission
- Sports for All Commission
- Working Group for the Revision of the Olympic Charter
- Philatelic Working Group (stamps)
- Coordination Commission for the Olympic Games
- Study Commission for the Preparation of the Olympic Games 1996
- Study Commission for the Preparation of the Olympic Games 1998
- Council of the Olympic Order
- C.A.S. Court of Arbitration for Sport

SOURCE: Comite International Olympique. 1990. *Olympic Movement Directory 1990*. Lausanne: Comite International Olympique. pp. 36–47.

THE INTERNATIONAL OLYMPIC COMMITTEE (IOC) BOARD

PRESIDENT
Juan Antonio Samaranch

DIRECTOR GENERAL

SECRETARY GENERAL

DIRECTORS
Sports Director
Director of Olympic Solidarity
Director of Information
Director of Legal Affairs
Director of the Olympic Museum
Director of NOC Relations (National Olympic Committees)
Director of Internal Management
Marketing Director

SOURCE: Comite International Olympique. 1990. *Olympic Movement Directory 1990*. Lausanne: Comite International Olympique, p. 6.

In addition, Sport Canada and Fitness Canada administer three programs whose object is to engineer social change through sport:

- The Women's Program
- The Sport Marketing Program
- The Official Languages Program.

The *Women's Program* was established to improve the status of women in sport and physical activity, recognizing that women are not equally represented in any aspect of sport. The Women's Program reflects the government's commitment to encouraging the development of opportunities for women in all areas of fitness and sport, as outlined in the *Women and Sport* policy of Sport Canada.

The *Sport Marketing Program* encourages individual sports organisations to seek financial support from the private sector, thus easing the burden on public funds.

The Future of Sport Organization

Carol Anne Letheren sees the future changes in sport structures being focused on the relationships between and among organizations, principally government and sport. "The bureaucracy that has really grown is in government. It has become a huge structure and it should be a facilitator and a service organization to those private sector entrepreneurial organizations whose responsibility it is to govern sport."

She feels government should provide funding but not create and manage the amateur sport organizations on a day-to-day basis. She outlines how sport has evolved over the past three decades.

"In the 60s it was the decade of heavy volunteer involvement—'the kitchen table' approach in the community. After the Mexico Games, the Task Force made recommendations that provided the base for the 70s, and it was the decade of the professionalization of sport with full-time management and administration of sport with sport coming together in one centre.

"In the 1980s that structure and professional layer was never rationalized as to how the professionals and volunteers would work together—the strength was the professional side. There were too many structures, too many full-time people, and there was a take-over by the professional layer and the pulling back of the volunteer.

"The 1990s will be a decade of getting the balance back. We'll now rationalize the bureaucracies, the professional layers and the volunteer strength and power we have in this country. I think Canada was a country built on the pioneer spirit. It is a country of volunteers, we are a nation that does give ... In our office we agree to give 25–30% of our time to volunteer effort. No country can accomplish what this country has accomplished without volunteers. In Canada we have too small a population base. We don't have the economic stature that the United States has and we never will have.

"The Calgary Games are touted world wide, and the one single thing that they are touted for is the volunteer spirit. Albertville (the site of the 1992 Winter Olympics) makes reports to the IOC: in every report they make they say they are getting a lot of helpful advice from Calgary, and we are getting good volunteer spirit within our community. I think we have even contributed to the world wide effort in terms of this magical quality we possess."

Quotations from a personal interview with the author, June 1991.

The *Official Languages Program* was established in 1983 in order to encourage sport and fitness organizations to become permanently bilingual. This program was formulated to address what was felt to be under-representation of francophones in Canadian sport.

A wide variety of sport and fitness activities are covered by Fitness Canada. Along with mainstream sports such as basketball, cycling and gymnastics, a variety of organizations are included—the Canada Sports Hall of Fame, Canadian Square and Round Dance Society, Royal Life Saving Society of Canada, Federation of Silent Sport, Canadian Association for Disabled Skiing, and events such as the Arctic Games.

Provincial Responsibilities for Sport

Provincially, sport, recreation and fitness normally falls under the responsibility of the various provincial ministries of tourism and recreation. The division responsible for community programs, sports

~ SPORT PROFILE ~

Richard (Dick) Pound—A Realist about Olympic Idealism

b. 1942, St Catherines, Ontario. Dick Pound spends a great deal of time at sport banquets, committee meetings and conferences, but his interest in sport began in a small B.C. town where everybody liked to swim. Pound began winning races and ended up competing at the Olympics in 1960 and winning at the Commonwealth Games in 1962.

After finishing law school and a degree in accounting, he was invited to be secretary to the Canadian Olympic Association—a post he held from 1968 to 1977. In 1977, he became President of the COA and in 1978, after the Montreal Olympics, he became a Canadian IOC member.

When asked how he became involved in the IOC, he explains: "Because as a young IOC member I didn't have enough sense to keep my mouth shut. I kept saying we're not doing this right. We need to be better organized. Finally, in 1984 President Samaranch

said: 'You do it.' He knew I had a legal and business background to deal with the television negotiations and that I would be straight and above board. I felt that, although the IOC is not a business, it has to operate in a business-like fashion."

Dick Pound brings a great deal of enthusiasm to any discussion of the Olympic Movement. When asked if the positive drug tests at Seoul spoiled the image of the Olympics, he explains firmly: "We (the IOC) are prepared to test and disqualify. People recognize that the Olympics are only two weeks out of four years and that we can't solve all the problems. We, however, made our message clear. We are not going to accept cheating. The fastest man in the world tested positive and we didn't make an exception."

Some people find it surprising that this quiet, very Canadian man holds the number two spot in world sport. "I'm

an idealist and at the same time I have both feet on the ground. For international sport to flourish, you need support from the public and private sectors encouraging people to identify with the Olympic movement. I speak two and a half languages (English, French and Spanish) and as a Canadian I come from a country that isn't a super power. There is an Asian saying that is often quoted at international meetings 'When elephants fight, it is the mice and the rabbits that get killed.' It's been important for the Olympic movement to get the political side in perspective and President Samaranch, with his diplomatic background, has done that."

Dick Pound is certain that Samaranch and former President Brundage will be acknowledged as two of the greatest IOC presidents. There are some who are waiting with interest to see what Pound's uniquely Canadian contribution will be.

and recreation provides advice and leadership in the development of community recreation activities and facilities, and the promotion of sport and fitness, principally through its support of amateur athletic associations. The division is also normally responsible for a wide range of activities, including such things as operating training programs, publishing manuals and providing leadership to municipalities and public and private recreation organizations. It also funds local facilities and sports governing bodies and support a varied number of programs in the area of recreation.

Other provincial ministries may also be involved in various aspects of sport and recreation activities. The provincial ministry in charge of consumer affairs is responsible for the area of business practices for companies in the private sector. The Ministry of the Attorney General is responsible for any new legislation. The Ministry of Natural Resources is involved where recreational, sport and fitness activities involve natural resources such as lakes, trails and parks, etc. Across Canada,

Dick Pound.

Richard (Dick) Pound, competitive swimmer, now Vice-President of IOC.

Proposed First Nations Sport Secretariat

Alwyn Morris, the Olympic kayacking gold medalist in 1984, says: "If you have it in you to dream, you have it in you to succeed." The creation of a First Nations Sport Secretariat is part of creating winners. Many aboriginal people hope that a Sport Secretariat will be formed in the immediate future.

In 1990, a Sub-committee on Fitness and Amateur Sport, headed by Dr. John Cole, held a series of public meetings and concluded that an Aboriginal Sport Secretariat should be established "to encourage the increased active participation of Aboriginals in national and international competitions." *Toward 2000* states that the federal government invest in its sport system "because sport forms part of our national identity and is an expression of our culture and who we are" (1988: 16).

The First Peoples' special needs, in all aspects, have been overlooked through much of the last four hundred years. There is a great deal of frustration across Canada because of this. Two things in 1990 helped bring First Peoples' concerns to centre stage: (a) Elijah Harper opposed the exclusion of aboriginal peoples as one of the founding nations in the Meech Lake Constitution discussions; and (b) the blockade at Oka in the summer of 1990.

The three main areas of concern for the Aboriginal Sport Secretariat, which combine government and private sponsorship, are:

- High performance—to develop at both the national and provincial level

- Community development— educational based sport development programs; community recreational programs

- International development— indigenous networking through sport and sporting venues; aboriginal sport secretariat (Morris, 1991).

Many native people want a comprehensive program to include sport, education and health concerns. This should be structured so that native groups work directly with the government, rather than having the directions come down from the government The special needs and concerns of the native communities mean special support and organization are essential. Many native children live far away from, or do not have access to, facilities, coaching and high performance centres. Additional issues of language, communication and finances (many children live in poverty where even the purchase of skates can be a serious hurdle) inevitably reduce the opportunities for young native athletes to become winners.

Alwyn Morris sees the linking of health, recreation and sport as part of the central goals of his foundation to encourage the full development of native children in all ways. The foundation wants to help raise the high school completion rates from 20%, so the children of the future can achieve the goals they want in all fields of endeavour.

The hope is that in the future native children can participate fully in recreational and competitive sport programs at the community, provincial, national and international levels. It is exciting to imagine that one day we may also see some of the games of the first peoples included in the

provincial ministries responsible for municipal affairs are involved in sport through financial subsidies of programs at the municipal level and through its support of planning and community development. Similarly, education ministries have an indirect impact on sport, fitness and recreational activities through the sports and fitness programs of the school boards, colleges and universities.

Other ministries and provincial offices would also be involved directly or indirectly in the administration of sports and recreation throughout each province.

Bread Not Circuses—The Toronto Olympics

For many, the Olympic Games are an important event—the highest attainable peak in the athletic world, an international festival of culture and sport, an apolitical event and a time for developing community spirit. For community groups trying to stop an Olympics from coming to their city, these sentiments are myths that perpetuate a false sense of what the Olympic Games are, who really benefits and what their impact will be.

By the early 1980s, there was a virtual explosion in the number of cities bidding for the rights to host Olympic Games. In 1978, Los Angeles was the only city willing to bid for the 1984 Olympics. Three cities bid for the rights to the 1988 Summer Olympics and six bid for both the 1992 Olympics and the 1996 Summer Olympics.

There have been direct challenges to the bids by community-based groups operating as broad-based coalitions. Consider this incomplete list: Amsterdam No Olympics and No Bread, No Games 1984–85; No to Barcelona Games 1985; Seoul Fighting for Tenants 1987; No Games in Lausanne 1985; Bread Not Circuses, Toronto 1988–90; No Olympics in Nagano, Japan 1990.

In Toronto, those taking an anti-Olympic stance argue that the Olympics are part of the most rapidly expanding sector of the entertainment industry. They argue that the Olympic Games are used for the benefit of business and corporate elites and that the Olympic Games should be dismantled to work towards creating a physical culture for the benefit of all people regardless of income, gender, race, sexuality, age or ability.

Toronto's Bread Not Circuses Coalition used the theme "Stop playing games with Toronto" and opposed the bid for the Games for these reasons.

- The Coalition focused attention on issues of poverty, de-industrialization and homelessness. It raised the question of why there were resources for the Olympics and not for things like affordable housing, battered women, poverty, pollution and jobs.

- The decision-making process was not open. The Board initially only had two women members and was made up primarily of corporate directors like Trevor Eyton and Galen Weston, who were similar in interests to the IOC board of directors with their memberships in international economic, corporate, military or aristocratic structures.

- Jobs would be temporary and unskilled in nature. Some of the jobs would be security related and would create a negative police-state environment.

- The Olympics since 1984 has acted like a private advertising corporation selling the rights to the Games and the Olympics for a clear profit. The IOC made $110 m. from the sale of television rights for the Calgary Winter Games and was expected to make a minimum of $366 m. from the Toronto Games. ABC paid $309 m. for the rights to broadcast the Winter Games in Calgary and in return gathered $360 m. from advertising sales. NBC paid $400 m. for the 1988 Summer Olympics and sold $550 m. worth of advertising. Other multinationals made initial huge investments between $7 m. and $13 m. buying into the IOC TOP program for the right to become sponsors with access to 164 nations. The Coalition felt that corporations were making an enormous profit from using the Olympics as a cheap and high profile venue for advertising. The Olympics were therefore not about athletics and community spirit but a major entertainment and advertising spectacle for multinational corporations.

- The Olympics do not pay their workers—the athletes—a full wage for their activity.

- It meant that community based sport is not being supported.

The Bread Not Circuses Coalition argued that it was not against sport but against the type of sport the Olympics represent s.

Two representatives were sent to the 96th Session of the IOC in Tokyo and lobbied the IOC members directly, held forums and demonstrations and even set up a tent in the lobby of the IOC hotel to remind everyone of the homeless in Toronto.

The Coalition brought attention to several issues—what should be a city's priorities; what is the nature of sport; how has Canadian sport been organized; and are we supporting elite sport at the expense of sport-for-all and non-competitive sporting activities?

Based on material provided by Jan Borowy, November 1990. Jan Borowy was a writer and researcher for the Bread Not Circuses Coalition.

The Commonwealth Games—Commonwealth of Nations

Although the idea of a Commonwealth or Empire Games was first raised by the Reverend Astley Cooper of England in July 1881, it was not until 1928 that actual plans were made to bring them about. It was a Canadian, Bobby Robinson, who brought sport representatives of the British Empire together and so the first British Empire Games took place in Hamilton, Ontario in 1930.

It is no accident that the Games to this day are called the "Friendly Games." The organizers declared:

- "(The Games) will be designed on the Olympic model, both in general construction and its stern definition of the amateur. But the Games will be very different, free from both the excessive stimulus and babel of the international stadium. They should be merrier and less stern than the Olympics, and will substitute the stimulus of novel adventure for the pressure of international rivalry."

The aim was to "unite countries from five continents in the spirit of friendship as inspired by the ideals of goodwill, understanding and peace amongst nations." To further these aims two interesting policies were included. No sports that were purely team sports would be added and there was to be no scoring by country as the games were to be "a contest between individuals not countries." However it should be noted that women were only allowed to compete in swimming events in Hamilton. Another concern from the very beginning was that the smaller nations with fewer athletes and limited financial resources must be included as well.

In 1933 the British Empire Games Federation came into being. They were called Empire Games because Britain considered herself to be the centre of an Empire. Some issues do seem to change very slowly. In the light of the struggles over apartheid in the 1990s, it is interesting to note that one of the first decisions made by the Empire Games Federation was to move the 1934 Games from South Africa to England, because of concern about the attitude of white South Africans towards black athletes from other countries!

The changes in the organization and the name—British Empire Games—reflected the changing relationships of the former colonies to Britain. In 1952 the name was changed to the *British Empire and Commonwealth Games* reflecting the new status of many participants. Previously Britain had directed their economic and political future and now they were independent countries.

The Commonwealth Federation also had to take stands on issues that could have divided the nations. In 1958 South Africa sent an all-white team to the Games. As a consequence the Constitution was amended to read clearly: "No discrimination against any country or person shall be permitted on the grounds of race, colour, religion or politics." South Africa never again participated in the Games, and in 1960 withdrew from the Commonwealth.

In 1966 the term Empire was dropped and the Games became *The British Commonwealth Games* reflecting the end of the days of the Empire and the importance of the British connection.

In 1974 the Games were renamed again and became the *Commonwealth Games* reflecting the principle of the equality of the participants. It is quite moving to see the opening parade of the Commonwealth Games and watch the contingents pass by. Sometimes as few as two or three individuals will represent their country, and they often get the loudest cheers. The changing name of the Games themselves reflects the changing international world. However some concerns have remained over the decades. It is the countries of Australia, Britain, Canada, and New Zealand that have hosted the Games most often. This reflects the fact that the more wealthy countries have dominated the Federation.

In 1930 Hamilton, Ontario helped provide funds for athletes to travel from Australia, New Zealand and South Africa. Members of the Federation today are concerned about these same issues and finding ways to subsidize or assist the smaller countries so they have a larger say within the organization.

Source: Quoted material from the Commonwealth Games Federation, 1991.

Planning Sport and Recreation at the Local Level

Local municipalities in Canada have provided sport and recreational facilities for over a hundred years. However, the focus has changed considerably over the last decade. In the past, it was assumed that subsidies would be given to sport and recreation facilities. Today, that premise is being challenged. In Canada sport administrators are having to evaluate priorities and expenditures in order to choose new strategies and goals for the future.

Today, there is often a conflict between the pressure to be self-financing and the need for subsidies. Most facilities do not recover their costs by means of user fees in Canada. Indoor facilities recover less than half their cost of operating but charges are kept low to encourage use. (Audit Commission for Local Authorities in England and Wales. 1989:7) What this means is that many local facilities, such as swimming pools, are presently being closed because they are too expensive to operate.

Underlying all this is a conflict between the *social service objective* and the *profitability objective* in sports. The private sector runs facilities and programs in order to make a profit. The public sector has broader objectives such as health promotion, the alleviation of social deprivation and such things as urban regeneration and the creation of nature areas.

In addition, local, provincial and federal governments have to evaluate their priorities in sport, fitness and recreational programs. What should be the balance between the money spent on high performance training and the money spent on encouraging fitness and health? Should facilities be run on a user-fee basis? What is to be done about all the aging facilities around the country? Should they be upgraded to meet contemporary safety standards or bulldozed to meet the criteria of modern health and fitness facilities? Evidently, funds must be spent in a number of different areas, and decisions about the best use of money can only be made after evaluating changing needs and demographic profiles.

The International Connections

Canada's sports structures are linked directly to international sport organizations. These international organizations are based on specific sports, such as the International Badminton Federation, International Skating Federation, and so on. These organizations in turn are linked with the International Olympic Committee, usually referred to simply as the IOC. One hundred and sixty countries are part of the Olympic organization.

THE COMMONWEALTH

The Countries Affiliated with the Commonwealth Federation

- Australia
- Bahamas
- Bangladesh
- Barbados
- Belize
- Bermuda
- Botswana
- British Virgin Islands
- Brunei
- Canada
- Cayman Islands
- Cyprus
- Dominica
- Falkland Islands
- Gambia
- Ghana
- Gibralter
- Grenada
- Guernsey
- Guyana
- Hong Kong
- India
- Isle of Man
- Jamaica
- Jersey
- Kenya
- Lesotho
- Malawi
- Maldives
- Malta
- Mauritius
- Montserrat
- Namibia
- New Zealand
- Nigeria
- Norfolk Islands
- Northern Island
- Pakistan
- Papua New Guinea
- Scotland
- Seychelles
- Sierra Leone
- Singapore
- Solomon Islands
- Sri Lanka
- St. Helena
- St. Kitts
- St. Lucia
- St. Vincent
- Swaziland
- Tanzia
- Tonga
- Trinidad and Tobago
- Turks and Caicos
- Tuvalu
- Uganda
- Vanuata
- Wales
- Western Samoa
- Zambia
- Zimbabwe

Politics and the Olympics

Sport and politics have never been separate. From the beginning of the modern Olympics when Baron Pierre de Coubertin agreed to hold the Games in Athens rather than his choice, France, to the present, we find political conflicts taking place. Below is a brief outline of some of the political conflicts with the International Olympic Committee over who should participate and how the Games should be organized. The names and faces change but the conflicts continue.

- no games in 1916 because of World War I.
- the creation of a separate Women's Olympics because of their exclusion.
- the creation of the Workers Sporticades because of the exclusion of working people from the Games.
- controversy over the German Nazi government excluding Jews in the 1936 Olympics.
- no Games in 1940 and 1944 because of World War II.
- Egypt, Iraq and the Lebanon boycotted the 1956 Melbourne Games because of the British and French take-over of the Suez Canal; and the Netherlands, Spain and Switzerland boycotted the Games to protest the Soviet Union invasion of Hungary.
- In Mexico City, two American athletes were thrown out of the Games for raising the issue of racism against black people.
- In Munich in 1972 Palestinians kidnapped 11 Israeli athletes and many were killed in an airport shoot-out.
- In Montreal in 1976 33 African nations boycotted the Olympics to protest South Africa's apartheid system.
- The United States boycotted the Moscow Olympics in 1980 because of the Soviet Union's invasion of Afghanistan.
- In 1984 the Soviet Union boycotted the Los Angeles Olympics.

The dream of participating in the Olympics is the driving force in many young athlete's lives. The movement in Canada's federally supported system has been towards an increasing emphasis on competition and records at the international level. Tied in with young athletes' thoughts of the perfect run, jump, swim or dive are the television images of the medal ceremony and the sound of their country's national anthem playing. The idea of being the best in the world is exciting and motivating. The Olympics, rather than the World Championships, often represent the pinnacle of success—the recognition of the supreme achievement.

The Olympics today is an extensive organization with connections to most of the countries of the world through the National Olympic Committees (NOCs). There are also links to cities in the context of bidding or planning for upcoming winter or summer Olympics. Connections to sponsors, television and other media and political officials are also part and parcel of the Olympic Movement.

The Executive Board that makes the major decisions includes the president, former diplomat Juan Antonio Samaranch and four vice-presidents: Prince Alexandre de Merode from Belgium, Keba Mbaye, a judge with the International Court of Justice in Brussels, Zhenliang

He from China, and Richard Pound of Canada. There are six other members and an administrator (Comité International Olympique, 1990:7).

The protocol list (or ranking status) is based on the date at which the individual member joined the IOC. In 1990, there were 90 members from around the world. Many of these members have titles of nobility or are members of the armed services. They are not political figures, like members of the United Nations. There are nine directors who report to the president, director general and secretary general.

In addition to these individuals, there are twenty commissions that handle specific aspects of the Olympic organization. These involve a range of activities, including preparation, finance, athletes and the media as well as controversial issues such as apartheid.

Canada's team at the Commonwealth Games in Auckland, New Zealand, 1990.

There are also individual athletes who make special contributions to changing sport structures who may not hold positions within the sport structures themselves. Sam Ramsamy, for example, is a South African who has lived in exile in London, England, for over twenty years. He has fought on a daily basis to force international sport bodies to recognize the racist policies in South Africa. Through his efforts to encourage the boycott of South Africa in sport, pressure has been kept on the South African government. Although he was recognized as an "outsider" to the elite and privileged IOC board, he now sits as a consultant on the IOC Apartheid Commission.

The basic principles of the Olympics are inspiring and exciting. The call to excellence and achievement is one that crosses all national boundaries. Yet, it has some critics. While the IOC formally is separate from national policies, the organization is fundamentally linked to international politics. The "Cold War" and other aspects of international economic politics have had a direct bearing on the Olympics. Also, while the IOC is opposed to discrimination in sport, some feel it has not done enough to fight racism. Similarly, women are also still enormously under-represented in all aspects of the Olympics, and many feel the IOC could play a larger leadership role in this area, even though the sport structures and organizations may reflect the cultural and social values of their countries.

Finally, in the international context, it is also important to mention the Commonwealth Games which, like the Olympics, take place every four years and bring together all the member nations of the Commonwealth. They are generally known as "the friendly games" because they are small and informal. There are fewer events than in the Olympics and fewer countries participate. The "big-time" giants— the United States, the Soviet Union and Germany—do not participate.

REVIEW

Questions

1. How can different sport organizations be classified?
2. What are the goals of Sport Canada and Fitness Canada?
3. How is the IOC linked with Canadian sports organizations?

Concepts

- formal organizations
- sport specific system model
- public funding
- private funding
- shamateurism

Discussion

1. Briefly outline the major debate in Canadian sport with reference to high performance sport and fitness/recreation.
2. If you were appointed the Minister of Fitness and Amateur Sport, what would be the priorities you would set for your Ministry?
3. How could the concerns of athletes be better integrated into Canada's sport structures?
4. What are the major criticisms or concerns about the huge growth in Canadian sport? Why do some people feel athletes are lost in the bureaucratic system?
5. What are the aims and concerns of organizations like Toronto's "Bread Not Circuses"?
6. What are the origins of the Commonwealth Games?

The Olympic Stadium, Montréal.

J. Le Clair.

Eric Lindros, drafted by the Quebec Nordiques in 1991.

Chapter Ten

THE BUSINESS OF SPORT

"Anytime you dispute with management, whether you're white, black, or indifferent, you're gone."
Chuck Harmon, professional baseball player in the 1950s

"The pros become a grind, a well-paying grind—you are being paid thousands of dollars a game—but a grind nevertheless. Winning is acceptable. Losing is costing somebody money. In the pros, I found, the game is very rarely fun."
Kareem Abdul-Jabbar, basketball star

"Women's downhill skiing is downright boring when compared to more daring men's races."
Headline of a sport article in the Globe and Mail *by Al Strachan March 14, 1991*

PROFILES IN THIS CHAPTER

- Barbara Ann Scott
- Hank Aaron
- Cito Gaston
- Eric Lindros
- Donald (Donnie) Meehan

Josée Chouinard, one of Canada's leading skaters.

The root of our interest in sport is a love for the sport itself. We may play or have played the sport or have a member of the family who does. Dreams and fantasies are intermixed with the sport experience. Heroism, excitement, hope and joy are all part of the magic of sport. Some people experience these feelings through their own participation. Others experience them vicariously through other athletes. It is on this foundation that the whole of the *corporate* sport world is built.

Sport as a Business

In our society, winning in sport is about much more than just winning athletic competitions. Increasingly, the financial component of sport has become important. The difference between placing first and second in some events can mean the difference between earning millions and not.

Clearly, all sports do not reward athletes to the same degree; nevertheless, winning in any major event makes an athlete more marketable. Increased exposure means that the athlete can demand

Amateur—To Be "Pure" and Untainted by Financial Rewards

Individuals who would be considered superstars today were not able to turn their national or international standing into considerable financial gain in the past. Two examples of this are Maurice Richard in hockey and Barbara Ann Scott in ice skating. The opportunity to take their great athletic talents off the ice and into financial areas was not available to them as it would be today. Richard's financial gains were restricted to his on-ice performance. There were none of the present-day promotional opportunities. Scott had to wait until her amateur career was finished before receiving financial benefits.

In many sports the stumbling block was the IOC's definition of what constituted an amateur. Careers would be terminated if there was any hint of professionalism. Athletes had to be "pure" and untainted by financial reward. Barbara Ann Scott had to return a car given to her after her Olympic success in 1948, even though it was given to her by appreciative supporters in Ottawa, because it might have jeopardized her amateur status.

One of the best known controversies over professionalism in amateur sport concerned the American runner Jim Thorpe. His Olympic medals were taken away from him because it was said that he had taken money for playing baseball while a high school student. His medals were only restored to his name after his death.

Today, an increasing number of sports have eliminated the categories of amateur and professional.

BILLIE JEAN KING—WOMEN'S TENNIS ADVOCATE

In the 1950s and 60s, many media experts claimed no one would watch professional women's tennis, asserting that it would not sell because it was boring and no one was interested. But Billie Jean King loved tennis and was sure they were wrong.

Billie Jean King argues that professional women athletes are at a particular disadvantage. No one expects only handsome men to play sports, but people still expect all women in the public eye to be especially attractive. She explains: "We're sweating, our hair is all quickly askew, and we don't have thirty-seven takes under ideal lighting conditions to get it just right ... As a young sixteen-year-old girl she was told by one of her idols: "You'll never be good because you're ugly, Billie Jean" (King, 1982).

Today, women's tennis is a big draw, thanks largely to Billie Jean King. Billie Jean King has had the last laugh.

more in appearance fees, and companies will compete to have the individual promote their particular product or service. As the earning power of top athletes has risen, so has their role or status within society. They too have become part of the commercial and corporate world.

In an attempt to analyze the business of sport, sociologists Curry and Jiobu have developed a description of sports as a business that has four elements:

1. *Sport is business, but it is a romantic one.* On some occasions, financial decisions are secondary to other factors such as tradition. Individuals will buy sport businesses and lose money, but they hold on to the investment because they like the publicity and rewards surrounding the games or sport. In some situations the owners are not even clear what their financial situation is (Cosell, 1986).

2. *Sport is a product that is sold.* The product is competition-entertainment. The owners hope to have winning teams that provide good entertainment. If a team constantly loses, fans may lose interest and stop watching the games or buying the tickets. Sometimes other elements are stressed. In professional wrestling, the emphasis is on providing entertainment rather than on competitive sporting activity. Sometimes the structure of the sport itself creates marketing problems—tennis scoring rules, for example, were simplified to provide a better spectator sport; football

Blue Jays and Maple Leafs—A Study in Contrasts

The recent history of Toronto's baseball team, the Blue Jays, and Toronto's hockey team, the Maple Leafs, is an interesting study in contrasts.

Although they have only been in Toronto for sixteen years, the Blue Jays are a success. Ed Prevost, President of Carling O'Keefe's operation in Montreal, said "the Blue Jays have become Canada's national team and the Expo's a regional team" (McKee, 1986). Labatt Breweries obtained a monopoly over baseball promotion in Canada when it entered a five-year deal with the Montreal Expos. Exact figures were not made public but the Expos' president said that "it was more lucrative than the five-year, $31.5 million contract that had been held by Carling O'Keefe" (Kidd, 1986). Clearly, John Labatt Ltd. wanted to solidify its baseball position. Labatt's position on the Jays is clear:

"Blue outsells our other brands [of beer] two to one, but whether that's because of the Blue Jays, we don't know. However as 45% owners, there's a positive association. We benefit, no question about that" (Foster & Miller, 1985:A6).

Certainly has become a popular sport and, with their successes, the Jays have developed loyal fans. The effective promotion of the team, its availability to the press, and its win/loss record have brought about this popularity.

The recent history of the Toronto Maple Leafs is a completely different story. The Leafs have a long and respected tradition. They were Stanley Cup winners in the 1960s, but because they have not been winners for a long time many have begun to turn away from the team.

There are a number of reasons for this state of affairs with the Leafs. In addition to their win/loss record, Harold Ballard, late owner of the Maple Leafs, did not use the modern marketing techniques. There are no Leafs' tickets available in supermarkets, for example. Hockey has been promoted as a man's sport and has not attracted families in the same way as baseball. Its image of fighting and brutality has discouraged younger fans to some degree. Ballard did not have a good relationship with the press for some time. Last but not least, of course, everyone loves winners. Teams don't have to win all the time, but with the Leafs there rarely seemed to be hope.

"To have a product, sport requires an even spreading out of the competition—all teams must have the potential of becoming champions, serious contenders, or at the very least, be able to be a 'spoiler' from time to time (a spoiler is a team that prevents other teams from winning championships by beating them)" (Curry & Jiobu, 1984:143).

In spite of their success, however, the Blue Jays management does not make money directly on the team. Bob Nicholson, the club's Vice-President of finance, said that the regular season of 1985 left the team $3 million in debt. The problem for the Jays is that two-thirds of their expenses are in American dollars (York, 1985). In 1991, the team generated an estimated revenue of $88.4 million (U.S.) including $32 million (U.S.) from television and radio agreements (Evans, 1991).

On the other hand, for the moment at least, the financial stability of the Leafs seems as strong as ever. Statistics show that although the Maple Leafs seem to live at the bottom of the Norris Division, the team is profitable. In 1984, the gate-receipts showed a $2,060,654 over two years. The average seat in 83–84 was $11.72. Of the 16,182 seats, 2,251 (14%) are gold seats with the highest priced tickets in the Norris Division at $18.50. Maple Leaf Gardens stadium was filled to 99.75% capacity. Maple Leaf Gardens stock traded at around $30.00 at the end of 1982. In February 1985, it was at $47.00 (Strachan, 1985). Dedicated fans fill Maple Leaf Gardens to capacity at each game despite the fact that the owners seem not to be concerned about the lacklustre performance of the team. No doubt this will change if the poor record continues, but in the meantime there may be little financial incentive on the part of the owners to reverse the Leaf's losing record.

provides "natural" breaks for the insertion of commercials; etc. Some have argued that association football (soccer) has proved harder to market because it does not provide "natural" breaks for commercials.

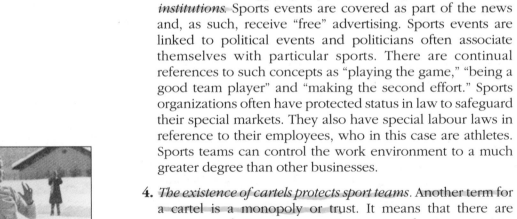

Barbara Ann Scott—Athletic Revolutionary on Ice

b. 1930, Ottawa, Ontario. Barbara Ann Scott impressed the judges and everyone else with the new style of athleticism she brought to the 1947 figure-skating world championship held in Stockholm.

She completed "three double-loop jumps in succession, (and) the perfect 6.0 marks awarded by two of the judges seemed merely a necessary confirmation of the roars of approval from 15,000 fans" (Cox, 1985: 28). It was said of her:

"Barbara Ann is executing spins, turns and jumps so far advanced they were unheard of ten years ago—even by men skaters" (ibid: 29).

In the following year (1948) she won the gold medal at the Winter Olympics in St. Moritz. Here was a skater who had an enormous impact on her sport. Canadians were certainly impressed with her skills.

Scott captured the imagination of the Canadian public. The city of Ottawa arranged to give her a car—a small

financial gain by today's standards. However, this was in violation of the Olympic regulations at that time. The head of the IOC, Avery Brundage, insisted she could not accept the car or she would lose her status as an amateur and would have to give up her gold medal. There was no choice for Barbara Ann Scott—she refused the car and kept the medal.

Barbara Ann Scott, winner of Olympic gold in figure skating, 1948.

3. *There is much support for sport in social, political and legal institutions.* Sports events are covered as part of the news and, as such, receive "free" advertising. Sports events are linked to political events and politicians often associate themselves with particular sports. There are continual references to such concepts as "playing the game," "being a good team player" and "making the second effort." Sports organizations often have protected status in law to safeguard their special markets. They also have special labour laws in reference to their employees, who in this case are athletes. Sports teams can control the work environment to a much greater degree than other businesses.

4. *The existence of cartels protects sport teams.* Another term for a cartel is a monopoly or trust. It means that there are agreements between companies to control prices, services and markets in some areas and to be independent in others. To control prices and markets artificially is against the law in other areas of the economy, since in the free market economy individuals and companies are supposed to compete in the context of an open market. However in sport the restriction of competition is entrenched in law (Curry & Jiobu, 1984).

This description is helpful in analyzing the various aspects of the business of sport today. Very few of us have ever seen balance sheets for the corporations that own our favourite teams. Many vaguely know that a brewery owns the Blue Jays but don't really care which

High Salaries in Baseball

Many suggest that high salaries will ruin the game of baseball. Dave Perkins of the *Toronto Star* argues that salaries, like Roger Clemens' $21 million dollar contract, will destroy baseball. "The ground is coming up fast, though. It can't be more than a couple of years away when the current TV deal ends and the cash faucet goes (comparatively) dry" (1991: C1). However the constant, repeated attacks on the salaries of professional athletes are not found in other areas of work. And it is important to keep in mind that athletes do *work* every day to generate the revenues they make for their corporations. Certainly, there are many executives in the United States who make sums equal to professional athletes and for much longer periods of time, without risk of injury or disability.

When we examine the rewards for athletes, there are various factors at play. The commercialization and marketing of sport as a whole (through such things as television and merchandizing) has contributed to the increased profitability of athletic performance. Athletes in turn have become increasingly assertive through the courts and their agents in pressing for better financial compensation. At the same time, they have begun to try to take advantage of their marketability by promoting various products, endorsements, etc.

THE WORLD SERIES

Reaching the world series makes a great deal of difference financially for a baseball team and the players:

"Players participating in the league championship series and the World Series share 60% of the gate receipts of the first four games of the series. The remainder will be split among the league office, the opposing club and the Blue Jays."

From the financial perspective, therefore, the Jay owners would be better off if the team lost a few games in the best-of-seven American League Championship and World Series and stretched each series to the maximum number of games ... the Jays' loss of more than $3 million could be reduced by about $2 million if the two series went the 14 games (York, 1985).

one. The focus is on the team and the players themselves. The fact that the sports teams exist to generate a profit or provide good publicity for the company seems very remote to the average fan. Nevertheless, in understanding sport, it is important to realize that, for the most part, sport today is big business and much of what happens in and around sport is determined by the business demands on sport.

Player Salaries in Professional Sport

It has become commonplace to see headlines such as "Superstar Gruber cashes in with $11 million Jays deal" (*Toronto Star,* February 13, 1991: Front page). In 1991, Kelly Gruber became the highest paid athlete in Toronto's history and the best-paid third baseman in the world with a package that guaranteed him $11 million over the next three years. He will earn an average of $3,666,667 each year. Bonuses could add up to an additional $250,000 ($50,000 for winning a regular season, playoff or World Series MVP Award; $50,000 for a Gold Glove or Silver Slugger Award; $25,000 if he places second through fifth in the MVP voting). This is a great deal of money by anyone's standards.

INCOMES OF AMERICAN ENTERTAINERS IN 1989

A number of highly-paid television, music and film entertainers follow sport closely but do not play sport professionally. In comparing their salaries, it might seem that professional athletes are underpaid relative to them.

Bill Cosby tops the list earning $60 million in 1989, while Michael J. Fox only made $10 million (Rosen, 1990: 54). Yet no one writes articles arguing that Cosby is ruining television or that Tom Selleck will destroy the film industry.

Here is a list of some of these figures, showing their favourite sport and their income in 1989.

- Bill Cosby, *Basketball*
  $60,000,000
- Sylvester Stallone, *Boxing*
  $38,000,000
- Jack Nicholson, *Basketball*
  $34,000,000
- Charles Schulz, *Hockey*
  $28,000,000
- Johnny Carson, *Tennis*
  $25,000,000
- Julio Inglesias, *Basketball*
  $22,000,000
- Bill Murray, *Baseball*
  $17,000,000
- Kenny Rogers, *Tennis*
  $13,000,000
- Michael J. Fox, *Hockey*
  $10,000,000
- Tom Selleck, *Baseball*
  $8,000,000
- Van Halen (5 members) *Tennis*
  $5,000,000

SOURCE: Craig Rosen. 1990. "Celebrities." *Inside Sports—Special Report: Sports and Salaries.* February 1990.

However, the headlines focus on the high salaries, not the low salaries. The salaries of players in the minor leagues are seldom listed at all. Articles and books that present the not-so-glamorous side of baseball get much less coverage. In *The Only TICKET Off the Island*, which is about baseball players in the Dominican Republic, Gare Joyce describes the limited options available to aspiring athletes there. He describes the differences between a talented American second-round draft choice and a Dominican player. The former will expect an $80,000 signing bonus, the latter has a much poorer bargaining position. As one scout explained:

> There's no draft, so there isn't a market value you can tag on him. A scout can offer him a couple of thousand bucks although he knows that the young Dominican has the same ability as that second-rounder in the States … The kid has to decide—sign, or wait. His family doesn't know anything about ball. And, if it's a poor family, for them two or three thousand bucks American looks like a lot of money, more money than they've ever seen at one time in their lives. The only person the kid can get advice from is the personal trainer and his commission (for the player being signed) is fixed at $300 a head (Joyce, 1990: 77).

These kinds of stories do not make the headlines. The focus of most of the articles about ball players is on the high salaries of the few at the top of the field.

One problem in discussing high-performance athletes and money is that all athletes are lumped together. A relatively unknown rower is lumped in the same category as the professional NHL player or an athlete who retires with a medal from figure skating. This is misleading. While it is true that, as a result of extensive sports coverage, they are all members of the sport entertainment system, they are not all rewarded in the same way. Perhaps the best parallel is the salary differentials between film and theatre where the remuneration actors and actresses receive varies enormously.

Many of Canada's top athletes face enormous financial difficulties in participating in their chosen sport. The glamour sports—like hockey, skiing and figure skating—get disproportionate attention and support. Athletes who compete in sports which have not been marketed so effectively, like speed skating and the biathlon, often face a difficult financial situation if they continue training. In the past, companies like Adidas would help to support athletes in return for their endorsement for the company's products. Until December 1984, Adidas paid $1,000 a month to various trust funds set up by the Canadian Track and Field Association. The athletes, Ben Johnson, Angella Taylor, Marita Payne, Molly Killingbeck, Desai Williams and Tony Williams were all members of the York Optimists Track Club

~ SPORT PROFILE ~

Hank Aaron—Broke Babe Ruth's Home Run Record

b. 1934, Mobile, Alabama. In 1952, when Hank Aaron signed with the Boston Braves, he received $350 a month, exactly the same salary he had been making while playing for the Indianapolis Clowns, the biggest attraction in the Negro Leagues. With the signing of the deal, the Clowns received $2,500 compensation immediately and $7,500 after 30 days. Aaron's signing bonus was a cardboard suitcase (Aaron, 1990: 38–39).

Twenty-two years later it was clear to everyone that Hank Aaron was going to break Ruth's record of 714 home runs. It might be expected that Aaron's only concern would be with breaking the record and maximizing its financial potential. In fact, any pleasure from the achievement was almost totally eliminated by concern about threats against himself and his family. The hate mail was hideous. The letters expressed racial hatred and anger at the breaking of the record. Some examples are as follows:

- Dear Jungle Bunny,
  You may beat Ruth's record but there will always be only one Babe. You will be just another Black f— down from the trees. Go back to the Jungles.

- Dear Brother Hank Aaron,
  I hope you join Brother Dr. Martin Luther King in that heaven he spoke of. Willie Mays was a much better player than you anyway!

- Dear Nigger,
  You're a real SKUM. You should still be in the Nigger Leagues.

The letters went on and on (Ibid: 233).

It was very hurtful to Hank Aaron that this title of obtaining the most home runs of any baseball player was not given the respect such an achievement warrants. It was as if he were being punished for his past outspokenness about racism and treated differently than if he had been white. It is especially amazing that Hank Aaron achieved this goal in spite of having played part of his career in the Negro Leagues and having faced overt discrimination. Babe Ruth did not have to overcome either of these obstacles.

Aaron says: "The people who cared most about the record were black people and, for the most part, they were not the ones who had the money to spend at the ballpark." It seemed as if this remarkable achievement did not get the same recognition because of the financial and marketing concerns of the North American market.

and received this funding. The total paid by Adidas was $175,000 a year. The athletes were to use Adidas products exclusively and in return were expected to be involved in marketing promotions. The company has since decided to drop the program:

> Our marketing research shows that over 70% of the people who buy sporting goods are not involved in sports. The market is now in leisure and active wear and these consumers do not relate to high performance athletes (Sokol, 1984).

Research for the company carried out two months before the summer Olympics found that most people knew Wayne Gretzky and Carling Bassett, but only 20% knew Alex Baumann and 4% knew Mark McKoy (Sokol, 1984).

Athletes need special allowances in order to train. Training typically takes up a good part of the day. The athlete has to get up early, take a substantial break from work during the day to train or train in the early evening. This is further complicated by Canadian weather. Added to this, it is often difficult to get permission from employers to

TABLE 10-1:

The Top Ten Earners in All Sports, 1990-91

Name	Position	Earnings
1. Buster Douglas	heavyweight boxer	$25,400,000
2. Mike Tyson	heavyweight boxer	$18,500,000
3. Ayrton Senna	formula one auto racer	$13,000,000
4. Nigel Mansell	formula one auto racer	$11,000,000
5. Alain Prost	formula one auto racer	$10,000,000
6. Evander Holyfield	heavyweight boxer	$8,000,000
7. John (Hot Rod) Williams	basketball player, Cavaliers	$5,000,000
8. Nelson Piquet	formula one auto racer	$5,000,000
9. Jim Kelly	football player, Buffalo Bills	$4,800,000
10. Jose Canseco	baseball player, Oakland Athletics	$4,700,000

These figures do not include deductions, expenses, additional incentives, personal sponsorships, or endorsement incomes. *Source*: "Sport Salaries" *Inside Sports*, April 1991:13.

Toronto Blue Jays.

Cito Gaston, major league player and manager of the Toronto Blue Jays.

leave work to participate in competitions both in Canada and abroad. Thus, many athletes find themselves in a situation where they are forced to live just at the poverty line or manage with support from others. Some athletes just give up. Other athletes decide that it is better to put time and energy into their studies which will provide definite opportunities in the future rather than put all the work and effort into the possibility of doing well in their sport, no matter how much they love the sport. The struggle is long and the support is limited. As a result, we often find that it is athletes who come from families with a higher economic standing who have the opportunity to train at the elite level.

This precarious position of most athletes has to be contrasted to the considerable amounts of money generated by television coverage of sports events like the Olympics, the Superbowl or Wimbledon. The amount of revenue professional athletes and amateurs generate for the business infrastructure they support—through ticket sales advertising, T-shirts, hot dogs, hamburgers, beer and popcorn, sport shows, news coverage, returns on facility investment, capital appreciation, franchises sold—is enormous. If we consider the earnings of these athletes in this context it seems that these athletes may be underpaid, especially when you consider that most athletes' careers are very short.

~ SPORT PROFILE ~

Cito Gaston—The Reluctant Manager

b. 1944. Cito Gaston always dreamed of playing in "the big leagues," even as a child. Yet, in the year he was born, 1944, there were no people of colour filling positions at any level in major league baseball.

In the same way that Jackie Robinson was Hank Aaron's role model, so Hank Aaron was Gaston's idol. Hank Aaron was one of the athletes who opened the way for other athletes of colour. Frank Robinson (the former Orioles Manager) has said that no one should ever have to suffer the kind of abuse he and others had to put up with while playing baseball in the South Atlantic League (the Sally League) in the 1950s. Death threats and abuse were common. None of the players at that time imagined the important positions that would be filled by black athletes within twenty years.

In the 1970s, Aaron and Gaston both played for the Atlanta Braves and Gaston says, "I was lucky enough to room with Hank." Although many black athletes have very much wanted opportunities to take front office jobs, it took Aaron three attempts to persuade Gaston to come out of retirement and return to baseball and a coaching job with the Braves.

If there is a pattern to Cito Gaston's life it could be that people want him to take jobs in baseball more than he does. In May 1989, the Blue Jays organization fired manager Jimy Williams and asked Gaston to step in. The Jays wanted him, the players wanted him, but it was Gaston who was hesitant. Initially, he agreed to

take on the job for a couple of weeks, but that time period extended to years. He was concerned about the affect of the job on his family, but the players support and the possibility of winning the World Series were persuasive factors.

Gaston believes "that anything you want to do you can do," but he never planned to be a coach or a manager. Looking back, he explains: "It was tough. I had two jobs (batting coach and manager). I had to deal with the media. But I knew the hitters. I didn't ask them to do anything they couldn't do."

To onlookers it seems there are three key factors that account for Cito Gaston's successes in a sport where few move from playing to managing.

1. Having been a player in the major leagues for ten years and having coached hitting for nine, he has obtained a broad knowledge of the game and its players.

2. He brings a respect for players not always found in professional sport. It is significant that he mentioned the importance of a "manager knowing when to give a pat on the back when things are going bad." When he was playing, some managers would not even look at him when he was having a hard time. He explained that looking away from the player does not help. He added that he thinks that "it is not necessary to scream."

3. He has a positive attitude and patience with intolerance. When questioned about racist attitudes, he clearly stated that it has not been part

of his experience in Toronto. He followed Bobby Cox (from Atlanta) whom he had played with and had been managed by, to Toronto. He is unusual among baseball people in that he does not immediately head south to the U.S.A. at the end of the baseball season. He has made his permanent home near Toronto and is married to a Canadian. He gently and firmly elaborated on the subject of those with biased attitudes by saying many of them profess to be quite religious. He smiled ironically as he asked, "Do they think that there are only people of one colour in heaven or in hell? Do they think everyone will be white or black?"

It is these characteristics of tolerance, thoroughness and commitment that led to Cito Gaston to become one of baseball's best managers. These are traits essential to success in a field that entails handling many different personalities in a public context.

The sportswriter George F. Will argues in his book *Men at Work: The Craft of Baseball* that closed systems like tenured universities, the diplomatic service, the military and baseball, encourage mediocrity. This cannot be said about baseball and Cito Gaston. When asked what has been the most special event for him he answered: "It was winning the American League East in 1985" (Wills, 1990). Perhaps part of Cito Gaston's success is that like many ballplayers he has the ability to make a difficult task look easy.

How the Purse Splits—Boxing, Tennis, Golf, Horse Racing

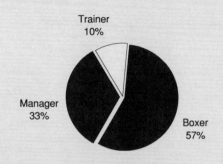

Trainer 10%
Manager 33%
Boxer 57%

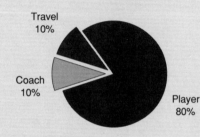

Travel 10%
Coach 10%
Player 80%

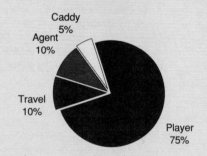

Caddy 5%
Agent 10%
Travel 10%
Player 75%

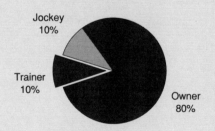

Jockey 10%
Trainer 10%
Owner 80%

Boxing

The promoter always pays the fighter's training and travel expenses. Any entourage expenses are picked up by the fighter, though many use part of their training expenses to offset the cost. If a fight is staged at a hotel, the hotel provides free rooms for the fighters.

Some notable exceptions include manager Emanuel Steward, who takes 40 percent of Thomas Hearns' purses; Angelo Dundee, who received only $175,000 from Ray Leonard's $10.8 million purse for the win over Marvelous Marvin Hagler; and now Bill Cayton, who gets 20 percent of Mike Tyson's purses (which he splits with Loraine Jacobs, widow of Tyson's co-manager, Jim Jacobs). Larry Homes and Michael Spinks, on the other hand, have been self-managed.

Tennis

Tennis coaches' pay varies widely. A well-known coach for a top player could earn $100,000 plus expenses and bonuses, while an unknown coach might make just $25,000 to keep a player in shape. Travel expenses, which include airfare, hotels and meals, are often offset by adoring jetsetters willing to pick up a top player's tab. Equipment, of course, not only is free, it is the vehicle for lucrative endorsement deals (from which an agent will generally take 25 percent).

Golf

Equipment, again, is free—at the very least. And agents generally also take 25 percent of a golfer's endorsement earnings.

Horse Racing

The jockey, in turn, has to dish out 25 percent of his earnings to his agent, plus additional fees to his valet (either a flat fee or a percentage of the purse; it's 5 percent in New York). The trainer pays his staff at his own discretion. The top five trainers in earnings in 1988 were: D. Wayne Lukas ($1,784,236), Shug McGaughey ($719,052), Jack Van Berg ($682,040), Charlie Whittingham ($619,508) and Woody Stephens ($497,135). ... and all the horses get is hay.

Source: Bill Ladson and Jeff Ryan, "How the purse gets split," *Sport,* June 1989:79

Scouting the Talent—the Dominican Republic

A central aspect of managing sport talent is finding it. Each sport has its own structure and methods of finding the athlete who will potentially help the team to achieve the championship. Key to success, particularly in team sports where there are large numbers of personnel, is information. Who are the new players? What are their strengths?

American professional teams even search other countries in order to find cheap talent. The Dominican Republic provides an interesting example of this development.

There are six teams in the Dominican League. One of them is the Blue Jays' La Romana Azucareros. The Jays' Epy Guerrero runs the baseball complex with eight instructors who also work as scouts. Most of those who stay at the complex during the week are 14–20 years old. There have been some complaints about these operations. However, teams like the Jays, the Phillies, the Dodgers, the Yankees, and the Brewers find them

useful. The financial aspect makes these programs very attractive. There is the possibility of developing talent slowly and inexpensively. As Epy Guerrero puts it:

"Money? Do you know what it costs the Yankees to operate our complex in San Cristobal (in Dominica) with eight instructors? 150,000 pesos. That's $50,000. Heck, you pay second-round draft choices that kind of money" (Gammons, 1985).

There have been increasing numbers of Latin players signed to play baseball. In fact, the numbers doubled between 1965 and 1985, although the U.S. State Department limits the total number of foreign baseball players to 500 for all 26 baseball leagues. Damasco Garcia is from Moca, in the Dominican Republic, and outlines the issue in this way:

"Almost every club has a scout looking for talent in the Dominican Republic … With the $200,000 it might take to sign a free agent from the June draft, you

can sign 20 Dominicans. From that, you can get three players as good as the free agents. Most of these guys are unemployed. If they sign it brings them a job and that supports a lot of people" (Millson, 1987:221).

Some people have severely criticized the way in which players have been signed from Latin America. They feel that it is unfair that youngsters aged fourteen and fifteen should be making choices while playing professional baseball, unable to speak English and with no opportunity to go to college to get an education.But the offers are very tempting to those living in conditions of widespread poverty.

The Latin Athletic Education Fund, set up by Donald Odermann, has tried to help Dominican athletes get an education. The reality for many in the Dominican Republic is that unemployment is widespread and any opportunity can seem advantageous.

The top ten earners across all sports are listed in Table 10-1. As might be expected, the huge prize money associated with heavyweight boxing dominates the top ten. Baseball and basketball players are also prominent in the top twenty earning positions. The top ten earners in baseball, football, hockey, basketball, boxing and Formula One Auto-racing are shown on page 242.

Strikes and Conflicts in Sport

The root causes for strikes in sport are the same as the reasons for strikes in other areas of employment. Those who work for the business feel that they want to get more for the work that they do. Today, professional athletes realize that they are part of an entertainment business that makes huge profits. Over the past few years, profes-

**AMERICA'S COOPERSTOWN BASEBALL —
AN UPSTART COMPARED WITH CANADIAN BASEBALL**

Baseball was played in Canada as early as 1838. The Canadian version was based on the English game of rounders and in its early years included an eleven member team and five bases.

In 1859 a Toronto writer explained: "Lacrosse is for younger socialites (while) baseball is just a sandlot sport, usually played by undesirables" (Filey, 1991: 12).

HOCKEY—POOREST PAID "BIG TIME" SPORT

Hockey is the poorest paid of the top four North American professional sports.

In spite of all the publicity surrounding Wayne Gretzky and his hockey talent, 1988 was the first year that Gretzky actually made it into the Top 100 earners.

Because of the domination of men in professional sport and the lack of women's professional team sport we find that there are few women listed in the Top 100 earners. Stefi Graf, the tennis player and the youngest member of the Top 100 list, was ranked 84 in the top 100 and earned $1,378,128 in 1988. Martina Navratilova was ranked 90th, earning $1,337,500 and it was her seventh year listed in the Top 100, the only woman to do this in any sport ("The Top 100" 1989:92).

EARNING A LIVELIHOOD THROUGH SPORT

The former head of Sport Canada, Abby Hoffman, puts the debate over high salaries for athletes in context when she explained: ... Of the 900 (carded) athletes we deal with and are supported by the program, this discussion is academic. We're talking fifty athletes across all sports who are in fact earning a livelihood" (Dewar, 1990).

The "Wayne" Gain

Bruce McNall bought the L.A. Kings hockey team in 1988 for $20 million. Previous owners had met with little success in making the team profitable. Canadian expatriate Jack Kent Cooke, who founded the franchise, despairingly used to say "the hundreds of thousands of one-time Canadians living in the Los Angeles area had moved there because they hated hockey" (Brunt, 1990: 79).

McNall, as the new owner, separated the hockey operation from the very successful L.A. Lakers basketball team, introduced new uniforms and decided he would buy Wayne Gretzky from Peter Pocklington and the Edmonton Oilers. Pocklington was facing the reality of an aging asset (Wayne Gretzky) with the knowledge that he owned a team which would sell tickets with or without Gretzky. Pocklington apparently refused to offer Gretzky a new eight-year, no-trade contract. McNall was prepared to offer $15 million dollars.

On August 9, 1988 the deal went through. Wayne Gretzky cried at the press conference. It was the end of an era for the Edmonton Oilers and for Gretzky. Only time will tell if the L.A. franchise will decline when Gretzky retires, but the figures certainly show what one very special super-star can do to an owner's bank balance.

"The Wayne Gain," as Stephen Brunt calls, it is as follows.

	1987–88	1988–89	1989–90
Average Attendance (capacity 16,005 seats)	11,667	14,875	15,875
Sold-out games	5	24	30*
Season's tickets	4,000	10,500	11,500
Ticket revenues/games	$108,000	$220,000	$350,000
Advertising revenues	$1 million	$2.5 million	$3 million
Television rights	$800,000	$2 million	$3 million

* estimated

Source: Stephen Brunt. 1990. "The Gretzky Effect." *Report on Business.* April: 74–80.

---

sional athletes have formed professional associations in order to put pressure on the owners to improve salaries and working conditions. Because they appear to be so highly paid, however, the press and the general public are often unsympathetic to their concerns.

What are the specific issues? They can be categorized into money, bonuses, freedom to choose place of work (free agency), and health and safety.

Most Athletes Living Below Poverty

A 1988 study on high performance athletes in Canada, completed by Ron Beamish and Jan Borowy at Queens University, throws some realistic figures into the picture. Instead of showing that athletes receive huge financial rewards for their work and skills, the study made it clear that the majority of Canadian athletes are living *below the poverty line*. The poverty line in 1987 was identified as $11,079. The maximum given to an athlete under the Athlete Assistance Program is $7800 a year. The key elements in the survey are:

- 78% of athletes are making less than $7,800 in sport related income;

- 63% of athletes earn less than $10,600 *from all sources of income combined*

- 70% of Canada's high performance athletes rely on others for financial support;

- more than half the athletes (54%) are either just balancing their total income (including the use of loans as sources of income) with their total expenses or else they are losing money; and

- financial constraint is one of the main reasons that Canadian athletes leave international sport (Beamish & Borowy, 1988: 3–4).

Beamish and Borowy argue that artists and performers have much greater protection as members of the Canadian Actors Equity as far as their work hours and time commitments are concerned. Athletes have to practice and train or they cannot compete. Canadian Actors Equity distinguishes between "performance days," "rehearsal days" and "free days." There is clear recognition for actors that the performance does not merely include the few minutes or hours of performance itself. The preparatory work is essential to performance.

BASEBALL SALARIES

Baseball salaries made a large leap in 1976. Increased profits from the growing television audiences account for this in part.

The other factor was the increasing pressure from player associations in all fields of sport. Free agency was central to this change. Twenty years ago athletes did not have agents and lawyers to represent their interests.

There is a story that Vince Lombardi was once faced with a player's lawyer who wanted to speak about his client's salary. Lombardi turned around and left the room. When he returned a few minutes later he told the lawyer "Your player has been traded." Lombardi did not want players to argue with whatever he thought was appropriate.

Alienation from work is something nearly every single working person feels at some point in his or her working life. Some employees feel it every day. What does it mean specifically for professional athletes?

1. *The athlete does not have control over sport.* Professional athletes do not control their industry, its marketing, goals, conditions or organization. An example of lack of control is the use of astro-turf—most players would prefer to play natural grass to help reduce injury. The owners of teams and stadiums prefer the astro-turf because it is cheaper to maintain.

2. *Sport becomes a means of earning a living and a job.* Sport stops being something that is fun and enjoyable and becomes a necessary performance.

~ SPORT PROFILE ~

Eric Lindros: Talent For Sale—The Battle For Control

b. 1973, London, Ontario. Eric Lindros has been described as another Wayne Gretzky. But at eighteen he was already 6'5" tall, weighed 230 pounds and identified himself as more like Marc Messier—physical and skilled.

Some described him as a lazy player, not understanding his ability to watch for opportunities and move with the openings. Many recognized his special talent and even before he began his professional career he was at the centre of the first of two battles over how his career would proceed.

Despite being forewarned that Lindros would choose an alternative, the Soo Greyhounds selected him in the 1988 OHL draft. Lindros and his parents were concerned that the required bus travel would prevent him from continuing his academic "fast track" program which would give him earlier entry into university. Unfortunately, his refusal to leave the program and move to the Soo angered the community. Lindros stuck to his guns and the Ontario Hockey League finally changed its regulations and passed the Lindros Rule so he could be traded as part of a package to the Oshawa Generals.

In the championship finals between the Oshawa Generals and the Greyhounds in May 1991, Lindros found himself facing an extremely hostile crowd. Many in the Sault felt that he had rebuffed the town by refusing to play. Signs all around the arena declared "Eric, does your Mummy know where you are?" The boos and yells were loud and security was tight. Many were concerned that

some in the crowd might lose control. Throughout all this, Lindros remained focused on the game, played well and ignored the jeers. He showed the same composure four months later in Quebec during the Canada Cup and his next major hockey battle.

The last placed team, the Quebec Nordiques, drafted Eric Lindros. He and his agent Rick Curran explain that they told the Nordiques management before, during and after the draft that he would not play in Quebec. They drafted him anyway. He refused to go and Lindros was in the middle of another struggle.

In Quebec, fans felt Lindros had thumbed his nose at French Canadians. There were many boos. There were talks of death threats. A hockey issue was turned into a national incident (some claimed at the Nordiques' instigation). Even the Canadian Prime Minister passed comment on the Lindros refusal.

Eric Lindros reiterated to the media that it was a combination of factors—"part of it is economics, part of it is the political situation and part of it is my perception of the track record of the Quebec Nordiques organization" (*Fire and Ice,* 1991). Curran's description of a franchise player illustrates how valuable a commodity Eric would be for any NHL club: "A franchise player contributes to the financial success of the club. Because of his status and charisma, combined with his on-ice performance, he can bring people in to sit in otherwise empty seats. Everyone wants to see this young

man play, and this is a revenue-producing opportunity for ownership" (Donaldson, 1991: 22).

Clearly, Lindros knows that he, like any other athlete, is selling himself when he signs a long-term contract. On several occasions he has described himself as "a piece of meat." However, despite this acknowledgement, he recognized that his skill allowed him the chance to achieve a balance in his career—to receive a fair economic return for his ability to perform on behalf of a team, while living in an environment of his choice.

Athletes in other sports change sponsors, coaches and training locales. Unfortunately for Eric Lindros, his goals conflict with the business of hockey whose rules happen to be the most restrictive of any professional sport. Observers are divided. Players wish him all the best, as they all may stand to benefit. Many fans feel players are already overpaid, but few have ever signed contracts that bind them to a city, an owner and a group of fellow employees. There is no going back and the terms of employment are one sided.

One thing is clear, Eric Lindros is making his way in hockey and his own unique contribution to the sport.

Source: Based on material provided to the author by Rick Curran, Eric Lindros's agent.

Soo Greyhounds—David and Goliath

Sault Ste. Marie is a city of 80,000 on beautiful Lake Superior in Northern Ontario. Hockey is part of the fabric of the community and the Junior-A Soo Greyhounds team is the main sport in town.

Most boys play hockey and most residents know or know of the team members who attend the local schools. Here Gretzky is just one of the many players who have passed through the system.

Sault residents care about hockey, so in June 1988 when it was clear Phil Esposito and a group of American businessmen had decided to sell the team to Compuware in Detroit, a number of Sault professional and businessmen were galvanized into action. The scenario took on the characteristics of a modern-day David (the small community of the Sault) and Goliath (American giant Compuware).

The usual OHL franchise price is approximately $400,000–450,000. Compuware was offering one million dollars to the Esposito group. Undaunted, Doctor George Shunock, a local dentist, decided he had to save the team. Four elements were essential for success: (1.) Speed—there were only 28 days to match Detroit's offer to purchase. (2.) Shunock needed individuals to invest immediately and directly. He lined up a group of ten investors who were willing to contribute $50,000 each. (3.) the "Save the Greyhounds" campaign had to obtain extensive community support and sell three-year seasons tickets at $600 each. Here Algoma Steel, the biggest employer in the Sault, set up a payroll deduction scheme to ease such an expensive outlay. (4.) The city, represented by Mayor Joe Fratesi,

agreed to guarantee a $400,000 loan. Support for this was obtained because the price of a Junior-A team is $450,000, excluding the team, and the City was to share in various money-making projects linked to the team.

Stage One was successful, and in less than four weeks the money was raised and the community saved the team—it did not move to Detroit. The next stage was to turn the team into winners. Sherry Bassin, the former manager of the Oshawa Generals, was brought in, and he in turn retained Ted Nolan as the head coach. By good management and astute trades, the team was strengthened. Nolan was able to encourage his players with the same fierce determination he had as a player.

The Greyhounds lost Eric Lindros when he refused to play for the team, but they obtained three Oshawa General players, two draft picks and $80,000 in his place. Nolan was able to develop the talent of his players and encourage the kind of tough, "get them in the corners" kind of attitude he had as a player.

May 1991 brought great excitement to the city. Many lined up in the pouring rain and stayed through the night in order to get tickets for the final game. That night the Soo Greyhounds defeated the Oshawa Generals, won the Ontario Championship and the Cup. The cheering in the Memorial Gardens in downtown Sault Ste. Marie made peoples' ears ring. The citizens and the team had shown everyone that they had made the impossible come true and that everyone in the Sault had come out a winner.

Eric Lindros

Greyhounds: Sherwood Bassin, Director of Operations; George Shunock, President.

SCOUTING THE TALENT

The search for new players is always on. Baseball teams, for example, use individual scouts or pool information through scouting bureaus. Author Hugh Alexander sums up the characteristics of good scouts:

"To be a scout, or to be a baseball person, you have to have a good memory. I wasn't blessed with much education, but I do have a great memory. You can name any player you want to, go back as far as you like, and immediately—now I'm not bragging—immediately I can see that player on the field. I can picture him at the plate, or at shortstop, or wherever. A pitcher, I'll tell you about his delivery" (Kerrane, 1985: 33).

Cito Gaston, manager of the Toronto Blue Jays, has the same ability. He and his coaching staff can discuss each individual player and his performance and each play after any completed game.

The Reserve System

The reserve system has been the cause of many complaints on the part of professional athletes. The system was created by team owners and league administrator to regulate: (1) how players are selected, traded and sold by teams; and (2) how players are legally tied to the teams holding their contracts.

Briefly, there are four purposes to the reserve system:

The draft—Players cannot choose where they want to go. The hockey player Darryl Sittler, for example, cried publicly on learning that he would have to make yet another move.

The standard contract— Every player must sign one to become part of the league—the player cannot "quit" and leave the team, but the owner can terminate the contract at any time.

The commissioner/president—The commissioner is the arbitrator if there are disputes between players and owners—this person is hired by the owners, however.

Free agency— After a contract has expired, a player cannot switch to any team during the "option" year without the permission of that player's own team. Even when the player becomes a "free agent," the purchasing team must compensate the player's team in the form of cash, other players, or future draft choices for the team's "loss" (Coakley, 1982:175).

There is a great deal of argument between the player and owners over this system. Players feel that they do not have control over their lives. Owners feel it is essential to ensure well-organized and profitable leagues and they are very worried about salaries increasing. Court cases show that there have been boycotts of free agents—it seems that teams have not picked up players from other teams if the players are free agents.

3. *The employer-employee relationship separates people from each other.* Owners, managers and coaches have pressures on them and it becomes hard for either side to see the other's point of view. Owners compete with each other to control markets and profits and athletes vie with one another for jobs.

4. *Performance takes precedence over health.* Because the emphasis is on performance and winning, concerns about being healthy, rested and recovered from injuries become secondary. Drugs can appear to offer an easy solution.

These problems lie at the root of much of the conflict between owners and athletes. Lack of control can result in resentment over the buying and selling of players between teams; the pressure to perform every time can undermine players' enjoyment of the game itself and can lead to conflict with managers and owners; and the need to win can lead to players, coaches and mangers ignoring health and safety.

Individual Vs. Team Sports

In many ways life is more difficult for individual competitors than for those who play team sports. Individual athletes have to manage their own careers, promote themselves and their sport, and cover their own expenses in ways athletes who are team members do not. Golfers, for example, appear to make large sums of money from the large purses offered at such events as Canadian Professional Golfers Association championship (purse of $125,000). However, the only other event in Canada with a purse over $100,000 is the British Columbia Open. The Canadian Professional Golfers Association wants more prize money and 72-hole games (rather than the usual 54 in Canada) to allow the development of more Canadian golfing talent and to get more tournaments recognized by international golfing associations (Shoalts, 1987).

Dan Halldorson is the president of the CPGA's Tournament Players Division. He won $83,876 (U.S.) on the U.S. Tour in 1986 and $36,118 (Canadian)

in Canada. Halldorson earned $593,894 (U.S.) in his first eight seasons, with 1985 his best year, $112,102 (U.S.). He comes close to doubling his tour earnings with play elsewhere and off-course endorsements and appearances. He signed with the International Management Group in December (1986) and notes that, "People forget our expenses. When you count everything, including a home, it costs around $75,000 a year to play the Tour now. Travel is very expensive" (McKee, 1987:B3).

The difference financially for non-team sports is, of course, the fact that all expenses related to competing have to be met by the athlete. The huge figures listed at competitions and matches are reduced by the athlete's expenses. Athletes lose a sizeable portion of their income. The way the purse is divided in boxing, tennis, golf and horse racing is shown on page 234.

NHL'S TOP SIXTEEN EARNERS, 1991-92

Below are the NHL's top sixteen annual earnings for the 1991-92 hockey season. Earnings include: base salary plus signing bonus (if any) paid out this season and deferred income (if any) allocated to this season. The dollar amounts listed below are mixed; that is, U.S. clubs pay their players in American funds and Canadian clubs, unless otherwise specified, pay their players in Canadian funds.

1. Wayne Gretzky, L.A.	3,000,000
2. Mario Lemieux, Pit.	2,338,000
3. Pat LaFontaine, Buf.	1,600,000
4. Brett Hull, StL.	1,500,000
5. Steve Yzerman, Det.	1,500,000
6. Kevin Stevens, Pit.	1,375,000
7. Denis Savard, Mtl.	1,250,000
8. Patrick Roy, Mtl.	1,200,000
John Cullen, Har.	1,200,000
10. Ray Bourque, Box.	1,196,000
11. Scott Stevens, N.J.	1,155,000
12. Chris Chelios, Chi.	1,100,000
Luc Robitaille, L.A.	1,100,000
14. Mark Messier, NYR	1,084,000
15. Paul Coffey, Pit.	1,000,000
Doug Wilson, S.J.	1,000,000

Source: The Toronto Star, October 31, 1991.

Although other aspects are important, much of the attention is naturally focused on salaries and pensions. A professional athlete is unlike employees in other fields who can expect to have increases in salary with increasing experience. With the passing of each day, athletes know they are getting nearer forced retirement. They know that they cannot beat the clock.

As the average professional athlete's career is four years, players are naturally very concerned about pensions. In the past, athletes made little money during their playing careers and could not promote themselves or products as athletes do today. As a result, many well-known athletes from the past have no pensions at all, or very small ones.

The Top Earners in Various Sports, 1990-91

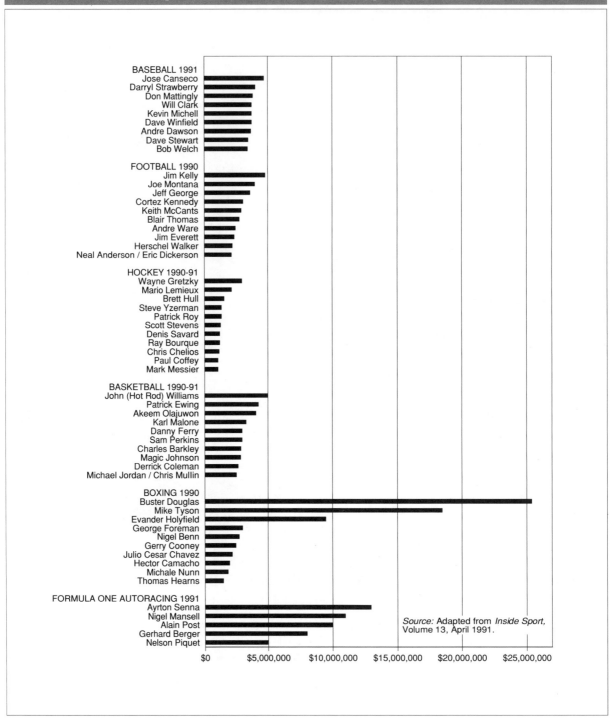

Source: Adapted from *Inside Sport*, Volume 13, April 1991.

In the baseball strike of 1985, the players wanted one-third of the owners' annual television revenue to go into a pension fund for players. The players wanted $60 million dollars out of the $1.1 billion six-year television contract. They agreed to $33 million, a $17 million annual increase over 1981. In the area of salaries, the players got a $60,000 minimum wage. In 1970, average ⸱ alaries were $29,000 but after 1976 salaries rose quickly to reach an average of $363,000 in 1985 (Quinn, 1985:30).

Health and Safety

When athletes are competing, the one thing they do not want to think about is injury. An injury at any time has the potential to end an athlete's chance of earning a living and doing the very thing he or she loves.

Unfortunately, records have not been kept to track the long-term effects of professional or high performance sport on athletes' health. While they are competing their health is of concern to everyone—the athletes, the coaches, the sport organization and the owners. After retirement there is little interest because the health of the athlete does not affect anyone else.

Ron Mix, a former NFL football player, is now a lawyer and often acts on behalf of many former players. He has uncovered some shocking statistics. He has found that:

> Veterans of the National Football League end up somewhere between 50% and 65% disabled. The most common source of this disability is a knee injury which, combined with a bad back (for instance), equals 50% disability. Approximately 20% of my clients will be rated 100% disabled. Most of them are unable to even stand or sit for a prolonged period. Total knee and hip replacements are common. Fused spines are a given; chronic searing headaches a plague (1987: 55).

In these circumstances, it is not surprising that disputes arise, sometimes involving strike action by players. These athletes were the epitome of strength and toughness. These were the men who never backed off. Ignoring the risks, they made that second effort. They are the heroes and gladiators of modern times. The reality is they are young men in pain, disabled, no longer capable of doing the athletic feats we so admired. No human body can support the punishment of professional football—each large knee that belongs to a linebacker is as fragile and delicate in its workings as the knee belonging to the smallest and most fragile looking gymnast.

THE HEALTH AND SAFETY ISSUE

In the 1990s, there has been an increase in the use of surgery for a "quick fix."

Sport is unusual in that athletes *are expected* to take potentially dangerous risks to compete and do their job. In all other areas of work, employees *do not* have to take risks that endanger their health. There are stringent health and safety regulations and committees to ensure that companies abide by safety regulations. Mostly, athletes have to take the job and the terrible conditions that may go with it.

It is important for doctors, athletes and coaches to investigate the health risks of playing professional sport. Increasingly, athletes and their representatives are collecting information on health concerns. Eventually, we may see law suits against team owners who do not act in the best interests of their players' health.

Donald (Donnie) Meehan—Important Agent for Players and the Industry

b. 1951, Montreal, Quebec. Donnie Meehan is a member of a small group of sixty people who are not very well known to the public—hockey agents.

He began working for Alan Eagleson's law firm in the 1970s in the area of corporate law, taxation and arbitration. In 1982, he opened his own legal practice specializing in providing services to professional hockey players. He chose hockey because he liked the game.

Meehan explains that not all agents are lawyers: "But I think a number of the successful agents are lawyers. When I look at my law practice today I would think perhaps my greatest strength would be the contacts and experience that I have in the industry and the people that I know, plus of course the legal presence as well."

Meehan has 75 clients who are players in the NHL (out of a total of 575) and another 50 players in other leagues. Most of these players sign a two-, three- or four-year deal. He, like other agents, charges 3% of the player's income to draw up the NHL contract and a further 3% for administering and managing the other aspects of a player's financial commitments.

Meehan works long hours. The phone rings constantly in his office and "the grind" continues at home where he takes calls through the evening. The secret to his success, he feels, is that he works hard.

Central to the career of hockey players is the contract that every player signs in the NHL and "that document embodies all the terms of the collective bargaining agreement between the NHL and the NHLPA (National Hockey League Players Association). The contract governs all players. There are very few personal services contracts in hockey—less than one percent of hockey players have them." Contracts may also be signed between NHL Clubs and personal corporations.

Agents focus on monetary considerations as well as personal and team bonuses which are included in the standard contract. Donnie Meehan includes a variety of factors in negotiating the best hockey contract: "the player's presence with the team, his success to date, his meaning to the community, his relevance to the market place (by making comparisons with another player of the same age with similar statistics and similar success to date) as we would rate the player throughout the league and draw comparisons. O bviously some of these issues would be tangible, others would not be tangible ... Salary disclosure in the NHL is part of the collective bargaining agreement—so at any given moment we have full knowledge and understanding of what everybody makes within the game."

Meehan's personal style is quietly reassuring. He could talk about clients and investment portfolios but he prefers to talk about his friendships within the industry.

"Often people don't really understand fully what we do. The contractual component of our work only takes up about 20% of our time. Athletes who come into the professional league are often eighteen and it is difficult for them to be responsible and think about a wide range of issues — including income tax, reciprocity treaties between Canada and the United States, disability insurance, etc."

"We do our best to have heart-to-heart discussions about the advisability of buying an expensive car. We feel obligated to try and ensure they are successful financially when they leave the game."

"Athletes depend on us not necessarily just for legal advice, they depend upon our judgement and friendship — that's more important in many respects than anything else. To gain their respect they have to believe in you as a professional ... but beyond that we have to gain their trust. If anything it is also more than a lawyer-client relationship. It becomes a big-brother-good-friend relationship, because we provide guidance with a lot of different issues."

"We are involved with every aspect of their professional career. But clearly the issues are different at eighteen from those of a mature player at twenty-five."

Quotations from a personal interview by the author, September 1991.

Sport is unusual in that athletes *are expected* to take potentially dangerous risks in order to compete or do their job. Ron Mix outlines these issues for professional football players powerfully.

> (They) do not have a day that is free of some degree of injury and pain; a group of men for whom the cumulative trauma and stress add up to a life expectancy that is believed to average 55 years, as compared with 70 for American men in general (1987: 55).

Unfortunately, the fact that many soccer players, football players, baseball and hockey players end up hardly able to walk is not of great interest to the general public. Any athlete who raises the issue may be dumped from their team in favour of another athlete who is barking at his or her heels for the same job.

Many health and safety risks are not immediately apparent. Who knew in the 1960s about the serious side effects of steroids? Who can imagine that the pressure on the knees may mean an inability to walk down the street ten years later. When you are young, fit and athletic it is hard to imagine being disabled and hobbling about. As with smoking a cigarette, the consequences seem so distant and the fun and pleasure so immediate. It is important that doctors, athletes and coaches thoroughly investigate the health risks of playing professional sport.

Women Athletes, Minorities and the Media

Part of maximizing your successes as an athlete lies in exposure and promotion. We know of Ben Johnson because we have seen him race on television and we have seen his picture on the front of magazines. We know about the Toronto's Blue Jays and the Leafs because they are in the press all the time. We know Madonna and her music for the same reasons. However, women are not promoted and marketed as fully and as effectively in the sports business as their male counterparts.

The Amateur Athletic Foundation of Los Angeles conducted research on women's and men's sports coverage during a six-week period on a local television station during the summer of 1989. This included the "Final Four" of the 1989 NCAA women's and men's basketball tournaments and the women's and men's singles, women's and men's doubles, and the mixed doubles of the 1989 U.S. Open tennis tournament (Wilson, 1990: 1). Although the researchers found that the coverage deliberately tried *not* to be overtly sexist, there were major differences between the coverage of women's and men's events. The research found a number of significant differences in the presentation of women and men's sport events.

GLADIATORS OR HOCKEY SLAVES

In the early days of hockey a bucket of water was kept behind the bench and "When a player was cut, he skated to the bench and had his wound sponged off. Games were rated by how red the water in the bucket became" (Cruise & Griffiths, 1991: 53).

Eddie Shore, who was born in 1902 in Fort Qu'Appelle, Saskatchewan, is a legend as a hockey player and known for his incredible toughness (or some might say today—foolish commitment to the game). It's said about him: "He bled almost every night ... Shore's bloody inventory included 978 stitches, rounded out by a fractured back, a fractured hip, a collarbone broken at least twelve times, a nose broken fourteen times and five broken jaws. The only teeth he had left were far—very far—back in his head."

Players were expected to play while injured and were not allowed to have evaluations from their own doctors. They were expected to play at all times and ignore any reservations about safety. There were no helmets and little protection as compared with today. Even the goalies did not wear masks. Their usage was not common until the mid–1960s.

CHANTAL PETITCLERC— BRONZE MEDALLIST

Chantal Petitclerc made the front page of the papers after winning the bronze medal in the 800 metre wheelchair event at the World Track and Field Championship in September 1991. But she did not have a Team Canada uniform and was not included in the Athletics Canada "Canada Proudly Presents" publicity brochure.

Petitclerc would like to be treated like the other athletes who represent her country. When interviewed she said: "It will come" (Goodspeed, 1991).

Athlete Information Bureau.

Chantal Petitclerc wants to be treated like other athletes who represent Canada.

A. *Televised Sport News*:

- Women were presented as humorous sex objects in the stands, but not as athletes.

- Men's sports received 92% of the air time; women's sports 5%; gender-neutral topics 3%.

- More attention was given to women as comical targets of the newscaster's jokes or as sexual objects, eg. women spectators in bikinis.

B. *Women's and Men's Basketball*:

- Significant differences in the quality of technical production tend to trivialize the women's games, while framing men's games as dramatic spectacles of historic significance.

- The quality of production, camera work, editing and sound in men's basketball were superior to that for women's games.

- Slow motion replays were utilized more often in men's games (18 per game versus 12.7 per game), from more than one angle and with graphics.

- Viewers of men's basketball games were more often informed of relevant statistics than in women's games (24.3 on-screen graphic statistics and 33.3 verbal statistics for a total of 57.6 per game versus 9.3 graphic on-screen statistics, 29 verbal statistics, for a total average of 38.3 statistics per game).

- The network produced openings which framed men's and women's events differently. Men's basketball contests were framed as dramatic spectacles of historic import. By contrast women's basketball contests were given the feel of neighbourhood pick-up games.

C. *Tennis and Basketball*:

- Women players constantly were "marked" verbally and visually and were verbally treated as children. Male athletes of colour shared some of this kind of treatment.

- Gender was verbally, visually and graphically marked (eg. " *Women's* National Championship") an average of nearly 60 times per game in women's basketball, and never was marked in men's games.

- Women athletes frequently were referred to as "girls" and "young ladies." Men athletes, never referred to as "boys," and usually were called "men," "young men" and "young fellas."

NHL Players Association

A number of former NHL hockey players are currently involved in a legal battle over pensions. This court case epitomizes the long history of struggle between hockey players and the owners of the NHL teams.

After years of attempts to obtain exact information as to the amount of money in the Players Pension Fund and how it was managed, former hockey greats like Gordie Howe found to their surprise that: "All-Star game proceeds are not contributed to the Pension Society. Rather, such proceeds are used to pay a portion of pension administration costs incurred by the plan sponsors *(the twenty-one NHL clubs)*... The annual All-Star games had been a tradition since 1930, and though the players *were never paid for their appearances*, they believed that a substantial portion of the proceeds from each game had been going into their pension plan since 1947" (Cruise & Griffiths, 1991 [Emphasis added]).

Hockey players each season signed the standard contract: they were paid only for six months, excluded from off-season athletic activities and were forced to participate in promotional activities for the Club and League without extra pay (ibid: 79). Incredible as it might seem today, hockey players "weren't allowed to have a copy of their contract! With permission from their general manager they could look at it, but simply requesting the opportunity branded them as troublemakers" (Ibid: 81). Also, players were not allowed to talk to other team members—it was labelled "fraternization." Typically, there was no negotiation over a contract. The general manager made an offer during training camp and the player signed (ibid: 150).

However, in spite of difficulties and fear of reprisals, there is a long history of player "uprisings," even if they are not well-known.

- 1910: the National Hockey Association crushed an attempt by the tough player, Art Ross, to create a union. The league imposed a salary ceiling of $5,000 a season for each team, and any player who did not agree would be cut (ibid: 14).

- 1925 play-offs: the Hamilton Tigers threatened a strike when their contracts specified 24 games and the season was extended to thirty without additional pay (ibid: 15).

- 1946: players met to organize a pension fund and Clarence Campbell (the new president) took it over and said any union member would not be eligible for benefits (ibid: 15).

- 1956: a National Hockey League Players Association was formed. The owners labelled the participants "traitors" and "communists." The players filed an anti-trust suit, like all the other major sports had done. The management of the Detroit Red Wings claimed the team might fold and the Detroit players withdrew from the association. With increasing pressure on individual team members, combined with claims that there was no money from the new television revenues, the association failed (ibid: 111). David Cruise and Alison Griffiths argue in their book *Net Worth* that the owners ended up not

benefiting from the huge potential of television revenues (like basketball, baseball and football) partially because they could not stand the thought of the increased independence of the players if a similar "star system" was created (ibid: 118).

- 1966: the NHL granted six franchises — Los Angeles, San Francisco, Minneapolis-Saint Paul, Pittsburgh and St. Louis.

- 1967: second NHLPA formed. The Young Lions of the Toronto Maple Leafs, some of the most talented hockey players ever (Billy Harris, Carl Brewer, Bob Braun and Bob Fulford) decided to try to improve their situation, spurred on by the hateful practices of Punch Imlach. For these efforts they were eventually traded and some feel that the Leafs never recovered from these decisions.

- 1971: World Hockey Association formed and the American Department of Justice began an investigation into hockey to see if the sport was in violation of the Sherman Anti-Trust Act (ibid: 270).

- 1974: a settlement was reached between the NHL and the WHA so the reserve clause system, which previously tied players to one team for life was dismantled, in favour of an option clause at the end of the player's contract.

- 1981: a boycott was threatened to obtain a share of the money from the oldtimers benefit (ibid: 20).

- 1990: former players initiate a law suit over the pension fund.

MARQUEE PLAYERS AS "MEAL TICKETS"—"ROCKET" ISMAIL

In September 1991, "Rocket" Ismail of the Toronto Argonauts received a concussion while playing against Dan Wicklum of the Calgary Stampeders. Afterwards a memo was sent to all CFL teams with instructions to be "careful" with high-price league talent.

"Many marquee players in this league have been lost to injury due to unnecessary actions and we can ill afford for this to happen" (*Battlecry*, 1991).

Wayne Gretzky put it even more bluntly. "Fans in the CFL are paying good money to see the Rocket play and the players should realize he's a meal ticket ... Guys like (Wicklum) better wake up" (Hunter, 1991).

Canadian women runners at Seoul Olympics in 1988.

- In the tennis commentary, women athletes were called by only their first names 52.7% of the time, while men were referred to by only their first names 7.8% of the time.

- In basketball, first name only descriptions by commentators were patterned along lines of race as well as gender. Women 31 times, men 19 times and all of the nineteen referred to men of colour. First names only were never used while discussing white, male basketball players.

- Martial metaphors and power descriptors, comments on strength and weakness were also unequal (Wilson, 1990).

These differences are important issues to address if the view of women's sport is to change. If women are demeaned, if events are not taken seriously by the media, it is unlikely the participants in the events, no matter how talented, will find sponsors and convert athletic skills into financial reward. To market women athletes effectively it is necessary to present women's athletic events very differently. It would be hard to imagine, for example, men's college basketball without the grand music, the impressive statistics and the serious reverence for the event. Should it be otherwise for women's events?

Images of women vary in sport. There is the image of the tough, strong, competitive athlete who is viewed as masculine and defeminized. There is also the delicate, petite athlete who is expected to compete in sports that stress delicacy and grace. These stereotypes put women athletes at one end or the other. Football teams have players of all sizes and shapes. Linemen may weigh 300 pounds and have huge wrist, arm and waist measurements, while receivers may be 150 pounds lighter and six inches shorter. Boxers compete in a multitude of categories and all these images of men are viewed as "normal." The same should be expected for women. This image of slim and pretty women is promoted further in advertisements for men's sporting products. A pretty girl and a muscular trim body are lumped together to help sell any product—from running shoes to windsurfing boards. They are also to be seen at any sports show and in swim-suit magazines each spring. Our society is in transition in its ideals as to what images of women are acceptable. No doubt, present-day images will go the way of the spittoon and cigarette ads.

The same applies for visible minorities. In the past visible minorities did not have the opportunity to market themselves, either because they were excluded or they did not have control over their careers. Muhammad Ali, for example, in the early part of his career, as Cassius Clay, was owned by nine white businessmen and received a very small percentage of the prize money he made.

Disabled athletes are increasingly frustrated about their lack of recognition. Events are rarely covered well in the media and there are at present no prime-time disabled sports events. Few able fans even stop to evaluate the challenge of getting from house-to-car-to-workplace while disabled. If these basics are only slowly being recognized, it is not surprising that the triumphs resulting from the dedicated training of disabled athletes often pass unnoticed.

Sport, as a business activity, would be more attractive if the undercurrent of racial and sexual discrimination were not present. It is the responsibility of owners and managers to ensure that all athletes are treated as equals in terms of access, the position they play and the rewards they receive.

THE HIGHEST PAID PLAYER OF ALL TIME

In 1920, Frank Frederickson was an amateur hockey player in the Canadian air force who made extra money by playing the violin. The last piece of music he played as a professional musician was the hit tune of the day "Ain't we got fun" and a few minutes later he signed a contract and turned pro with the Victoria Cougars, of the Pacific Coast Hockey League. The next day he resigned from the air force and prepared to move to Victoria. His signing contract was for $2,500 a season.

In those days many men had incomes of only a few hundred dollars for themselves and their families. By the time Victoria won the Stanley Cup in 1925, Frederickson was *the highest-paid player in the league* with the huge salary of $4,000 a season (Kearney, 1985: 53).

REVIEW

Questions

1. What comparisons can be made between the working lives of athletes and those of actors and entertainers?
2. Why is disability a concern for high-performance and professional athletes, when they appear to be fit and healthy?
3. In what way is the media coverage of women's and men's sports different?
4. What are some of the causes of strikes in professional sport?
5. Why do baseball franchises operate farm teams in places like the Dominican Republic?

Concepts

- cartels
- strike
- average salaries
- reserve system
- health and safety issues
- alienation
- marketing

Discussion

1. Describe the key business aspects of professional sport?
2. Explain why marketing is central to how sport is defined?
3. Discuss the causes of the frequent strikes and conflicts in sport?
4. What kinds of changes are needed to improve the way women and minorities athletes are presented in the media?

Susan Nattrass, Canada's consistent medal winner in trap-shooting.

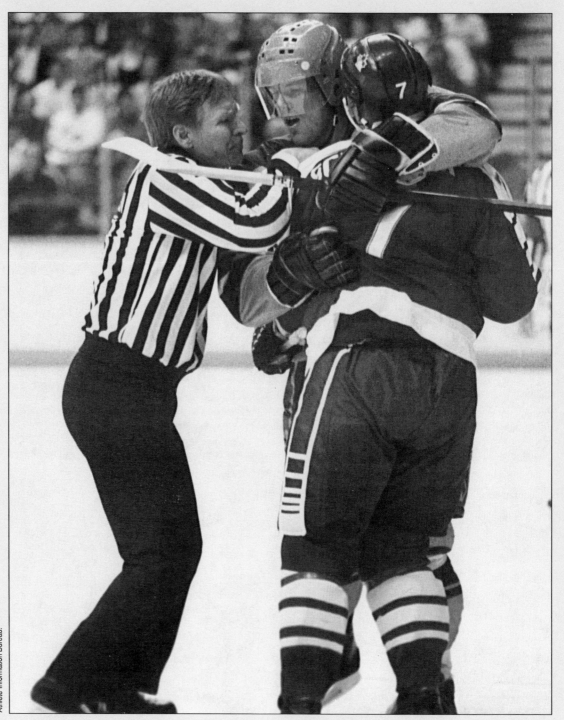

Unfortunately, violence has become a part of
North American hockey.

Chapter Eleven

VIOLENCE AND AGGRESSION

"Violence is the name of the game. Half the time I was just trying to hold my own. And no matter how hard I tried, I could never find a nonviolent way to hit a guy."
Conrad Dobler, NFL lineman

"The structure of sport ... actually promotes deviance."
D. S. Eitzen, sport sociologist

"I like playing football because I like to hit people without going to jail. It's a lot of fun. I do like hitting people and the game itself. It's more competitive and more team oriented. I like to be around people."
Toronto Argonauts football player

Conrad Dobler entitled his autobiography *They Call me Dirty.* He was labelled a dirty player and was known for his acts of intimidation in football.

There's just no room for politeness during a war ... There were about two seconds left in the 1974 season finale between the Giants and Cardinals, and all along the line of scrimmage, New York players began offering congratulatory handshakes for our 26–14 victory. When Pietrzak (of the New York Giants' team) reached across to shake my hand, I punched him in the throat. He was totally stunned. Then, when the gun went off, I stuck out my hand and said, "Thanks." The game was officially over at that point. With two seconds left, the war was still in progress" (Dobler, 1989:24). (parenthesis added)

Dobler argues he was paid to be the meanest, toughest lineman and to dominate his opponents by any physical or psychological method in order to bring about a win.

The press and various sectors of the sport industry often complain about the current level of violence in sport. The players are criticized for not upholding "proper" sporting values and bringing discredit upon the sport itself. In some sports the fans are criticized as well, as in the case of British soccer.

Athlete Information Bureau (Ted Grant).

For the fun or it—Tae Kwando, popular martial art.

WHO IS A DEVIANT?

Deviant behaviour is behaviour that goes against the normative behaviour of a particular society or of a particular sub-group within a society. In the context of sport, definitions of normality vary. In comparing a sport such as tennis with international rugby or NFL football, we can see that the appropriateness of physical contact is extremely varied.

For example, a hockey player who hooks or spears another player may receive a penalty, which simply means time off the ice. A hockey player who pounds another player to the ice and hospitalizes him may find himself in court facing an assault charge. There is a code of behaviour for hockey players and a style of fighting which is understood by the players.

However, a fight that leads to bruising is different from a fight that leads to death. Deliberate behaviour leading to death is an example of an individual violating a salient norm.

All societies have rules about expected social behaviour. There are also punishments for what is labelled inappropriate or deviant behaviour.

Definitions of Aggression

In most walks of life, people are usually clear when they use the term "aggression." An "aggressive" salesperson is one who goes after the customer, does not take a "no" easily and tries many different methods to make a sale. It is usually meant as a complimentary term and suggests that the person is a "go-getter." There is certainly no hint of the salesperson pressing the customer up against the wall, intimidating in a physical way or harassing the client verbally.

When we turn to sport, however, the dividing line between aggressive play and violent play is not clear cut. The court cases that have taken place over the issue of aggression in sport have involved violent action where the intent was to hurt and the action was not part of the hustle and tussle of aggressive play. **Violence in sport**, then, refers to aggressive behaviour designed to injure others.

There are a number of different theories about the nature and root causes of human aggression. The two main schools of thought are the "biological" and the "social (or cultural)."

Some researchers see violence as being innate to the human species. Many look to animals to make comparisons and conclude that humans are predetermined to be aggressive in the sense that they will inevitably have conflict and come to blows. Konrad Lorenz, the author of *On Aggression*, defined aggression as the fighting instinct in beast and men which is directed against members of the same species (Lorenz, 1969:ix). Lorenz argues that from observing animals it is clear that:

> intra-specific aggression assists the preservation of the animal species. The environment is divided between the members of the species in such a way that, within the potentialities offered, everyone can exist … The community is so organized that *a few wise males, the "senate,"* acquire the authority essential for making and carrying out decisions for the good of the community (Lorenz, 1969:38) (Emphasis added).

Lorenz then jumps from animals to humans. In making comparisons between species, it is possible to use animal behaviour to justify any particular position. One could equally, for example, argue that because female lions bring down the kill it is therefore "normal" for men to be kept by women! The underlying assumption is that violence is an inevitable aspect of animal *and* human behaviour.

Most social scientists, on the other hand, argue that it is necessary to look at the social factors that encourage violence in sports. Such factors include: expectations about winning, expectations about violence itself by players, coaches and the media, fans and sports organizations; and expectations about the role that athletes play. For

Penalty Minutes Tell the Tale

Penalty minutes, taken as a guide to violent behaviour, clearly indicates what is happening in hockey. *Penalty minutes have increased 92% in ten years.* In the 1977–78 season, the number of penalty minutes per game were 27.5. In the 1987–88 season, there were 52.8 penalty minutes per game (Swift, 1988:59).

There are a combination of factors which have affected the nature and extent of hockey penalties.

* *The expansion of the National Hockey League from six teams.*

The creation of a much larger organization meant it was essential to include many more players with the very special skills necessary to play hockey. It is easier to find athletes who can fulfil aggressive roles than match the talent of athletes like Wayne Gretzky or Bobby Orr.

* *The marketing pressures of a broader based hockey system.* The introduction of hockey into markets where the intricacies and

skills of hockey were unfamiliar and unknown changed the game itself.

* *Intimidation works in the short term.* If players are concerned about their safety and gratuitous violence, concentration falls off. Players such as Schultz and Semenko emphasize that their tactics are designed to reduce the effectiveness of the opposing team.

those who hold this approach, violence in sports is shaped and determined by social values and it is not a residual animal instinct that is inherent in humans. For this reason, they argue it can be eliminated from sport and society.

Hockey Violence

Although football players tackle and attempt to bring down the other player by using force, "recognized" fights are discouraged. Ice hockey, on the other hand, is quite different. Intimidation, both by means of "good body checks" and fist-fights, is an expected and integral part of the game.

The sports writer E.M. Swift has described hockey violence, as distinct from competitive play, in this way:

> Your kid is likely to see a potentially crippling cross-check to the back of an unsuspecting player. Or a savage elbow to the bridge of the nose. Or a carefully placed butt-end of the stick to the jaw. Maybe even a broken neck.

> ... It will be grotesque, unsportsmanlike and unrepentingly vicious. And it will probably be on display at the next game you attend, and the next, and the next, because the owners, the officials, the managers, the coaches and the players themselves confuse violence with toughness and will not put an end to the mayhem in their sport (Swift, 1988:56).

AN INTIMIIDATING HIT!

In a highly publicised football incident, Jack Tatum gave Darryl Stingley a hit which has left him paralysed to this day.

He said about the incident:

I"t was one of those pass plays where I could not possibly have intercepted, so because of what the owners expect of me when they give me my pay cheque I automatically reacted to the situation by going for an intimidating hit" (Cited in Coakley, 1982:73).

HIGH COST OF INSURANCE

As a consequence of the number of injuries, Alan Eagleson, the former head of the NHL Players' Association, had concerns about disability coverage.

Before 1986, every player in the league was eligible for $175,000 if he suffered a career-ending injury. The best deal Eagleson could make when he negotiated the (1988) contract was disability coverage of $150,000 for players 22–26 years old who had played at least 70 NHL games; $120,000 for 27 year-olds; $90,000 for $28 year-olds; $60,000 for 29 year-olds; and $30,000 for players 30 and over. The premiums, of course, have increased (Swift, 1988:58).

Lloyd's of London, the NHL insurance company, is concerned about the violence even if the NHL management is not.

Violent Hockey Incidents, 1988

October 23	Edmonton's Mark Messier extracted four teeth from Vancouver's Rich Sutter, with the blade of his stick.
October 27	Philadelphia Flyer right wing Rich Tocchet used his thumb to gouge the left eye of rookie defenseman, Dean Chynoweth.
October 29	New York Ranger defenseman, James Patrick, crosschecked Flyers', Ron Sutter, in the face, breaking his jaw and giving him a concussion.
October 30	Ranger defenseman, David Shaw, hit Pittsburgh's Mario Lemieux in the chest with his stick.

SOURCE: E.M. Swift. 1988. "Blood and Ice." *Sports Illustrated.* December 5:58.

A review of incidents shows that there have been changes in the numbers of incidents of hockey violence. According to Brian O'Neill, the NHL official in charge of disciplinary actions, there were significant increases in the year of 1988. All of these incidents and numerous others caused serious physical injuries to players—they were not merely roughness as a result of tough play. After some of these incidents, a player was suspended. Highly-regarded hockey star Mark Messier, for example, has been suspended three times in five years (Swift, 1988:58).

Hockey player Dino Ciccarelli, who played with the Minnesota North Stars, was the first NHL player to go to jail for an assault that took place on the ice. Ciccarelli was convicted of assaulting Luke Richardson of the Maple Leafs in Toronto. He hit Richardson over the head with his stick and punched him in the face during a game. He was given a $1,000 fine and one day in jail, although he in fact actually spent less than two hours in jail (Zgoda, 1988:3).

The NHL officials have tended to view hockey fights (or assaults) as part of the game. The attitude of the North Star President Lou Nanne is typical of many NHL officials who view the courts as interfering: "He [Ciccarelli] already served a 10-game suspension. That cost him over $25,000" (Murphy, 1988:34). NHL President John Zeigler said that the league's punishments have been more severe than the court's because a ten-game suspension without pay is the equivalent of a $40,000 (U.S.) fine (Hale, 1988:3).

Violence In Basketball

NBA basketball has also had its share of fights. Basketball used to be referred to as a non-contact sport, but this has changed in recent years.

David Stern, the NBA Commissioner argued for the reintroduction of three officials on the basketball court because of the fighting. There used to be three officials in the 1978–79 season but the program was dropped because of expense (McCallum, 1988:73). Adding the additional fifteen officials would cost $1,500,000 (McCallum, 1988:76).

The NBA has begun to impose heavier fines and more suspensions for violent acts. In 1987 only one player, Boston's Robert Parish, was suspended, whereas in 1988 many more incidents were punished (McCallum, 1988:74). Fines. of course, can easily be paid—it is the suspensions that concerns coaches because they weaken the team and fans don't not want to miss out on seeing their favourite players.

Some players even see the courts as interfering. Tiger Williams, a former NHL player also charged with assault in 1976 (but acquitted), sees the issue very simply: "You consent to assault when you lace up your skates" (Hale, 1988:3). And he says this as a former enforcer.

Expectations about Violence in Sport

Dave Schultz, who played hockey with the Philadelphia Flyers, is probably one of the best known hockey "enforcers." The videotapes of his fights are still popular. He describes a fight with Brad Park in a semi-final game with the New York Rangers in his book entitled *The Hammer: Confessions of a Hockey Enforcer.* Schultz did not like Park, but the key factor in his attacking Park was related to the need to win.

> In the sixth game I caught up with him. I ran him in the corner and got a piece of him. As the play turned up the ice, I checked him again and knocked him down. Then I stood over his body. I was worked up. I wanted more of Park. I worked myself free of a linesman and, while the other linesman held Park down, I belted him four good ones in the stomach before the officials pushed me to a neutral corner. This fight had a bit of a personal grudge to it, and lots of blind rage, *but I also knew that to take Park off with me to the penalty box would be a good trade for the Flyers*. And I had the incentive—if we beat the Rangers we would get five thousand dollars apiece and move into the finals (Schultz, 1983:6) (emphasis added).

Here Schultz traded off the time with Park in the penalty box against the risks. These strategies paid off. Using Schultz in this way the Flyers did better than anyone had thought they could. The intimidation and the fights worked. They also sold tickets.

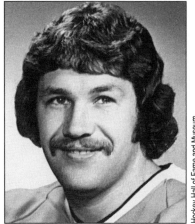

Dave Schultz, a hockey "enforcer" now questions the widespread hockey violence.

Hockey Hall of Fame and Museum.

CHAMPIONS TOGETHER— HORSE AND RIDER

Ian Millar of Perth, Ontario, on his fifteen-year-old gelding, Big Ben, won the Du Maurier Ltd. International Grand Prix (the richest show-jumping event in the world) in 1987 and again in 1991. In riding it is the magical mix of rider and horse that wins competitions.

Big Ben has won $1.4 million during his career, which to the surprise of everyone he even continued after abdominal surgery. Millar explains: "I want to make sure everyone knows who the true champion is. It's this magnificent horse. He's one of the best show jumpers that ever lived. I can't tell you how lucky and blessed I feel to have been able to escort this horse around courses" (Smith, 1991: C6).

Dave Semenko, who played hockey with the Edmonton Oilers for eight years on the same line as Wayne Gretzky, becomes annoyed when people label him Gretzky's bodyguard. "I wasn't anybody's personal bodyguard. I was a member of the Edmonton Oilers hockey club. And if anybody on my team needed help, I was there to help them" (Semenko, 1989:71). He saw himself as a team player. As far as Gretzky was concerned, Semenko says:

> And there's one of the big secrets to the successful life of number 99. You can't hit him. He's got built in radar. In the early days, there were all sorts of guys around who wouldn't have hesitated if they got the chance to take his head off, but they never got the chance. People couldn't cheap-shot Gretz because he never lost track of where everybody else was out there. ... Aside from that one shot (from Bill McCreary), I never saw Gretz get levelled in nine seasons (Semenko, 1989:73).

Semenko learned that his contribution was not specifically scoring goals but in other ways.

> There were nights when it seemed that if I fought, we won the hockey game. It seemed to shift the momentum of the game. I always wanted to think I could shift it another way, say by scoring the winning goal. But when a team's down and the game's really dead, a couple of big hits or a guy winning a fight can really fire a team up (Semenko, 1989:23).

Players know they are expected to do whatever is necessary to win. Although Schultz as a young athlete had not been a fighter, in the NHL he found that:

> The more I fought, the more I felt the need to fight some more. The pressure was real. I only got compliments when I fought. I became more obsessed with fighting than I did with scoring goals (which I had done pretty well in the minors and amateur hockey), and I became known as the Hammer (Schultz, 1983:9).

Even the fans sometimes criticize "soft" players who do not live up to the rough and tough image. Some hockey players from Sweden, for example, have been called "chicken Swede" or "cream puffs" (Smith, 1983:39). The media play a role in condoning violence as well:

> Some fans in North America are so devoted to the idea of hockey as a rough sport that it is easy for them to be misled, particularly by the press. Hockey reporters in North America are always concentrating on concepts such as courage, when 99% of the time it is not the moral quality of courage that is at issue but only the physical fact of tolerance to pain. Am I exhibiting any special kind of courage if they knock me unconscious to the ice and carry me off on a stretcher and later I return to the game. No, I am a hockey player ... Courage has nothing to do with it (Smith, 1983:39).

A Particularly Bad Example

Under the coach Bill McCartney the Colorado football team went from seven wins in three seasons to three Bowl appearances in four seasons. He has a winning team. However, many of his players did not have halos above their heads.

An incomplete list of the incidents in which his players were involved included:

Between February 1986 and 1989 over 24 players were arrested for such offences as trespassing and rape.

Miles Kusayanagi (1984–85) is awaiting trial on rape and kidnapping charges.

Chris Symington (1985-87) pleaded guilty to menacing and was thrown off the team in 1986 for drunk driving.

Anthony Weatherspoon (1986–88) was charged with second-degree criminal trespass and kicked off the team for a positive drug test in 1988.

Sam Sutherland (1986–87 & 89) received a six-month deferred sentence and agreed to undergo anger-control therapy after pleading no contest to a charge of assaulting his former girlfriend. A second charge of assault was dropped by another woman. He was suspended for the 1988 season.

JoJo Collins (1988) pleaded guilty to brawling after he assaulted an Air Force cadet.

J.J. Flannigan was arrested for threatening to kill a passerby, but charges were dropped. Then he was arrested for assaulting a woman and pleaded no contest to a 3rd degree assault charge.

Marcus Reliford was charged with rape and burglary (Reilly, 1989:32–34).

In the hope of avoiding more of these incidents, since March 1989 all players have been required to attend a one and a half hour date-rape seminar (Reilly, 1989:34).

Sexual Assault and Athletes

There has also been considerable concern about the violent attitudes of athletes outside the context of sport competition. Keith Horne, a freshman guard on the Texas-San Antonio basketball team, was charged with attempted murder after allegedly beating and trying to strangle a female hotel employee after his team's double overtime defeat (Kirshenbaum, 1989:17). Incidents of assault like this are not rare.

> In a 1986 survey of 350 (American) colleges, the *Philadelphia Daily News* found that athletes had been implicated in at least 61 sexual assaults between '83 and '85. The paper calculated that football and basketball players were 38% more likely to be implicated in such crimes than the average male student (Kirshenbaum, 1989:17).

These events cannot merely be dismissed as random incidents. These cases are coming to light in spite of the attempts of coaches to cover up and protect talented but aggressive players.

Some people blame the coaches and their tolerant attitude. Lefty Driesell had a nation-wide reputation as a very successful, tough recruiter and coach. He was the basketball coach at Maryland State University. In 1983, he called a women student three times to try to

Sexual Assault and Student Life

There are a number of aspects to the issue of sexual assault and student life.

- *The previous lack of concern about this crime.* It is only recently that the extent of this problem has been recognized. Often "jocks" were viewed simply as energetic, sexually-active young men.

- *Different values about appropriate male and female behaviour.* Males are expected to be outgoing or aggressive to succeed, particularly in sport. Such attitudes have led to sexual aggressiveness.

- *In the past "a man's home is his castle."* It was assumed that a man had the right to do what he wanted. Sexual assault was not even a crime between a husband and wife.

- *Safety* Most college campuses are very spread out with wide open spaces and a minimum of security. Often students jog, run, bicycle, and exercise on campus without regard to personal safety.

- *In most assault cases the victim is known to the person who commits the crime.* It seems that many of the incidents that involve campus or school athletes are in the "date-rape" or "acquaintance-rape" category. The athlete is known to the woman and the context is studying, the residences, campus bars, celebration parties, after game get-togethers, etc.

In a context where most women would expect to feel safe—their own places of study—it seems that administrators have been reluctant to address safety concerns for fear of scaring off prospective students.

---

persuade her *not* to lay a charge of sexual misconduct (within the university) against one of his player. As a result, she decided to lay a harassment complaint against Driesell, who subsequently was reprimanded by the university (Kirshenbaum, 1989:18).

All the usual values about good behaviour and setting examples sometimes fall by the wayside.

> Big-time athletics is creating an atmosphere conducive to those type of things. These athletes are put on a pedestal. They are given almost free rein to do what they want as long as their teams are in the Top 20 (Kirshenbaum, 1989:18).

A blind eye is often turned to incidents, even with the police, if the athlete is part of a winning team. There are often no sport sanctions for even illegal behaviour.

Sexual assault in the context of sport is a crime that has often been covered up, and it has only slowly begun to be taken seriously. One typical example of this increasing concern is an article published in the spring of 1991 entitled "Male Athletes and Sexual Assault." The author Gerald Eskenazi points out that there are a significant number of assaults on women in the context of college life, including collegiate sport.

~ SPORT PROFILE ~

Victor Davis—He Swam like a Shark, Positive Aggressiveness

b. 1964, Guelph, Ontario; d. 1989. Victor Davis was born on February 10, 1964 and died in a car accident in December 1989, at the young age of twenty-five. Victor Davis was respected as a fierce and committed competitor. He represented the positive aggressive aspects of competitive sport. He was also known for his pride and loyalty to Canada. So great was this concern, he had a Canadian flag tattooed on his chest.

Davis became labelled the "Bad Boy" of swimming after an incident at the Commonwealth Games in Brisbane, Australia, in 1982. Davis "was enraged by the disqualification of the winning Canadian 4 x 100 medley relay team for a premature start. In the presence of the Queen, Davis kicked a deck chair and stormed out of the pool area, sending towels, plants and a trash bin flying, amid a string of obscenities" (A Century 1986: 134).

In 1984, at the LA Olympics, he was beaten by the American Steve Lundquist in the 100 metres, by 34/100 of a second. There were no histrionics. He was courteous and polite. Davis merely said: "I swam the race I wanted to swim. Steve just swam faster" (ibid,1986: 134).

Four days later Davis broke the 200-metre record by almost two seconds and won the gold medal. He explained that he wanted to be remembered as a "hungry young Canadian athlete, not a caveman" and his wish came true.

In cases where women have made accusations of rape, the athlete usually denies it. In the cases where team members are accused of gang rape, the members usually deny together. Claire Walsh, the director of the sexual-assault recovery program at the University of Florida, points out: "In every single case, they will deny there was gang rape but admit there *was* group sex" (Eskenazi, 1991:222). It is usually team members who are involved and they stand together and explain it was all a misunderstanding. In a case with the Washington Capitols hockey team, a women claimed she was raped by three players in a limousine. The case received a great deal of publicity in the press, but charges were not filed against the players.

Ken Dryden has said that the special position of athletes influences how they feel about getting caught up in inappropriate behaviour:

It's really a sense of power that comes from specialness, reputation, money—whether he's an athlete, business man, or entertainer, anyone who finds himself at the centre of his world feels a sense of impunity—that no matter where the chips fall, they won't fall on him (ibid:223).

The situation can be made more complicated by factors of social class and race. Generally, athletes on scholarships in the United States have fewer financial resources than residential campus students, many of whom come from more wealthy families.

Athlete Information Bureau (Ted Grant).

Victor Davis, tough competitor, winner in swimming.

CREATING NEW SOCIAL VALUES

It is worth keeping in mind that behaviour that would be considered totally unacceptable today was formerly commonplace. There were numerous contests involving the killing or baiting of animals. Also, throwing at cocks, cockfighting, bull-baiting and bull chasing was common (Holt, 1989:16, 17, 18). "By the standards of our day the level of violence tolerated in sports was remarkable. This was true whether we look at contests between beasts or between men" (Holt, 1989:18). In fact fighting was the singular most popular sport (Holt, 1989:18).

This is not to minimize the seriousness of violence in many sports today. Quite the contrary. One significant difference is that today sport is a national and international industry that has far-reaching effects throughout our society. This vast sports industry creates values as well as reflects them.

Athlete Information Bureau.

Jim Worrall, Canadian boxer at the Olympics.

"Razor" Ruddock—The Killer Instinct

Some boxing promoters, apparently oblivious to the life and death hazards of their sport, argue that Canada's Donovan "Razor" Ruddock lacks a "killer" edge. He is too "gentle" and Canadian.

Promoters like Norman Henry believe: "Most boxers don't have a killer instinct. The warriors do — Mike Tyson does, Joe Frazier did. Razor is more of a pure boxer. He's surprised to find he can be a puncher. Of course you wouldn't get a killer instinct in Canada or Jamaica. If Razor'd grown up in a fight atmosphere in the ghetto, he would have had it more ..." (Brown, 1991: 64).

Mike Tyson, on the other hand, the former world heavyweight champion, known as the "Ice Man" is not even six feet tall, but he weighs 215 pounds and fights, it seems, without fear. Numerous newspaper and television commentators point to Tyson's childhood — robberies, muggings and jail time. Some argue that a "good boxer" has to have fire in his belly to win. It is the determination and desperation of ghetto life and poverty that help fighters succeed.

Outside the ring it appears that Tyson continues his commitment to control through his physical strength. Tyson has a long history of documented physical conflicts outside the boxing ring against both women and men: February 1986, June 1987, August 1988, September 1988, October 1988, December 1988, April 1989, August 1990, November 1990 and July 1991. Some have gone to court; some are in process (Sarenco, 1991).

In 1991, Tyson was charged with the rape and confinement of a woman contestant in a beauty pageant he was judging. Tyson's response to the latest charges was: "I train hard, then I go out and have fun. I'm not going to stay in the house" (Sarenco, 1991: C1).

Many women's groups were upset by Tyson's response. Ruth Jones of NOW (National Organization of Women) explained: "Of course he's innocent until proven guilty. But what sticks in the craw is we get to see him go on about his life, making money, getting the publicity and having a good time.

Coaches and Sport Violence

As we have seen, the coaches often set the tone for what is considered to be appropriate behaviour. A study was done on 900 football players between the ages of fifteen and eighteen. Players were asked if they agreed with statements in reference to violence in Association Football. The study suggests that many athletes will do the things a coach asks them to do (Smith, 1983). A very special trust is built up between coaches and players.

Dave Schultz was coached by Freddie Shero when he played for the Flyers in the 1970s. Schultz admired the man at that time: "History will show that Freddie was one of the most significant innovators among hockey coaches for his introduction of videotape as a coach-

Athletic Performance and Sexual Activity

Some coaches still maintain that sport and sexual relations do not mix, arguing that athlete's dedication to training must supersede other aspects of the athlete's life. This argument is centuries old. Everyone knows the story of Delila cutting off Sampson's hair, the symbol of his manly strength.

In the past, in many sports, sexual relations prior to major sporting events has been cited as the cause of poor athletic performance. "Many players drank themselves into a stupor after games, but if they violate the sex taboos they were in deep trouble. At the time, everyone, from arm-chair athletes to physicians, was convinced that athletes lost their "legs" or endurance if they engaged in sexual intercourse before competition … someone … would be delegated to approach the player, his wife or both to discuss their "problem." " (Cruise & Griffiths, 1991: 73)

Even in the 1990s, during the 1990 World Soccer Cup the Italian soccer team was told they were expected to abstain from all sexual activity in order to give the team an edge. Part of Muhammad Ali's mythical image was his isolation in training camp before big fights. Football players used to have bed checks before big games.

Today, most coaches recognize all this as myth. Most feel that an athlete's sexual behaviour is part of the athlete's private life and is not to be discussed publicly or as part of a training program. The only exception might be a discussion of contraceptive methods that would affect the possibility of the athlete becoming a parent.

ing aid, and his importing of the best of the Soviet style of play to North America" (Schultz, 1983:93). However, Schultz is now angry for the part Shero played in influencing him to play violent hockey.

> … he (Shero) also poignantly illustrates the extent to which individuals will go to produce a winning franchise, an end product that is revered and sanctioned by everyone who participates in the NHL (Schultz, 1983:93).

Tiger Williams, the NHL hockey player, on the other hand, takes full responsibility for his own violent behaviour. Williams' family had little money but they were known as fighters. He got his nickname, Tiger, from the way he played hockey and he explains: "but what I was most tigerish about, deep down, was the need to earn some money. It hurt like hell that my dad didn't have a car. It hurt like hell, and it was a wound that never really healed" (Williams, 1984:27). Williams was similar to many poorer Canadians who loved hockey and also saw hockey as a chance at upward social mobility and an entrance to a better life for themselves and their families.

Williams also describes his community and family life as one where no one backed off using their fists. "There was always violence: in the pool hall, in the workplace, at a bar and on the ice" (Williams, 1984:40). Williams learned to fight the other players and the fans in his home town of Flin Flon, Manitoba. He was picked up by the Toronto Maple Leafs, but was soon sent to the minors. He knew he could not be a Bobby Orr, and good fights were essential to enable him to stay in the NHL.

Athlete Information Bureau (F. Scott Grant).

Intensity is part of competition—Canadian women's rugby team.

SUPERSTITION IN SPORT

Because so much of sport is unpredictable, it is hardly surprising that many sports people are superstitious.

Outsiders joke about rabbits' feet but most sports people prefer to talk about "habits" or "routines" (McCallum, 1988:88). If things are going well, an athlete may decide a particular sweatshirt is lucky or that it is unlucky to cross baseball bats, etc. Some superstitions are rooted in time. Not stepping on the foul line recalls the childhood tradition of not stepping on a crack. The crack represented the opening of a grave, so stepping on a crack might be stepping in the grave of a family member (ibid:89).

Athletes subscribe to a variety of superstitions. The hockey player Phil Esposito dressed the same way for each game and used all kinds of good luck charms, such as shamrocks. He also believed in the Italian tradition of the evil eye or *malocchio*.

Some lovers of hockey feel angry about the violent kind of hockey that is being promoted. The Toronto writer Jim Proudfoot feels that fights sell tickets and this is the root of the problem.

> The truth is that the NHL's business is entertainment, not sports. The product placed on the ice is one which, in the NHL's point of view, will be purchased by the most people possible. And because those potential customers are now Americans, ignorant of hockey, the end result may well resemble something more readily marketable, like roller derby or wrestling (Proudfoot, 1986).

Coach Reggie Dunlop's ex-wife put it very succinctly, in the film *Slap Shot*, "Any fool can fight." Non-hockey "experts" do relate to the fights and buy the tickets and, as Jim Proudfoot outlined, fights do help teams with poor hockey skills to do better. Shero encouraged Schultz to develop his enforcer style. If a fight was needed, Schultz would be tapped on the shoulder. He was not told to go and fight, but everyone knew what his job was. " … not a word was spoken. Freddie liked it; my teammates liked it; and, most of all, the fans loved it" (Schultz, 1983:82). The tickets sold well.

Fan Violence

A study in the United States compared the fans at an Army-Navy football game and the fans at an Army-Temple gymnastics meet. A number of variables were taken into account in the comparison—age, frequency of attendance, number of companions, distance travelled, etc. It was found that the hostility levels of the football fans were greater after seeing the game than those of the fans who went to the gymnastics meet. The conditions were similar, but it seems that "the increase in hostility is due to the nature of the observed event; watching an aggressive sport leads to an increase in hostility among spectators" (Chu, 1982:42–43).

European-style football, soccer, is not aggressive in the way North American football is, but there have recently been a number of terrible incidents resulting in deaths and injuries of fans. The most recent incident happened at Sheffield's Hillsborough Stadium in England in 1989. This particular game was the English Football Association Cup semifinal between Liverpool and Nottingham Forest. This was not the first time that Liverpool fans were involved in a terrible football incident. The catastrophe was particularly severe because so many of the individuals who died or were injured came from the same community. Moreover, many were literally suffocated against metal crowd-control barriers and, as they were dying, the photographers and television cameras recorded the horror.

After the deaths and injuries resulting from the Liverpool fans' fighting at the Heysel stadium in Belgium in 1985, English clubs were

The Hillsborough Tragedy

Prior to the commencement of the soccer match at Hillsborough Stadium in England, an estimated crowd of 4,000 was pressing against the gates. The stadium itself held 50,000 fans. It was a few minutes before three and the game was about to start.

The fences around the perimeter of the field were set up to protect the soccer teams from invading fans, some of whom would throw things or attack players and officials. The police cordoned off the different clubs. The fans were not expected to be responsible for behaving well, the police were expected to act as the peacekeepers. If things became unruly the police procedure was to allow the crowd to rush in, without paying. The owners and managers of the facilities, of course, do not want this to happen.

On April 15, 1989 at Hillsborough, the police were very concerned about the growing crowd outside and opened the gate. The crowds flooded onto the terraces. They began to press upon the crowd already pushed up against the crowd-control barriers and that is when people began to die, suffocated by the pressure of the crowd. As police and observers yelled at the crowd to return they were ignored. Fans in other sections of the stadium could not see what was going on at all. Some got annoyed when the game was cancelled, thinking that the cancellation was due to hooliganism. The police then had to line up to prevent the two groups of fans from fighting while people were dying.

All of this took place in a matter of minutes, from approximately 2:57 to 3:06 on a Saturday afternoon. There was no intercom system to alert people, the police were slow to realize what was happening, and there were inadequate medical facilities available. When the first stage of the report came out the police were severely criticized; however, the management and organization of the facility escaped blame.

banned from the competitions of the European Football Union until 1990–91. Even after Heysel, fans from Germany, Holland and England in Dusseldorf in 1988 used the football match as an opportunity to express hostility. West German neo-Nazis wore modified swastikas, Dutch hooligans shouted anti-Semitic slogans, and the British attacked everyone. Windows were broken, property damaged and the atmosphere was generally violent. Thousands of police were kept in position (Gammon, 1988:50).

There are a number of factors that help to account for the particular violence of British soccer. A review of these helps to suggest measures to reduce fan violence.

1. Team identification. There is greater identification on the part of fans with teams than with individuals. In Canada, people tend to go to see sporting events with a few friends or their family. Sometimes a group will go from work; the composition of the group is small and varies very often from game to game. Usually the tickets are bought in advance. Some drinking may take place, but drunkenness is usually not tolerated. Often wives, girlfriends and children may be included. The seats may not be particularly comfortable, but there are seats. There are food and washroom facilities available and, increasingly, the stadiums or arenas are covered and heated. British fans, on the

Police escort the "away team" after a Tottenham Hotspurs match in England, 1990.

Soccer Stadium Deaths

April 15, 1989	Hillsborough Stadium, Sheffield, England. 93 deaths, 200 injured. People were crushed against immoveable barriers.
January 2, 1989	Glasgow, Scotland. 66 deaths. Fans were crushed at the end of a game as some fans were leaving and others were trying to return to see a late goal.
March 12, 1988	Katmandu Stadium, Nepal. 90 deaths, 700 injured. Spectators were trampled when rushing for cover during a violent hailstorm when the exits were locked.
March 10,1987	Tripoli, Libya. 20 deaths. Fans fled from knife-wielding ruffians and a wall collapsed.
May 29, 1985	Heysel Stadium, Brussels, Belgium. 39 deaths, 400 injured (mainly Italians). People were crushed or trampled during fighting between Liverpool & Juventus fans at a European Cup Final.
May 26, 1985	Olympic Stadium, Mexico City. 10 deaths, 29 injured. Fans were trampled in a panic.
May 11, 1985	Bradford Stadium, England. 56 deaths, 200 injured. A fire started by a cigarette set the wooden stands on fire.
May 24, 1965	Lima, Peru. 300 deaths, 500 injured. A Peruvian goal was disallowed. Police used tear gas, and spectators trying to flee were crushed against locked exit gates.

Source: Adapted from Reuter. 1989. "Tragedy at Sheffield Stadium the latest in series of disasters." *The Sunday Star*. April, 16:A14.

other hand, most often attend soccer games as club members. Fans go in groups and identify very strongly with their own team. Soccer seating is on the basis of which team you support. Fans of opposing teams are segregated. An "enemy" supporter will be "evicted" if pointed out to the police, and then asked to sit in the correct supporter's section. The intense emotion, attachment and anger associated with British soccer is hard for Canadians to understand. There is a tremendously strong emotional tie to the home team. As soccer games have become increasingly known for roughness on the part of fans, so the fan base for soccer has become narrower. Today few women and children attend games. This contrasts, for example, with the marketing strategy (discussed in a previous chapter) of the Toronto Blue Jays who, by opening a new franchise, tried to encourage everyone to come to baseball games—men, women, young and old. The supermarkets have been a focus of ticket sales and the image of baseball has been that of a family event. Any unpleasant behaviour at the event is discouraged because of this family appeal.

In England, for some fans, a small minority, it is considered "normal" to say, "Let's go to the match and have some fun." Fun can include having a "punch up" with opposing club team members.

2. Manliness. In many countries maleness is closely identified with sport. "The most popular nineteenth-century games and contests—football, hockey, lacrosse, track and field, and boxing—were termed 'the manly sports'" (Kidd, 1987). For soccer fans in England, the games provide opportunities to manifest maleness too. Describing bold exploits at games is part of the folklore. One soccer "hooligan" explains what happened in the Shed at Leatherhead, which is an area where fans stand on open terraces to watch the game.

> 'Yeah it was easy,' I said. But the truth was that my heart was beating at a hundred miles per hour and I was petrified. In order to go to the toilet I still had to walk past the stand they [the other team's fans] were in. I was saved that problem by everyone peeing against the wall behind the Shed terrace at half-time (Ward 1989:23).

The excitement, the police presence and the nervousness over the potential of violent outbreaks provide appeal and interest to some fans. It is during these incidents that male identity and bravery to go "steaming in" are established. "Steaming in" is the rush of fans on the terraces when they force their way against other fans already in position. To stand your ground and not show fear are important rituals that can be quite dangerous and lead to physical injury. Clothes usually identify the origins of the fans, even the apparently harmless question "What's the time?" may establish the identity of one fan to another as friend or foe.

3. Scoring. Some have argued that scoring methods may increase fan frustration when scores are very low, as they have been traditionally in soccer. It has been suggested that it would be better to have higher scores to reduce fan frustration and encourage more positive participation. This position has been put forward with respect to hockey as well. Higher scores also make a more marketable product.

4. Social conditions. One chief cause of soccer violence in Britain lies in the structures of the communities from which the fans are drawn. Soccer fans, at least the ones who go to matches, are not like other young people who are studying in colleges and universities and are convinced they have a successful career path mapped out. The groups are isolated at the lower end of the socio-economic ladder with few places to go, little money and a considerable sense of frustration stemming from the realization that upward social mobility might not be an automatic part of their lives.

5. The Facilities. Another major factor contributing to these terrible disasters is the condition of the facilities within which the soccer matches take place. The stadiums are old and in poor condition.

GAMBLING ON YOUR OWN TEAM

Pete Rose was a respected athlete and often referred to as Charlie Hustle. His dedication to competition, his will to win and his toughness made him many fans during his baseball career. He lost this respect and admiration because of his gambling and tax problems. It appears that Rose was a gambling addict and this led him to behave in ways that ended his job as manager of the Cincinnati Reds and put him in jail.

J. Le Clair.

Paul Gascoigne and the Tottenham Hotspurs, London, England, 1990.

Unlike stadiums in Canada, which must be made of concrete with seats of metal or plastic, many of the stadiums in England are built entirely of wood. The fire which raged quickly through the wooden stands at Bradford stadium in 1985 was a good example of the potential danger. There are also sections in the stadiums where there are no seats at all and fans must stand for hours, often in the pouring rain. On top of this, sometimes there are few washrooms, so people urinate wherever they can. It is common to go to pubs and drink before the games begin and little food is available inside the stadiums.

6. Ticket management. The very system of ticket management at British soccer matches creates crowd control problems. In Canada, it is considered usual to purchase a ticket for a sports event in advance, through a computerized system of ticket generation. In England, it has been usual for non-season ticket holders to turn up at an event and purchase the ticket on the spot. There are few turnstiles and usually they are not automated. Thus, you have people without tickets eager to get into the stadium, not wanting to miss the beginning of the match, not guaranteed a seat and possibly drunk as well.

In light of the recent tragedies, many changes have been made to improve the stadiums in Britain since 1989—the removal of field barriers, more seats, better communication systems and more medical and emergency facilities.

Cheating and Gambling

Cheating is inevitable when there is an over-emphasis on winning. It can take many forms. High sticking and slashing in hockey is one example where creating injuries can help you win if you can get away with it. Cheating involves getting around the rules or breaking them. There are a number of areas in sport that involve cheating.

1. *Recruitment in schools.* Rules are bent if not broken in order to sign promising talent.
2. *Cheating in games.* This most often takes the form of trying to get away with as much as possible. It can be against opposing teams, against team members, or simply by being violent. It can be done by modifying equipment—for example, rewiring a fencing competition so you can score higher or putting material on the ball in baseball.

Gambling is also a significant aspect of sport for many fans. The Super Bowl is the biggest betting event in the United States. In 1989, $4-5 million dollars was bet legally in Nevada and another $5 billion illegally on the Super Bowl (Cassidy & Richards, 1989:D6). Bets are made on everything from the point spread to the distances of field goals. Much of the betting takes place in office pools.

Elizabeth (Liz) Ashton, equestrian Olympic competitor.

Elizabeth Ashton.

~ SPORT PROFILE ~

Elizabeth (Liz) Ashton—Intense, Aggressive Competitor

b. 1950, Lancashire, England, grew up in Toronto, Ontario. Liz Ashton became interested in horses initially because her brother was riding. She enjoyed jumping right from the very beginning. She describes her own love of riding in this way. "I loved the relationship with the horse and training to become a professional athlete. Like caring for a child, I liked watching the horse develop—the care, the animal's maturation, and seeing your rapport develop. I always know the type of horse I can develop the best relationship with."

By fourteen years of age, Ashton knew she wanted to be on the national team. Unlike many other athletic youngsters whose friends shared the same interests, not many of her friends rode. Her role model was Jim Elder. He was one of her instructors and "he helped me go where I wanted to go and at eighteen I made the team."

Ashton continued jumping until 1975 when she then faced the problem of finances. She switched to competing in three-day events because of the expensive nature of horse jumping.

Liz Ashton is a thoughtful and careful planner. She manifests the characteristics of an aggressive athlete who pursues goals regardless of the obstacles on or off the course. She is aggressive in the positive sense of being committed to a goal and obstacles do not deter her.

At eighteen, she had already realized that the costs of competition were beyond the budget of her supportive family. She went into business. She took horses for training and during that period commuted from Orangeville to Toronto to attend university. She smiled as she said: "My poor mother never had a car. I stole her car!"

In the early 1970s she went to work in Virginia (one of the great riding centres in the United States) and got some training as well. Here she was exposed to the international circuit.

Throughout her competitive career Ashton juggled her long-term goals, her financial concerns and her love of riding competition.

She wanted to become a vetinarian. She applied to the University of Guelph. At that time there were only two women and 102 men students enroled. She was accepted, but decided to seek a degree in physical education at the University of Toronto since she could also ride competitively while there.

As the costs of competing kept going up, Ashton's family continued to provide additional support. Her father retired and they turned their farm into a business, breaking and training thoroughbred race horses. "If they had the money, they would willingly have bought me a $100,000 horse."

Commercial sponsors for riders were not available at that time. To help the financial situation, in 1973 she applied for "a real job" and headed up the Equine Program at Humber College in Etobicoke, which opened with 85 students and established a national reputation. "The college was generous and allowed me the flexibility to do what I had to do to be competitive."

Liz Ashton is an adventurous pioneer in other ways. Men dominated equestrian events. Most young women gave up competitive riding in their teens to pursue other activities. She was one of the few women representing her country on national equestrian teams and was one of a handful of women to hold an exercise rider and trainer's licenses at the thoroughbred track. Through this complicated balance of interests she worked full-time. She competed internationally until 1985.

Today Liz Ashton is the Vice-President Academic at Sir Stanford Fleming College in Peterborough, Ontario, where she continues her dedicated commitment to hard work, innovation and excellence. Ashton is a living example of how the aggressive pursuit of goals can benefit others.

Quotations from a personal interview by the author, May 1991.

~ **SPORT PROFILE** ~

Gilles Villeneuve—Quebec Champion Race Car Driver

b. 1952, St. Jean, Quebec; d. 1982 on the track at the Belgium Grand Prix. Gilles Villeneuve loved speed from the beginning. His family remembers when he sat "on his father's knee in the car and urged him to go 'faster Daddy, faster' and 'pass him, pass him'" (Donaldson, 1982: S6).

Villeneuve began racing snowmobiles and became the Canadian champion in 1973 and world champion in 1975. He then switched to cars, moving from Formula Ford, Formula Atlantic and then to Formula One racing and the Grand Prix circuit where he continued to be equally successful.

Although he was the first Canadian to win on the Grand Prix circuit and he expected to earn over $3 million in 1982 (the best paid Canadian athlete at that time), he always saw Berthierville, Quebec, as his home. "No matter what happens money won't matter. We won't change. We're just ordinary Quebecoise and enjoy the simple life" (Donaldson, 1982: S6).

In a sport where many die, Gilles Villeneuve claimed that Grand Prix driving was nowhere near as frightening as snowmobile racing. In snowmobiles, he argued, "unless you are in the lead, you can hardly see a thing because of the snow being blown up—but you have to plunge ahead anyway" (Villeneuve, 1982: 6). He did say in 1977: "I am always aware of the possibility that this sport could kill me at the next corner ... It's something I live with" (Donaldson, 1982a: S1).

In May 1982, while in practice at the Belgium Grand Prix, his reputation as a driver's driver could not save him. His Ferrari hit a car driven by Jochen Mass of West Germany and his car "somersaulted 150 metres into a sandbank. The force of the crash disintegrated the red Ferrari and snapped the safety harness, throwing Villeneuve another 30 metres across the track into a steel catch-fence ...

Villeneuve suffered a broken neck and severe head injuries. He died seven hours later without regaining consciousness" (Donaldson, 1982a: S1). Bits and pieces of the wreckage of the Ferrari were strewn along the asphalt for some 200 metres. There in the middle of the track was the utterly destroyed chassis, shorn of all bodywork, with only the right rear wheel remaining and the centre front of the car sheered off at the point where the steering wheel once was" (Donaldson, 1982b: S1).

Teddy Mayer, the U.S. co-managing director of the McLaren racing team, knew Villeneuve well. He gave him his first Grand Prix race. Mayer said of Villeneuve: "I think he was one of the most talented and aggressive drivers that I've ever seen. He always gave 100%. He was probably the ultimate racing driver in his attitude" (Donaldson, 1982a: S1).

But danger is always a factor for the drivers. After the crash the Grand Prix Drivers Association met to work on safety problems. In these practice sessions Villeneuve was averaging just over 200 kilometres an hour. The question has to be asked if the death of these athletes is really necessary merely to have an exciting sport?

Although gambling is a part of many sports, ~~it is important to the gambling and sport industries themselves that sport be considered free from corruption~~. Any hint of fixed games puts the entire sport industry at risk. The 1919 incident with the Boston "Black" Sox, where some baseball players took bribes, hangs like a shadow over sport. If games are rigged fans will stay away. In Canada, the Stanley Cup playoffs are the biggest focus for gambling. There are no figures on the amounts gambled, since office pools handle most of the betting.

At Florida State University various infractions of NCAA rules took place, including team members accepting bribes to shave points and quarterbacks placing bets. Some players received under-the-table payments and there were drug sales between team members. The quarterback Kyle Morris and another teammate placed bets on college football teams in amounts of $25-100 dollars each week. Morris said "the betting really didn't seem like that big a deal. All of a sudden it just exploded, and we were shocked. It is like the Pete Rose thing. It's just as big as far as college ball is concerned" (Sullivan, 1989:42).

Risk and Danger in Sport

For many people, the enjoyment of risk is part of their enjoyment of sport. The risk can be from such activities as boxing, football, hockey, gymnastics or figure skating. Two interesting examples of perceived risk are boxing and bungee-jumping.

Bunjee-jumping, a "sport" developed by the Dangerous Sports Club of Oxford is based on vine jumping in the South Pacific, where men must show their courage as part of their passage rites into manhood. (It is not really a sport because there is no competitive component.) In bungee-jumping the participant ties an elastic cord (the bungee cord) around his or her ankles and then jumps off a bridge or crane. The usual fee is around $85.00 (or more if you wish a video of the proceedings). The risk appears to be considerable since the drops are usually at least one hundred feet. Most of those who have bungee-jumped explained that the reason they had done so was they thought it would be exciting. They were thrill-seekers.

The actual risk in bungee-jumping is quite limited. The bungee cords are tested by a safety committee. Each jumper is weighed three times and their bungee cord is colour coded. "With this calibration it is possible to determine the lowest point a jumper will descend to within one per cent of the jump height. This means that the lowest point can be determined within 0.4 of a metre if the jump is from a 40 metre height." On the jump cage, "an electronic lock is automatically activated and is only disengaged after bar codes on the bungee cord and main webbing are read by a computer. The computer-controlled lock must receive the correct information before the electronic lock is opened." Each employee has safety and medical training. At the 1991 Canadian National Exhibition in Toronto there was not one injury during the whole period the jump was in operation. World Bungee International Ltd. had been in operation two years by 1991 "without a single incident of a customer being hurt." Andy Veazey, the manager of the CNE jumps, takes pride in his company's safety record and that the turn around time per jump is only three minutes!

Boxing is a fairly modern sport. In theory, there are many safeguards to protect boxers from harm, but often these rules in amateur and professional boxing are overlooked. One myth about the sport is that the larger the glove, the safer the sport. In fact, the

Gilles Villeneuve, champion Formula One race car driver.

Canada's Sports Hall of Fame.

MAGIC JOHNSON—AIDS TESTING

After basketball player Earvin (Magic) Johnson made the announcement that he had tested positive for the HIV virus in November, 1991, many athletes began to re-think safety issues.

In the past athletes and coaches were casual about such things as sharing towels and taking care of minor scrapes and cuts. Now athletes are wondering if they should be more careful.

Some athletes are even arguing that they would be in favour of aids testing. Dan Ferrone of the Toronto Argonauts expresses views held by other players: "We (football players) share a lot of sweat sucking on the same Gatorade bottles and passing from hand to hand to hand when you touch someone. It's supposed to be safe, but with all that blood and sweat splashing around, it makes you wonder. I really think we should be tested to help stop the spread of disease" (Zwolinski, 1991: B5).

We may see a redefinition of contact sports based not on a new caring for the athlete but on a new interest on safer and healthier sport.

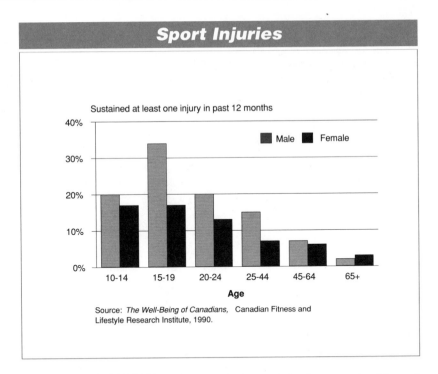

Sport Injuries

Sustained at least one injury in past 12 months

Source: *The Well-Being of Canadians,* Canadian Fitness and Lifestyle Research Institute, 1990.

Bungee-jumping at the Canadian National Exhibition, Toronto, 1991.

J. Le Clair.

larger the glove, the heavier the weight and the heavier the blow. A 1991 Ontario study found numerous violations: fighting without "passports" (a list of a fighter's medical and fight history); daily weigh-ins overlooked (these ensure fighters of similar weight fight one another); injury waiver forms unsigned by boxers or parents; irregular documents; and children fighting adults (Starkman & Edwards, 1991: C1). In professional boxing, names are changed, medical checks are not completed and termination of fights to prevent injury are slow to take place, even in fights with prize money as little as a few hundred dollars. The Canadian, American, British and Australian Medical Associations all feel that boxing as a sport should be banned because its sole purpose is to deliberately injure the opponent.

Often we accept and take for granted risks related to sporting activities. Tackling in football and checking in hockey, for example, have always been there. Young athletes are trained in techniques to hit or check. Sometimes the coach encourages athletes develop this aspect of their performance.

Many athletes in the past played sports without eye or head protection, an unacceptable risk today. Probably the best example is that of goalies playing hockey without masks. Until the 1960s, no one wore masks. Pucks smashing into faces, missing teeth, and gruesome stitches were all an accepted part of the hockey. It is the pioneer Jacques Plante who decided, after appalling injuries to his face, to

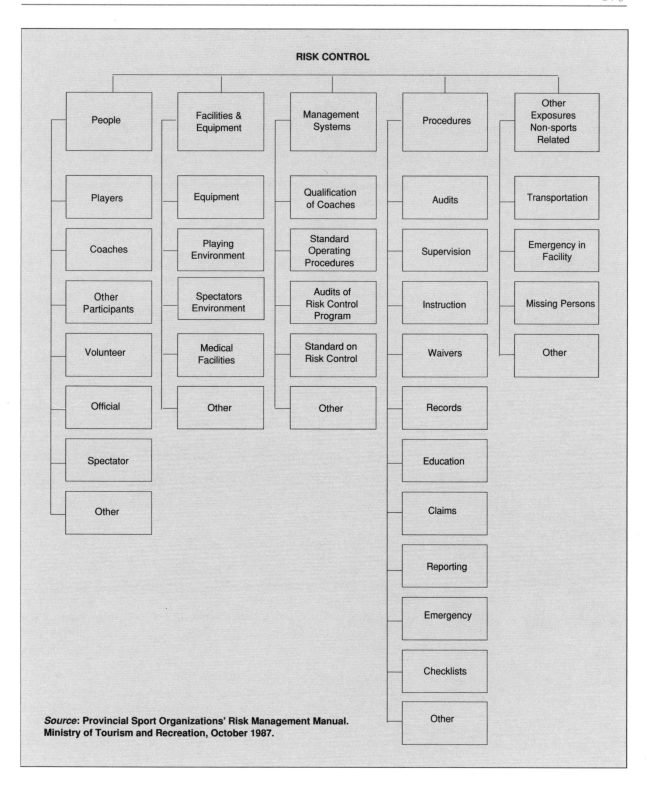

RISK CONTROL

People	Facilities & Equipment	Management Systems	Procedures	Other Exposures Non-sports Related
Players	Equipment	Qualification of Coaches	Audits	Transportation
Coaches	Playing Environment	Standard Operating Procedures	Supervision	Emergency in Facility
Other Participants	Spectators Environment	Audits of Risk Control Program	Instruction	Missing Persons
Volunteer	Medical Facilities	Standard on Risk Control	Waivers	Other
Official	Other	Other	Records	
Spectator			Education	
Other			Claims	
			Reporting	
			Emergency	
			Checklists	
			Other	

**Source: Provincial Sport Organizations' Risk Management Manual.
Ministry of Tourism and Recreation, October 1987.**

wear protection. He designed a simple mask and insisted he would not play unless he could wear it. Today, very few would step onto the rink without a mask, and especially not goalies.

Susan Goodman, a researcher in the area of risk management, has outlined the key aspects to consider in evaluating the risks associated with any sport activity. If the sport organization or school follows each step in evaluating its own physical activities, it is possible to reduce risks and injuries.

The standard of care required in physical education and sport revolves around three factors:

- the instruction to the participant or athlete
- the supervision of the activity, and
- the maintenance of facilities and equipment.

By being a prudent risk manager in these three areas, the risk of injury, and the severity of any injury that does occur, can be greatly reduced. By maintaining these precautions, a facility's insurance costs also may be lower.

Risk management is a planning function. It involves identifying the potential risks and hazards and taking steps (eg, safety inspections, first-aid training, and the use of protective equipment) to reduce any risks. The risk control chart on page 272 outlines the areas to consider in planning activities in order to reduce risk. Removing liability by having athletes merely sign a waiver is not a satisfactory solution to the problem of risk. The risk of accident and injury can be reduced significantly through the study, establishment and implementation of safety procedures and practices (Goodman, 1990).

What is acceptable?

The question of what is violence and what is legitimate aggression, what is a safe or unsafe activity, initiates considerable controversy. This debate is not one that will be resolved easily through discussions. It involves wider issues about the nature of sport, masculinity and femininity, and about the application of rules and regulations in sport.

For many sports, physical contact is part of its history and appeal. However, as our tolerance for violence of all sorts is reduced in every area of society, so the question of physical contact within sport will come under greater scrutiny. It is not just a question of legal liability and the signing of waiver forms but the moral or ethical issue—to what lengths should athletes go in order to perform and win.

Athlete Information Bureau (E. Langsley).

Sports injuries are all too common—
Canadian women's hockey.

REVIEW

Questions

1. How does the pressure to win help to increase the likelihood of violent behaviour?
2. What are the biological and cultural explanations for violence in sport?
3. What are some of the key social factors leading to soccer violence?
4. Why is the discussion of violence in sport important?
5. Why is gambling on the part of players and coaches an issue of concern?
6. Why is it important to evaluate and manage risk in sport and physical activity?

Concepts

- aggression
- deviant behaviour
- cheating

Discussion

1. Briefly discuss the biological and cultural explanations for aggression and violence in sport.
2. Discuss what you think are the main contributing factors in the increase in hockey violence in recent years.
3. Describe a situation you participated in or observed where the sport or physical activity risk might have been handled or evaluated better by the organizing coach, educator, sponsor or volunteer?

Ben Johnson beating Carl Lewis at the 1988
Olympic Games in Seoul.

Chapter Twelve

DRUGS AND SPORT PERFORMANCE

"They figured if one pill was good, three or four would be better, and they were eating them like candy."
Dr. John Zeigler, the introducer of anabolic steroids to American athletes in the 1950s

"Athletes often refer to these (anabolic-androgenic steroids) as 'the breakfast of champions,' which shows just how prevalent and innocent athletes feel AAS use is."
Dr. Robert Voy, M.D. former Chief Medical Officer U.S. Olympic Committee

"Performance standards—this is not a question for government, it is question for sport. It is a sport issue that we now have such inflated records. Some of them will never be beaten in our lifetime and that's a question for sport to deal with."
Carol Anne Letheren. Canadian Chef de Mission at Seoul in 1988, IOC member and President of the Canadian Olympic Association

PROFILES IN THIS CHAPTER

* Ben Johnson

* Bill Crothers

* Angella Issajenko

* Charlie Francis

E rgogenic aids are used in all aspects of human life. People use music to increase production or increase sales. Better designed seats are installed in cars and trucks to facilitate driving. In the same way athletes have used different kinds of substances and practices to improve their performances.

The will to improve performance is fundamental to success in any sport. The central problem in discussing ergogenic aids is the question of where to draw the line as to what is banned and what is acceptable. Is the use of special diets with extra supplements of vitamins and proteins, cheating? Is the use of visualization when the athlete imagines the perfect run, the perfect shot, the perfect hit, cheating? Is using the latest kind of hi-tech material, a new kind of bicycle metal, or newly designed bob-sled runner, cheating?

Angella Issajenko—seventh in the world in 1979.

~ SPORT PROFILE ~

Ben Johnson—Fastest Man in the World?

b. Falmouth, Jamaica. Ben Johnson is probably one of Canada's best-known athletes. The face of this powerful runner is recognized in all countries as the winner of the popular 100-metre sprint event in the 1988 Summer Olympics held in Seoul, South Korea.

However, news that Johnson tested positive on a drug test three days later shocked Canada and the world. His denial of drug use, the subsequent Dubin inquiry and Johnson's eventual admission of drug usage became the centre of the world-wide controversy over the use of performance-enhancing substances in sport.

It might be argued that the "Johnson incident" was a focal turning point in sport. The issue of drug use had to be addressed—the need to win was making many athletes feel it was essential to take drugs. Johnson, as it turned out, was not very different from many other athletes, but he was caught.

Since then Johnson has been working hard in two areas: informing young people about the harmful effects of drug use and training for competition, as he still hopes to compete and win internationally now that his ban has been lifted.

Despite the drug-use incident, there can be no doubt that Ben Johnson is popular and one of Canada's top athletes. The personal example he has set subsequent to the Seoul Olympics in the face of great media pressure shows his determination and commitment to competition. He understands what went wrong and how important it is for there to be controls to ensure that performance-enhancing drugs are not a part of Canadian and international sport.

The question of performance enhancing substances is intimately linked with the need to win. If athletes feel that the pressure to win is overwhelming, then the temptation to use the miracle pill is great. If the focus is on the process of performance and the *competition* itself, then the ethical issue of drug use comes into much sharper focus. However, it must be remembered that the system of sport at nearly all levels is set up to stress winning. The rewards and the recognition lie at the feet of the first place winner.

Drug Use and Misuse

Athletic performance comprises three aspects: (1) energy production—short-term, as in sprints; and long-term, as in marathons; (2) energy control—the athlete must perform different tasks in changing conditions (eg. shooting, horseback riding, golf) and not become anxious; (3) energy efficiency through better techniques, (eg. swim strokes or better designed bicycles) (Williams, 1989:6). Regardless of the sport, the athlete is attempting to improve his or her performance in competition.

Athletes use the word "doping" to describe the use of drugs. The origin of the word comes from the Dutch word "dop". It was first recorded in an English dictionary in 1889 "as a narcotic mixture of opium used for race horses" (Goldman, 1987: 26).

Athlete Information Bureau (R. Pilon).

Ben Johnson, 100 m. gold medal winner 1988 Olympics (rescinded).

Drug Misuse and Drug Dependency

Many parents are concerned about drug use in general, not only in the context of sport. Across Canada, teachers and parents are addressing this concern.

In 1985 a number of parents formed a volunteer, non-profit organisation called the Peel Parents Against Drugs. This group reflects the increasing concern by many people about the use of drugs.

Their program defines the terms related to drug use as follows:

- A "drug" is anything other than "food" which is taken to change the way the body or mind works.

- The most commonly used drugs are "psychoactive" drugs. These are taken to change the way a person feels, acts or thinks.

- The three "psychoactive" drugs which are most commonly used by Canadian youth are: alcohol, tobacco and cannabis (marijuana, hashish, grass, etc.).

- Alcohol and drug abuse is the use of a drug which causes problems at school, on the job, with family and friends, or with one's health.

- Drug-related problems often occur because a person becomes dependent on the drug. That means the drug becomes so important to the person that the person cannot manage without it.

For the typical college student the problem is clearly defined. A student who needs to drink beer to "feel good" at parties, gets in a fight with parents about being home late and has a hangover in the morning has a serious substance or drug problem. Alcohol use is the most serious substance abuse problem that exists in Canada. There is much discussion in the media about crack and cocaine and the devastation it creates, but the drug that causes the most destruction is legal—alcohol. Part of the problem is that this drug use is everywhere, and it is presented as "natural" or normal. A guest comes to watch the ball game and the first thing offered is a "brew." Usually part of being a good host is to offer a drug! But many do not view beer, scotch or coolers as drugs. Until recently it was also considered courteous to offer cigarettes at the same time.

In "self-reporting" research on drinking in Canadian high schools (completed in 1979) statistics showed that: "about 77% of students drank alcohol at least once in the past year ... 25% of the drinkers had been drunk at least once in the past month and 33% had taken as many as five drinks on a single occasion. ... a few trends are obvious. More high school students are drinking then in the past and much of the change is accounted for by girls beginning to drink" (Smart,1985:21).

One study on adults over 18 "found that 98.9% of those aged 20 to 24 were drinkers" (Smart, 1985:24). Drinking is considered a normal part of student life. A worrying aspect of these figures is that drinking quantities and frequencies are usually under-reported (Smart, 1985:26).

The choice of drug that the athlete might use is determined by the kind of activity the athlete is involved in. If short, sharp bursts of energy are needed then muscle bulk is advantageous and the activity does not need oxygen. A good example of this kind of activity is sprinting, as in the 100-metres. The opposite of this kind of activity is long-distance running, as in the marathon. Energy is required over a 2-2½ hour period and oxygen management is important. If a marathon runner and a sprinter stand side by side it becomes quite easy to tell which kind of running event each competes in. The sprinters are usually fairly short and well muscled. The long distance runners tend to be thinner and long limbed.

Ergogenic is derived from the Greek words *ergon* (work) and *gennan* (to produce).

Hence, erogenic is usually interpreted as work-producing or work-enhancing. (Williams, 1989:5)

Bill Crothers—A Fighter for Honest Sport

b. 1940, Markham, Ontario. In the 1960s Bill Crothers was recognized as one of the best middle-distance runners in the world. He held Canadian and world records at a variety of distances—440 yards, 660 yards, 880 yards, 1,000 yards, 800 metres and 1500 metres. He was a strong runner who managed to keep a reserve of energy for the end of a race.

In the 1964 Tokyo Olympics Crothers was beaten in the 800 metres by his main competitor, the New Zealander Peter Snell. Snell's time was 1: 45.1 and Crothers ran it in 1: 45.6 (Wise, 1974: 235). In the following year, Crothers beat Snell twice—one was a brilliant race at Varsity Stadium in front of a home town crowd.

Crothers was at the centre of a drug controversy in the sixties. Canadian athletes were very frustrated with the coaches, managers and officials of track and field at that time. The Canadian track officials were even nicknamed "the badgers" by the athletes. Most talented athletes left to train in the United States. When athletes learned that Bill Crothers was

studying to become a pharmacist they would often talk to him about drugs, anabolic steroids in particular, and this was in the 1960s. At that time, it was the athletes competing in the strength sports of athletics—the shot put, hammer throw, discus and javelin events—who were interested in the potential advantages of drug use.

One incident was indicative of the period. Lloyd Percival was a highly successful track and field coach in Toronto. Crothers and four other athletes asked the Track and Field Association to investigate if Percival was giving Dexedrine (an illegal drug) to athletes. The Central Ontario Track and Field Association suspended Percival from amateur athletics. Percival in turn sued the COFTA officials. The case only took one day, Percival's suspension was dropped. (Batten, 1971: 109).

In charges of drug use there must be evidence to support the charge. Use of drugs like steroids were not against the law. They were banned in sport but if provided by a doctor there was nothing improper in their use.

Bill Crothers, called "The Crusader," by his former teammate Bruce Kidd, has continued to work on behalf of athletes and their interests, as well as working towards drug-free sport.

Some of the issues Crothers was concerned about as a young athlete continue to be important today. Crothers gave testimony at the 1989 Dubin inquiry into drug use in Canadian sport. He is convinced that attitude is very important to an athlete's sense of confidence. "Athletes are influenced not just by the results. If the athlete thinks he or she is getting an advantage it helps their willingness to put up with discomfort."

Bill Crothers points out something that is often overlooked in the 1990s. "No Canadian is running faster than I ran twenty-eight years ago on a crushed brick track." Crothers feels it is important for young athletes to realize that drug use is not a requirement for success and this is from a winning, "clean" champion.

Quotations from a personal interview by the author, November 1991.

Today, after the Seoul positive test of Ben Johnson, many people think of steroids as the drug typically used by athletes. Prior to that incident there was a great deal of publicity surrounding cocaine use by professional athletes. The court cases involving the baseball player Vida Blue, football player Eugene "Mercury" Morris, and the hockey player Robert Probert received a great deal of publicity. However there are many different kinds of drug misuse. The one discussed the least, and probably the most prevalent because it is legal, is alcohol.

When is a drug a drug? The term "drug" is commonly used to refer to any medical substance. For our purposes, **substance misuse** in sport refers to putting various substances in the body in order to improve sport performance.

Five Classes of Performance-Enhancing Aids

1. Nutritional aids	• amino acid supplements • carbohydrate loading • water	Used primarily to increase muscle tissue, increase muscle energy supplies, and increase the rate of energy production in the muscle
2. Physiological aids	• alkaline salts • blood doping • oxygen	Used primarily to increase the rate of energy production in the muscle and to counteract the accumulation of fatigue products
3. Pharmacological aids	• amphetamines • anabolic steroids • caffeine	Used for both physiological and psychological reasons
4. Psychological aids	• hypnosis • imagery • stress management	Used to improve mental conditions conducive to success and to help reduce those mental factors that can impair performance
5. Mechanical and biomechanical aids	• body composition • clothing • equipment	Used primarily to improve the mechanical efficiency of human movement, possibly saving both physical and mental energy

SOURCE: Melvin H. Williams. 1989. *Beyond Training: How Athletes Enhance Performance Legally and Illegally*. Champaign, Illinois: Leisure Press:8 & 34

Drug Use in Sport

Television commercials advertise the use of pills for the instant relief of everything from headaches to stomach aches. It is a small step from expectations about instant pain relief to similar expectations of instant results on the track. Expectations about instant muscles and instant performance rewards are closely linked. Steroids, as performance enhancers, are seductively appealing. The consequences of use, like those of alcohol and cigarettes, seem remote. Warnings are often viewed as scare-mongering.

In looking at the healthy, fit bodies of athletes it is hard to realize the abuse to which high performance and professional athletes subject their bodies. The compulsion to win and the narrow focus of competition often blinds athletes to the world around them. In her book, appropriately entitled *Running Risks*, Angella Issajenko describes trying a whole range of substances in order to become the best in the world. In her case, steroid use may have led to a susceptibility to injury. The very drugs which she took to succeed may in fact have reduced her chances of success.

Canadian Olympic Association.

Bill Crothers, one of best middle-distance runners in the mid-1960s.

~ **SPORT PROFILE** ~

Angella Issajenko—The Addiction to Winning

b. 1958, St. Andrew, Jamaica. Angella Issajenko is on record as one of Canada's most successful athletes. She is a six-time record holder in the women's indoor 60 metres, holds the world record in the indoor 50 metres, and ranks fourth in the world in the 100 metres. She has broken fifty Canadian records and was a Canadian champion twenty-four times, as well as being the female athlete of the year twice (Issajenko, 1990: 2). She trained with Ben Johnson at the Mazda Optimist Track and Field Club with coach Charlie Francis. Some call her a champion, others a cheat.

Angella Issajenko opens up her book *Running Risks* with a quote from Christopher Marlowe: Run slowly, slowly, horses of the night:/ The stars move still, time runs, the clock will strike, / The Devil will come, and Faustus must be damned.

Issajenko was an athlete who decided to make her deal with the Faustus of the sport world — the chemical industry. She used the steroids or medications recommended by the team doctor, Dr. Jamie Astaphan. She also used a multitude of self-prescribed drugs in the hope their use would lead to her winning more races.

Like many in high performance sports at that time, her coach Charlie Francis thought success at the international level was only possible by using drugs. Although by 1987 Issajenko worried about her drug program, "Not one of us really knew what the hell we were taking any more" (Issajenko, 1990a: C14). She explains: "To criticize Jamie would have been to criticize his medicinal concoctions: a key to BJ's (Ben Johnson's) success.

Who could argue with that? What was good for BJ was good for all of us, and there was no better reminder than the sponsorship packages and group promotions that (agent) Larry (Heidebrecht) kept digging up … It did not occur to me that the brutal workouts and heavy drug dosages were perfectly tailored to BJ's physique and nobody else's."

As a key witness in the Dubin Inquiry Angella Issajenko felt she could say with some authority: "I knew that Dubin had absolutely no idea what it takes to be a successful athlete — or more accurately, what it takes to be a successful Canadian amateur athlete at the international level … For ten years from 1978–1988, a few seconds here and there were the story of my life."

The other part of athletics at that time was the drug use. "There were no doping controls that could not easily be circumvented in the dog days of August 1981" (ibid: 126). The pressure to win and keep fit were enormous. Issajenko describes the panic of trying to get ready for competition. She tried a variety of vitamins and injections. "None of it helped. My hamstring was not mending. The World Cup was three days away. For the first time, I decided to try a technique called hot-shotting. To an extent, it was the same thing I had tried to achieve with the cocaine and the black beauties — the kick start just before a race.

"Cocaine and amphetamines were minor versions, however, of the true hot-shot, an injection of aqueous-testosterone. This is testosterone based in water, so the

effect on your body is instant. I wanted to come out of the blocks like a missile with a rocker engine boost … [Issajenko came fourth.] As far as I was concerned, my experiment with hotshotting had failed … Every time I tried it, I injured my hamstring."

Like many athletes, Issajenko found that the very drugs that were expected to help her win caused injuries because of the artificially increased size of the muscles. The short-cuts through drugs were not as effective as she hoped.

But in the fall of 1981, in spite of the drugs, or because of them—no one will ever know — she was ranked 5th in the world in both the 100 and 200 metres. Issajenko went from doctor to doctor trying to find good drug advice.

"Steroid-dependent would be a more accurate description of my state of mind by 1983 … I simply began steroids and began serious training at the same time. The truth is, I no longer knew if I could run without steroids, and if I was addicted to anything, I was addicted to winning" (Issajenko, 1990a: C14).

Issajenko will never know what she might have achieved drug-free. She does say with some pride: "that Fall, the magazine *Track and Field News* came out, as it does every year, with the world rankings for amateur athletes. I was seventh in the world in the 100-metres. That was for the 1979 season, when I was "clean" (Issajenko, 1990: 90). No one can take that away from her.

Athletes become drug dependent once they become convinced that the only way to win is with drugs. The dependency lies not in a craving for the fix, but in the belief that a win is not possible without the assistance of a particular drug.

Physicians and Athletes

All physicians who treat athletes are provided with a list of banned drugs or medications. The list is quite extensive. There is a specific section which is entitled "Sports medicine information: drug use and competition." It provides:

> Abbreviated information for athletes, coaches, medical practitioners on the safe, restricted and banned use of drugs in amateur sport is provided. The user is cautioned that the lists are not complete. New products are continually introduced on the market and the list of banned substances is periodically revised. Additional information may be obtained from the Sport Medicine Council of Canada …

If the doctor is not familiar with the updated banned substances, in prescribing a drug for a fairly minor complaint, the physician may put an athlete in a position where the athlete may test positive for a banned substance. The range of products and the regulations used by the Sport Medicine Council of Canada are complex. Some products may be taken any time, others taken only under strict supervision and medically justified conditions, and still others are completely forbidden. If an athlete has a cold and takes an over-the-counter product, a positive test may result. Examples of this might be the use of cold pills, cough syrups, or decongestants containing codeine which is a banned substance. Some products for the treatment of asthma are allowed and others are not. Some products can be used in an aerosol form only. Local anaesthetics that are injected can be used in certain forms, such as procaine, Xylocaine or Carbocaine. These must be medically justified and written details have to be submitted in order for an athlete to continue after injury in a competition.

Just as the law with regard to the health and safety of workers with restricted chemicals has been criticized, so some people are critical of the manner in which drugs are banned in sport. Some feel that drugs should be banned from sport altogether. Others in the sport field feel that it is impossible for non-medical people to decide what a doctor should or should not prescribe and that the *health risk* is the only basis upon which a drug should be banned (Savage, 1989:14).

The issue is very complex and highly controversial. For example beta-blockers, used by marksmen and archers to steady their hands, are also used in the field of music (Jeffers, 1989:C11). The moral

THE PLACEBO EFFECT

Values and beliefs about substances and techniques have an impact on performance too. The mere belief that a particular substance or technique will help will often lead to a better performance.

The **placebo effect** is the impact of taking a non-effective substance and believing it to be helpful.

Macmillan of Canada.

Angella Issajenko, "If I was addicted to anything, I was addicted to winning."

~ **SPORT PROFILE** ~

Charlie Francis—Canada's Famous Coach

Charlie Francis is known around the world as Ben Johnson's coach but he is also a former Canadian sprint champion who at 22 ran the 100 metres in 10.1 seconds. This was in 1971.

A year later, at the Olympics, Francis saw the advantages other international athletes had: "There were tracks of all surfaces—dirt, grass, and synthetic. The big national teams had weight rooms staffed around the clock with specialists and masseurs. Starters were available for practices at all times. The 1972 Olympics revealed one more area where sophisticated training programs had a leg up on the rest of the world: the use of anabolic steroids" (Francis & Coplon, 1990: 36).

Later in the decade when Francis began to coach he was determined that his Canadian athletes would have every training advantage. Some of those he coached were the international competitors Ben Johnson, Angella Issajenko, Mark McKoy, Desai Williams and Tony Sharpe.

Francis was also an innovator. He evaluated training approaches from a new perspective. He brought in *reduced* distance running, sprints at full speed, introduced massages and got winning results (ibid: 62). He trained males and females together. One of the young people he coached was Angella Taylor (Issajenko). She was so fast he hoped she would win a medal in the 1980 Olympics.

Francis explains: "Numbers define one's place in the track world. Now our place was receding—and I felt sure I knew why. Angella wasn't losing ground because of a talent gap. She was losing because of a drug gap, and it was widening by the day … An athlete could not expect to win in top international competition without using anabolic steroids (ibid: 83).

Charlie Francis knew that there was no serious drug testing in track and field. Athletes and coaches openly used drugs. "As I saw it, a coach had two options: he could face reality and plan an appropriate response, or he could bury his head in the sand while his athletes fell behind" (ibid: 83). Francis felt steroid use would make competition fairer for Issajenko and it was better for her to use drugs under controlled, medical conditions than to use the black market, as so many athletes were doing, especially as the medical community were claiming that there were few side effects to steroid use (ibid: 84).

Charlie Francis and his athletes then began their steroid programs of cycling on and off the drugs for greater effectiveness and to avoid positive drug tests. Steroids have clearance times and Francis would switch dosages to pass the tests. "To bridge the gap to race day, however, some athletes might switch to testosterone, for which there was no test until 1983; or take probenicid, which effectively masked steroid use and would be banned only in 1987; or add growth hormone for which there is no test. (Partly as a result of such manoeuvres, only a tiny percentage of steroid users have ever been caught)."

Since Ben Johnson's positive drug test, Francis' statements that drug use is rampant in sport have been verified. The Soviets had pre-event drug testing facilities of their own; the East Germans had a doping research program with "18 professors, 24 assistant professors, 132 doctors, and 240 staff people" (ibid: 285). Drug use in sport is a problem everywhere in the world. Manfred Donike of the IOC is quoted as saying: "The Russians know a few drugs, the East Germans are much more sophisticated, but the Americans are world champions of doping" (ibid: 286).

Charlie Francis feels that because track and field is big business now, the television stations call the shots. On the one hand, they want drug-free family entertainment and, on the other, they want new world records which are drug dependent. Certainly, it is clear to everyone that international sport was not committed to drug-free sport. Random drug testing would have been a first step and it was not taken. In Canada there were many rumours about the phenomenal successes of Francis' athletes and their amazing physiques, but it was only during the Dublin inquiry that drug issues were finally addressed publicly.

Francis does not challenge the issue of drug use because it seems the message he got from the whole sport system was "We like winners. No questions asked." Not many people would agree with Francis, but his explanation needs to be addressed. "Given the pressures of the day, I believe I would choose the same course again. And I'd have plenty of company—and a venerable tradition on my side" (ibid: 86).

Drug-Testing: A Cat and Mouse Game

There are many difficulties associated with testing for drugs. For which drugs should tests be done? What tests can reasonably be done if the cost for each test is in the $200–$300 dollar range? What can be done when masking agents are used to obstruct accurate testing?

One of the biggest drug scandals took place in Caracas, Venezuela in 1983;

... when fifteen athletes from ten countries (the United States, Cuba, Canada, Colombia, Nicaragua, Argentine, Puerto Rico, Venezuela,

Chile, and the Dominican Republic) were disqualified and stripped of twenty-three medals. ... Moveover, when told of the sensitivity of the tests—able to detect traces of scores of drugs used months, even years, before the test—twelve American athletes withdrew from the competition and went home (Goldman 1987:22-23).

The business of drug testing is like a cat and mouse game. But it has serious consequences because the lives and health of many young people are at stake.

THE FATHER OF STEROID USE IN NORTH AMERICA

Dr. Zeigler is the father of steroid use in North America. He found out about steroid use in 1956 from the Soviets and felt that it was unfair (in the context of the cold war) that the Soviets were beating the American athletes by using drugs. He worked with the drug company Ciba Pharmaceutical (now Ciba-Geigy) to develop an anabolic steroid and the drug was made available to American athletes (Goldman, 1987:94).

What he could not foresee, and later very much regretted, was that athletes would think that if a few pills were good more would be better. "They figured if one pill was good, three or four would be better, and they were eating them like candy" (ibid:94). Everyone wanted to use them!

question of the legitimacy of their use is thus raised—Is it right that a wonderful musical performance is drug-enhanced, but performance enhancers are not allowed in sport?

The Desperation to Win

Lovers of sport ask themselves why athletes like Johnson and Issajenko felt it was essential to use banned substances. What were the reasons for these decisions? It is important to examine what factors might have been part of these decisions.

In many sports, success is linked to being strong and powerful, so there is a great temptation to take drugs to improve strength and performance. Also, as mentioned previously, Sport Canada funds athletes on international competitive standards. As a result, an athlete has to rank against *international* competitors who may be using performance enhancing drugs.

Until 1988, many fans were under the impression that the East Germans, the Americans and the Soviet athletes were obviously just much better than Canadians—due to their bigger budgets, larger populations (with the exception of East Germany) and sport traditions. It has become increasingly clear with each new revelation that there was no such thing as a level playing field.

Apart from the obvious physical benefits, there are a number of aspects in the use of performance-enhancing drugs that help to account for their wide spread use.

Charlie Francis, introduced successful new techniques for training athletes.

Athlete Information Bureau (R. Pilon).

The Range of Drug Misuse

Sport doctor Bob Goldman outlines the amazing range of substances that athletes use or have used in attempts to improve performance.

- *Diuretics*—help athletes to make their weight categories; are also used to counteract fluid retention due to steroid use, Dangers: they can lead to electrolyte and fluid imbalances.

- *Blood boosting or blood packing*—removing 1200 cc. (approximately a quart) in advance and then replacing just the red cells increases the oxygen carrying capacity of the blood—may increase blood clotting and danger of infection.

- *Rectal Injections of air*—to increase swimmers buoyancy.

- *Alcohol*—previously thought that it aided oxygen consumption and performance—now it is accepted that it decreases performance.

- *Marijuana*—thought to help

athletes relax—dangers are that perception of improved performance are often incorrect and it distorts time and visual perceptions.

- *Amphetamines*—elevates mood and increases muscle tension, heart rate and blood pressure—dangers to the heart has lead to death.

- *Cocaine*—used as a stimulant and to conquer fear—dangers are that it is highly addictive. Professional teams worry about the consequences of addition.

- *Stimulant*—extremely addictive.

- *Alkalies*—help to neutralize the accumulation of acids in the bloodstream during physical exertion (the burn). Useful for middle distance runners. These include sodium bicarbonate, sodium citrate and potassium citrate.

- *Phosphates*—thought to bring

about feelings of euphoria and reduce fatigue.

- *Beta-adrenergic receptors*—propronolol, librium, valium, alcohol and sevax are used by ski jumpers, trap shooters, golfers and archers to slow down the heart.

- *Caffeine*—speeds up the cardio-vascular system—addictive and very dangerous.

There are a range of other substances that are thought to be useful, but there has been considerable debate about their usefulness and harmfulness. Food products like gelatin, glycine, fruit juices, oxygen, sugar, carbohydrate-loading, and DMSO—Dimethyl Sulfoxide use.

HGH (Human Growth Hormone) was the most popular substance under consideration in the late eighties (Goldman, 1984:97-111).

ANABOLIC STEROIDS

What are anabolic-androgenic steroids?

- anabolic refers to the muscle building characteristics of synthetic hormones

- "andro" comes from the Greek word for "man" or "male" and "genic" means producing, so androgenic refers to masculinizing or male hormonal effect. They are derivatives of the natural male hormone testosterone (Voy, 1991:13).

1. *Pre-testing support*. In a number of countries, there were extensive support systems that allowed athletes to receive banned substances and then undergo their own test in a national sport laboratories *before* any test by the IOC or outside testing facilities. This meant that scientists, doctors, coaches and trainers were helping the athletes avoid detection. If they tested positive in the pre-testing lab, they could claim injury and drop out of their event. The system supported their drug use. In Canada the athletes did not have this possibility. Sport Canada took a public position in opposition to drug use and did not provide any pre-testing.

2. *Big crowds and big sponsors*. Sport, and track and field in particular, have become a popular money maker for promoters and for sport associations. Big names attract big crowds and sponsors. It is in everyone's interest not to have positive drug tests. Charlie Francis argues that competitors

and their coaches were informed in advance which meets would be tested so drug schedules could be planned in advance. "Since 1968, when the IOC initiated drug testing at the Olympics, it has recorded a total of six positives in track and field—an average of one per Games" (1990:291). There is too much at stake to delay competitions or put the "big names" under drug shadows. Everyone wants the larger revenues with no embarrassments to upset the money cart.

3. *The effectiveness of banned substances.* On the track and field circuit there was an old saying "If you don't take it, you won't make it" (Francis, 1990: 291). A problem with steroid use, according to Dr. Robert Voy, the former Chief Medical Officer for the US Olympic Committee, is that "Because anabolic-androgenic steroids are so effective, ... it is hard to find a placebo or another substance that subjects would take and not know they weren't getting the real thing" (Voy, 1991:22). Athletes often want to use the substances.

4. *The glitter of gold.* The rewards for everyone around sport are enormous for first-place wins. Tony Sharpe, one of the Mazda Optimist athletes whom Charlie Francis coached, said at the Dubin Inquiry "The glory is too sweet, the dollars are too much" (Francis, 1990:292). Athletes and coaches put in years and years of work to reach the pinnacle of competition and that first-place finish is so important for recognition and financial rewards. It has been reported that Johnson probably lost as much as ten million dollars as a consequence of his positive test at the Seoul Olympics. The rewards are there for everyone associated with the athlete. The coaches, the trainers, the sponsors, the families, the spouses, the clubs all stand to gain from successes. This often means that the athlete may not have impartial people around him or her. The bandwagon is fun to be on. Advising caution and restraint may not be what a rising star wants to hear either.

5. *The health consequences.* The health consequences seem remote to most athletes whereas the direct results in muscle growth seem immediate. There are parallels with the smoking issue. For many teenagers smoking seems glamorous and fun and the consequences of lung cancer, emphysema and early death are perceived as scare tactics on the part of coaches or parents. The list of permanent harmful consequences for steroid users is extensive. Unconfirmed stories of deaths related to liver cancer, kidney tumours, heart attacks abound and Dr. Voy, the former Chief Medical Officer for the United States Olympic Committee, says that death is possible (1991:23).

PROFESSIONAL PLAYERS' CONCERNS ABOUT DRUG-TESTING

The players associations are nervous about the idea that there should be widespread drug testing. They see it as an invasion of privacy.

They argue that other workers do not have to go through such tests. However, some players have agreed to drug-testing clauses. They have said in public that they have nothing to hide and it is not important to them.

"WE HAVE COME HERE TO SWIM, NOT SING."

A popular story of the 1976 Montreal Olympics involved the success of the East German women swimmers. When asked why so many of their women had deep voices (suspecting drug use), an East German coach replied, "We have come here to swim, not sing."

DYING TO WIN

Dr. Bob Goldman, former world-class athlete, leading steroid expert and chair of Athletes Against Drug Abuse Canada, asked 198 world-class athletes the following question before the 1984 Summer Olympics.

"If I had a magic drug that was so fantastic that if you took it once you would win every competition you would enter, from the Olympic decathlon to Mr. Universe, for the next five years, but it had one drawback—it would kill you five years after you took it—would you take the drug?"

Of those asked, 103 (52 %) said yes. Winning was so attractive that they would not only be willing to achieve it by taking a pill (in other words, through an outlawed, unfair method—that is, in effect, cheating), but they would give their lives to do it (Goldman, 1987:32).

Side-Effects of Steroid Use

The list of permanent, harmful effects of anabolic-androgenic steroid for users is extensive.

Unconfirmed reports of deaths related to liver cnncer, kidney tumours, heart attacks, etc. abound. Dr Voy, former Medical Offiecer of the US Olympic team, says that death is possible (1991:23).

Some of the possible side-effects are:

- Acne—systic acne can leave permanent scars on the face, body and trunk
- nervous tension, agressiveness, and psychotic states—paranoia and anti-social behaviour
- increased sex drive after initial usage but decreased sex drive after repeated use (often leading to psychologically induced impotence)
- breast development in males, also known as gynaecomastia (a permanent effect)
- gastrointestinal and leg muscle cramping
- headaches, dizziness, and high-blood pressure
- burning and pain on urination
- bizzare testicular or scrotal pain
- premature male baldness
- excessive body and facial hair growth among women
- atrophy of testicles and decreasing sperm production
- prostrate enlargement, causing urination to be difficult
- enlargement of the clitoris, the female organ analogous to the male penis (usually irreversible and many require surgical removal)
- disruption of menstrual cycle
- deepening of the voice (permanent in women)
- stunted growth among adolescents, basically due to premature stoppage of the expected growth of the long bones.

Drug-free Guy Greavette, Champion Canadian weight lifter.

Recreational, Restorative, and Addictive Drugs

Nearly everyone consciously uses drugs at some point. People take aspirin for headaches or cramps. Antibiotics help cure bronchitis. Others use drugs for entertainment. People have a glass of beer at a party or while watching a game. Although illegal, some people smoke marijuana while listening to music, etc.; others light up cigarettes and drink coffee. Sadly, sometimes these drugs become addictive and cause a great deal of harm. Anyone who has seen a smoker light up an old cigarette butt left in an ashtray the night before, or "rescue" a butt from the garbage, has seen an addiction. It is not an amusing sight.

Blood-Doping—A Rather Different Kind of Drug Use

Usually the term "drug" is used to refer to any medical substance. An interesting example of a rather different kind of drug use is that of blood doping. Sometimes it is called **blood boosting**. Is a person who has a transfusion of his of her own blood using a drug?

The American cycling team was under a lot of pressure in the 1984 Olympics. The Americans had not had wins in cycling since the turn of the century.

Millions had been put into the high-tech program and every edge was needed. The team members were encouraged to go through the process of blood boosting.

In this case blood was taken from other family members some time before the Olympics and given back to the athletes just before the competition. Having additional red blood corpuscles means that the blood can transport more oxygen and give endurance athletes an improved performance.

Under the Olympic regulations drugs are not allowed. However, technically blood is not a drug and therefore the Americans were not in violation of the rules. Afterwards, this whole area came under review and blood doping is now illegal in the Olympics.

Some "recreational drugs" are seen to be a part of the sport itself. The post-game beer in hockey is almost as much a part of the sport as the puck itself. Socializing after the game is true for amateur as well as professional players. For professional players there is the added pressure of being away from home, the games being in the evening, the loneliness of the hotel room and the tight timetables which provide little free time to do other kinds of things. Alcohol seems to make things easier. Athletes have easy access to recreational non-legal drugs. Hangers-on are usually only too willing to provide them.

Because of the nature of their work, professional athletes also use drugs to heal from injuries. *Restorative drugs* are an essential part of sports because there is pressure to get the injured athlete back into action as a productive team member as soon as possible. This pressure comes from the athletes themselves, from the sports industry and from management. In this respect, medical people are often seen as servants of the industry. On the one hand, they may want to do what is best for the long-term health of the athlete; on the other, the management, whether it is the owner seeing the $1.5 million-dollar wonder sitting on the bench or the coach who desperately wants to win, wants to see the athlete fully fit again. Anything that speeds up the recovery is useful. The athletes themselves feel the frustration of sitting on the sidelines and fear being considered malingerers.

Some players also regularly take drugs without questioning the long-term effects. Derek Sanderson is an example of an athlete who took steroids for a colitis problem in the early seventies and now can hardly walk. He maintains that he would have done anything to continue playing, and probably would have taken the drug anyway, even if he had known there were serious risks.

DRUG-TESTING IN BASEBALL

In 1985, the then Commissioner of baseball, Peter Ueberroth, said that he would like to bring mandatory drug testing to the major leagues. There is some drug testing in the minor leagues, but it is not on a consistent basis.

Ueberroth decided to conditionally suspended for one year seven Philadelphia players who were involved in drug dealing. The players had to donate 10% of their income to drug prevention programs, submit to random drug testing for the rest of their careers and fulfil 100 hours of community work in the next two years (Ueberroth, 1986). He wanted to send out a message to all players that the owners do not want to read more stories about baseball and drugs.

The Medical and Non-Medical Use of Drugs in Sport

The Sport Medicine Council and Sport Canada very clearly outline their concerns about drug use in their handbook, *Banned and Restricted Doping Classes and Methods*, which is given to each high-performance Canadian athlete .

The only reason that an athlete should be taking any drugs is for a clinical condition that is being treated by a doctor. The International Olympic Committee (IOC) and other international sport organizations started drug testing to protect amateur athletes from (a) the potential unfair advantage that might be gained by those athletes who take drugs to enhance performance and (b) the potential harmful side effects which some drugs can produce.

Drugs are put into three categories — banned, restricted and permitted. "Different sports may ban different drugs" and the athlete's doctor has to refer to the *Compendium of Pharmaceutical and Specialities* (CPS) for detailed information.

Athletes are told if they are in doubt about a drug they should not take it. However, it can be complicated. For example, Robitussin is permitted but Robitussin PS contains a banned substance (ibid: 2).

BANNED AND RESTRICTED DOPING CLASSES

SECTION I
IOC Banned Drugs
A. Stimulants
B. Narcotic Analgesics
C. Anabolic Steroids
D. Beta-Blockers
E. Diuretics
F. Blood Doping

SECTION II
A. Injectable local anaesthetics
B. Asthma and Respiratory Ailments Drugs (Beta-agonists)
C. Corticosteroids
D. Caffeine
E. Alcohol
F. Marijuana

SECTION III
Permitted Drugs that are NOT currently banned.

- Analgesics (painkillers)
- Antacids
- Antibiotics
- Anti-asthmatics
- Anti-convulsants (anti-epileptics)

- Anti-depressants
- Anti-diabetics
- Anti-diarrheals
- Anti-fungals
- Anti-histamines
- Anti-inflammatories
- Anti-nauseants
- Anti-ulcer
- Anti-viral
- Contraceptives
- Cough syrups and lozenges
- Decongestants
- Eye/ear drops
- Haemorrhoidal preparations
- Laxatives
- Migraine medications
- Muscle relaxants
- Ointments/creams/lotions
- Sedatives
- Tranquilizers
- Vaginal preparations

Source: Banned and Restricted Doping Classes and Methods. 1989. Sport Medicine Council of Canada. Minister of Supply and Services: 3–9. (Modified)

COCAINE ADDICTION.

Recently, medical doctors have become increasingly concerned about cocaine addiction. Unlike other harmful substances, cocaine addiction can take place in a few weeks, rather than in a few years. It is a much more powerful chemical than was initially realized.

Amphetamines are also regarded as part of the sport industry. Jim Bouton, the baseball player, describes players popping them like smarties in his book *Ball Four, Plus Ball Five*. A study of professional football players in the 1970s found that two thirds of the players occasionally or regularly took amphetamines (Curry & Jiobu, 1984:222). The difficulty is, of course, that athletes cannot afford to have days where they perform below average. They are not expected to have poor days. The pressure is there to perform and to perform well at all times.

Work Fair, Clear the Air—Smoking

Smoking cannot be separated from health and fitness. It is the major cause of ill-health in Canada.

Increasingly, more and more cities are passing by-laws against smoking in public places. More workplaces are creating smoke-free environments. The difficulty is, however, that smoking is not like preferring the CBC over NBC. Once the person begins smoking, an addiction develops and there is evidence that smoking is a harder addiction to treat then heroin. It takes the average smoker nine attempts before he or she finally quit.

On the other hand, fewer people are smoking nowadays. Twenty years ago over 50% of the male population smoked; now it is around 35%, depending on the age group. Unfortunately, one segment of the population is responding to the advertisements aimed at it, and that is young women. Advertisements of products such as Virginia Slims, etc., are working.

Everyone claims that they know the hazards of smoking and will usually quote the example of lung cancer. Yet, there are many other smoking-related illnesses that are not mentioned. Heart disease is one of them. Contrary to the general belief that smoking calms people's nerves, it in fact puts the body under great strain. Smoking one cigarette raises the heart rate by twenty beats a minute and the effects linger for about 25 minutes. With the constriction of the blood vessels, reduced oxygen in the blood stream and the contaminants in the smoke itself, the heart is put under considerable stress (Glover & Shepherd, 1983: 284).

Work fair, clear the air

Of course there are those who say "I want to enjoy life now, who cares." Sadly, included in that group are athletes. Athletes are no more resistant to advertisements than the rest of the population. Some athletes, because they are fit, parade their athletic ability as proof of the non-harmful nature of smoking. Obviously, they have not read the long-term studies.

Some addicted smokers justify their smoking by proclaiming their "right to smoke in the privacy of their own closet." Increasingly, of course, it is unsocial behaviour to smoke in public places. However, even second-hand tobacco smoke is lethal. Women who never smoked themselves but who are married to men who smoke at home die at a higher rate from lung cancer than non-smokers, even though they never smoked themselves. Children are away from school more often and get coughs and colds more frequently if they live in a home with adults who smoke.

Because it is now known that second hand smoke is a killer to non-smokers, just as cigarettes are killers for smokers, we are seeing more and more communities pass legislation and municipal by-laws to prohibit smoking in order to reduce health risks. The assumption is that employees in the workplace have the right to work in a smoke-free environment.

WOMEN, ALCOHOL AND SPORT

Results from an American study on women athletes found that only 50% of women in the general public drink alcohol, but 76% of women athletes surveyed as part of the Women's Sport Foundation study by Hazelden-Cork had drunk alcohol within the last thirty days (*Women's Sports and Fitness*, 1987:26).

Ethics and Technology—How Good Are You, Really?

Carol Anne Letheren, who was chef de mission at Seoul in 1988 and is also an IOC member, sees drug use from the perspective of a lifetime in sport. She sees drug use as an ethics and technology issue which undermine the athlete's ability to know the genuine limits of his or her ability. She feels it is essential that the sport system takes responsibility for its role vis-à-vis the athlete and focus on education and, where necessary, rehabilitation.

"At Seoul what we were really observing was not drugs in sport but ethics and technology. We see young people who are dedicating sometimes maybe fifteen years of their lives, seven or eight hours a day, seven days a week to arrive at a moment of time in history where they want to perform the ultimate, and their absolute personal best. There's only one gold medal. They are looking for that competitive edge that will make them the best they can be at that moment … Compare that to an Ivan Boesky, a Donald Trump or anybody in any competitive field who is seeking the competitive edge and athletes are going to look for the tools and the opportunities in some way."

If technology can give that competitive edge to an athlete and success means gold medals and financial rewards, the question becomes what should be done about it. Letheren explains: "Now we're at a crossroads and we have to make choices. Technology is going to offer us a series of opportunities that are going to help us. The question becomes what do we have inside us that allows us or helps us to make wise choices,

so we can decide that a particular technology is inappropriate because if I indulge in it I'm cheating."

She does not see the athlete in isolation however. Each athlete operates within the wider sport system. "The sport system has to say we're dealing with young people and it's our responsibility to help them to make those wise choices. One can't turn around to the athletes and say it's your problem, you suffer the penalties, you take all the blame because you took those steroids and the rest of us are absolutely clean. There's nothing we have to do—it's your problem. I just don't buy that."

Letheren is convinced that the ethics and technology issue in sport involves education and changing values. "We're dealing with an educational issue, an awareness issue. If you want to cheat go ahead. You may win and you may get away with it, but you are going to live the rest of your life knowing that you got there unfairly, number one. But also you're going to live the rest of your life never knowing how good you are. You'll never know how good you are because you've chosen to use, in that case, an artificial substance or a chemical substance to help you get your body to a state that will give you that edge.

We're never going to get rid of drugs in sport—the wreaths in Olympic sport at the end of the day are so coveted, People can say it's because of the greed and money, but that's not formally correct. In most sports our athletes are not going to make a great deal of money. The issue is more a personal one of competitive drive—the goal is so individually

driven. There is a tremendous responsibility on the individual and I think there is a tremendous responsibility on the system surrounding that individual to create the best possible environment for that person to grow as a person as well as an athlete."

For those athletes who try to beat the system she argues for rehabilitation, but an end to government funding. "We should help the athlete rehabilitate. They should understand the seriousness of what they've done, but they should have a chance to come back. These are young people and I think that a second chance is everything. The punishment has to fit the crime. These people are not criminals. I do not believe in a lifetime ban for first-time steroid use, not at all, but fior a second offense, yes."

Quotations from a personal interview by the author, July 1991.

Eat to Win—Diet and Nutrition

Weight gain is linked to the kinds of food that we eat. Foods contain six major nutrients: fats, carbohydrates, proteins, minerals, vitamins, and water. Only three of these—fats, carbohydrates and proteins—contain energy (Measure of Fitness, 1985: 8).

The average diet should consist of:

- 60% carbohydrates
- 30% fats
- 10% protein

What most people consume is:

- 46% carbohydrates
- 42% fats
- 12% protein
  (*Measure of Energy*, 1985: 8)

In other words, although people eat good quanitites of food in North America, it often consists of the wrong balance of foods. In the past, dieters would often avoid eating such things as pasta, believing that it was fattening. Now we know that it is an important source of complex carbohydrates. Elite athletes are turning away from the traditional steak and potatoes to foods such as pasta and salads.

Tennis player Martina Navratilova is a high performance athlete who changed her diet to correspond with the new understanding of nutrition. She is a fan of Dr. Robert Haas, who is a proponent of the high carbohydrate diets. He maintains that each athlete should have a blood chemistry profile done—to obtain better performances and to evaluate risks of diet-related diseases. The five vital values he thinks should be of concern are: total cholesterol, high-density lipoprotein (HDL) cholesterol, glucose (blood sugar), triglycerides (blood fats), and uric acid.

Haas' diet aims to improve these values so that peak performance can be reached by athletes (Haas, 1983: 38–39). Hence, he called his book *Eat To Win*. Some nutritionists have criticized his work and feel that traditional guidelines are better.

Alcohol and Sport

Alcohol is a long-standing social problem. A study on average Canadians showed 77% of all Canadians drink and 26% admit they over-indulge from time to time. Even two out of every five fifteen-year-olds use alcohol once a month (Woolsey, 1986).

Generally speaking, alcohol has not been considered a serious problem in sports. In Canada, hockey and alcohol are of course very closely identified, if only because of the sheer number of beer commercials during televised hockey games. However, there has been little discussion in the press about alcohol and alcohol addiction among athletes. The focus has been on cocaine use. With the fatal car accident involving hockey player Pelle Lindbergh, the matter has

Sport and Pain

One aspect of sport not discussed a great deal is that of pain. Many professional athletes live with constant pain. Often recreational athletes take the view "no pain no gain" and push themselves to the point of injury.

Pain is the body's messenger to rest and recover. Often the handy pill bottle provides a seemingly quick and easy answer. The difficulty is that this short-term solution often holds a long-term danger. Hospitals and doctor's offices are full of athletes who "had to" go onto the field and "had to" play. The very pills that are supposed to help an athlete perform in fact create the greatest dangers because they mask the seriousness of the injuries. The body's alarm system is overridden by the painkilling drugs. Because athletes love their sport and because the sport industry often demands participation when injured, injuries are often exacerbated.

A sport where drug use of all kinds has been commonplace for thirty years is that of NFL football. Steroids and pain-killers have been widely used by players, and the consequences of this are now being seen. These apparently healthy men are in fact dying at a much younger age than the general population. It seems clear that the combination of drug use, increased body size by means of unusual weight lifting and the sheer physical abuse from the game is causing earlier deaths. The main reason for insurance claims from NHLers (who have played the required four years) who have died in their thirties, forties and fifties is cardio-vascular disease. It appears that arterial-sclerosis associated with steroid use may be the culprit.

Thomas Henderson played football with the Dallas Cowboys. He was a linebacker who liked to hit. It wasn't until his rookie year as a professional that he himself received a bad hit — a helmet directly into his hip. "I never wore hip pads or rib pads so I took it right on the bone. I thought he'd broken me in half" (Henderson, 1987: 91). Henderson couldn't even walk. He received an injection of cortisone, two injections of Xylocaine and two Codeine IVs. "I got up off the table, bent to the left, bent to the right. I didn't feel a damn thing. No pain, no discomfort, no nothing." He then went out and scored a touchdown, the Cowboys won 37–31 and he won the Big Play award for the Game.

"No one told me that I wasn't going to be able to walk Monday or Tuesday ... "On Monday I couldn't even practice. When you get hurt in the NFL the real pain comes on Wednesday. The day after the game you're basically okay, just generally sore. Tuesday you're okay. Wednesday the pain really sets in. Especially when they have anaesthetized an area, because it takes that long for the cortisone and the Xylocaine to wear off. By the third day your body just refuses to be ignored any more.

"They gave me another shot of Xylocaine and another shot of cortisone and some more codeine IVs and I got hooked. By the third week of the NFL I got hooked on drugs that made me not feel. The first feelings that I knew I could anaesthetize were the feelings of pain. I didn't have to feel pain when I played this game. And the drugs they didn't give me I could get on my own."

Thomas Henderson, nicknamed "Hollywood" Henderson began to use cocaine as well. It was the beginning of a downward slope, which eventually led to his ruining his life. By 1980 he had been dumped by the Cowboys because his drug use was affecting his performance. In nine weeks, while playing for his new team in Houston, he spent $110,000 — his whole salary— on cocaine.

received more publicity. Other players have spoken up as well. Retired superstar Derek Sanderson has said that the lifestyle of hockey players is a major problem. Hockey players have:

> too much money, too much free time, boredom ... you'd be six hours on an airplane, I was drunk six hours. With the Bruins, we'd travel by train sometimes. What would you do? Play gin and drink (Woolsey,1986).

The drinking problem for some players starts as junior players. Sanderson himself, as a young athlete, did not believe in drugs or drinking because he was a dedicated athlete.

The hockey industry itself is starting to become more aware of alcohol problems. The Minnesota North Stars have banned beer from their dressing room and the Flyers have been using a sport psychologist to develop other ways of relaxing after games (Woolsey, 1986). In the past, players thought that drinking beer helped replace lost body fluids, not realizing that it caused further dehydration.

Making a Difference

More and more scientific evidence shows that there are real dangers associated with drugs used to enhance sport performance, yet many athletes continue to ignore the dangers. Angela Issajenko, the Canadian sprinter, has said "if athletes don't see other athletes dropping dead, they do not believe the dangers" (Macleod, 1989:13). Yet, West German heptathlete Birgit Dressel died at twenty-six, after over 400 injections of many kinds of drugs including vitamins. A Swedish body builder died at twenty-eight with the arteries of a seventy-year-old after steroid use (Macleod, 1989:13).

Some members of the International Amateur Athletic Foundation (IAAF) feel that widespread use of random drug testing will solve the problem of drug use. However, random drug testing can only be part of the solution. It would seem necessary to attack drug use among athletes from a number of different directions. What is required above all is a renewed education program at all levels in sport—including owners, managers and coaches.

A complete program for dealing with substance abuse must involve the following elements:

1. *Education of athletes, coaches, physicians, parents and the media about risks and consequences.* If we make comparisons with the highly addictive use of cigarettes, it is clear that change takes place slowly. Drug-free competition has to be consciously and persistently encouraged and promoted and rewarded—through schools, colleges and universities and through the sports programs themselves.

2. *Random doping tests are essential and should be administered both within and outside competition.* Most people keep to the speed limit but there are always those who want to speed. The police monitor cars and use speed traps to ticket those who break the speed limit. There will always be athletes who will try to beat the system, therefore the

Francis Farrugia (Max Body Sports).

Anja Langer, world-class Dutch competitor at a body-building competition in Toronto.

STEROIDS WIDELY USED

Dr. Voy, former Chief Medical Officer of the US Olympic Team, claims anabolic steroid use is almost universal in sport.

"In fact, the only Olympic sports where I have not witnessed AAS use have been table tennis, women's field hockey, men's and women's figure skating, equestrian events and women's gymnastics. When I'm asked which sports' athletes take steroids, I usually answer, 'You show me a sport where increased power, endurance, or speed can possibly benefit the athlete, and I'll show you a sport where AAS use exists'"(Voy, 1991:17).

expenses related to testing should be viewed as an inevitable part of running high performance programs.

3. *Change carding criteria.* If government financial support is based on performances that are the best in Canada, rather than world rankings, then the desperation to cheat in order to get funding will be reduced. Some athletes felt that Athletics Canada was hypocritical in holding up Charlie Francis' team as models to follow when it was widely suspected that they were using steroids. It seemed to some that the message was "win and don't tell us how you do it."

4. *Health and safety.* Athletes should never be expected to harm their health in order to win and thus bring fame and glory to Canada or their sponsors. Perhaps in twenty years time, people will look back on this period and view our expectations of athletes and performance in the same way we read with horror the stories of animal abuse in the nineteenth century.

5. *Ethical debate.* Unless the issues are on the table and athletes feel they are free to discuss the questions of drug use, ethics and politics, it is very difficult for change to take place in sport. Many athletes feel unable to speak up about the things that seem unfair to them. Many other fields have constant debate about ethical issues—doctors, teachers and even lawyers discuss the ethics of their professions. Sport has become bureaucratized and professionalized and perhaps it is time for greater regulation and ethical discussion on a more formal basis.

6. *Personal responsibility.* With increased education and a system that expects and supports ethical non-cheating behaviour, athletes will themselves choose to reject drugs. Personal responsibility comes when those in responsible positions act responsibly and set examples for others. Athletes take great personal pride in their achievements and will respond favourably to any opportunity to display greater personal responsibility in these matters. Greater support should also be given to athletes in areas of nutrition, training and equipment so that athletes feel they are getting the best support available.

It is sad to think that the love that so many feel towards physical activity and sport has been lost in a quagmire of suspicion and doubt. Because attitudes about high performance sport spill over into recreational sport the consequences are all the more worrying.

If we are unable to solve the problem of drug use, then competitive sport will lose its undisputed charm for many people. Those who succeed will not be applauded but suspected of wrong-doing (Macleod, 1989:12). Often when a new record is broken, disparaging comments are made about drug use. People do not accept or relish physical triumphs as they once did in the past. All athletes now have this question mark hanging over their performances—Was the athlete clean?

Testing for substance abuse will remain a central part of the battle to ensure a "level playing field" in sport, but clearly more is required. With each new technological breakthrough in this area comes the chance of avoiding detection. There has to be a strong, clear message from the most senior sport administrators and politicians that drug use in sport will not be tolerated.

BODY BUILDING?

A student research paper done in Toronto gyms in the mid 80s found that nearly half the amateur bodybuilders were using steroids. In the area of professional bodybuilding competitions, it is thought they are an essential tool. In fact there is a growing movement of bodybuilders who compete in "natural" events without using chemicals. They find it necessary to establish a separate competition!

REVIEW

Questions

1. What are performance enhancers?
2. What is the primary cause of the use of performance-enhancing drugs?
3. When does drug use become a problem?
4. What is the substance, widely used and legal, that causes the most problems in Canadian society?
5. What are anabolic-androgenic steroids? What are some of the reasons that athletes have used steroids?
6. What are the side effects of steroid use? Why do athletes continue to ignore warnings about drug use?
7. What are some of the other drugs that are used to enhance performance?
8. How can drug testing and education help to eliminate drug misuse in sport?

Concepts

- performance enhancer
- testing
- ergogenic aids
- blood boosting
- psycho active drugs
- anabolic-androgenic steroids

Discussion

1. What are the factors that lead athletes to use banned drugs?
2. What might you do if you were head of Sport Canada and had to address the problem of athletes using drugs?
3. Why is it important to encourage drug-free sport and physical activity?

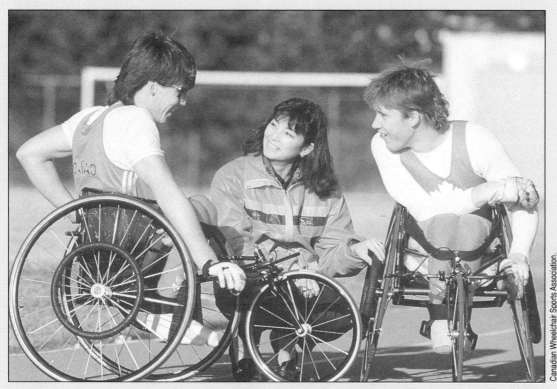

Jamie Cody and James Baker in training.

Playing field hockey can be fun for both the winners and losers if the spirit is right.

Chapter Thirteen

WHERE IS SPORT GOING

"A map of the world that does not include utopia is not worth even glancing at."
Oscar Wilde

"A demanding activity can test to the limit our bodies as well as our minds. ... Each of us has to find this activity for himself (or herself). It may be mountain climbing, running or sailing, or it may be something quite different. The important thing is that we should perform ourselves rather than watch others."
Roger Bannister, the first athlete to run the four-minute-mile.

Sport is under the microscope. As the pain of the Ben Johnson incident fades into memory, Canadians are evaluating what sport should be and what are the costs to the athletes who compete at the high-performance level. Is sport corrupt? Should there be less violence in hockey? Should drug testing be compulsory? There is debate, argument and more debate.

All this is a positive development. Instead of having a sense of regret or loss about how sport used to be, discussion can focus on what it is and what it could be. In this concluding chapter, we will consider the direction of sport in the 1990s and beyond.

The Potential of Sport

As we have seen throughout earlier chapters, sport experience is rooted in the culture and society where it takes place. Expectations, hopes and even the execution of sports are influenced by the social organization of sport and values about who will participate in physical activities and how.

Much of the anxiety we feel about sport is related to the great changes taking place in Canada and throughout the world. In Canada, we have experienced a major economic downturn (combined with a

Sport for a cold climate—Pierre Harvey, champion cross-country skier.

Athlete Information Bureau (J. Gibson).

Changes in the World Of Sport

If we look back in time we see that many profound changes have taken place in Canadian sport. Just over a hundred years ago a person attending a sport event would have lived in a society where the following would have been taken for granted:

- Considerable cruelty towards animals was the norm: baiting animals or watching animals fight to the death was considered acceptable.

- Brutality within sport was common. Fist fights without gloves were common. Fights were long and bloody. Safety rules were non-existent.

- The right to vote was limited to men and restricted by property requirements. All men were certainly not treated equally. Political rights were not an automatic part of citizenship. Only certain sporting activities were open to competitors. Classifications on the basis of amateur and professional status had most to do with economic status and work.

- Women suffered even greater discrimination, with the additional load of childbearing, poorer wages (if they were able to work) and public institutionalization of their inferiority. Their second class status was automatically assumed. Exclusion and inequity are the terms that best describe women's lives in those days.

- Children very often went to work at a very early age. There was no institutionalized recognition of a period of childhood play. The special talents of their nimble fingers and small bodies were often utilized in very primitive conditions to aid in a family's survival or to increase profits for a company owner.

- Freedom to work where and when you liked did not exist. Slavery in many societies reduced some to chattels, or pieces of property. Work contracts restricted a person's freedom, so that often an individual might be forced to work for the same person or company for many years as an indentured servant.

- Long work days were the norm, usually six days a week. Most people had little free time or leisure time due to the hard necessity of working to survive. There were very clear divisions between the leisurely pursuits of the "leisured classes" and the rest of the population which struggled on.

- Education was not compulsory for all children. The ability to read and write effectively was a privilege of the well-to-do. For many it was hard to be effective in obtaining access, input or control over sport structures.

- Many children and adults went hungry and were poorly clothed.

There were no extensive institutionalized governmental support systems for the disabled, the elderly or the unemployed. Money for leisure time or physical activities was not available.

- There were no entrenched civil or human rights as we know them to-day. Employers, schools and individuals could effect racist or discriminatory behaviour and there was no recourse in the courts. There was no guarantee of access to resources, training, competition or the rewards associated with sport.

- Sport and physical activities were very narrowly defined. Working people had their activities and the leisured classes had theirs. The public images of sport in the press were for the most part white and male. Participation was more the norm than commercialized spectator sport before the days of electric light and modern city transit systems.

~ SPORT PROFILE ~

Angela Bailey—A Voice for Sport

b. 1962, Coventry, England; currently a Canadian living in Toronto, Ontario. Angela Bailey's love of running developed as an eleven-year-old when she won a local championship race. But it was at sixteen years of age in Canada that she decided to become serious about competition.

Bailey realized that running could provide an opportunity to do other things as well. "I like everything about running. I'm good at it. It provided an opportunity to travel and also meet interesting people."

In the 1980s Bailey found herself in the middle of a situation which was unacceptable. All around her athletes were using drugs. Like the runner Bill Crothers before her, she went to the sport authorities at the national level in 1983 to tell her story. However, no one seemed interested. She tried at various times in 1984, 1985, and 1986, but nothing happened. It seemed as if everyone in sport was happy with the winners.

"I went to where things should be done. I was in there to compete. I had problems competing clean … Everyone who wanted to know, could find out about drugs."

Asked whether it bothers her that things were not fair, she replies quietly and firmly: "Nothing's fair in life, being black and a woman I realized that many things aren't fair. I have a God-given talent and I wanted to use my potential. I try to do my best. What I am proud of is my 10.98 drug-free 100 metres. Everyone said no athlete could go under 11 flat—everyone knew that, and I proved them wrong in Budapest in 1987. It was also very special to win the Olympic silver medal in the 4 x 100 in the 1984 Olympics."

In looking at the new athletes entering the world scene Angela Bailey has this to say: "It's good that athletes like Mike Smith and his generation can speak up to the press (about drugs) and be listened to—no one will be hiding their heads in the sand. Choices are available and people are now aware of the consequences."

Quotations from a personal interview by the author, November 1991.

new tax on consumers), with no lasting recovery in sight. We have also experienced Meech Lake (involving the future unity of Canada and Quebec) and "Oka" (involving the First Peoples' continuing struggle over land claims). As well, we have experienced the continuing degradation of the environment and the struggle to redress the damage. Internationally, these years have brought war on a grand scale (in the Gulf), the spectre of nuclear annihilation, as well as mass starvation in parts of Africa. We have also witnessed remarkable popular uprisings for democracy in Eastern Europe and the Soviet Union. These are unsettling events, and we can be certain the next decade will be quite different from the previous one.

Most people did not foresee these changes and most never thought that such profound change could take place so quickly. In the same way, many people are struggling to re-evaluate ideas and approaches to sport. Society is changing, and so is our perception of sport and physical activity. It is only by analyzing what is taking place around us, throughout Canada and the world, that it is possible to evaluate whether we like what we see or if we want to change it.

Angela Bailey.

Loves to run—Angela Bailey in her winning form.

To Stamp Out Incentives for Athletes to Cheat

Globe and Mail Editorial

The doctor who administered performance-enhancing steroids to Canadian sprinter Ben Johnson has been reprimanded, and another chapter in the country's shameful sport story closes. Whether Canada can turn the page to develop an effective strategy to deal with the moral crisis in amateur sport and make an impact as a world crusader against doping is the next question.

Dr. George Mario (Jamie) Astaphan's licence to practice medicine has been suspended for 18 months for violating Ontario's Health Disciplines Act, chiefly for his involvement in steroid programs. He said he cared for athletes who would have taken drugs with or without his assistance. Those who counsel improper drug use should be dealt with severely, and by its strict policing Canada has discouraged drug use by athletes and complicity by sports officials, coaches and doctors. But in the absence of measures to tackle incentives for athletes to cheat, the anti-doping message is not complete.

There has been little change to policies and practices in the sport world that are at the root of the problem. In Canada, where a revamped amateur sport system and legislation to improve the control of anabolic steroids are promised this fall, government support for athletes continues to be tied with world rankings.

The commercial gain that comes from athletic excellence—outlined last year in the Dubin Royal Commission into the Use of Drugs and Banned Practices—offers a strong impetus to bend the rules.

A new report by the federal government, titled *Values and Ethics in Amateur Sport: Morality, Leadership and Education*, looks further at cheating by athletes and finds "confusion about morality, a vacuum in leadership and a lack of education focused on values and ethics." There is simply a premium on winning, it says. "Those values that once motivated participation in amateur sport, for instance the quest for personal growth and excellence, have usurped by other values, those of winning, fame and money."

There are different interpretations of ethics in sport in the international sphere, the report says, "Fairness" can mean playing by the rules, doing what everyone else does or doing "whatever you can get away with."

The new Minister of State for Fitness and Amateur Sport, Pierre Cadieux, says he believes that, armed with a new strategy, Canada can influence the world to adopt strict anti-doping standards, an idealistic goal that has already met resistance from the world sport community. The International Skating Union has threatened to pull the junior world championship out of Canada rather than agree to this country's drug testing protocol.

The anti-drug message is having some success internationally, largely with the help of changing political systems. Sport bodies in Eastern Bloc countries that cooperated in cheating in the past no longer offer the secrecy, finances or bureaucracy under which drug use can flourish. As well, countries such as Britain, Australia and West Germany have held their own Dubin inquiries or set up agencies to police drug use.

The motivation for cheating, as well as mechanisms to stop the use of performance-enhancing drugs, must be strongly addressed in an anti-doping strategy for Canada, which can in turn educate the world. Dealing with the crisis in sport is a question of values as well as pharmacology.

Source: Globe and Mail, June 8, 1991.

What is the potential, the possibility, the future of sport? There are a number of exciting possibilities for sport in the future. For one thing, today, we have much more sophisticated tools to study sport, athletes and fans. The computer, psychologists, sociologists, anthropologists, historians, statisticians all facilitate the greater understanding of the social context of sport. It is through accurate information that a greater understanding can come about and changes can be made.

~ SPORT PROFILE ~

Juan Antonio Samaranch—Innovative IOC President

b. 1921, Barcelona, Spain. Juan Antonio Samaranch became head of the International Olympic Committee (IOC) in 1980. At that time the Olympics were in trouble. Few cities wanted to host the Olympics (only Los Angeles bid in 1978), the Soviets were about to boycott the 1980 Olympics and there were many complaints about the amateur / shamateur/ professional categories.

Samaranch is the past president of the Spanish roller-skate hockey association (Barber, 1988: 84). He is also a banker and career diplomat. He was Spain's ambassador to the Soviet Union and brings a delicate touch to the often tricky political conflicts that take place in the name of sport.

In the political arena, he tried very hard to persuade the Soviets to participate in the 1984 Los Angeles Olympics, without success. But the Olympics went on regardless. He also managed to get the Taiwanese to compete using the Olympic committee flag, and so the People's Republic of China agreed to participate as well (Barber, 1988: 84). Then North Korea wanted to co-host the 1988 summer Olympics and boycotts were threatened by the communist bloc. However, despite these obstacles, the 1988 Seoul Olympics went smoothly.

Samaranch also decided to allow "professional" athletes to compete. His view was: "Professionals have been in the Olympics for a long time. What we are doing now is telling people the truth about athletes' status. We want everything clean and clear" (Barber, 1988: 85).

After the incredible financial success of the privately funded Los Angeles Games, where $240 million was made to be distributed to sports organizations, the IOC under Samaranch decided it had to control its own marketing. "In 1985 it hired a Swiss firm, International Sports, Culture and Leisure Marketing (ISL), to oversee the global marketing of all Olympic properties, chiefly the five-ring logo" (Barber, 1988: 86).

An innovative president at a time when the IOC greatly needed it, Samaranch leaves a distinct mark on the history of the Olympics.

A simple example of this is the question of fan safety in football stadiums. Research on the movement of people in crowds, completed by the Canadian National Research Council, indicates that the government requirements for British stadiums, based on engineering guidelines, does not fit with the research on what people actually do in stadiums (Canter, Comber & Uzzell, 1989:97). The fact that people choose to go down the right side of a staircase, even if the left side is open, can dramatically change flow patterns (Canter et al, 1989: 96). The old stadiums with their narrow stairways, small door openings and cramped corridors could not possibly provide adequate fast escape for fans *regardless of the hooligan nature of the fans.* This has great significance for the planning of facilities and the understanding of crushes with soccer "hooligans."

Accurate research of this kind means that taxpayers' money can be used more effectively. The $160 million dollars to be provided by the British government to improve safety and comfort at soccer stadiums, in the wake of the Hillsborough disaster, can be spent where it is most useful (Funds for soccer safety, March 21, 1990:A19).

International Olympic Committee (Jean-Paul Madeder).

Juan Antonio Samaranch, President of the International Olympic Committee.

A Success Story: Women in Sports

It has been said that the reason we don't see as many female teenagers in the parks and participating in sport activities is because they are not interested. A group of people in Ottawa decided to investigate the truth of this.

When we examine what happens to girls and physical activities in Canada we find there are common patterns in nearly all communities:

- less encouragement to participate in the same range of activities as boys (at all ages from family, teachers, friends or the media);
- less encouragement to develop the full range of basic motor skills and therefore specific skills as a base for sport participation;
- a lower level of performance expectations;
- fewer choices and opportunities;
- fewer facilities and less funding (male dominated sports like hockey and football get more of everything);
- less media coverage; less visibility and more emphasis on appearance;
- fewer role models;
- myths about of sport being dangerous to women, although there is no evidence for this.

The examination of sports activities in Ottawa revealed that males participated at a higher rate than females (61% versus 39%); males were better serviced; female youths (aged 13-17) had the lowest participation rate; females tended to participate in individual, non-competitive activities and males in competitive, group activities; females were more likely to participate in activities which had a fee and were more expensive (*On the Move I Program*, 1989:16).

Various groups and government departments combined their efforts to support the *Women and Sport* program. These were the City of Ottawa, Women's Program Fitness, and Amateur Sport and Women in Sport Leadership and Sport Canada. The *On the Move Program* was designed to reach "inactive or semi-active" girls who would not normally be involved in organized sport.

A two-year pilot program began in 1985 with the City of Ottawa, the Ottawa Board of Education, and parents in the community working together. Soccer, softball and volleyball were the chosen sports, but soccer was later dropped because it was well supported in other programs. A Sportsline was included—a telephone number Ottawa residents could call to get information about what programs were offered. The idea was to find out if participation rates would increase if programs were offered specifically for young girls.

The program is not the typical sport program where the emphasis is on competition and choosing the best in order to have winning teams.

Once the girls are "hooked" on the fun of playing on their team, they begin to develop sport skills, to come out to practices and even to attend occasional training workshops. However their primary interest is in playing and sport participation can teach more than just sport skills. It can instill important values and behaviour such as teamwork, discipline, cooperation and fair play (*On the Move II Guidebook*, 1989:8).

The program was extremely successful: 650,000 people were surveyed and the impact of the new program was considerable.

- there was a 10% increase in female sport participation between 1983/4 and 1986/7;
- there was a 19% increase in female participation in the program cluster (group oriented, inexpensive and competitive) targeted by the Women and Sport Program;
- volunteer support was high (800 hours of volunteer support);
- leadership training and coaching programs meant that eighty-five women had participated in training programs (*On the Move I Program*, 1989:20).

What this program shows very clearly is that if programs are tailored to meet the interests and needs of young women, they will participate in larger numbers. The social and cultural conditions which encourage boys to "naturally" participate are not automatically in place in local community, recreational and school programs. If children can be encouraged to become active and have fun through physical activity their lives will be enriched. Once people have been taught basic physical skills they can then branch out into competitive sport, coaching or what ever they choose.

More and more communities across Canada are implementing this program. Different sport activities are chosen according to cultural and geographic factors and the facilities and programs already in existence.

Athlete Information Bureau (T. O'Lett).

Canadian women's hockey team members celebrate victory.

In the future, sport can be a vehicle for greater understanding between societies. The gathering of teams from different countries allows people to see the similarities and shared heritage of the human race. The dedication, commitment and training of all athletes is universal. While a person is admiring the dedication and commitment of an athlete in competition, aspects which individualize that person are lost for the moment. The fact that people speak another language, are of a different religion, colour or sex fades in the context of their struggle with gravity, the elements, time and competitors. Even at the height of the "Cold War," Soviet hockey players earned the respect of Canadians with their hockey skills. Indeed, the table tennis tournaments between Chinese and American athletes in the 1970s was a genuine breakthrough in the political isolation of China.

Sport can also be a vehicle for the expression of the uniqueness of the culture and tradition of a society. Canadian hockey is different from Soviet hockey. Sumo wrestling is not part of the Canadian tradition, whereas lacrosse is. The television coverage of the Arctic Winter Games bring the values and sports of the northern communities into homes across Canada. Unknown games are presented and the emphasis on friendship rather than competition is clearly seen. Also the teams of Alaska, the Soviet Union and Greenland participate in competition as well as those from Canada. It is evident to all that the northern peoples across the political boundaries share a great deal.

Sport can also be re-defined through the greater media coverage of events that are unfamiliar to us. Television and its new on-site technology can bring into everyone's home activities that are remote to us. Media coverage shapes and defines what sport is and how we perceive it. Coverage of previously unknown activities allows viewers a window on the world.

~ SPORT PROFILE ~

James Naismith—Sports Innovator and Inventor of Basketball

b. Almonte, Ontario. Dr. James Naismith is the inventor of basketball. Most people assume he is American since Springfield, Massachusetts, is the location of the Naismith Memorial Basketball Hall of Fame. However, Naismith grew up in Almonte, a small town south of Ottawa, Ontario, and attended McGill University in Montreal.

When he was asked to design an indoor activity for the physical education students at the YMCA in the winter of 1891, he thought back to his childhood. The children in Almonte used to throw pebbles at the ducks that sat on rocks in the river. They also played another game called "duck on the rock" that involved throwing "stones at an apple or a pumpkin, or any other reasonable duck facsimile, placed on a three-foot high rock behind the local blacksmith shop … the most efficient way to hit the target

involved tossing the stone lightly overhand with an arc" (Davidson, 1991: C6).

The first games had nine players per side and thirteen posted rules. James Naismith asked the superintendent, Pop Stebbins, to get two boxes for the goals. He returned with two peach baskets, which were nailed up (A century, 1991: 29). The game was popular with both women and men from the start. It was also popular as a spectator sport and within four years there were professional teams. But there were problems with enthusiastic fans who directly interfered with the games by grabbing the ball, etc. As a result "chicken-wire enclosures were erected around the courts and the games were played inside 'cages' which is why basketball players for generations have been known as 'cagers'" (Ward, 1991: 63).

Many wanted to call the game Naismith ball but Naismith would not hear of it. One of the first players called it "basket ball" and so the name was adopted (Ward, 1991: 63). 1991 marks the 100th anniversary of the creation of the game. To the annoyance of Almonte residents, Americans are claiming: "Unlike other sports, basketball began as a purely American game, but has leaped all boundaries to become a truly international sport" (Ward, 1991: 60). In 1992 professional basketball players will be competing in the Olympics for the first time.

James Naismith is an example of a person who came up with a new sports idea. That idea opened a wealth of positive experiences for people of all ages around the world.

Canada's Sports Hall of Fame.

James Naismith, a century of slam-dunks.

Sport can also be a force in shaping the values of our society, not only for young people but adults as well. This has already happened to some degree. Courageous individual athletes like Terry Fox, Justine Blainey, Jackie Robinson and Fanny Rosenfeld have helped re-define what sport is. Similarly, lobby and pressure groups within sport, such as the Canadian Association for the Advancement of Women and Sport and Physical Activity, have brought about important changes in sport policy. Also, the current debate over the use of performance-enhancing drugs has raised wide-ranging questions of sport morality.

Can sport also become more open and more fair? Great strides have been made over the past fifty years. In professional sports we now see black and white athletes playing on the same teams. In the area of equality between the sexes, progress has been much slower, even though more than half the population is women. As a sign of the times, perhaps, the first international women's ice hockey competitions took place in March 1990. They were an overwhelming success. The media covered the games and the finals were shown on cable television.

The Focus of Canadian Sport

Many people have worked hard in and for their chosen sport, including administrators, scientists, coaches, trainers and educators. We have today a highly developed sports system in Canada that is producing top world athletes.

However, many athletes, sport administrators and educators are concerned about the focus of Canadian sport. The emphasis has switched to elite athletes and international competition, away from the "average" individual.

In a study of six national sport organizations Macintosh and Whitson conclude that there has been a shift to the professionalization of sport and an emphasis on records and high-performance sport with a de-emphasis on recreational, fitness and health aspects of physical activity. They see a growing focus on bureaucracy, the scientific evaluation of performance in the context of the government, the sport community and in physical education (Macintosh & Whitson, 1990: 122).

Macintosh and Whitson outline five key aspects of the formal organization of sport that tend to promote high performance sport over the health and recreational apects:

* the federal government and in particular ministers;
* the federal sport bureaucracy, including the deputy minister, the director-general of Sport Canada and sport consultants;
* the sport bureaucracy at the NSRC in Ottawa and the executive, technical and program directors of NSOs;
* the NSOs and umbrella associations such as the CAO and the Sports Federation of Canada and their voluntary executive members;
* key actors outside the formal structure (Macintosh and Whitson, 1990: 5–6).

DAILY HEALTH

With the aging of our population as a whole, the 1990s are likely to be a decade of increasing concern for health and physical activity. We are already seeing people turning to gentler kinds of exercise (badminton, croquet, golf) rather than continuing the more trendy but injury-prone activities of running and jogging. There is increased recognition of the need to have life-long health practices.

T'ai chi is an example of an integrated activity where the participant attempts to bring together the mental or meditative aspect and the physical. Some athletes focus on the martial art component but many train in order to develop their mental and physical well-being by listening to their bodies, rather than pushing their bodies and ignoring discomfort.

Over twenty years ago, the Canadian government made a commitment to advance sport in this country. This has resulted in a major expansion of sport and physical recreation that has benefitted every citizen. In these times of major cutbacks to reduce deficits, a renewed financial commitment at federal, provincial and local level will be required if the present momentum is to continue.

The definition of what is to be considered inappropriate behaviour in sport is also undergoing change. There are three areas that are undergoing change: safety, aggression or violence in sport, and performance enhancers or drug use.

Expectations about the appropriate risks in sport are being re-defined. Risks that were taken for granted only ten or fifteen years ago are now considered unacceptable. It is compulsory for hockey players at all levels, including the NHL, to wear protective gear. It is

The Spitfires—Fun, Competition and Integration

The Toronto Spitfires are a wheelchair basketball team founded in 1976 by Michael Bryce which he and his brother Bob Bryce now coach.

In wheelchair basketball, team members are classified into four basic groups from 1 to 4, with the most severe being the number four classification. Some teams use a point system with a maximum of 14 or 15 points allowed for the five players; other teams have an open point system.

The Spitfires operate on an open basis. As Bob Bryce explains: "We believe very strongly in integration—not only the integration of the disabled into the able bodied community but we believe very strongly it should take place the other way as well. It's very important that able people are integrated into the disabled community so that they can understand what is going on and that there aren't barriers. We've found that integration has been very effective over the years."

Another factor is player availability. "In a number of areas of the country there are not enough disabled people to make a team. Especially in eastern Canada we didn't have enough people to come out to play so we included abled people as well."

The team includes athletes at all levels and combines fun and competition. The coaches aim to develop skills so athletes can improve. There are different team practices and athletes can choose their preference. Monday and Thursday nights are for those developing their competitive skills. "Others might choose to stay with the Tuesday night fun night because they enjoy the evening and the social aspect. We provide low-level, mid-level and high-level competition." Also the team believes in integrating fully abled athletes with the disabled athletes to allow for the best competition possible.

Bryce elaborates that the team members are athletes first and want good competition. "But there are games at all levels so everyone can come out. Just as in abled bodied sport there should be a good farm system so everyone can participate and develop."

Quotations from personal interview by the author, October 1991.

Thomas Bazydlo.

Spitfires—wheelchair basketball team founded in 1976.

not considered a question of personal preference but a necessary part of participating in hockey. Some schools have dropped gymnastics programs because they feel that without the proper equipment and trained staff, the risks are too high. No longer do children fly through the air with thin mats on the floor with only a fellow student acting as spotter. Other schools have dropped football programs because of concerns about the high injury rates. These decisions are good ones and taken in the interest of children's safety.

On the other hand, attitudes toward aggression in sport are somewhat contradictory at this time. While fighting in hockey is denounced, the fights that do occur get special coverage on the news and sport clips. Athletes, like the hockey player Bob Probert, get special attention for their "aggressive" manner of playing. WWF wrestling is ridiculed because it is viewed as a spectacle rather than a sport, but "Hulk" Hogan is seen to be too tame by the under-tens, so new "more aggressive" wrestlers are promoted. John McEnroe was criticized for his rudeness to umpires and fans but this was used to help sell tennis tickets on the circuit. Athletes are seen as role models for children, but the influence of their behaviour is often of secondary importance to the promotion and marketing of the sport. Advertisers

Wheelchair Rugby—All Can Play

Wheelchair rugby was developed in 1977 by the players themselves and combines rules from rugby, volleyball, basketball and hockey. It used to be called MurderBall.

The Toronto Bulldogs Rugby team is co-ed and consists of athletes who are all trauma quadriplegics; that is, they became "quads" because of car accidents or illnesses. The Lyndhurst Cup, held at the hospital of the same name, allows patients to be exposed to the sport. Each year new athletes are drafted onto the team. The sport was developed by quadriplegics who were often left out of the faster sport of wheelchair basketball, played by less disabled paraplegics.

In many disabled sports the athletes are classified according to their disability and assigned points according to the classification. Up to 8 points are allowed for each team on the floor: an A athlete is assigned 1 point; a B athlete is assigned 2 points; a C athlete is assigned 3 points; etc.

Pawel Zbieranowski has coached the wheelchair rugby athletes for eleven years. He explains:

"The coach decides on the composition of the team by combining athletes of different disabilities. A classic team would consist of one C, 2 B's and an A athlete. Rugby is in the process of switching from one classification system to another. Basketball, swimming, track and field, weightlifting, archery and shooting all have unified international classification systems already in place."

The principle behind the classification is to allow as many athletes to participate as possible. By balancing out the strengths and disability levels of the participants the maximum number of players can participate.

The team competes across Ontario and has been the provincial champion eight years out of twelve. It placed second and third all the other times. The National champions have been "the powerhouse" team from Saskatchewan.

The Bulldogs have also competed in England and the United States. A considerable amount of time has to be spent on fund raising because of the expenses related to travelling and to the cost of obtaining wheelchairs.

"Each athlete has their regular daily wheelchair, but they must also purchase a court chair for competition. The court chairs cost anything from $1,500 to $3,000 dollars each. If they go into track and field ,chairs cost even more—$4,000 to $6,000 each. The money is raised on a private basis or, if the athlete is very good, he or she is able to obtain a small amount of money through the carding system."

The athletes are hoping to get recognition as an Olympic sport by 1996.

Quotations from personal interview by the author, October 1991.

and promoters want to turn a profit and violence and aggression help sell the sport. Still, there is some evidence that attitudes are changing. The fact that fewer children are entering hockey programs suggests that children and their parents are beginning to question sports programs that stress aggressive interaction.

Fan behaviour has also come under scrutiny. Police can help provide "safety" but even hundreds of police cannot control fan fighting and rowdiness. If a stadium is dangerous, the addition of more police will not significantly help. Fans will increasingly watch their sport on television. Sports managers and officials can make it clear that rowdy behaviour is unacceptable, but the ultimate responsibility lies with the fans themselves.

Opinion is divided about the use of performance-enhancing drugs. When is a drug not a drug? Does the use of mega-vitamins enhance performance? Where do the drugs used by asthmatic athletes fit in?

~ SPORT PROFILE ~

Michael (Mike) Smith—Anything Is Possible

b. 1967, Kenora, Ontario. Mike Smith is an athlete who competes to be "the best athlete in the world." This is the title given to the athlete who wins the gold in the decathlon—a gruelling two-day, ten-event competition.

The first day includes the 100-metre race, the long jump, the shot put, the high jump and the 400-metre run. The second day includes the 110-metre hurdles, the discus, the pole vault, the javelin and the exhausting 1500-metre race.

Smith grew up in the small town of Kenora where there were few facilities and none of the support you would expect for a high performance athlete. He trained at the Kenora recreation centre which had a cinder track and a long jump that consisted of an old rubber conveyor belt donated from a local pulp and paper mill. In spite of the facilities, Smith was an outstanding athlete in high school. He participated in basketball, track and field and football. In Grade 12 he was offered five football scholarships to American universities (Anything's Possible, 1991).

Andy Higgins, track and field coach at the University of Toronto, went to see Mike Smith in Kenora in 1985. Higgins told Smith's family that Mike had more raw talent than any seventeen-year-old he'd ever seen. Higgins encouraged Smith to leave Kenora and train in Toronto at the University of Toronto, outlining a plan of expectations for the following ten years. So far Mike Smith has far exceeded the expected pace and plans of Higgins.

Mike Smith has captured the imagination of Canadians. He is committed to excellence. He is from a small town which he still regards as home. He is polite as well as handsome. He also states publicly that he is "clean" and does not believe in drug use. Smith is someone Canadians feel they can be proud of. He epitomizes the romanticism of the past and the hope for the future of sport.

Smith has an extremely positive attitude that stems from his family. His parents explain: "We're more proud of him as a human being—the athletics is a bonus."

Smith is already a Canadian hero: "I'm pleased to be doing what I'm doing and achieving what I'm doing and staying clean."

Athlete Information Bureau (E. Langsley).

Michael Smith, new-style Canadian athlete and winner in the decathlon.

The sports community has to accept the fact that random drug testing must be a part of every sport, regardless of the additional costs of administering the tests. Also, perceptions about what is appropriate behaviour in sport are beginning to change as a result of educational programs. Ten or fifteen years ago many could never have imagined that smoking would be banned by means of municipal by-laws, but that is the case in many Canadian cities today. It has come about because of increased awareness and support from the general population.

The Canadian Olympic Association published "The Olympics and Playing Fair" in 1989. The theme of the publication is that Olympic ideals and cheating don't mix—"Real Athletes Don't Cheat." Although drug use may appeal to athletes who are tempted to be dishonest, essentially it is cheating. At the same time it is necessary for Canadians to understand why athletes have felt the pressure to cheat in the past. Bruce Kidd, the former middle-distance runner, argues that the carding system of Sport Canada demands that athletes be among the top in the world in order to get funding and that may pressure athletes to cheat (Hall & Ormsby, 1989:A5). It could be argued that the whole Ben Johnson affair would not even have been necessary if effective random drug testing had taken place and the widespread rumours about Johnson had been thoroughly investigated. If sport is seen to support cheating and corruption, it will be irreparably damaged.

What is the future of sport?

There are many contradictory themes and directions in sport of the 1990s. The fundamental question of what sport is and who will play it is under review. If you had undertaken a survey of the participants in 1896 and asked them if they could imagine an Olympics covered by a technological system through which millions of people could see live coverage of sport in their homes; where women and men both compete (even together in some events); where skin colour and the need to be a "gentleman" would be irrelevant; where it would be accepted that athletes should receive significant financial support for their work; where many "colonial" countries would win medals against the Europeans. All of this would have seemed truly in the realm of space fantasy. Yet, today all these things take place.

Part of the appeal of the Olympics is that it crosses the boundaries of national sports and individual sport teams. It transcends the local and encourages us, no matter how minimally, to reach further. If we can exercise our imagination and project an Olympics of the future, it is possible to see an Olympics quite different from the present.

Sport of the future will include a number of features not in the forefront today. These will become more prevalent in the coming decades.

- *Genuine equity between men and women in access to sport and sport participation.* The events might be different but the prizes, resources, trophies, coaching, funding will be equal.

- *The inclusion of disabled athletes as part of Olympic competition.* The recognition of athletic skill on the part of all athletes will be accepted, regardless of disability.

- *Greater participation of athletes both from indigenous or aboriginal peoples and from the Third World and countries with smaller budgets and populations.*

- *The inclusion of sports that are regional, local and traditional to countries other than Western Europe.* This could include such sports as Thai boxing, sumo wrestling, dog-sled racing, etc.

THE FOUR-STEP APPROACH TO LIFE-LONG FITNESS

Peter and Lorna Francis are researchers in the area of health and fitness. They are well aware of the high drop-out rate of those individuals who fail to commit to a regular exercise program or never even start at all. They argue that individuals must try to evaluate themselves and approach fitness from a life-long point of view.

They maintain that four key elements are basic to establishing an effective lifetime exercise program.

- Realistic, personal goal setting (What are my exercise goals?)

- Personalized fitness assessment (Is my body ready to achieve my exercise goals?)

- Discriminate exercise and physical activity. (What do I have to do to reach my goals?)

- Self-motivation. (What can I do to stick to my exercise goals?) (Francis & Francis, 1988: 7)

Philip Mo.

Fitness for life—increasingly everyone is getting in on the action.

- *An increased emphasis on cooperation and friendly cultural exchanges.* A decrease in the emphasis on nationalism and a greater focus on individual skill, especially in the light of the European Community where there are more cross-allegiances.

- *Sexual orientation will not be the subject of concern in access to sport or in sport participation.* The sexual orientation of a person will not be the basis for discriminatory behaviour in the form of verbal abuse and team or job selection.

- *An end to political boycotts because the Olympic Charter would not permit the participation of countries unless they have a commitment to the equity principles of the Olympic ideal.*

- *Salaries for athletes so that they would not have to face living below the poverty line in order to train for their own sport.* The differentiation between amateur and professional would no longer exist at all.

- *Extensive drug testing and a public commitment on the part of national and local sport organizations, coaches and educators for drug-free competitions.*

- *A greater emphasis on the non-contact nature of sport.* Sports such as boxing, where the intent of the competition is to harm the other competitor, will be banned. Sports like ice hockey and soccer will have severe penalties for athletes stepping over the line and harming fellow athletes. The focus will be, to a much greater degree, on the skill of the athletic endeavour rather than on aggressive force.

- *There will be much more governmental support for athletic interests and fitness.* Governments will see fitness and recreational activities as part of their overall health programs and as essential as an academic or technical education.

- *Encouragement of lifelong sport.* Physical activity will be expected for people of all ages. The separation and isolation of seniors will be a thing of the past.

It is to be hoped that the basic love that people have for physical activity will be translated into opportunities to express it and the rewards and benefits will be available to everyone.

Gaetan Boucher in victory.

REFERENCES

Aaron, Hank and Lonnie Wheeler. 1990. *I Had A Hammer: The Hank Aaron Story*. New York: Harper Collins Publishers.

Abdul-Jabbar, Kareem and Peter Knobler. 1985. *Giant Steps: The Autobiography of Kareem Abdul-Jabbar*. Toronto: Bantam.

Abel, Allen. 1984. "Cromartie no hit in Japanese ball." *The Globe and Mail*. May 26: S3.

Acosta, R.V. and L.J. Carpenter. 1985(a). "Women in Athletics: A Status Report." *Journal of Physical Education, Recreation and Dance (JOPERD)* 56(6): 30–35.

————— 1985(b). "Status of Women in Athletics: Changes and Causes." *Journal of Physical Education, Recreation and Dance (JOPERD)* 56(6): 35–37.

Adam, Barry. 1987. *The Rise of a Gay and Lesbian Movement*. Boston: Twayne Publishers.

Alfano, Peter. 1989(a). "Visions of the Pro's come early: The lure of the big contracts can leave academics behind." *New York Times*. March 9: D27, 30.

————— 1989(b). "When the alternative route is the way to go: Prep schools serve the colleges by delivering athletes ready, and eligible to play." *New York Times*. March 8: D27, 29.

————— 1989(c). "Prep schools deliver college athletes, ready to play." *New York Times*. March 8: D49, Journal of Physical Education, Recreation and Dance (51.

Allen, George. 1970. *Inside Football. Fundamentals, Strategy and Tactics for Winning*. Boston: Allyn and Bacon, Inc.

Allerdt, Erik. 1970. "Basic Approaches in Comparative Sociological Research" in Gunther Luschen (ed). *The Cross-Cultural Analysis of Sport and Game*. Champaign, Illinois: Stipes Publication Company. pp. 14–30.

Anderson, Dave. 1991. "The Knicks' Philosophy Professor." *New York Times*. June 2: 27.

"Arctic Winter Games." 1970. *North* 17. July-August: 40–41.

Armstrong, Pat and Hugh Armstrong. 1984. *The Double Ghetto: Canadian Women and their Segregated Work* (revised edition). Toronto: McClelland and Stewart.

Asken, Michael J. 1988. *Dying To Win: The Athlete's Guide to Safe and Unsafe Drugs*. Washington, D.C.: Acropolis Books.

Associated Press Sports Staff. 1976. *A Century of Champions*. New York: MacMillan Publishing Co. Inc.

Audit Commission for Local Authorities in England and Wales. 1989. *Sport For Whom? Clarifying the Local Authority's Role in Sport and Recreation*. London: Her Majesty's Stationary Office.

Banned and Restricted Doping Classes and Methods. 1989. A Joint Program of the Sport Medicine Council of Canada and Sport Canada. Ottawa: Minister of Supply and Services.

Bannister, Roger. 1989. *The Four-Minute Mile*. New York: Lyons & Burford Publishers.

"Baseball owners lost $31 million, professor says." *The Globe and Mail*. July 1, 1985.

Batten, Jack. 1971. *Champions. Great Figures in Canadian Sport*. Toronto: New Press.

Beamish, Rob. 1981. "Central Issues in the Materialist Study of Sport as Cultural Practice" in Susan L. Greendorfer and Andrew Jiannakis (eds). *The Sociology of Sport: Perspectives*. West Point, New York: Leisure Press. pp. 23–33.

————— and J. Borowy. 1988. *Q. What Do You Do For A Living? A. I'm An Athlete*. Kingston, Ontario: The Sport Research Group.

Beddoes, Dick. 1985. "Gretzky. Number 99." *Winners: A Century of Canadian Sport*. Canada: Grosvenor House Press Inc. pp. 136–138.

Bell, George G. and Andrew Pascoe. 1988. *The Ontario Government: Structure and Functions*. Toronto: Thompson Educational Publishing. Inc.

Bialeschki, Deborah M. 1990. "The Feminist Movement and Women's Participation in Physical Recreation." *Journal of Physical Education, Recreation and Dance (JOPERD)* 61(1): 44–47.

Binder, Deanna. 1986. *Come Together: The Olympics and You, Calgary 1988*. XV Olympic Games Organization Committee.

Bird, Heather. 1987. "Paralysed cyclist gets $500,000 plus $4,000 a month for life." *The Toronto Star.* January 31: A3.

Bird, Larry and Bob Ryan. 1990. *Larry Bird. Drive. The Story of My Life*. Toronto: Bantam Books.

Birrell, Susan. 1990. "Women of Colour, Critical Autobiography, and Sport" in Messner, Michael A. and Donald F. Sabo (eds). 1990. *Sport, Men and the Gender Order: Critical Feminist Perspectives*. Champaign, Illinois: Human Kinetics Books. pp. 185–200.

Blaikie, David. 1984. *Boston. The Canadian Story*. Ottawa: Seneca House Books.

Blair, Suzanne. 1985. "Professionalization of Attitude Toward Play in Children and Adults." *Research Quarterly for Exercise and Sport* 56(1): 82–83.

Boutilier, M.A. and L. San Giovanni. 1984. *The Sporting Woman*. Champaign, Illinois: Human Kinetics Publishers.

Bouton, Bobbie and Nancy Marshall. 1983. *Home Games: Two Baseball Wives Speak Out*. New York: St. Martin's/Marek.

Bouton, Jim. 1982. *Ball Four Plus Ball Five*. New York: Stein and Day Publishers.

"Brian Orser's long, lonely skate. He wants to be the best in the world and it's costing his parents $15,000 a year." 1990. *The Globe and Mail*. December 6: A1, 2.

Brill, Debbie and James Lawton. 1986. *Jump*. Vancouver: Douglas & McIntyre.

Brown, Ian. 1991. "The Razor's Edge." *Saturday Night*. October: 62–115.

Brown, Jim and Steve Delsohn. 1989. *Out of Bounds*. New York: Zebra Books.

Brunt, Stephen. 1991. "Fergie" *The Globe and Mail*. July 6: D1-4.

————— 1990. "The Gretzky Effect." *Report on Business*. April: 74–80.

————— 1989. "Island's charms help university lure outsiders into cage." *The Globe and Mail*. November 1: A18.

————— 1986. "To be the best." *The Globe and Mail*. January 18: C1, 5.

Bryant, Rosalie and Eloise McLean Oliver. 1974. *Complete Elementary Physical Education Guide*. New York: Parker Publishing Company.

Bryden, Wendy. 1987. *Canada at the Olympic World Games*. Edmonton: Hurtig.

Bucher, Charles A. and William E. Prentice. 1986. *Fitness for College and Life*. Toronto: Times Mirror/Mosby.

————— 1985. *Fitness for College and Life*. Toronto: Times Mirror/ Mosby College Publications.

Budd, Zola and Hugh Eley. 1989. *Zola: The Autobiography of Zola Budd*. London: Partridge Press.

Burstyn, Varda. 1990. "The Sporting Life." *Saturday Night*. March: 42–49.

Byrne John, Keith Hammonds, Ronald Grover, James Treece and Jo Ellen Davis. 1988. "The 25 Highest Paid Executives." *Business Week*. May 2: 50–54.

Calhoun, Don. 1981. *Sports Culture and Personality*. West Point, New York: Leisure Press.

Calleja, Frank. 1986. "Insurance threat hangs over recreational groups." *The Toronto Star*. January 28: 6 West.

Campbell, Murray and James Christie. 1988. "Size of TV staff proves measure of NBC's clout." *The Globe and Mail*. September 17: A15.

Campbell, Neil A. 1982. "High school blossoms into top hockey nursery." *The Globe and Mail*. October 26: 53.

Canter, David, Miriam Comber and David L. Uzzell. 1989. *Football In Its Place: An Environmental Psychology of Football Grounds*. London: Routledge.

Carlson, Alison. 1991. "When is a woman not a woman." *Womens Sports & Fitness*. March: 24–29.

Carter, Kelly. 1991. "Jennifer Capriati. A Breath of Fresh Air." *The National Sports Review*. March 4: 55–57.

Cashmore, Ernest. 1982. *The Black Sportsmen*. London: Routledge & Kegan Paul.

Cassidy, Mike and Gary Richards. 1989. "Hyped-up bettors Bowl-ing for dollars." *The Toronto Star*. January 16: D6.

Celebration '90: Gay Games III and Cultural Festival. 1989. Vancouver, B.C.: Official Press Kit No. 1 (March).

Chapman, Currie and Randy Starkman. 1988. *On the Edge. The Inside Story of the Canadian Women's Ski Team*. Toronto: McGraw-Hill Ryerson.

"Cherry threatens suit over "racist" label." 1989. *The Montreal Gazette*. February 21: E1.

Chisholm, Patricia, Russell Wangersky et al. 1989. "Destroying the Middle Class." *Maclean's*. November 6: 56–62.

Christie, James. 1991. "Underwriters Play Major Role in Sports." *The Globe and Mail*. March 20: C10.

———— 1990. "Letheren elevated to IOC position." *The Globe and Mail*. September 21: C14.

———— 1989(a). "Hockey brothers took different paths." *The Globe and Mail*. February 14: A21.

———— 1989(b). "Anything but spartan." *The Globe and Mail*. February 13: D4.

———— 1988. *Ben Johnson. The Fastest Man On Earth*. Toronto: McClelland, Bantam Inc.

———— 1986. "CAHA wants fun put back in hockey." *The Globe and Mail*. September 9: D1.

Chu, Donald. 1982. *Dimensions of Sport Studies*. Toronto: John Wiley and Sons.

Clark, William. 1987. "Can our schools meet the fitness challenge?" *The Sunday Star*. January 25: A1.

Clayton, Deidra. 1982. *Eagle. The Life and Times of Alan Eagleson*. Toronto: Lester & Orpen Dennys.

Clement, Wallace. 1975. *The Canadian Corporate Elite: An Analysis of Economic Power*. Toronto: McClelland and Stewart Ltd.

Coakley, Jay. 1986. *Sport in Society: Issues and Controversies* (2nd edition). St Louis: Times Mirror/Moseby.

Cochrane, Jean, Abby Hoffman and Pat Kincaid. 1977. *Women in Canadian Life: Sport*. Toronto: Fitzhenry and Whiteside Ltd.

Cohen, Neil. 1989. "The Sport 100 Salary Survey." *Sport*. June: 75–96.

Cohen, Stanley. 1980. *Folk Devils and Moral Panics: The Creation of Mods and Rockers*. Oxford: Martin Robertson.

Commission of Inquiry into the Use of Drugs and Banned Practices Intended to Increase Athletic Performance. Ottawa: Minister of Supply and Services.

Commonwealth Games 1966–1990. 1990. Number of Events by Gender. Ottawa: Sport Canada.

Comité Internationale Olympique. 1990. "Olympic Movement Directory." Lausanne, Switzerland.

Considine, Tim. 1982. *The Language of Sport: A Handy Dictionary of Sporting Terms*. London: Angus and Robertson Publishers.

Cordes, Kathy. 1988. "The Ritual of the MesoAmerican Ballgame." *Journal of Physical Education, Recreation and Dance (JOPERD)*. November/December: 44–47.

Cosell, Howard and Peter Bonventre. 1986. *I Never Played the Game*. New York: Avon.

Cowley, Joyce. 1971. *Pioneers of Women's Liberation*. New York: Pathfinder Press.

Cox, Graham. 1985. "Barbara Ann Scott: The Girl Who Changed Figure Skating Forever" in *Winners A Century of Canadian Sport*. Toronto: The Grosvenor Press: 28–29.

Creighton, Judy. 1990. "Fitness trails wind through malls." *The Toronto Star*. March 24: K2.

Cresap, McCormick and Paget/Barnard. 1986. *Toronto as Host to the 100th Anniversary Olympics: A Feasibility Study*. Toronto: CMP/Barnard.

Cruise, David and Alison Griffiths. 1991. *Net Worth: Exploding the Myths of Pro Hockey*. Toronto: Viking.

Crystal, Graef S. 1988. "CEO Pay." *Fortune*. June 6: 68–80.

———— 1988. "The Wacky, Wacky World of CEO Pay." *Fortune*. June 6: 68–80.

Cunningham, Mary and Fran Schumer. 1984. *Powerplay: What Really Happened at Bendix*. New York: Fawcett Gold Medal.

Curry, Timothy J. and Robert M. Jiobu. 1984. *Sports: A Social Perspective*. Englewood Cliffs, New Jersey: Prentice-Hall Inc.

Davidson, James. 1986. "Sunshine and slapshots. Hockey by the beach new southern delight." *The Globe and Mail*. February 22: C1, 4.

———— 1985. "Academy breeds success. Learning the slopes at ski school of hopes." *The Globe and Mail*. November 23: C4.

Davidson, Neil. 1985. "Harry Jerome. The Man Who Made It Alone." *Winners: A Century of Canadian Sport*. Canada: Grosvenor House Press Inc. pp. 49–50.

"Davis inquiry to hear 25 witnesses." 1990. *The Toronto Star*. April 2: A12.

Davis, Laurel R. 1990. "Male Cheerleaders and the Naturalization of Gender" in Messner, Michael A. and Donald F. Sabo (eds). 1990. *Sport, Men and the Gender Order: Critical Feminist Perspectives*. Champaign, Illinois: Human Kinetics Books. pp. 153–162.

Dayton, Laura. 1990. "What Price Glory?" *Women's Sports & Fitness*. March: 52–55.

de Swarte, Lyn Guest. 1988. *Women and Sport: From Fitness for Fun to International Competition—The Pleasures and Pressures for Women To-Day*. Wellingborough, Northamptonshire: Grapevine.

de Varona, Donna. 1990. *Women and Triathlon*. Keynote Address: Disney World. International Triathlon Union 1990.

Deacon, James. 1991. "To be the best: Canadian Rower Silken Laumann tops her class." *Maclean's*. August 19: 37.

DePauw, Karen P. 1990. "PE and Sport for Disabled Individuals in the United States." *Journal of Physical Education, Recreation and Dance (JOPERD)* 61(2): 53–57.

Devereux, Edward. 1978. "Backyard Versus Little League Baseball: The Impoverishment of Children's Games" in Rainer Martens (ed). *Joy and Sadness in Children's Sport*. Champaign, Illinois: Human Kenetics Publishers. pp. 115–131.

Dewar, Elaine. 1990. "Unsportsmanlike Conduct." *Toronto Life*. January: 33–41, 59–72.

Dobler, Conrad and Vic Carucci. 1989. *They Call Me Dirty*. New York: Jove Books.

Donaldson, Gordon. 1991. "A piece of the action." *Business Journal*. April: 20–25.

Dryden, Ken. 1983. *The Game*. Toronto: Totem Press.

————— and Roy MacGregor. 1989. *Home Game: Hockey and Life in Canada*. Toronto: McClelland & Stewart.

Dubin, Charles L. 1990. *Commission of Inquiry into the Use of Drugs and Banned Practices Intended to Increase Athletic Performance*. Ottawa: Minister of Supply and Services.

Duncan John. 1989. "Surveying the Damage, But First the Bad News." *When Saturday Comes: The Half Decent Football Magazine*. June, No. 2: 82–5.

Dunphy, Catherine. 1989. "Ontario women set for key conference." *The Toronto Star*. September 19: B1.

————— 1986. "Hockey parents. The fun and the fury." *The Toronto Star*. December 6: G1.

Dyer, K.F. 1982. *Catching Up the Men: Women In Sport*. London: Junction Books.

"Echoes From The Cave." *The National Sports Review*. March 4, 1991.

Edgerton, Robert B. 1979. *Alone Together: Social Order on an Urban Beach*. Los Angeles: University of California Press.

Edwards, Harry. 1985. "Beyond Symptoms: Unethical Behaviour in American Collegiate Sport and the Problem of the Color Line." *Journal of Sport and Social Issues* 9 (Summer/Fall): 3–13.

————— 1973. *Sociology of Sport*. Homewood, Illinois: Irwin Dorsey Ltd.

————— 1970. *The Revolt of the Black Athlete*. New York: The Press.

Eichler, Margrit and Jeanne Lapointe. 1985. *On the Treatment of the Sexes in Research*. Ottawa: Social Sciences and Humanities Research Council.

Eitzen, D. Stanley and George H. Sage. 1986. *Sociology of North American Sport*. Dubuque, Iowa: Wm. C. Brown.

Encyclopedia Britannica. 1982. *Britannica. Book of the Year*. Chicago: University of Chicago.

————— 1981. *Britannica. Book of the Year*. Chicago: University of Chicago.

Erikson, Kai T. 1966. *Wayword Puritans: A Study in the Sociology of Deviance*. New York: John Wiley and Sons Inc.

Eskenazi, Gerald. 1991. "Male Athletes and Sexual Assault." *Cosmopolitan*. February: 220–223.

————— 1972. *A Thinking Man's Guide to Pro Hockey*. New York: E.P. Dutton and Co. Inc.

Evans, Mark. 1991. "When Will the Bubble Burst? Skyrocketing player salaries raise concerns about the future of sport." *The Financial Post*. September 2: 2.

Fawcett, Margot (ed). 1977. *Canadian Sports Annual*. Toronto: Corpus Publishers.

Feldman, Julien. 1991. "Fitness agency tones up Canada." *Financial Times*. December 2-8: 14-15.

Ferguson, Bob. 1985. *Who's Who in Canadian Sport*. Toronto: Summerhill Press Inc.

"50% Polled say runner knew he took steroids." 1989. *The Toronto Star*. January 30: A9.

Figler, Stephen K. 1981. *Sport and Play in American Life. A Textbook in the Sociology of Sport*. Toronto: Saunders College Publishing.

Filey, Mike. 1991. "Looking Back at "The Canadian Game." 1991 Baseball All-Star Game. Special Supplement. *The Toronto Star*. July 8: 12–14.

Finley, M.I. and H.W. Pleket. 1976. *The Olympic Games: The First Thousand Year*. London: Chatto & Windus

Fischler, Stan. 1985. *Offside. Hockey from the Inside*. Toronto: Methuen.

Fisher, Matthew. 1985. "Crazy Canuck. For the Love of Speed." *Winners: A Century of Canadian Sport*. Canada: Grosvenor House Press Inc. pp. 108–114.

Fitness and Amateur Sport Annual Report 1987–1988. 1989. Ottawa: Fitness and Amateur Sport.

Flynn, George L. (ed). 1973. *Vince Lombardi on Football*. New York: Galahad Books.

Foster, Jim and David Miller. 1985. "Blue Jays loss cost Metro a big bundle." *The Sunday Star*. October 20: A6.

Francis, Charlie and Jeff Coplon. 1990. *Speed Trap: Inside the Biggest Scandal in Olympic History*. Toronto: Lester & Orpen Dennys.

Francis, Peter and Lorna Francis. 1988. *If It Hurts, Don't Do It*. Rocklin, California: Prima Publishing and Communications.

Frayne, Trent. 1985. "Cox's brave new world." *The Globe and Mail*. October 22: D2.

————— 1979. *Famous Women Tennis Players*. New York: Dodd, Mead & Co.

————— 1973. *Famous Hockey Players*. New York: Dodd, Mead & Co.

————— and Peter Gzowski. 1965. *Great Canadian Sports Stories: A Century of Competitions*. Toronto: The Canadian Centennial Publishing Company Ltd.

Freysinger, Valeria J. 1990. "A Lifespan Perspective on Women and Physical Recreation." *Journal of Physical Education, Recreation and Dance (JOPERD)* 61(1): 48–51.

"Funds for soccer safety." 1990. *The Globe and Mail*. March 21: A19.

Gammon, Clive. 1988. "Those Thugs Again." *Sports Illustrated*. June 27: 49.

Gammons, Peter. 1985. "Dominican Republic: Baseball is a passion and much, much more." *The Sunday Star*. February 10: F3.

Garfield, Charles A. and Hal Zina Bennett. 1984. *Peak Performance: Mental Training Techniques of the World's Greatest Athletes*. Los Angeles: Warner.

Gay Olympic Games. 1982. San Francisco.

Giddens, Anthony. 1987. *Sociology: A Brief but Critical Introduction* (2nd edition). New York: Harcourt Brace Jovanovich, Publishers.

Gilbert, Bill. 1988. "Competition: Is It What Life's All About?" *Sports Illustrated*. May 16: 86–100.

Glassford, R. Gerald. 1970. "Organization of Games and Adaptive Strategies of Canadian Eskimo's" in Gunther Luschen (ed). *The Cross-Cultural Analysis of Sport and Games*. Champaign, Illinois: Stipes Publishing Company. pp. 70–84.

Godbey, Geoffrey. 1981. *Leisure in Your Life: An Exploration*. Toronto: Saunders College Publishing.

Golenbock, Peter. 1990. *Personal Fouls*. New York: Signet Books.

Goodman, Dr. Bob and Patricia Bush and Dr. Ronald Klatz. 1987. *Death in the Locker Room: Steroids, Cocaine and Sports*. Tuscon: The Body Press.

Goldman, Paul. 1983. *Sporting Life: An Anthology of British Sporting Prints*. London: British Museum Publications.

Goldstein, Wesley. 1985. "Jackie Robinson. Breakthrough." *Winners: A Century of Canadian Sport*. Canada: Grosvenor House Press Inc. p. 27.

"Gooden's wage will top them all." 1989. *The Toronto Star*. February 9: B3.

Goodspeed, Peter. 1991. "Loneliness of Canada's wheelchair medallist." *The Toronto Star*. September 11: A1.

Gordon, Alison. 1984. *Foul Balls*. Don Mills, Ontario: General Publishing Co. Ltd.

Goyens, Chrys and Allan Turowetz. 1981. *Lions in Winter*. Markham: Penguin.

Graham, George. 1990. "Physical Education in U.S. Schools, K–12." *Journal of Physical Education, Recreation and Dance (JOPERD)* 61(2): 35–39.

Gretzky, Walter and Jim Taylor. 1984. *Gretzky: From the Backyard Rink to the Stanley Cup*. New York: Avon Books.

Griffin, Pat. 1989. "Homophobia in Physical Education." *Canadian Association of Health, Physical Education, Recreation and Dance (CAHPERD)* 55(2) March/April: 27–31

Grossman, David. 1987. "Runnymeade recruits players, rival says." *The Toronto Star*. January 29: H6.

Gruneau, Richard. 1983. *Class, Sports and Social Development*. Amherst, Mass.: University of Massachusetts Press.

Haas, Robert. 1983. *Eat To Win*. New York: Signet.

Hagedorn, Robert (ed). 1983. *Essentials of Sociology*. Toronto: Holt, Rinehart and Winston.

Hale, Jeff. 1988. "Hockey and Law at Odds Again." *Hockey News* 42 (September 16): 3.

Hall, Daniel G. 1981. *The Freedom-Seekers. Blacks in Early Canada*. Agincourt: The Book Society of Canada Limited.

Hall, M. Ann, Dallas Cullen and Trevor Slack. 1990. "The Gender Structure of National Sport Organizations" in *Sport Canada*. Occasional Papers. December (Vol. 1, No. 2).

————— and Dorothy Richardson. 1982. *Fair Ball: Towards Sex Equality in Canadian Sport*. Ottawa: Canadian Advisory Council on the Status of Women.

Hall, Michael H. and Darla Rhyne. 1988a. *Leisure Behaviour and Recreation Needs of Ontario's Ethnocultural Populations*. Toronto: Ministry of Tourism and Recreation.

Hansen, Hal and Roger Gauthier. 1988. "Reasons for Involvement of Canadian Hockey Coaches in Minor Hockey." *The Physical Educator* 45(103): 147.

Hansen, Rick and Jim Taylor. 1987. *Man In Motion*. Vancouver/Toronto: Douglas and McIntyre.

Harding, Mark. 1985. "1984 Olympics. Canada's Golden Summer." *Winners: A Century of Canadian Sport.* Canada: Grosvenor House Press Inc. pp. 131–135.

Hargreaves, Jennifer A. 1987. "Victorian Familism and Formative Years of Female Sport" in J.A. Mangan and Roberta J. Parks (eds). *From 'Fair Sex' To Feminism.* London: Frank Cass and Co. Ltd. pp. 130–144.

Harper, Tim. 1988. "Fonyo raised millions, can't outrun troubles." *The Toronto Star.* January 5: A16.

Healy, Timothy Reverend. 1988. "It's Too Much, Too Soon." *Sports Illustrated.* September 5: 142.

Henderson, Karla A., G. Ann Uhlir and Donald Greer. 1990. "Women and Physical Recreation." *Journal of Physical Education, Recreation and Dance (JOPERD)* 61(1): 41, 42.

Henderson, Thomas "Hollywood" and Peter Knobler. 1987. *Out of Control: Confessions of an NFL Casualty.* New York: G.P. Putnam.

Hill, D. 1989(a). *Out of His Skin: The John Barnes Phenomenon.* London: Faber and Faber.

Hill, David. 1981. The Freedom-seekers: Blacks in Early Canada. Agincourt: The Book Society of Canada.

Hockey, Robert V. 1985. *Physical Fitness: The Pathway to Healthful Living.* Toronto: Times Mirror/Mosby College Publishing.

Hockey News 43 (January 26, 1990): 31–74.

"Hockey Scores Few Points According To Sports Survey." 1991. *The Globe and Mail.* October 22: C12.

Hoffman, Dale and Martin Greenberg. 1989. *Sport$biz: An Irreverent Look at Big Business in Pro Sports.* Champaign, Illinois: Leisure Press.

Holt, Richard. 1989. *Sport and the British: A Modern History.* Oxford: Clarendon Press.

Hood, Bruce. 1988. *Calling the Shots.* Don Mills, Ontario: General Publishing Co. Ltd.

Houston, William. 1991. "Baseball old boys' network." "Truth & Rumours." *The Globe and Mail.* July 16: C11.

——— 1989. *Inside Maple Leaf Gardens: The Rise and Fall of the Toronto Maple Leafs.* Scarborough, Ontario: McGraw-Hill Ryerson Ltd.

——— 1989. "No 'money' goalies in Canada." *The Globe and Mail.* January 10: C4.

——— 1988. "A Discriminating Case: Report claiming NHL unfair to French Canadians has balanced share of strong points, weaknesses." *The Globe and Mail.* August 7: D2.

Houston, William. 1988. "French Canadians suffer NHL discrimination: report." *The Globe and Mail.* August 7: A1.

"How Many Athletes are High?" 1987. *Women and Fitness* 9 (April): 26.

Human Rights Code, 1981. May, 1989. Ministry of the Attorney General. Toronto: Queen's Printer.

Hynes, Mary. 1988. "Rave reviews for village, thumbs down for kimchi." *The Globe and Mail.* September 16: A24.

"In the arena of big time athletics, a younger act." 1989. *New York Times.* March 5: Y1

Inside Sport. 1991. Vol. 13 (April).

Issajenko, Angella. 1990a. "Coping with an addiction to winning." *The Globe and Mail.* September 27: C14.

Issajenko, Angella as told to Martin O'Malley and Karen O'Reilly. 1990. *Running Risks.* Toronto: Macmillan of Canada.

Jackson, Reggie and P. Gammons. 1987. "We have a serious problem that isn't going to go away." *Sports Illustrated* 66 (May 11): 40–48.

——— and Mike Lupica. 1984. *Reggie: An Autobiography.* New York: Villard Books.

Jeffers, Alan. 1989. "Musicians worried by drug abuse." *The Globe and Mail.* January 21: C11.

"Jelinek urging athlete funding." 1987. *The Globe and Mail.* June 17: D3.

Jensen, David. 1985. "Marilyn Bell. The Underdog Champion." *Winners: A Century of Canadian Sport.* Canada: Grosvenor Press. pp. 35–36.

Jones, Wally and Jim Washington. 1972. *Black Champions Challenge American Sports.* New York: David McKay Company, Inc.

Joyce, Gare. 1990. *The Only Ticket Off the Island.* Toronto: Lester & Orpen Dennys Limited.

Kamm, Josephine. 1958. *A Biography of Miss Buss and Miss Beale. How Different From Us.* London: Bodley Head.

Kane, Mary Jo. 1990. "Female Involvement in Physical Recreation—Gender Role as a Constraint." *Journal of Physical Education, Recreation and Dance (JOPERD)* 61(1): 52–56.

Katz, Sidney. 1955. "Strange Forces Behind the Richard Hockey Riot." *Maclean's* 68 (September 17): 11–15, 97–110.

Kaufman, Michael. 1987. *Beyond Patriarchy: Essays by Men on Pleasure, Power and Change.* Toronto: Oxford University Press.

Kalcham, Lois. 1988. "Quebec to eliminate competitive hockey for kids under 12." *The Toronto Star*. November 10: A23.

Kearney, Jim. 1985. *Champions. A British Columbia Sports Album*. Vancouver/Toronto: Douglas & MacIntyre.

"Keith opens pool she helped build." 1989. *The Globe and Mail*. July 19: A7.

Kerrane, Kevin. 1985. *Dollar Sign on the Muscle: The World of Baseball Scouting*. New York: Avon.

Khan, Imran. 1989. *All Round View*. London: Pan Books Ltd.

Kidd, Bruce. 1990. "The Men's Cultural Centre: Sports and the Dynamic of Women's Oppression/Men's Repression" in Messner, Michael A. and Donald F. Sabo (eds). 1990. *Sport, Men and the Gender Order: Critical Feminist Perspectives*. Champaign, Illinois: Human Kinetics Books. pp. 31–44.

———— 1989. "Today's Tradition Echoes The Past: Taking Pride in an Honest Effort." *University of Toronto Magazine*. Winter: 9–11.

———— 1987. "Sports and Masculinity" in Michael Kaufman (ed). *Beyond Patriarchy: Essays by Men on Pleasure, Power, and Change*. Toronto: Oxford University Press.

———— 1977. "Left Runner." *Canadian Dimension*. September: 36–37.

Kidd, Kenneth. 1986. "Carling O'Keefe denies it shed Expos' TV rights to save money." *The Toronto Star*. January 31: E1.

Kimieckik, Jay. 1988. "Who Needs Coaches Education? U.S. Coaches Do." *The Physician and Sports Medicine* 16(11): 124–136.

King, Billie Jean and Kim Chapin. 1974. *Billie Jean*. New York: Harper and Row Publishers.

Kinsella, W.P. 1982. *Shoeless Joe*. Boston: Mifflin Company.

Kinsman, Gary. 1987. *The Regulation of Desire: Sexuality in Canada*. Montreal: Black Rose Books.

Kirshenbaum, Jerry. 1989. "An American Disgrace." *Sports Illustrated*. February 27: 16–19.

Klapper, Joseph T. 1963. *The Effects of Mass Communication*. Chencoe: The Free Press.

Klatell, David A. and Norman Marcus. 1988. *Sports For Sale: Television, Money and the Fans*. New York: Oxford University Press.

Klein, Stanley. 1987. *Ideology in Illness and Healing: A Study of Diabetes Management*. The School of Social Work, McGill University Montreal: Unpublished M.A. Research Report.

Kline, Kimberly A. and Maureen R. Weiss. 1987. "Perceived Competence and Motives for Participating in Youth Sports: A Test of Harter's Competence Motivation Theory." *Journal of Sport Psychology* 9: 55–65.

Knoppers, Annelis. 1989. "Coaching: An Equal Opportunity Occupation?" *Journal of Physical Education, Recreation and Dance (JOPERD)*. March: 38–43.

Kop, Ken E. August, 1989. "Ken E. of the Kop (with the Lager Top)." *Red Issue. The Voice for United Fans Everywhere*.

Kramer, Jerry. 1968. *Instant Replay: The Green Bay Diary of Jerry Kramer*. New York: Signet.

Kulicke, Stephen and Pat Califia. 1982 "in the True 'Olympic' Tradition: The Gay Games." *The Advocate*. October 14: 29–35.

Ladson, Bill and Jeff Ryan. 1989. "How the Purse Gets Split." *Sport*. June: 79.

Landes, David S. 1983. *Revolution in Time: Clocks and the Making of the Modern World*. Cambridge, Massachusetts: The Belknap Press of Harvard University Press.

Lapointe, Kirk. 1986. "Children not fit enough, doctors say." *The Toronto Star*. December 27: E2.

Lazarsfeld, Paul F., Bernard Berelson and Hazel Gaudet. 1960. *The People's Choice: How the Voter Makes Up His Mind in a Presidential Campaign*. New York: Columbia University Press.

Lea, John, Roger Matthews and Jock Young. 1987. *Law and Order: Five years on*. Middlesex Polytechnic: Centre of Criminology.

———— and Jock Young. 1984. *What is to be Done About Law and Order?* Harmondsworth, Middlesex: Penguin Books Ltd.

Leigh, Mary H. and Therese M. Bonin. Spring, 1977. "The pioneering role of Madame Alice Milliat and the FSFI in establishing International Track and Field Competition for women." *Journal of Sport History* 4(1): 72-83.

Lenskyj, Helen. 1987. "Canadian Women and Physical Activity, 1890-1930: Media Views" in J.A. Mangan and Roberta J. Parks (eds). *From 'Fair Sex' to Feminism*. London: Frank Cass and Co. Ltd. pp. 208–234.

———— 1986. *Out of Bounds: Women, Sport and Sexuality*. Toronto: Women's Press.

———— 1988. *Women, Sport and Physical Activity: Research and Bibliography*. Ottawa: Minister of State, Fitness and Amateur Sport.

Leonard, George. 1977. *The Ultimate Athlete: Re-visioning Sports, Physical Education and the Body*. New York: Avon.

Leonard, William II and Jonathan Reyman. 1988. "The Odds of Attaining Professional Athlete Status: Refining the Computations." *Sociology of Sport Journal* 6: 162–169.

Letheren. Carol Anne. 1991. "Technological Pursuit in Sport" in *Critical Choices! Ethics, Science and Technology*. Henry Wiseman, Jokelee Vanderkop and Jorge Nef. Toronto: Thompson Educational Publishing.

————— Nov 3, 1989. "Marketing Sport After Seoul.ø *Sports Administration International 1989*. Montreal: Mathieu Letheren Associates.

Lever, Janet. 1978. "Sex Differences in the Complexity of Children's Play." *American Sociological Review* 43(4): 471–483.

————— 1976. "Sex Differences in the Games Children Play." *Social Problems* 23(4): 478–487.

————— 1975–76. "Sex differences in the games children play" *Social Problems* 23(4): 478–487.

Li, Peter S. 1988. *Ethnic Inequality in a Class Society*. Toronto: Thompson Educational Publishing, Inc.

Lipsyte, Robert. 1975. *Sportsworld. An American Dreamland*. New York: Quadrangle/The New York Times Book Co.

Lieber, Jill. 1990. "Free-Fall from the Top." *Sports Illustrated*. October: 83–91.

Lorenz, Konrad. 1969. *On Aggression*. London: Metheun.

Louis, Victor and Jennifer Louis. 1980. *Sport in the Soviet Union* (2nd edition). Toronto: Pergamon Press.

Luschen, Gunther. 1970(a). "The Interdependence of Sport and Culture" in Gunther Luschen (ed). *The Cross-Cultural Analysis of Sport and Games*. Champaign, Illinois: Stipes Publishing Company. pp. 85–99.

————— 1970(b). "Sociology of Sport and the Cross-Cultural Analysis of Sport and Games" in Gunther Luschen (ed). *The Cross-Cultural Analysis of Sport and Games*. Champaign, Illinois: Stipes Publishing Company. pp. 5–13.

MacAloon, John J. 1988. "A Prefatory Note to Pierre Bourdieu's 'Program for a Sociology of Sport'." *Sociology of Sport Journal* 5(2): 150–153.

Macntosh, Donald and David Whitson. 1990. *The Game Planners: Transforming Canada's Sport System*. Montreal/Kingston: McGill-Queen's University Press.

————— 1990. "Interschool Sport Programs in Canada." *Journal of Physical Education, Recreation and Dance (JOPERD)* 61(2): 58–64.

————— 1989. "Female Participation in Ontario Inter-University Sport Programs." *Canadian Association of Health, Physical Education and Dance (CAHPERD)* March/April: 7.

————— 1987. "Are sport scholarships sneaking into Canada?" *The Toronto Star*. July 13: A13.

MacLeod, Iain. 1989. "Drug Abuse." *Athletics*. June: 12–13.

Majors, Richard. 1990. "Cool Pose: Black Masculinity and Sports." in Messner, Michael A. and Donald F. Sabo (eds). 1990. *Sport, Men and the Gender Order: Critical Feminist Perspectives*. Champaign, Illinois: Human Kinetics Books. pp. 109–114.

Makin, Kirk. 1987. "Lawyer defends whites-only scholarship." *The Globe and Mail*. March 20: A14.

Mangan, J.A. and Roberta J. Parks. 1987. *From 'Fair Sex' to Feminism: Sport and the Socialization in the Industrial and Post-Industrial Era's*. London: Frank Cass and Co. Ltd.

"Manitoba cage coach riled by rule at games." 1985. *The Globe and Mail*. August 21: S3.

Manley, Elizabeth and Elva Clairmont Oglanby. 1990. *Thumbs up*. Toronto: Macmillan of Canada.

Marshall, Tyler. 1987. "Fair play. Changes in England's mood." *St. Peterburg Times*, November 8: 28A.

Martens, Rainer (ed). 1978. *Joy and Sadness in Children's Sport*. Champaign, Illinois: Human Kenetics Publishers.

Masse, Linda. 1986. "Nancy's upwardly mobile." *The Globe and Mail*. July 15: D1.

Mathabane, Mark. 1986. *Kaffir Boy: The True Story of a Black Youths Coming of Age in Apartheid*. New York: New American Library.

May, John Bentley. 1991. "Tin God." *The Globe and Mail*. February 16: D1–4.

Mays, Willie and Lou Sahadi. 1989. *Say hey. The Autobiography of Willie Mays*. New York: Pocket Books.

McCabe, Nora. 1988. "Olympic official with a mission. Woman leader makes history without a fuss." *The Globe and Mail*. September 17: A14.

McCallum, Jack. 1988a. "Green cars, black cats and Lady Luck." *Sports Illustrated*. February 8: 86–96.

————— 1988b. "Disorder in the Court." *Sports Illustrated*. February 8: 73.

McSherry, Sheryl. 1990. "Personal Correspondence." Olympic Job Opportunity Program, United States Olympic Committee.

McCrone, Kathleen E. 1987. "Play Up! Play Up! And Play the Games! Sport and the Late Victorian Girls' Public Schools" in J.A. Mangan and Roberta J. Parks (eds). *From 'Fair Sex' to Feminism*. London: Frank Cass and Co. Ltd. pp. 97–129.

McDermott, Barry. 1987. "Switching Signals." *Life Magazine*. November: 43–46.

McDonald, Lanny and Steve Simmons. 1987. *Lanny*. Toronto: McGraw-Hill Ryerson Limited.

Mckee, Ken. 1987. "Cholesterol count worries Dan Halldorson." *The Toronto Star*. February 18: B3.

————— 1986. "Carling drops Expo's telecasts, Labatt's moves in." *The Toronto Star*. January 31: B5.

McQuaig, Linda. 1987. *Behind Closed Doors: How the Rich Won Control of Canada's Tax System*. Markham, Ontario: Viking.

Mead, G.H. 1934. *Mind, Self and Society*. Chicago: University of Chicago Press.

Messner, Michael A. and Donald F. Sabo (eds). 1990. *Sport, Men and the Gender Order: Critical Feminist Perspectives*.Champaign, Illinois: Human Kinetics Books.

Metcalfe, Alan. 1987. *Canada Learns to Play: The Emergence of Organized Sport, 1807–1914*. Toronto: McClelland and Stewart.

Miller, Casey and Kate Swift. 1981. *The Handbook of Nonsexist Writing: For Writers, Editors and Speakers*. New York: Barnes & Noble.

Mills, C. Wright. 1970. *The Sociological Imagination*. Harmondsworth: Penguin.

Mills, Jack. 1989. "Do agents help or hurt? Sound advice and protection for players." *New York Times*. March 5: 59.

Millson, Larry. 1987. *Ballpark Figures. The Blue Jays and the Business of Baseball*. Toronto: McClelland and Stewart.

————— 1985. "Caudill's deal near $8 million." *The Globe and Mail*. February 21: M7.

Milton, Steve. 1985. "Japanese fans praise skaters in quiet fashion." *The Toronto Star*. March 4: B5.

Ministry of Tourism and Recreation, Fitness Ontario. 1985. *Measure of Fitness*. Toronto: Fitness Ontario.

————— 1983. *Sport and Recreation in Ontario*. Toronto: Fitness Ontario.

————— 1986. *Physical Activity Patterns in Ontario III: A Research Report from the Ministry of Tourism and Recreation*. Toronto: Ministry of Tourism and Recreation: 5–9.

————— October 1987. "Provincial Sport Organizations: Risk Management Manual." Ministry of Tourism and Recreation.

Mix, Ron. 1987. "So Little Gain for the Pain." *Sports Illustrated*. October 19: 54–69.

Morris, Alwyn. 1991. First Nations Sport Secretariat Proposal.

Mrozek, Donald J. 1987. "The Amazon and the American 'Lady': Sexual Fears of Women as Athletes" in J.A. Mangan and Roberta J. Parks (eds). *From 'Fair Sex' to Feminism*. London: Frank Cass and Co. Ltd. pp. 282–298.

Murphy, Austin. 1988. "North Star on Ice." *Sports Illustrated*. September 5: 34.

Murphy, Robert. 1989. *Cultural and Social Anthropology: An Overview* (3rd edition). Englewood Cliffs, New Jersey: Prentice-Hall Inc.

Nagler, Jack. 1989. "Skater Manley busy on her feet." *The Globe and Mail*. November 29: A19.

National Basketball Association. September, 1991. "Personal Correspondence."

National Hockey League Player's Association. 1989. Personal correspondences, September 21.

Navratilova, Martina and Mary Carillo. 1983. *Tennis My Way*. New York: Charles Scribner's Sons.

Neff, Craig. 1989. "Overtown." *Sports Illustrated*. January 30: 9.

————— 1988. "Pay for Play." *Sports Illustrated*. April 18: 21.

NHL Official Guide and Record Book. 1984–85 and 1983–84 editions.

Neill, Sue. 1990. *The Canadian Sport System—From Concept to Reality*. Sport Canada: Government of Canada.

"No scholarships in varsity program." 1989. *The Toronto Star*. October 25: F1.

Norman, A.V.B. and G.M. Wilson. 1982. *Treasures From the Tower of London*. London: ND Humphries Ltd.

Office for Disabled Persons. 1989. *Word Choices: A Lexicon of Preferred Terms for Disability Issues*. Toronto: Queen's Printer.

Oliver, M. 1980. "Race, Class and the Family's Orientation to Mobility Through Sport." *Sociology Symposium* 30: 62–86.

Oliver, Thomas. 1984. "Dr. J scores twice with Coca-Cola." *The Globe and Mail*. February 9: S6.

The Olympics and Playing Fair. 1989. Ottawa: Canadian Olympic Association.

"On the Move I Program." 1989.

"On the Move II Guidebook." 1989.

Oppenheim, A.N. 1966. *Questionnaire Design and Attitude Measurement*. New York: Basic Books Inc.

Orlick, Terry. 1982. *The Second Cooperative Sports and Games Book*. New York: Pantheon Books.

————— 1978. "Why Eliminate Kids" in Rainer Martens (ed). *Joy and Sadness in Children's Sports*. Champaign, Illinois: Human Kenetics Publishers. pp. 145–151.

———— 1978. *Winning Through Cooperation.* Washington: Hawkins & Associates Book.

———— and C. Botterill. 1975. *Every Kid Can Win.* Chicago: Nelson-Hall.

Ormsby, Mary. 1989(a). "Drug-free athletes speak out: 'Giving it your best is winning'." *The Toronto Star.* May 10: A4.

———— 1989(b). "Fans make it happen in U.S. colleges." *The Sunday Star.* October 29: G7.

———— and Joseph Hall. 1989. "Hoffman urges salaries for athletes." *The Toronto Star.* January 14, 1989: B4.

———— 1985(a). "Field hockey coach rehired but her role to be examined." *The Toronto Star.* October 10.

————. 1985(b). "Van der Merwe to be reappointed field hockey coach." *The Toronto Star.* October 9: B9.

———— 1985(c). "Field hockey feud to end to-day." *The Toronto Star.* October 8.

———— and Joseph Hall. 1989. "Pressure to win made drugs almost essential, coach says." *The Toronto Star.* May 10: A4.

———— and Mark Zwolinski. 1989. "Money, crowds. The American dream. $10 million fuels Michigan … Blues manage on $300,000. College football, a tale of two systems." *The Toronto Star.* October 25: F1, F11.

Orr, Frank. 1989. "Liz Manley still skating strong." *The Toronto Star.* November 29: A19.

———— 1988. "Manley turns her silver medal into gold." *The Toronto Star.* November 29: F4.

"Orser takes his first step backward. Canada's brightest hope slips in Games spotlight." 1988. *The Toronto Star.* February 22: B4.

Oxendine, Joseph B. 1988. *American Indian Sports Heritage.* Champaign, Illinois: Human Kinetics.

Page, Shelley. 1989. "Best marathon swimmer set to beat Lake Ontario." *The Toronto Star.* September 3: A4.

———— 1988(a). "Vicki tops $300,000 goal at last. But few at victory parade for Great Lakes champion." *The Toronto Star.* September 2: A7.

———— 1988(b). "What makes Vicki swim." *The Toronto Star.* July 28: A20.

———— 1988(c). "Ontario swimmer to raise funds by crossing all 5 Great Lakes." *The Toronto Star.* June 25: A21.

Parrish, Wayne. 1984. "Tearful Winner Salutes Lovell." *The Toronto Star.* August 2: F4.

Parsons, Talcott (ed). 1964. *Essays in Sociological Theory.* New York: Free Press.

Patmore, Angela. 1979. *Playing on Their Nerves. The Sport Experiment.* London: Stanley Paul & Co.

Pease, Dale and Jocelyn Drabelle. 1988. "Pre-Entry Coaching Expectations of Women and Men." *Journal of Physical Education, Recreation and Dance (JOPERD).* April: 30–32.

Peel Parents Against Drugs. PAD. 1990. *A Parent Handbook.* Brampton/Bramalea: Kinsmen Club of Brampton/Bramalea.

Pelto, Pertti J. 1973. *The Snowmobile Revolution: Technology and Social Change in the Arts.* Menlo Park, California: Cummings Publishing Company.

Pena, Nelson. 1989. "Cycling gets Sexy." *Bicycling* 8: 29–32.

Pena, Nelson. 1989. "For Men Only: How Cycling Makes you a Better (or worse) Lover." *Bicycling* 8: 30–31.

———— 1989. "For Women Only: Cycling's Impact on Your Sex Life." *Bicycling* 8: 32.

Penner, Mike. 1989. "The Man with the Golden Arm." *Men's Fitness.* October: 74–77.

Perkins, Dave. 1991. "Baseball's well will run dry if money madness continues." *The Toronto Star.* February 11: C1.

Pesmen, Curtis. 1989. "Corporate Sponsorships: The New Name of the Game." *Sport.* June: 82.

Phinney, Richard. 1985. "Australian tour lift for Canadians." *The Globe and Mail.* June 15: S3.

Pineo, Peter and John Porter. 1967. "Occupational Prestige in Canada." *Canadian Review of Sociology and Anthropology* 4: 24–40.

Plan for Equality Between Women and Men in Sport in the 1990s. 1990. Stockholm: Swedish Sports Federation.

Pleiss, Kathy. 1986. *Cheap Amusements: Working Women and Leisure in Turn-of-the-Century New York.* Philadelphia: Temple University Press.

Podborski, Steve and Gerald Donaldson. 1987. *Podborski.* Toronto: McClelland and Stewart.

Porter, Bob M.P. and John Cole M.P. Chairmen Sub-Committee on Fitness and Amateur Sport. 1990. *Amateur Sport: Future Challenges.* Second Report of the Standing Committee on Health and Welfare. Social Affairs, Seniors and the Status of Women.

Porter, John. 1967. *The Vertical Mosaic.* Toronto: University of Toronto Press.

Prescott, Eileen. 1989. "The Networks Fight Back, Finally." *The New York Sunday Times.* March 5: 20.

Pronger, Brian. 1990. "Gay Jocks: A Phenomenology of Gay Men in Athletics" in Messner, Michael A. and Donald F. Sabo (eds). 1990. *Sport, Men and the Gender Order: Critical Feminist Perspectives.* Champaign, Illinois: Human Kinetics Books. pp. 141–152.

———— 1990a. *The Arena of Masculinity: Sports, Homosexuality, and the Meaning of Sex.* Toronto: Summerhill Press.

Proudfoot, Jim. 1986. "NHL allows violence because it sells." *The Toronto Star.* February 22: C1.

———— 1985. "Gaetan Boucher: The Winning Habit." in *Winners: A Century of Canadian Sport.* Toronto: The Canadian Press and Molsons.

Quinn, Hal. 1985. "Baseball Fans Strike Out." *Maclean's.* August 19: 30–31.

Ramsamy, Sam. 1982. *Apartheid: The Real Hurdle (Sport in South Africa and the International Boycott).* London: International Defence and Aid Fund for Southern Africa.

Reed, William. 1989. "A New Proposition." *Sports Illustrated.* January 23: 16.

Reilly, Rick. 1989. "What Price Glory?" *Sports Illustrated.* February 27: 32–34.

Rhoden, William C. 1990. "Job insecurity: A chill wind blows through the coaching profession." *International Herald Tribune.* August 24: 17.

———— 1989(a). "At the top level of play, it's often all work. Capacity demands on high school stars make competing a very serious business." *New York Times.* March 7: B9–10.

———— 1989(b). "Recruiting Extends Its Reach." *New York Times.* March 6: C1, 4.

Rinehart, James W. and Seymour Faber. 1987. *The Tyranny of Work: Alienation and the Labour Process* (2nd edition). Toronto: Harcourt Brace Jovanovich.

Riordan, James. 1980. *Soviet Sport: Background to the Olympics.* Oxford: Basil Blackwell.

Robbins, Stuart G. 1990. "Physical Education in Canadian Schools." *Journal of Physical Education, Recreation and Dance (JOPERD)* 61(2): 34–38.

Robinson, Laura. 1991. "Sports talk excludes women." *The Globe and Mail.* July 8: A13.

Rogosin, Donn. 1987. *Invisible Men: Life in Baseball's Negro League.* New York: Atheneum.

Rosen, Craig. 1990. "Celebrities." *Inside Sports.* Special Report: Sports and Salaries. February 1990: 54.

Ross, James, Russell R. Pate, Carl J. Caspersen, Cheryl L. Damberg and Michael Svilar. 1987. "Home and Community in Children's Exercise Habits." *Journal of Physical Education, Recreation and Dance (JOPERD).* November/December: 85–92.

Rounds, Kate. 1991. "Where Is Our Field of Dreams?" *Ms.* II(2) (September/October): 44–45.

Rusk, James. 1986. "Game a national passion. Go Victor wins China's heart." *The Globe and Mail.* January 13: A8.

Ryan, Allan. 1991. "Superstar Gruber cashes in with $11 million Jays deal." *The Toronto Star.* February 13: A1, C1.

Sage, George H. 1990. "High School and College Sports in the United States." *Journal of Physical Education, Recreation and Dance (JOPERD)* 61(2): 59–63.

"Salary Survey." 1988. *US News and World Report.* April 25: 66–76.

Salter, Michael A. 1980. "Play in Ritual: An Ethnohistorical Overview of Native North America" in Helen B. Schwartzman (ed). *Play in Culture: 1978 Proceedings of the [4th annual meeting of the] Association for the Anthropological Study of Play.* West Point, New York: Leisure Press. pp. 70–83.

Saraceno, Jon. 1991. "Ex-Champ barrels ahead with lifestyle." *USA Today.* September 10: C1.

Sarick, Lila. 1988. "Lake Ontario last leg for swimmer. Awkward on land, Keith is graceful in cold, hostile water." *The Globe and Mail.* August 28: A1, 14.

Savage, Bruce. 1989. "Banned Drugs." *Athletics.* June: 14.

Schiller, Bill. 1988. "Gold doesn't spell success in Olympics." *The Toronto Star.* March 5: B1.

Schultz, Dave and Stan Fischler. 1983. *The Hammer: Confessions of a Hockey Enforcer.* New York: Berkley.

Scott, Terry. 1985. "Maurice Richard: The Rocket" in *Winners: A Century of Canadian Sport.* Toronto: Grosvenor House & Canadian Press. pp. 37–42.

Seagoe, May V. 1970. "Children's Play as an Indicator of Cross-Cultural and Intra-Cultural Differences" in Gunther Luschen (ed). *The Cross-Cultural Analysis of Sport and Games.* Champaign, Illinois: Stipes Publishing Company. pp. 132–137.

Searchinger, Brian. 1985. "The Trial of Eddie B." *Cyclist.* July.

Semenko, Dave and Larry Tucker. 1984. *Looking Out for Number One.* Toronto: Stoddart.

Sennet, Richard and Jonathan Cobb. 1973. *The Hidden Injuries of Class.* New York: Vintage Books.

Sex Discrimination Act 1975. Chapter 65. 1975. London: Her Majesty's Stationery Office.

Shimizu, Jhana. 1988. "A Comparison of Open-Ended and Closed-Ended Questioning Systems." *Recreation Research Review* 13 (Special Issue: Research on understanding the implications of research design decisions.) (4): 22–27.

Shipsides, Ardith. 1988. "Negative and Positive Wording of Attitude Statements: A Study of Their Effect on Responses." *Recreation Research Review* 13 (Special Issue: Research on understanding the implications of research design decisions.) (4): 23–27.

Shoalts, David. 1987. "Golf pro's shoot for higher purses." *The Globe and Mail*. February 18: D5.

"Showdown at Shoal Creek." 1991. *The National Sports Review*. March 4: 28–29.

Siegel, Linda. 1989. "Ben Johnson case questions validity of I.Q. tests." *The Toronto Star*. June 20: A15.

Sigesmund, Jory. 1984. "Minor hockey people love the Japanese culture." *The Globe and Mail*. January 23: S10.

Silverman, Al. 1968. *Sports Titans for the Twentieth Century*. New York: G.P. Putman's Sons.

Simon, Robert L. 1985. *Sports and Social Values*. Englewood Cliffs, New Jersey: Prentice-Hall Inc.

Sipes, Richard G. 1973. "War, Sports and Aggression: An Empirical Test of Two Rival Theories." *American Anthropologist* 75: 64–86.

"Skating success comes cheap for Orser. He's 'frugal', sport director says." 1988. *The Toronto Star*. February 15: B5.

Slater, Tom. 1989. "Cherry's bite eats 'em alive: 'I'm a beer hall kind of a guy'." *The Toronto Star*. December 16: B1, B4.

Smart, Reginald G. 1985. *The New Drinkers: Teenage Use and Abuse of Alcohol* (2nd edition). Toronto: Addiction Research Foundation.

Smith, Beverley.1991. "Big Ben a rich winner." *The Globe and Mail*. September 9: C6.

————— 1989. "More cash sought by coaches group." *The Globe and Mail*. January 14: A19.

————— 1988. "Top figures paid for U.S. coaches." *The Globe and Mail*. January 19: D1.

Smith, Michael. 1983. *Violence and Sport*. Toronto: Butterworths.

Smith, Richard. 1989. "Advisers suggested for hockey." *The Globe and Mail*. January 16: A16.

Smith-Rosenberg, Carroll and Charles Rosenberg. 1987. "The Female Animal: Medical and Biological Views of Women and Their Role in Nineteenth Century America" in Mangan, J.A. and Roberta J. Parks (eds). *From "Fair Sex" to Feminism*. London: Frank Cass and Co. Ltd. pp. 13–37.

Sneider, Daniel. 1985. "Japanese baseball all business." *The Toronto Star*. October 17.

Snyder, Eldon and Elmer A. Speitzner. 1989. *Social Aspects of Sport* (3rd edition). Englewood Cliffs, New Jersey: Prentice-Hall Inc.

————— 1983. *Social Aspects of Sport* (2nd edition). Englewood Cliffs, New Jersey: Prentice-Hall Inc.

Sokol, Al. 1985(a). "Rick Hansen. A Man in Motion." *Winners: A Century of Canadian Sport*. Canada: Grosvenor Press Inc. p. 139.

————— 1985(b). "Teen motorcyclists tempting death in defiance of Taiwan's spartan life." *The Toronto Star*. October 3: L2.

————— 1985(c). "Lovell embarks on campaign to cure the spinal-injured." *The Toronto Star*. May 30: H2

————— 1985(d). "Stroking towards Seoul." *The Toronto Star*. March 9: C7.

————— 1984. "Adidas cancels track subsidies." *The Toronto Star*. October 17.

Sopinka, John. 1984. *Can I Play? The Report of the Task Forces on Equal Opportunity in Athletics 11*. Schools, Colleges and Universities.

Spencer, Metta. 1981. *Foundations of Modern Sociology*. Scarborough, Ontario: Prentice-Hall Canada.

Sport Canada. 1990. 1988 Olympic Games. Countries Placing in the Top 8. Sokol, Al. 1985. "Lovell embarks on campaign to cure the spinal-injured." *The Toronto Star*. May 30: L9.

————— 1986(a). *Sport Canada Policy On Women in Sport*. Ottawa: Fitness & Amateur Sport.

————— 1986(b). *Sport Canada Athletic Assistance Programme: Policy and Guidelines, 1986–1987*. Ottawa: Government of Canada, Fitness and Amateur Sport.

"Sports Medicine Information: Drug Use and Competition." 1989. *Compendium of Pharmaceuticals and Specialties* (24th edition). Toronto: Canadian Pharmaceutical Association. pp. GY15, GY16.

St. Hilda's Budget. 1985. St. Hilda's College, Oxford. Archives.

Starkman, Randy and Peter Edwards. 1991. "Amateur boxing officials are on the ropes." *The Toronto Star*. April 13: C1-C11.

Statistics Canada. 1987. "Earnings of Men and Women 1986." Ottawa: Minister of Supply and Services.

Staurowsky, Ellen J. 1990. "Women Coaching Male Athletes." in Messner, Michael A. and Donald F. Sabo (eds). *Sport, Men and the Gender Order: Critical Feminist Perspectives*. Champaign, Illinois: Human Kinetics Books. pp. 163–172.

Stefaniuk, Walter. 1987. "363,000 children under 14 in Ontario live below the poverty line, Task Force told." *The Toronto Star.* January 24: B5.

Stephens, Thomas and Cora Lynn Craig. 1990 "The Well-being of Canadians: the 1988 Campbell's survey on well-being in Canada is a longitudinal follow-up of the 1981 Canada Fitness Survey." Ottawa: Canadian Fitness and Lifestyle Research Institute.

Stock, Curtis. 1990. "Cherry doesn't stand in the middle." *The Calgary Herald.* January 26: F2.

Story, Alan. 1987. "Why the dreams for justice do not die." *The Toronto Star.* January 24: B5.

Stoynoff, Natasha. 1991. "7,000 cheer for "spirit" of bullfighting at Listowel." *The Toronto Star.* June 3: A3.

Strachan, Al. 1990. "Son a junior version in name only." *The Globe and Mail.* September 1: A10.

————— 1986. "Mecker takes aim at hockey Canada." *The Globe and Mail.* December 29: C1, 5.

————— 1985(a). "Card Shark. Herzog rides high in role of bumpkin." *The Globe and Mail.* October 19: C2.

————— 1985(b). " Leafs winners at bank last season." *The Globe and Mail.* February 19: S1.

Straw, Sandy. July 26, 1990. Women in Sports and Physical Recreation Project (WISPR) Report. City of Toronto, Parks and Recreation Department.

Suinn, Richard M. 1983. "Body Thinking: Psychology for Olympic Champs" in *Psychology in Sports: Methods and Applications.* Minneapolis, Minn.: Burgess Publishing Co.

————— 1983. "Body Thinking: Psychology for Olympic Champs" in *Psychology in Sports: Methods and Applications.* Minneapolis, Minn.: Burgess Publishing Co.

Sullivan, Robert. 1989. "Gambling, payoffs and drugs." *Sports Illustrated* 71(18) (October 30): 40–45.

"Superstar Gruber cashes in with $11 million Jays deal." 1991. *The Toronto Star.* February 13: A1.

Swift, E.M. 1991. "Why Johnny Can't Play." *Sports Illustrated.* September 23: 61–72.

————— 1988. "Blood and Ice." *Sports Illustrated.* December 5: 56.

Talbot, Margaret. 1990. "Women and Sport: The Many Dimensions of Power." Plenary paper presented at the First World Summit on Women and the Many Dimensions of Power. Montreal, Quebec.

Taylor, Bill. 1991. "Out of the Game." *The Toronto Star.* June 28: F1.

Taylor, Lawrence and David Falkner. 1987. *LT: Living on the Edge.* New York: Warner Books.

Taylor, Rt. Honourable Lord Justice. 1989. "The Hillsborough Stadium Disaster, 15 April 1989." *Interim Report.* (Presented to Parliament by the Secretary of State for the Home Department, August 1989.) London: Her Majesty's Stationery Office.

Thomas, Carolyn E. 1983. *Sport in a Philosophic Context.* Philadelphia: Lea and Febiger.

Thompson, Allan. 1990. "Vancouver tops Metro in carrying home costs." *The Toronto Star.* March 23: F1.

Thornton, James S. 1990. "Sexual Activity and Athletic Performance: Is There A Relationship?" *The Physician and Sportsmedicine* 16(3):

"The Top Twenty." 1989. *Sport.* June.

"Toronto: Setting the Pace For A Smoke-Free Workplace." By-law No. 23–88.

"Tragedy at Sheffield Stadium the latest in a series of disasters." *The Sunday Star.* April 16: A14.

Tretiak, Vladislav. 1987. *Tretiak: The Legend.* Edmonton: Plains Publishing Company.

Trottier, Andre. 1987. "Results of a National Survey on Physical Education in the Provinces." *Canadian Association of Health, Physical Education and Dance (CAHPERD).* November/December: 8–9.

Tully, Shawn. 1988. "American Bosses are Overpaid." *Fortune.* November 7: 121–136.

Turnbull, Alison. 1988. "Woman enough for the Games?". *New Scientist.* September 15: 61–64.

Tutko, Thomas and William Bruns. 1976. *Winning is Everything and Other American Myths.* New York: MacMillan Publishing Co. Inc.

Tygiel, Jules. 1983. *Baseball's Great Experiment: Jackie Robinson and His Legacy.* New York: Oxford University Press.

"Ueberroth penalizes drug-linked players." 1986. *The Globe and Mail.* March 1: C3.

Valvano, Jim and Curry Kirkpatrick. 1991. *Valvano: They Gave Me A Lifetime Contract, and Then They Declared Me Dead.* New York: Pocket Books.

Voy, Robert and Kirk D. Deeter. 1991. *Drugs, Sport, and Politics.* Champaign, Illinois: Leisure Press.

Walker, Bill. 1984. "Cyclist Jocelyn Lovell thrilled to go home." *The Toronto Star.* May 12: A3.

Wall, A.E. 1990. "Fostering Physical Activity Among Canadians with Disablities." *Journal of Physical Education, Recreation and Dance (JOPERD)* 61(2): 52–56.

Walwin, James. 1986. *Football and the Decline of Britain.* London: Macmillan.

Ward, Colin. 1989. *Steaming In: Journal of a Football Fan.* London: Sports Pages/Simon & Shuster.

Water Sports for the Disabled. 1983. Water Sports Division. British Sports Association for the Disabled. Wakefield, West Yorkshire: E.P. Publishing Ltd.

Washington, Sharon J. 1990. "Provision of Leisure Services to People of Colour." *Journal of Physical Education, Recreation and Dance (JOPERD)*. October: 37–39.

Watson, A.W.S. 1983. *Physical Fitness and Athletic Performance: A Guide for Students, Athletes and Coaches*. London: Longman.

———— 1983. *Physical Fitness and Athletic Performance: A Guide for Students, Athletes and Coaches*. London: Longman.

Webster Encyclopedic Dictionary of the English Language. 1965. Chicago: Consolidated Books.

Webster's New Ideal Dictionary. 1978. Chicago: Consolidated Books.

Whannel, Garry. 1983. *Blowing the Whistle. The Politics of Sport*. London: Pluto Press.

"What Jobs are Worth Around the Country." *US News & World Report*. April 25, 1988: 68–74.

Whitaker, Kevin W.V. 1981. "Marxist Cultural Analysis: A Case for the Symbolic" in Susan Greendorfer and Andrew Jiannakis (eds). *Sociology of Sport: Perspectives*. West Point, New York: Leisure Press. pp. 43–52.

Whittemore, Hank. 1985. "My Daughter, The Competitor." *Parade Magazine*. July 28: 4–7.

Who we are? What we do? How we work? Toronto: Ontario Women's Directorate.

Whyte, Heather D. 1988. "What Canada's Top Executives Earn." *Financial Post*. April 11: 12.

Will, George F. 1990. *Men At Work. The Craft of Baseball*. New York: Macmillan Publishing Company.

Williams, Doug and Bruce Hunter. 1990. *Quarterblack: Shattering the NFL Myth. Autobiography of Doug Williams First Black Super Bowl Quarterback*. Chicago: Bonus Books.

Williams, John, Eric Dunning and Patrick Murphy. 1984. *Hooligans Abroad. The Behaviour and Control of English Fans in Continental Europe*. London: Routledge & Kegan Paul.

Williams, Melvin, H. 1989. *Beyond Training. How Athletes Enhance Performance Legally and Illegally*. Champaign, Illinois: Leisure Press.

Williams, Tiger and James Lawton. 1984. *Tiger*. Toronto: Seal.

Wilson, Hugh. 1988. "The Legend of the Scholar-Athlete." *McGill News*. Fall: 5.

Wilson, Wayne. 1990. *Gender Stereotyping in Televised Sports*. Los Angeles: Amateur Athletic Foundation of Los Angeles.

Winners: A Century of Canadian Sport. 1985. Toronto: Grosvenor House.

Wise, S.F. and Douglas Fisher. 1974. *Canada's Sporting Heroes*. Don Mills, Ontario: General Publishing Co. Ltd.

Wiseman, Henry, Jokelee Vanderkop and Jorge Nef. 1991. *Critical Choices: Ethics, Science and Technology*. Toronto. Thompson Educational Publishing.

Wishnietsky, Don and Dennis Felder. 1989. "Coaching Problems: Are Suggested Solutions Effective?" *Journal of Physical Education, Recreation and Dance (JOPERD)*. January: 70.

Woman in Sport Leadership: An Issue for Sport. Summary of a National Level Survey. 1990. Ottawa: Sport Canada: Women's Program.

"Women's groups take aim at Tyson." 1991. *The Toronto Star*. September 11: C5.

Woolsey, Garth. 1985. "Battling booze in the NHL." *The Sunday Star*. February 16: E3.

Wright, J.R. 1984. *Urban Parks in Ontario Part II: The Public Park Movement (1860–1914)*. Ottawa: Ministry of Tourism and Recreation.

Wulf, Steve. 1989. "A man in command." *Sports Illustrated*. October 30: 30–35.

York, Marty. 1985. "Title quest puts Jays in debt." *The Globe and Mail*. September 27: S1.

Zeigler, Earle. 1989. "Let's Preserve Educational Sport in Canadian Higher Education." *Canadian Association of Health, Physical Education and Dance (CAHPERD)*. May-June: 24.

Zeman, Brenda (ed). 1988. *To Run with Longboat: Twelve Stories of Indian Athletes in Canada*. Edmonton: GMS2 Ventures Inc.

Zgoda, Jerry. 1988. "Ciccarelli Goes to Jail." *Hockey News*. September 16: 3.

Zurcher, Louis A. and Arnold Meadow. 1970. "On Bullfights and Baseball: An Example of Interaction of Social Institutions" in Gunther Luschen (ed). *The Cross-Cultural Analysis of Sport and Games*. Champaign, Illinois: Stipes Publishing Company. pp. 109–131.

INDEX

Printed in Canada